The Post-Reform Indian Economy

The Post-Reform Indian Economy
An Unfolding Story

Edited by   SOUMYEN SIKDAR

Orient BlackSwan

All rights reserved. No part of this book may be modified, reproduced or utilised in any form, or by any means, electronic or mechanical, including photocopying, recording or by any information storage and retrieval system, in any form of binding or cover other than in which it is published, without permission in writing from the publisher.

THE POST-REFORM INDIAN ECONOMY: AN UNFOLDING STORY

ORIENT BLACKSWAN PRIVATE LIMITED

Registered Office
3-6-752 Himayatnagar, Hyderabad 500 029, Telangana, India
e-mail: centraloffice@orientblackswan.com

Other Offices
Bengaluru, Chennai, Guwahati, Hyderabad, Kolkata,
Mumbai, New Delhi, Noida, Patna, Visakhapatnam

© Orient Blackswan Private Limited 2023
First published by Orient Blackswan Private Limited 2023

ISBN 978-93-5442-458-8

Typeset in
Minion Pro 11.5/13.5
by Le Studio Graphique, Gurgaon 122 007

Printed in India at
Thomson Press, New Delhi 110 020

Published by
Orient Blackswan Private Limited
3-6-752 Himayatnagar, Hyderabad 500 029, Telangana, India
e-mail: info@orientblackswan.com

In memoriam
Prof. Amitava Bose

Contents

List of Tables and Figures	*ix*
List of Abbreviations	*xv*
Publishers' Acknowledgements	*xxi*
Acknowledgements	*xxiii*
Introduction	*xxv*
SOUMYEN SIKDAR	

1. India's Growth Cycles—Resolving Some Theoretical and Empirical Issues   1
   MIHIR RAKSHIT

2. The Volatility of India's Catch-Up Growth   35
   A Discussion
   ASHIMA GOYAL

3. Measuring the Trend of Economic Well-Being in India in Recent Decades   76
   ASIS KUMAR BANERJEE

4. Do Stock Markets Signal Real Economic Performance?   106
   A Theoretical and Empirical Note
   ABHIRUP SARKAR AND AGNIRUP SARKAR

5. Yield Curve and Economic Activity   129
   ABHISHEK NARESH, JONG KOOK SHIN AND CHETAN SUBRAMANIAN

6. Inflation and Stabilisation Policies in India 154
   DEBASHREE CHAKRABORTY AND
   AMBAR GHOSH

7. Indian Inflation 198
   An Econometric Exploration with Disaggregated Price Data
   DIPANKOR COONDOO AND
   PARAMITA MUKHERJEE

8. India's Trade and Foreign Investment Policy 235
   Evolution and Current Issues
   ALOK RAY

9. Balancing the Pushes and Pulls of the Impossible Trinity 287
   Capital Flows, RBI Intervention and Exchange Rate in India
   PARTHA RAY AND PARTHAPRATIM PAL

10. Changing Dynamics of Intergovernmental Fiscal Relations in India 322
    Emerging Issues and Challenges
    PINAKI CHAKRABORTY AND SHUBHAM GUPTA

11. The Natural Environment in India 342
    Good Laws, Bad Practices
    ANUP SINHA

Notes on the Contributors 365
Index 369

Tables and Figures

Tables

1.1	Macroeconomic indicators over 2003–11 and 2011–15	19
2.1	Comparing Latin America and Asia	45
2.2	Comparing China and India	49
3.1	Average MPCE at current prices in the rural and the urban sectors in India in various NSSO survey years (Rs)	91
3.2	Index of average MPCE at current prices, the price deflator and the index of real average MPCE in the rural sector in India in various years (Base: 1983)	92
3.3	Index of average MPCE at current prices, the price deflator and the index of real average MPCE in the urban sector in India in various years (Base: 1983)	92
3.4	Rural and urban shares (per cent) in population in India	93
3.5	Index numbers of average real MPCE in India in various years (Base: 1983)	93
3.6	Cumulative quintile shares in the distribution of MPCE in India	94
3.7	Coordinates of generalised Lorenz curves of the distribution of MPCE in India in 1983 and 2004–05	95
3.8	Value of the well-being measure $W = \mu(1 - G)$ in India in various NSSO survey years	97
3.9	Qualitative trend of economic well-being in India as per any scale monotonic Lorenz consistent well-being function	98

3.10 Qualitative trend of economic well-being in India as per any scale monotonic fuzzy Lorenz consistent well-being function — 99

4.1 Short run relationship between log MK and log PCY — 123

5.1 Result from probit regression of Indian periods of recession on Indian term spread — 137

5.2 Result from probit regression of Indian periods of recession on US term spread — 138

5.3 Estimated values of US (large economy) parameters from Bayesian estimation — 147

5.4 Estimated values of Indian (small economy) parameters from Bayesian estimation — 148

5.5 Standard deviations — 148

5.6 Correlation of Indian GDP growth and lagged and future term spreads (Model) — 150

6.1 Annual percentage growth rate of GDP at market prices based on constant local currency — 158

6.2 Interest rates and growth rates in the US — 159

6.3 Average growth rate of real GDP and average interest rates in the US economy — 160

6.4 Growth rate of GDP, net FDI, foreign portfolio investment, government consumption and gross fiscal deficit (GFD) — 164

6.5 Exchange rate of the Indian rupee vis-à-vis the US dollar (monthly average) — 165

6.6 Commodity composition of India's imports percentage share — 166

6.7 Composition of India's external debt (as percentage of total external debt) — 167

7.1 Weights of components in inflation — 201

7.2 Summary of stationarity test results — 207

7.3	HEGY test results for WPIHL, WPICORE, NCPIHL and NCPICORE	211
7.4	VAR estimation on components of CPI inflation	212
7.5	VAR estimation on components of WPI	214
7.6	CPI inflation and components of GDP	215
7.7	WPI inflation and exchange rate	218
7.8a	Regression for WPI headline and core inflation	222
7.8b	Regression for NCPI headline and core inflation	223
8.1	Trade/GDP ratio of India and China during 1980–2014	241
8.2	India's top 7 major trading partners in 2016–17 (in US$ billion)	242
9.1	India's balance of payments (US$ billion)	296
9.2	Some metrics of forex reserves of select countries, end of 2017	307
9.3	Estimates of sterilization coefficient	310
10.1	Devolution, grants and aggregate transfers to states	329
10.2	Cess and surcharge	333

Figures

1.1	Trade cycle in an economy	6
2.1	Country structure and growth paths	42
2.2	Fuel imports (% of merchandise imports)	47
2.3	Monthly foreign equity flows and the BSE Sensex	66
5.1	Correlation between the US and Indian bond yield	131
5.2	US yield spread and periods of Indian recession	135
5.3	India yield spread and periods of Indian recession	136
5.4	Predictive power for Indian recession using Indian yield spread (12 months in advance)	138

5.5	Predictive power for Indian recession using the US yield spread (12 months in advance)	139
5.6	Forecast of Indian recession using the US yield spread (12 months in advance)	139
5.7	Prior and posterior distributions of large and small economies' technology and demand persistence	149
6.1	Determination of Y and P	170
7.1	Movement of WPI inflation components	200
7.2	Movement of CPI inflation components	200
7.3	Movement of New CPI and WPI 2011 Inflation Components (m-o-m)	209
7.4a	New CPI inflation and the moments of relative price distribution	220
7.4b	WPI inflation and moments of relative price distribution	220
7.5a	WPI headline inflation and skewness of relative price changes	221
7.5b	WPI headline inflation and SD of relative price changes	221
A7.1	Relative price distribution of new CPI commodities subgroups for 2012 to 2018	231–232
A7.2	Relative price distribution of WPI commodities for 2013 to 2018	233–234
9.1	The impossible trinity	289
9.2	Net capital inflows to EMEs (percentages of nominal GDP)	292
9.3	Use of macroprudential tools	294
9.4	Long term trends in India's current account (% of GDP)	295
9.5	India's BOP indicators (% of GDP)	297
9.6	FDI and FPI in India's capital account of BOP (US$ million)	298

9.7	Composition of FPI in India (INR billion)	299
9.8	Exchange rate of INR with respect to four major currencies (vertical axis values in reverse order)	300–301
9.9	Indices of real effective exchange rate (REER) of the Indian rupee (36-currency bilateral weights) (monthly average)	302
9.10	RBI's sale and purchase of foreign exchange (US$ million): Outstanding net forward sales (−) / purchase (+) at end of month (US$ million)	304
9.11	Foreign currency reserves (US$ billion)	306
9.12	Debt flows in various forms	313

Abbreviations

ADD	Anti-Dumping Duties
ADF	Augmented Dickey–Fuller test
AE	Advanced Economies
AI	Aggregate Investment
AIC	Akaike Information Criteria
AIIB	Asian Infrastructure Investment Bank
ANON	Anonymity
ASEAN	Association of Southeast Asian Nations
BJP	Bharatiya Janata Party
BOP	Balance of Payments
BPO	Business Process Outsourcing
BRI	Belt and Road Initiative
CAC	Capital Account Convertibility
CAD	Current Account Deficit
CIS	Commonwealth of Independent States
CP	Consumer Price
CPI	Consumer Price Index
CPI–AL	Consumer Price Index for Agricultural Labourers
CPICORE	Core CPI
CPIFD	CPI Food
CPIFL	CPI Fuel
CPIHL	Headline CPI
CPI–IW	Consumer Price Index for Industrial Workers
CSO	Central Statistics Office
CSS	Centrally Sponsored Schemes
CST	Central Sales Tax
DIPP	Department of Industrial Policy and Promotion
EBA	Everything but Arms
ECB	External Commercial Borrowing
EIA	Environmental Impact Assessment

EM	Emerging Markets
EMEs	Emerging Market Economies
EXCHRT	Exchange Rate
FC	Finance Commission
FCA	Foreign Currency Assets
FCAC	Fuller Capital Account Convertibility
FDI	Foreign Direct Investment
FEMA	Foreign Exchange Management Act
FERA	Foreign Exchange Regulation Act
FFC	Fourteenth Finance Commission
FII	Foreign Institutional Investors
FLC	Fuzzy Lorenz Consistency
FMCG	Fast-moving Consumer Goods
FPI	Foreign Portfolio Investment
FRA	Forest Rights Act
FRBM Act	Fiscal Responsibility and Budget Management Act
FTA	Free Trade Agreements
FX reserves	Foreign Exchange reserves
GDCF	Gross domestic capital formation
GDP	Gross Domestic Product
GDPAG	Agricultural GDP
GDPNAG	Non-agricultural GDP
GFC	Global Financial Crisis
GFCE	Government Final Consumption Expenditure
GFCF	Gross Fixed Capital Formation
GFD	Gross Fiscal deficit
GSDP	Gross State Domestic Product
GSP	Generalized System of Preferences
GST	Goods and Services Tax
GSTN	Goods and Services Tax Network
GTR	Gross Tax Revenues
GVA	Gross Value Added
HH Index	Herfindahl–Hirschman Index

IBC	Insolvency and Bankruptcy Code
ICR	Interest Coverage Ratios
ICT	Information and Communications Technology
IMF	International Monetary Fund
IP	Interest Payments
ITeS	Information Technology Enabled Services
KPO	Knowledge Process Outsourcing
LC	Lorenz Consistency
LCR	Liquidity Coverage Ratio
LERMS	Liberalised Exchange Rate Management System
LTP	Lower Turning Point
LVR	Loan-to-Value Ratios
MCA21	Ministry of Corporate Affairs e-Governance initiative
MFN	Most-Favoured Nation (tariff)
MGNREGA	Mahatma Gandhi National Rural Employment Guarantee Act
MMRP	Modified Mixed Reference Period
MON	Monotonicity
MPC	Monetary Policy Committee
MPCE	Monthly Per Capita Expenditure
MRP	Mixed Recall (or Reference) Period
MSME	Micro, Small and Medium Enterprises
MSP	Minimum Support Prices
MSS	Market Stabilisation Scheme
NABARD	National Bank for Agriculture and Rural Development
NAFTA	North American Free Trade Agreement
NBER	National Bureau of Economic Research
NBFC	Non-Bank financial institution
NCLT	National Company Law Tribunal
NCS	Net Cess and Surcharge
NDA	National Democratic Alliance

NDA	Net Domestic Assets
NDCF	Net Domestic Capital Formation
NDP	Net Domestic Product
NEP	New Economic Policy (1991)
NFA	Net Foreign Assets
NGO	Nongovernmental Association
NITI	National Institution for Transforming India
NPA	Non-performing Assets
NSFR	Net Stable Funding Ratio
NSFR	Net Stable Funding Ratio
NSSO	National sample Survey Office
OECD	Organisation for Economic Cooperation and Development
OPEC	Organization of the Petroleum Exporting Countries
PC	Private Consumption
PCB	Pollution Control Boards
POL	Petroleum, Oil, Lubricants
PP	Phillips-Perron test
PPP	Public-Private Partnership
PPP	Purchasing Power Parity
PRI	Population Replication Invariance
PSB	Public Sector Banks
QE	Quantitative Easing
QR	Quantitative Restrictions
R&D	Resource and Development
RBI	Reserve Bank of India
RCEP	Regional Comprehensive Economic Partnership
RDB	Rupee Denominated Bonds
REER	Real Effective Exchange Rate
RPV	Relative Price Variability
RR	Revenue Receipts
RTI	Right to Information

RTP	Reserve Trench Positions
SD	Standard Deviation
SDR	Special Drawing Rights
SEBI	Securities and Exchange Board of India
SEZ	Special Economic Zone
SK	Skewness
SLR	Statutory Liquidity Ratio
SMON	Scale Monotonicity
TFC	Thirteenth Finance Commission
TOR	Terms of Reference
TPP	Trans-Pacific Partnership
UAE	United Arab Emirates
UK	United Kingdom
UNCTAD	United Nations Conference on Trade and Development
UNEP	United Nations Environmental Programme
URP	Uniform Recall Period
USMCA	United States-Mexico-Canada Agreement
USSR	Union of Soviet Socialist Republics
UTP	Upper Turning Points
VAR	Vector Auto Regression
WP	Wholesale Price
WPI	Wholesale Price Index
WPICORE	Core WPI
WPIFD	WPI Food
WPIFL	WPI Fuel & Power
WPIHL	Headline WPI
WTO	World Trade Organization
ZA Test	Zivot-Andrews Test

Publishers' Acknowledgements

The publishers would like to thank the Indira Gandhi Institute of Development Research (IGIDR) for their kind permission to reproduce in this volume, Ashima Goyal's 'The Volatility of India's Catch-Up Growth: A Discussion' (Chapter 2), in a revised form. The IGIDR had first published this as an IGIDR Working Paper with the title 'What Explains the Volatility of India's Catch-up Growth?' in 2019.

The publishers also extend their gratitude to the Indian Institute of Management Bangalore (IIMB) for their kind consideration, which has enabled the reproduction (with revisions) of Chapter 5 in the present volume titled 'Yield Curve and Economic Activity' by Abhishek Naresh, Jong Kook Shin and Chetan Subramanian. The IIMB had first published it as IIMB Working Paper No. 579.

Acknowledgements

As editor of this volume, I take this opportunity to record my deep gratitude to all the contributors, participants and the reviewers of the workshop titled 'Perspectives on the contemporary Indian economy', held at the Indian Institute of Management Calcutta on 21–22 February 2019, for their very sincere efforts, which culminated in the present volume. Special word of thanks goes to the editorial team at Orient BlackSwan, especially Nilanjana Majumdar and Debangana Pal for their help and cooperation. Finally, I thank my wife Paramita and daughter Paramgama for their support throughout the endeavour.

Introduction

The editor of yet another book of essays on the post-reform Indian economy may legitimately be asked to justify the product. Aren't interested readers already drowning in the deluge of material in newspapers, magazines and social media? Aren't there enough such books already on this subject? The blunt answer is no, especially when we consider the evolving global scenario and the dynamics of the emerging market economies therein and BRICS in particular. The field is ever open for serious academic intervention and exploration. Given the richness and complexity of our post-reform development experience, there is always room for a fresh look even at age-old issues. And, of course, new and interesting facets keep on appearing all the time as local and global economic conditions change. The flourishing state of academic research and publication on the contemporary Indian economy, therefore, should come as no surprise. There is another reason why the flow of new publications is likely to get a boost. The year 2021 marked three decades of economic restructuring and reforms, initiated in 1991 by the government headed by P. V. Narasimha Rao. The first serious attempts at reform were made in the 1980s, but in depth and coverage they were far exceeded by the policy changes of 1991. No area of economic activity had been left untouched and the consequences of that momentous decision are still playing out with far-reaching rippling effects.

These consequences continue to fascinate and exercise the intellect of economists and other serious social scientists in all parts of the world. At the same time, very significant changes have been happening on the world stage too, namely slow recovery from the destruction wrought by the Global Financial Crisis of 2008, China's rise as a formidable economic force, the steady retreat from WTO-led (World Trade Organization) multilateralism in tandem with a gradual but clearly noticeable erosion of faith in democratic institutions among the polity. Therefore, books on the politics and economics of India, China and other emerging economies will keep on coming with new perspectives emerging continuously as new issues appear and old issues branch out in new directions in novel forms. Social scientists, observers and policy makers may look forward to living in interesting times. We are confident that this volume will continue to serve as a source of important information and fresh insights, a concise but solid presence within a very lively discourse.

A quarter century after 1991, two other critical decisions were again implemented, this time by the government headed by Narendra Modi. These are: demonetisation of rupee notes of denominations 500 and 1000 in November 2016 and the introduction of the nationwide Goods and Services Tax (GST) in July 2017. It was not just that a new type of tax was brought into the existing framework of Centre–state fiscal relations. The framework itself was significantly modified. This certainly merits careful scrutiny and assessment.

In happier pre-Covid days, a small number of Calcutta economists, belonging to different age groups, met informally but regularly (on an average frequency of once a month) to discuss current (mostly) macroeconomic issues of the country. Members took turns making brief presentations, which were followed by free-flowing but intense discussion. Topics ranged over a wide spectrum—methodologies of measuring GDP (Gross Domestic Product), its growth and inflation, consequences of rising inequality in income and wealth, desirability of inflation targeting, the link between the stock market and the real economy, policy interventions in the spheres of foreign commerce and investment, petroleum pricing and fertiliser subsidy, just to give a small sample. The idea for the present collection of essays had its origin in one such meeting. Some members volunteered to contribute on subjects of their interest. After some deliberation, the following broad themes were selected: quantification and volatility of Indian growth, inequality and well-being, real-financial interaction, inflation measurement and inflation targeting as policy, trade, foreign investment and exchange rate policies, recent changes in Union–state fiscal relations and management of environmental resources.

Writings on India's macro economy today seem to fall into two broad types. The type that appears in professional journals is often technically demanding, requiring a knowledge of advanced mathematical methods such as dynamic optimisation, and the other type tends to be too descriptive (and simplistic), avoiding analytical modelling altogether. It was decided to avoid this bias by striking a middle position so that for following the basic logic, no knowledge of advanced economic theory or mathematics (or econometrics for that matter) would be essential. To expand the scope of the volume, the editor approached a few other research-active economists of the country for contributions, indicating possible areas for treatment. All of them, without exception, agreed to do so. Then on 21–22 February 2019, a formal conference was organised in the Indian Institute of Management Calcutta under the aegis of its Centre for Development and Environment Policy, where the first drafts were presented and discussed. Revisions were done in light of the comments received there, and Orient BlackSwan very enthusiastically accepted the final manuscript for publication.

It should be noted that the project was conceived and the writings and revisions were done before the world was hit by the Covid-19 pandemic. Most unfortunately but inevitably, the great unforeseen shock caused considerable delay and uncertainty in the process of production. In view of the changed situation, the idea of adding new material on the implications of the pandemic for the themes treated was considered but ultimately rejected, chiefly because the work was already fairly deep into production. It was unanimously felt that there was enough of value in it for the reader interested in India in the decades preceding the pandemic.

Out of a rather large (but generally unremarkable) crop, let us pick three important recent volumes offering experts' views on the Indian economy in pre-Covid times. This may help provide a perspective on the book in the context of current available literature. They are, *What the Economy Needs Now*, edited by A. Banerjee, G. Gopinath, R. Rajan and M. Sharma (2019); *A Concise Handbook of the Indian Economy in the 21st Century*, edited by A. Goyal (2019); and *The Path Ahead: Transformative Ideas for India*, edited by A. Kant (2018). Like the present volume, all three focus on the nation's achievements and failures in select areas of particular concern to policy makers and the general public. There is similarity in the graph–table–plain English style of exposition too. The targeted audience seems to be broadly similar. But several topics of critical importance that receive in-depth coverage in our collection are either absent or receive less attention (or attention from different angles) in these other members of the set. These include: methodological issues relating to growth measurement and volatility of our growth dynamics (Chapters 1 and 2), trend in inequality-adjusted economic well-being in India in recent decades (Chapter 3), stock markets and real economic performance (Chapters 4 and 5), statistical exploration of inflation with disaggregated price data (Chapter 7), current issues of India's trade and foreign investment policies against the backdrop of China's rise as an economic superpower on one hand and the growing global discontent with sweeping liberalisation and WTO-led multilateralism on the other (Chapter 8), assessment of the Reserve Bank of India's (RBI) policy efficacy within the confines of the impossible trinity confronting an economy open to both foreign trade and international capital flows (Chapter 9) and GST and the associated changes in Centre–state financial relations. The evaluation of inflation and stabilisation policies using a suitably modified Keynesian analytical framework in Chapter 6 is also something unique to this volume.

At this point what is not on offer should also be made clear. The volume was never intended to be a comprehensive handbook on the post-reform Indian economy. (The economy is so big and complex that even comprehensive handbooks are forced to leave out many interesting aspects.) There are, for example, no chapters on poverty (incidence and measurement), competition policy, human capital development, banking sector issues, labour and land market reforms, infrastructure finance and problems faced by small and medium enterprises. Demonetisation was discussed but dropped chiefly because it was felt that instead of being a well thought-out long-term policy initiative, this was of the nature of, and intended to be, a draconian one-time shock. The transformation of Centre-state fiscal relationship is however retained for scrutiny. Two prominent and undesirable features of India's growth over the past quarter century—sectoral imbalances and non-inclusivity—have naturally attracted a great deal of attention from researchers and analysts. The first is not included in this volume, but inequality does get its proper share of attention in the context of injudicious exploitation of natural resources and as part of the broader notion of well-being of a society. Use of this more general concept of welfare is also a novel contribution not found in any essay of the other three books cited or elsewhere in the literature.

Let us take an overview of the critical issues covered by our contributors. First is the issue of growth. Although GDP growth is no longer considered the be-all and end-all of development, growth continues to be of interest because it is undeniably a necessary condition for sustained improvements in the standard of living of a country. Given this importance, it is not surprising that quantification of growth and its refinement continues to be an important part of research of Indian economists and statisticians.

Over the period of 2003–04 to 2007–08, India clocked an average real GDP growth rate of 8.9 per cent, a very impressive figure second only to that of the other Asian giant, China. The Global Financial Crisis brought it down to 4.1 per cent in 2008–09. It picked up to a better level in the next couple of years, but long-term deceleration set in subsequently. Meanwhile, the base year was changed to 2011–12 (from 2004–05) coupled with some other definitional changes. Serious questions have been raised about the reliability of official figures based on these changes. For example, calculations using the new methodology give growth of 6.9 per cent for 2013–14, but it has been shown that the old base and old definitions would have set it at 4.7 per cent only. A discrepancy of this magnitude is very difficult to accept. Another area of discontent is the widening gap between figures reported in the National Sample Survey and the National Accounts Statistics. But there are other equally important methodological issues which are not adequately highlighted in current literature. Mihir Rakshit addresses some of these less discussed issues in Chapter 1, 'India's Growth Cycles—Resolving Some Theoretical and Empirical Issues'.

Rakshit does much more than simply analyse the ups and downs of GDP growth from an economist's perspective. Going beyond (and behind) the numbers, he raises fundamental questions about the standard methodology used to quantify Indian growth dynamics. These questions are not about the well-known National Sample Survey–National Accounts Statistics discrepancies, or choice of the base year, or the inclusion or exclusion of certain items from this category or that. They delve much deeper along different dimensions. The faulty methodology is rooted in neglect of the consequences of the structural features of developing economies, which, in turn, leads to a faulty understanding of the behaviour of the economy over the short and medium terms. In the school of structuralist macroeconomics, the interaction between demand-constrained (fix-price) manufacturing and supply-constrained (flex-price) agriculture has important implications for short-term variations in output and prices (a good exposition is provided in Taylor 1983). These insights are routinely ignored in our official formulations of growth problems. Instead, there is almost a total reliance on supply side explanations favoured by the International Monetary Fund (IMF) and the World

Bank. These methodological inadequacies, Rakshit argues, cause misspecification of the turning points of growth cycles and prevent correct identification of the sources of expansion or slowdown in output and employment. The implication for correct policy formulation is not difficult to understand. It is also lamentable that the Central Statistics Office (CSO) has so far failed to produce de-seasonalised time-series estimates for quarterly GDP and its components. Had that data been available, some of the quantification pitfalls could have been avoided. Growing real and financial sector imbalances during the boom phase, much of it policy-induced, exacerbated by both domestic and international factors, were seriously responsible for the subsequent deceleration in growth. Critical analysis of these factors with emphasis on misguided policy measures form a substantial part of the chapter.

The next chapter by Ashima Goyal, 'The Volatility of India's Catch-Up Growth: A Discussion' is in many respects complementary to Rakshit's. To catch up fast with the developed world, sustained (real) growth at 8 per cent or above over an extended period is necessary. Given its rich demographic dividend and other strengths accumulated over the reform years, this was not beyond India's grasp. Unfortunately, this has not materialised. The growth path has been conspicuously erratic. China seems to have done much better in this respect. Persistent high growth over 2003–08 in India was followed by periods of low growth, robust recovery and then a slide back and stagnation again. This does not portend well for the prospect of becoming a 10 trillion-dollar economy by 2030. Goyal provides a comprehensive examination of the factors that may have contributed to the erratic nature of our performance. Interesting points of comparison between India and China and, more generally, Latin America and Asia are highlighted. Damaging policy failures are discussed. Supply shocks have been relatively large and could not be adequately offset because fiscal and monetary policy remained essentially conservative. One major limitation is that in deference to the out-dated

World Bank mantra of 'Stabilize, Privatize, Liberalize', the focus remained on fiscal prudence and structural reforms despite the prolonged slowdown after 2011.

The majority of economists investigating the persistent deceleration of the Indian economy have identified demand deceleration as a major contributory factor (along with the government's preoccupation with supply side policies and a global recession in the background), of which consumption slowdown is in turn one major component. And widening inequality in favour of the wealthier classes that have relatively lower propensities to consume has acted as a brake on consumption growth. Apart from this purely functional role in income generation, inequality has a separate ethical dimension too. It is morally unacceptable as a promoter of exclusion in a society blighted by centuries of oppression, exploitation and exclusion. Supported by the works of Amartya Sen, Martha Nussbaum and other scholars, this dimension has gained wide recognition as essential criteria for judging the performance of any modern economy. This brings us to the third chapter of the book by Asis Kumar Banerjee, 'Measuring the Trend of Economic Well-Being in India in Recent Decades'. Another aspect of the link between inequality and social welfare via the impact on the environment is discussed by Anup Sinha in the last chapter on environmental policies of the land.

In the course of her discussion Goyal at one point states that '...absence of true economic inclusion, despite full political inclusion, is the biggest failure of Indian democracy.' The chapter by Banerjee is an innovative contribution to non-inclusion and welfare. Measurement of inequality and its time trend in India is a fertile field of research. Analysis of economic well-being or welfare is a lagging area, comparatively. A natural hypothesis to start with is the idea that the well-being of a community varies positively with its mean income and inversely with the inequality in the distribution of that income. Proceeding further, one soon runs into the classic problem of intersecting Lorenz curves. It is possible to have a situation of two income (or expenditure) distributions where neither Lorenz-curve dominates the other. Banerjee overcomes the problem by introducing the concept of fuzzy Lorenz-dominance and extends the scope of existing results in a significant manner. The theoretical innovation is applied to rank economic well-being in India over three recent decades. The result is that over 1983 to 2011–12 there is no positive monotonic trend in well-being, although it increased over 1983 to 1993–94 and over 2004–05 to 2011–12. It is not possible to unambiguously rank the periods 1993–94 and 2004–05. Fuzzy Lorenz-dominance is a novel contribution of this chapter to the existing literature on inequality and its welfare consequences.

While the importance of deepening and maturity of financial activities for overall development is well recognised in general terms, attempts at more precise validation have produced mixed results for the emerging market economies. In addition to giving a good overview of current research in this area, the next two chapters throw interesting new light on real-financial sector interaction in India. Both combine theoretical modelling with empirical evidence from India and other countries. Using the asset pricing model of Robert Lucas, Sarkar and Sarkar in Chapter 4 titled 'Do Stock Markets Signal Real Economic Performance? A Theoretical and Empirical Note', explore whether there is a tight link between stock market capitalisation and the real per capita income of an economy. The answer is no, generally, but in the non-trivial case of two states there is indeed a monotonic relationship. The exact nature, positive or negative, is governed by the degree of risk aversion. The theoretical model is tested using data for 33 countries over the period 1988–2018. Surprisingly, for India the relation is strongly positive and significant. This interesting result points the way to further research in this important area.

In Chapter 5 titled 'Yield Curve and Economic Activity', Abhishek Naresh, Jong Kook Shin and Chetan Subramanian establish two interesting results. First, long-term interest rates in India show high degree of co-movement with their US counterparts in the post-reform period. Second, the US yield spread is a better predictor of Indian business cycles than the Indian yield spread. This is a novel contribution to the sparse literature on cycle forecasting in India. And needless to say, the results on the interlinks between Indian and US interest rates are of considerable relevance to monetary policy exercises in India.

The New Economic Policy ushered in after the reforms attached critical importance to fiscal prudence in the form of stringent caps on the fiscal deficit–GDP ratio. Borrowed unquestioningly from the orthodoxy of the neo-liberal or new classical school of economics, it has become firmly entrenched with the passage of time. Since 2015, the Reserve Bank of India has adopted inflation control (inflation targeting) as the major objective of monetary policy. Using a Keynesian framework suited to the Indian context, Debashree Chakraborty and Ambar Ghosh in Chapter 6 titled 'Inflation and Stabilisation Policies in India', show that the costs of inflation get magnified by inflation targeting and with rigid adherence to fiscal prudence. This is a valuable contribution to the contemporary policy literature on India. The analytical framework used is a Keynesian one which differs fundamentally from the one used in the preceding two chapters, which is new-classical in its use of micro-level optimisation as the fundamental building block. Many economists today would consider only the latter approach as 'scientifically valid', but the editor is not in agreement. In our judgment, the Keynesian framework with its emphasis on nominal rigidities and quantity adjustments in the short run is better equipped to handle macroeconomic questions of developing economies. Chapter 6 demonstrates its ability to clarify a crucial policy question of such an economy.

Indian inflation continues to be the subject matter of the next chapter, Chapter 7 titled 'Indian Inflation: An Econometric Exploration with Disaggregated Price Data' by Dipankor Coondoo and Paramita Mukherjee. Under inflation-control, the focus of policy has recently shifted to tracking CPI (Consumer Price Index) inflation rather than headline WPI

(Wholesale Price Index) inflation. This brings up interesting issues in its wake, both statistical as well as economic. For example, when the structure of relative prices changes due to some shock or structural changes in the economy, expenditure on more expensive commodities is likely to fall. But the CPI, being based on a fixed set of weights will falsely show a rise in the overall price level. Also, it has been noted that during some decades there has been a significant mismatch between the WPI headline inflation and CPI inflation in terms of variation in prices of the component indexes. All these are of considerable relevance to the RBI which has set inflation as the primary target of monetary policy.

The analysis of Coondoo and Mukherjee (using monthly data for the period 2006–18) goes a long way in clarifying these issues. In broad terms the study does two things, both of which are quite novel in the context of the existing literature. First, it discusses the role of individual component indexes in driving WPI and CPI changes and second, after tracking the temporal movement of relative prices at a disaggregated level (for both WPI and CPI), it examines how overall inflation is related to such relative price movements. Rigorous econometric analysis using disaggregated commodity price data enables them to throw new light on the short-run dynamics of inflation. The distribution of relative prices in India has generally been asymmetric with a positive skewness in some years and negative skewness in others. One interesting result is that significant amount of variation in both CPI and WPI inflation is explained by the skewness of relative price changes. On the policy question, the study suggests that the RBI should track CPI core inflation along with headline inflation as the core inflation has influence on other components of headline inflation.

Openness to foreign trade in goods and services and (to a lesser extent) unrestricted cross-border asset transactions have become critical elements of our commitment to liberalisation and globalisation. True to this commitment, India's involvement in the global economy, both in trade and investment, has been increasing steadily over time. Aspects of this very significant development are the focus of exploration in Chapters 8 and 9. Alok Ray in Chapter 8 titled 'India's Trade and Foreign Investment Policy: Evolution and Current Issues' examines the evolution of the country's trade and foreign investment policy with focus on the sharp break in 1991. He also provides an in-depth analysis of a number of very important questions that the nation is facing at the current juncture where the benefits (and hence the sustainability) of globalisation and multilateralism are being seriously questioned. These span the issues of selective protectionism, greater exchange rate management, strategic regional groupings and liberalisation of the foreign investment regime. How India and China, the two emerging giants of Asia, choose to address these critical issues is likely to be of great moment for the world at large. The essay sets out with clarity the essential elements required for a better understanding of these emerging uncertainties.

Partha Ray and Parthapratim Pal in Chapter 9, 'Balancing the Pushes and Pulls of the Impossible Trinity: Capital Flows, RBI Intervention and Exchange Rate in India', cover the interesting narrative of India's efforts to balance the pushes and pulls of the celebrated impossible trinity where the RBI's interventions, capital account restrictions and monetary policy interplayed with oscillations in market forces to determine the exchange value of the rupee. It is a story of commendable success in holding a steady course in waters that were choppy at the best and violently turbulent at the worst. The chapter is an illuminating and comprehensive overview of the RBI's performance in handling truly messy choices involving exchange rates, sterilisation, and capital controls on cross-border flow of funds. Certainly, there are lessons here for prudent macroeconomic management in an emerging market economy.

Federal fiscal relations in India have undergone significant alterations in recent years. Three major changes are: abolition of the Planning Commission and creation of the NITI Aayog, fundamental changes in the transfer system by providing higher tax devolution to the states based on the recommendations of the Fourteenth Finance Commission, and a constitutional amendment to introduce the GST. These changes have far-reaching implications for Centre-state fiscal relations and provisioning of public services. Pinaki Chakraborty and Shubham Gupta in Chapter 10, 'Changing Dynamics of Intergovernmental Fiscal Relations in India: Emerging Issues and Challenges' undertake a detailed review of the major issues regarding fiscal balance and debt sustainability in pre-Covid India.

After decades of almost complete neglect in the development discourse, the importance of efficient management of environmental resources in supporting healthy and sustainable growth is finally getting the attention it deserves. But, as is to be expected, there is debate on the design and implementation of 'efficient management'. The final essay takes a close look at environmental management in India. Anup Sinha in Chapter 11, 'The Natural Environment in India: Good Laws, Bad Practices', discusses the salient features of environmental protection and how it might conflict with the 'business as usual' model of economic activities. Environmental stress, which has increased over the years despite strict laws, is examined in the context of depletion of natural resources and their implications for social welfare. Also taken up for discussion is the process through which rising inequality has generated different types of stresses from different segments—from wastages created by consumerism and ecosystem damages to excessive and inefficient exploitation of natural resources by the very poor. A wide chasm has developed between the letter of the law and what happens on the ground. The author concludes with a brief account of alternative courses of action that could possibly bridge this gap.

As already mentioned, the book was conceived and gestated before the pandemic. However, it was not designed to cover all major macroeconomic aspects of pre-Covid India. The aim was to present before the reader analytical explorations in some critically important areas combined with a probing look at policy options and actions. Lucid treatments by acknowledged experts in diverse areas have brought to fruition that ambition of the editor.

It is over to the reader now.

REFERENCES

Banerjee, Abhijit, G. Gopinath, R. Rajan and M. S. Sharma (eds). 2019. *What the Economy Needs Now*. New Delhi: Juggernaut Books.

Goyal, A. (ed.). 2019. *A Concise Handbook of the Indian Economy in the 21st Century*. New Delhi: Oxford University Press.

Kant, A. (ed.). 2018. *The Path Ahead: Transformative Ideas for India*. New Delhi: Rupa Publications.

Taylor, Lance. 1983. *Structuralist Macroeconomics*. New York: Basic Books.

1

INDIA'S GROWTH CYCLES—RESOLVING SOME THEORETICAL AND EMPIRICAL ISSUES*

Mihir Rakshit

Introduction

The chapter discusses the nature and drivers of India's GDP growth over the first one-and-a-half decade of the new millennium.[1] On the basis of the year-on-year variations in incomes, the period was marked by two broad phases: a booming phase of GDP growth, which was followed by a steep slowdown

---

*This is a revised version of a paper presented at Jadavpur University in March 2018. I am indebted to members of the seminar for their helpful comments.

and stagnation. The economy experienced persistently elevated growth averaging 8.9 per cent over 2003–08. Thanks to the outbreak of the Global Financial Crisis, 2008–09 saw GDP growth plummeting to 4.15 per cent from 9.83 per cent in the previous financial year. However, there was a robust recovery from the very next year, with growth jumping to 8.4 per cent in 2009–10 and rising further to 10.3 per cent in 2010–11. Thus despite the 2008–09 dip, India's average growth during the eight year period (2003–11) was an unprecedented 8.4 per cent (see various issues of Economic Surveys and RBI reports).

The prolonged boom was followed by a sharp slowdown and sluggish growth during 2011–14, with the GDP recording growth rates of 6.7, 4.72 and 4.98 per cent respectively in the three successive years. The sluggish phase continued (as per the old series) till the mid 2014–15 so that the average growth over this three-and-a-half-year period was 5.45 per cent compared with 8.4 per cent posted during the earlier phase. From mid-2014–15, there was some recovery until mid-2017–18. However, because of intractable data-related problems and initiation of major policy measures like demonetisation and GST, our reference period has not been extended beyond mid 2014–15.

The discussion of the temporal behaviour of the Indian macro economy during the period under review in the rest of the chapter is conducted as follows. By way of clearing the deck, the following two sections draw attention to some serious theoretical and methodological pitfalls or inadequacies characterising the large majority of both official and unofficial studies of India's economic performance—inadequacies that cause misspecification of phases of growth cycles, especially their upper and lower turning points; make the analysis largely tautological; and stand in the way of identifying the primary sources of variations in GDP over the short and the medium run. In the context of these observations, the next section examines some salient features of the Indian economy over the reference period and provides a preliminary assessment of the proximate factors affecting growth. The fifth section analyses the interplay of domestic and international economic factors, including policy changes in fostering real and financial sector imbalances during the booming phase of the economy, and sowing the seeds of slowdown and stagnation. The concluding section summarises the main findings of the chapter, both analytical and empirical, and draws some policy lessons.

Explaining Short-Term GDP Growth: Some Common Pitfalls

Changes in short-term growth is generally examined in terms of year-on-year (y-o-y) variations in quarterly GDP at constant market prices or/and factor costs. In order to assess the merit or deficiency of such explanations, we need to address two questions:

(*i*) Why focus on quarterly (and not say monthly, yearly or half-yearly) GDP?

(*ii*) If the quarter is indeed the appropriate time unit for studying the macro behaviour of the economy, what is the rationale of considering y-o-y rather than quarter on quarter (q-o-q) changes in GDP?

There is in fact a long tradition of analysing the temporal behaviour of the macro economy on the basis of time series of quarterly GDP and its components. Such analyses owe their origin to the Keynesian theory under which, (*i*) output is governed by aggregate demand; (*ii*) aggregate demand is generated by autonomous expenditures (expenditures that are not dependent on current income, as distinguished from induced spending that is governed by current output) and the multiplier process they give rise to; and (*iii*) the overwhelming part of the multiplier in advanced countries works out over a period of around three months.[2]

This perspective suggests, as we shall discuss in the next section, a whole host of inadequacies in usual explanations of India's growth dynamics. Sans any economically meaningful distinction between the autonomous and induced components of expenditure, the 'explanation' degenerates into tautology, shedding little light on the causal connection underlying the formation of aggregate demand. Second, there is little attempt at a close assessment of differences between and the intertwining of demand and supply side effects of shocks, relating to changes in investment or in domestic and external economic environment, including policy stance. Third and perhaps the most important is the oversight of major macro implications of some structural features of the Indian economy. The resulting analysis of both the short- and medium-run behaviour of the country's economy, it is not difficult to see, can hardly be illuminating.

Uses and Abuses of Data for Macro Aggregates

No less serious are the pitfalls arising from use of y-o-y changes in quarterly GDP and its components for explaining the growth cycle. Such uses run against the dictates of macro-theoretic considerations concerning data required for examining cyclical fluctuations over a reference period. We have already noted how and why use of data for quarterly GDP is legitimate when output is demand-determined. Were production governed entirely by supply-side factors à la Say's law or Solovian growth models, for identifying sources of GDP growth and its variation, three months would hardly be the appropriate unit period: the period would be too short for examining the supply-side consequences of growth of labour forces, technological changes, formation of human capital or accumulation of machinery and equipment.

Again, given the importance of agriculture even now in countries like India and the long lag between the sowing and harvesting seasons, a non-negligible part of production during a quarter would not be demand-determined. As structuralist macroeconomics underlines, this has a major consequence for formation of demand for non-agricultural products both directly and indirectly through changes in relative prices. Thus, a harvest failure not only reduces farmers' demand for industrial goods and services but rising food prices also force farm and non-farm households to cut their consumption of other products. The important point to note in this connection is that, before one uses quarterly data for analysing macro behaviour of countries like India, it is necessary to modify the mainstream one-sector model to take account of differences across sectors in the role of demand and supply constraints as also in the nature of price formation (Rakshit 1982, 1989; Taylor 1983).

Misspecification of Cyclical Changes

It is also important to recognise that analysis based on y-o-y changes in quarterly output is bound to yield a distorted view of the behaviour of the economy with misspecification of phases and turning points of growth cycles. In the context of the near-universal use of y-o-y variations in GDP and its components in discussions of India's macro performance, some elaboration of the indictment appears to be in order at this stage.

Consider first the simple case where production is demand-determined and income-generation period is roughly a quarter. Macro econometric models based on such a Keynesian framework focus on sequential q-o-q changes in quarterly income and explain its temporal behaviour in terms of (*i*) policy or other shocks, domestic and external; (*ii*) changes in autonomous components of expenditures (apart from those under [*i*]), including lagged or spill-over effects of income on demand in subsequent periods.[3] In such explanations, not only have y-o-y changes in macro aggregates no role, but their use generally results in erroneous results relating to nature of cyclical fluctuations.

In Figure 1.1, the curve *YY* denotes a typical trade cycle in an economy. Over the period T_1T_4, the upward and downward phases of the economy are *AB* and *BC* respectively with *A* as the lower and *B* as the upper turning points. However, when one focuses on y-o-y rather than q-o-q changes in income, the upper turning point would seem to have occurred at A_1 (at $T=t_1$), not A (at $T=T_1$) and the lower turning point at B_1, not B. The corresponding upward phase would seem to be A_1B_1 over the period t_1t_3.[4] In fact, so far as q-o-q growth is concerned, its declining phase occurs at $T=T_2$, much earlier than T_3 (or t_3). Quite clearly, the longer the time interval for estimating GDP growth, the more pronounced would be the misspecification of phases and turning points of growth cycles. The difficulties of identifying the drivers of fluctuations would correspondingly be greater. In sum, the length of the period over which changes in GDP are measured needs to be based on macro-theoretic considerations. These suggest that when output is demand-determined, the q-o-q, not the y-o-y GDP growth, is the relevant time series for fruitful analyses of cyclical variations and their sources.

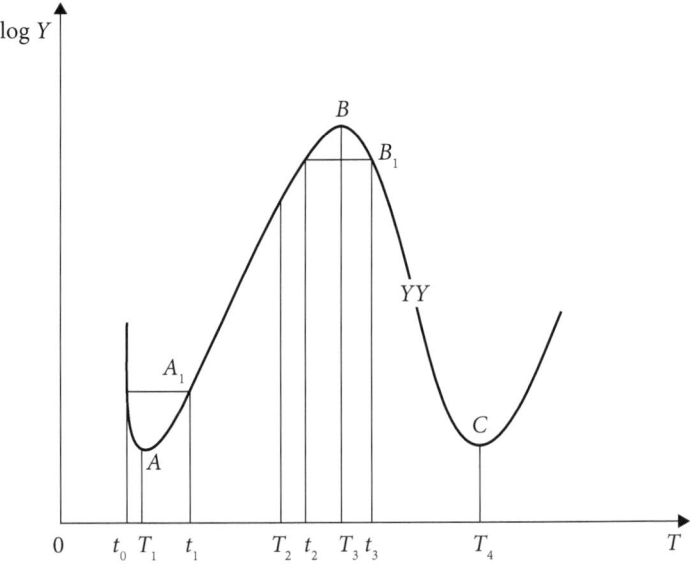

Fig. 1.1: Trade cycle in an economy

Source: Author

The main justification for using the y-o-y rather than the q-o-q growth data is perhaps the bias in the latter due to seasonal factors. If so, the remedy lies in using q-o-q changes in deseasonalised quarterly macro magnitudes, something the OECD (Organization for Economic Co-operation and Development) estimates for India's GDP (at constant market prices) and some of its components. The CSO's (Central Statistics Office) failure to provide estimates of deseasonalised time series for quarterly GDP and its components reflects poorly on the state of macroeconomic research in India, and since supply of official statistics is demand-determined, it is the paucity of rigorous research in macroeconomics that must be at the root of such major gaps in India's official statistics.

The time series of y-o-y growth of quarterly output levels, aggregate and sectoral, is also used for explaining supply side factors driving GDP growth. Our earlier observations relating to differences in output lags across sectors suggest that such supply-side explanations of output growth are grossly inappropriate, something we shall elaborate in the next section.

How Not to Explain GDP Growth

The inadequacies resulting from the use of the time series of quarterly GDP and its components are undoubtedly important. Much more serious however is the weakness in the analytical underpinning of the studies that prevents them from identifying basic factors and the mechanism behind temporal variations in the economy. Consider for example the analysis in the Reserve Bank of India's *Monetary Policy Reports*, one of the foremost publications on India's economic performance. The report explains the growth of GDP at factor costs and market prices in terms of contributions of different components of GDP. Thus growth of aggregate output is viewed to arise from changes in output (gross value added) in different sectors, e.g., agriculture, industry and services (and their subsectors), the contribution of each sector being its growth times the share of the sector in total output. It is calculated/analysed similarly for changes in aggregate demand (GDP at market prices). Such explanation, it is obvious, is tautological and sheds little light on the chain of causation: *ex post* GDP (at factor costs or market prices), let us recall, is necessarily equal to the sum of its components. The basic flaw in the analysis consists in the absence of (*i*) any distinction between the autonomous and the induced components of GDP;[5] and (*ii*) identification of sources of change in the autonomous components and their quantitative significance. Such deficiency in its turn may be traced to the fact that the analysis lacks a solid theoretical foundation.

To see how, consider first the RBI analysis of aggregate demand, universally viewed to be the main driver of income over the short run. Explanation of the change in aggregate demand runs in terms of variation in (*i*) private consumption (PC) (*ii*) government final consumption expenditure (GFCE); (*iii*) aggregate investment (AI), private and public; and (*iv*) net exports (NE). Such classification, a moment's reflection suggests, is hardly helpful in unearthing the sources of changes in GDP. Clubbing components of aggregate demand under (*i*), (*ii*) and (*iii*) blurs the distinction between the autonomous and induced components of expenditures. Thus, while GFCE is largely autonomous, PC depends mostly on disposable income. In examining changes in PC, one thus needs to consider government policy initiatives relating to taxes and transfers and other factors affecting the relation between income and household consumption. So far as investment is concerned, it is necessary to distinguish between (*i*) fixed investments and accumulation of stocks; and (*ii*) public and private sector addition to machinery and equipment. While investment in inventories is mostly induced, fixed investments are by and large autonomous. Factors driving public and private sector investments in fixed capital are also generally quite different. Finally, focusing on net exports instead of exports and imports separately defies macroeconomic logic, remembering that purchases from abroad depend primarily on domestic income and hence are induced; but exports, being governed by income of the country's trading partners, need to be treated as autonomous. The pitfalls in the RBI analysis resulting from clubbing of such disparate expenditures can, it is clear, be due primarily to quite inadequate appreciation of the theory of aggregate demand.

The RBI analysis of supply-side factors is no less problematic. The change in GDP at factor cost (or GVA [gross value added]) is explained in terms of contributions of agriculture, industry and services (and their subsectors). Here also the explanation, as in the analysis of demand side, is tautological. A most glaring gap in the discussion of demand- and supply-side factors is the absence of any link between the two: the reader is left wondering how the two sets of factors, which are apparently quite distinct, generate the same level of GDP (except for indirect tax-less subsidies). Since the macro-theoretic issues arising in this context are fundamental for examining India's short- and medium-run growth dynamics, a few words on their nature and implications seem necessary at this stage.

Consider the standard demand-side explanation of GDP. In this case, causation runs from expenditure to output and income with no separate role of supply-side factors in governing GDP. Production in different sectors is governed by distribution of aggregate demand across sectors, which in its turn depends on relative prices and income elasticities of demand for different goods and services.[6]

In sharp contrast, when production is supply-constrained (due to say wage-price flexibility), for identifying sources of temporal variation in GDP, one has to consider changes in labour, capital and technical conditions. Even in this case, focusing on changes in sectoral output could be highly misleading; given the addition to productive capacity of the economy, its sectoral distribution depends on composition of demand and hence does not indicate the basic factors behind GDP growth.

Coexistence and Interaction of Demand- and Supply-side Constraints

There are several reasons why analysing the demand- and supply-side factors separately, without taking cognisance of their interaction, could be seriously misleading. In countries like India, most industrial goods and services are demand-determined. But there are two major sectors—agriculture and petroleum—where production is supply-constrained and these constraints play a major role in governing demand and hence output in other sectors. For an adequate appreciation of the role of the two supply constraints looming large on the Indian macro economy, it is necessary to take account of the nature of their operations.

In view of the time lag between sowing and harvesting, agricultural output in the short run is largely independent of current demand; climatic conditions in general and the monsoon in particular tend to make agricultural output vary widely over time. The supply shocks, whatever be their source, tend to have large effects on demand for and hence production of non-agricultural goods and services. This occurs in three ways. First, though agriculture's share in GDP (total GVA) is only around 13–14 per cent, nearly 50 per cent of Indian households are dependent on incomes originating in this sector for their livelihood. Hence the direct, demand-debilitating impact of a fall in farmers' earnings on other sectors tends to be disproportionately large. Again, since (a) demand for agro-products, especially food grains, is both price and income inelastic and (b) agricultural prices are market clearing, shocks by way of (say) a crop failure cause spiralling agricultural prices and a sharp diminution in demand for industrial products and services. Under what we called elsewhere the dual adjustment process (Rakshit 1982), with market-clearing price adjustments in agriculture and output adjustments in other sectors, the importance of the cutback in demand for non-farm products due to sharp rise in agricultural prices can hardly be overemphasised. Third, given the large weight of agro-products, especially foodgrains, in the Consumer Price Index (CPI), raising agricultural prices push up the CPI inflation, forcing the government and the central bank to adopt contractionary measures, making the fall in demand for non-farm products steeper. The other supply-side factor having a major impact on the Indian macro economy is international petroleum prices. There are several routes through which global price shocks are transmitted to the domestic sector. First, since India's imports of crude oil and chemical fertilisers[7] are substantial and demand for both are relatively insensitive to prices, a hardening (or softening) of international oil prices raises (or lowers) the country's import bill and sets a negative (or positive) foreign trade multiplier in motion. Second, with low price elasticity of demand for petro products, upward (or downward) revisions of petroleum prices would reinforce the contractionary (or expansionary) process through a fall (or rise) in demand for other products. Third, if the pass-through of oil price increases (or decreases), it raises (or lowers) the inflationary pressure which often prompts the central bank to initiate dear (or easy) money policy. The result is further contraction of aggregate demand.

Fortunately for the Indian economy, there are fairly strong countervailing forces that tend to moderate volatility of domestic income due to gyrations of petroleum prices in the international market. A most important reason for hardening of oil prices is expansion in global economic activity. But such expansion also tends to boost exports and reins in contractionary forces unleashed by surge in oil prices. The countervailing force operating through exports is of particular significance for India, given her proximity to the oil-rich Middle East countries. Again, expansion of income in advanced and oil-producing nations provides a fillip to the flow of NRI remittances which constitute a non-negligible source of household consumption and investment. In fact, instances abound when the net impact of an adverse oil shock on the Indian economy was benign, not malignant (Rakshit 2007).

Identifying Drivers of the Growth Cycle

In the context of the discussion in the two previous sections, we first try to disabuse some widely held views regarding the nature, especially the phases and turning points, of the growth cycle during the reference period, pinpoint the proximate, autonomous components of demand and supply causing short term variations in GDP, and seek to identify the basic factors driving the components. Next, taking a broader view of the cyclical behaviour of the economy, we try to examine how imbalances, both real and financial, developed during the booming phase and how together with other factors, they ushered in a period of downturn and protracted slowdown.[8]

Short-Term Variations

Year-on-year changes in quarterly GDP at constant market prices suggest that the lower and upper turning points (LTP and UTP) of the growth cycle occurred at $Q_1(03-04)$[9] and $Q_1(11-12)$ respectively. However, on the basis of OECD estimates of deseasonalised quarterly GDP, the turning points, as discussed in the preceding section, occurred earlier than what is suggested by the time series of y-o-y growth (since OECD does not provide estimates of deseasonalised quarterly GDP at factor costs and its components, we are forced to consider the misspecification of the phase and turning points only of GDP at market prices). The LTP, according to the OECD time series was reached at $Q_4(02-03)$, not $Q_1(03-04)$. The q-o-q growth went up from 3.4 per cent in $Q_3(02-03)$ to 5.4 per cent in $Q_4(02-03)$ and accelerated to 8.2 per cent, 8.3 per cent and 23 per cent respectively in the three successive quarters. The misspecification of the conventional analysis relating to the UTP and the initial phase of the slowdown is much more pronounced. The q-o-q GDP growth started slowing down from $Q_2(10-11)$, not $Q_1(11-12)$, as is usually supposed (on the basis of y-o-y growth estimates). Quarter-on-quarter growth declined from 11.2 per cent in $Q_1(10–11)$ to 9.4 per cent in $Q_2(10–11)$ and continued to fall thereafter over the next five successive quarters. Given such misspecification, analysis of India's growth cycle based on the time series of y-o-y growth data cannot but be grossly distortionary. What about the triggers of the turning points and drivers of short-term variations in growth? The variations, we have noted earlier, could be due to operation of both demand- and supply-side factors. However, in the absence of data for deseasonalised quarterly GDP at factor costs and its components, we try to identify only the demand-side factors driving short-term growth.[10]

The enquiry is conducted in two stages. First, as suggested in the previous section, for analysing the short-term behaviour of aggregate demand, we focus on its autonomous components, the most important of which are (a) government final consumption expenditure (GFCE); (b) gross fixed capital formation (GFCF); and (c) exports.[11] As a first approximation, the contribution of the three autonomous components of q-o-q changes in quarterly GDP may be taken to be equal to the q-o-q growth of the components times their respective shares in total autonomous expenditure.[12] In order to appreciate the significance of GFCF etc. in total autonomous expenditure (rather than GDP), consider the simple Keynesian model with its standard notations (ignoring the distinction between GFCF and inventory investment[13]).

$$Y = C(Y) + I + G + X - M(Y) \quad (1)$$

While C and M are assumed to be dependent on Y, the other three components of Y are taken to be autonomous. A little rearrangement of terms and differentiating the two sides of (1) with respect to time yields

$$g_Y = (1/Y)(I + G + X)/(1 - C' + M')(\alpha_I g_I + \alpha_g g_g + \alpha_x g_x) \quad (2)$$

Where g_z denotes the growth rate of variable z and α_z is the share of z in total autonomous expenditure $A = I + G + X$. To see why $(\alpha_I g_I + \alpha_g g_g + \alpha_x g_x) = K$ (say) provides a good, first order approximation of GDP and respective contributions of autonomous expenditures, note that if C and M are linear functions of Y, K exactly equals g_Y. Quite clearly, for not too large temporal variations in Y, the difference between the estimated value of g_Y on the basis of K and the actual g_Y would be of a minor order.

Identification of changes in autonomous expenditure and their quantitative impact on aggregate demand constitutes, however, only the first step for an adequate analysis of short-term growth dynamics. At the second stage, we need to examine the factors behind changes in the three autonomous components themselves. These factors generally consist of domestic and international economic environment including governments' policy initiatives. It is important to recognise that they affect not only GFCE, GFCF and exports but also the relationship between GDP and other components of demand,[14] for example, household consumption and imports of goods and services.

Strictly speaking, the distinction between autonomous and induced demand is often a matter of degree, not of kind. While a part of C and M is generally autonomous (in the sense of not being induced by changes in GDP), investment and government expenditures could be positively impacted by rising GDP, the first due to improvement in business expectations, the second because of relaxation of constraints relating to targets for fiscal deficits as a ratio of GDP (as both the numerator and denominator of the fiscal deficit ratio declines). We thus need to (a) take cognisance of changes in autonomous components of C and M along with that in induced components of I and G; and (b) identify the temporal variations in the autonomous parts of GDP's components or in the relationship between Y and the induced components. Once we have identified these changes, the explanation of short-term growth, at the formal level, is similar to that in equation (2). But it is horrendously difficult to separate the autonomous from the induced parts and estimate contributions of the former.

However, taking account of ongoing and past developments which had major consequences for aggregate demand, it is possible to assess the main drivers of and their significance for short-term, q-o-q changes in quarterly output. The upsurge in output in the early 2000s, as already noted, started from $Q_1(02-03)$. The quarter also marked the beginning of a robust and prolonged growth in GFCF. Though the upward thrust in GDP growth was led by domestic investment, the role of external factors in the turnaround of the growth trajectory was not negligible. Thanks to the US expansionary policy in the wake of the burst of the dot-com bubble, and acceleration of global growth, India's exports of goods and services started rising at a rapid pace from the second half of 2002. The other, though relatively less important source of external stimulus to domestic demand, was the rise in household consumption and investment out of growing NRI remittances as the world economy entered its booming phase.

The salubrious international economic environment was thus an important factor in reversing the direction of India's growth trajectory. Much more important however, was the government policy relating to investment in general and infrastructural investment in particular. The late 1990s saw a step-up in public investment in power, irrigation, road, railways and transport and communication. But private investment, which formed the bulk of aggregate GFCF, remained lacklustre at the initial stage. It was the multi-pronged government support to private investment in infrastructure, especially through public-private partnership (PPP) from the early 2000s that, backed by the improving global economic and financial outlook, induced massive flows of private sector GFCF, which helped accelerate the upturn in GDP growth from $Q_1(03-04)$.

Contrary to popular perception, triggers of the downturn since $Q_1(10-11)$ were domestic, not external. Between $Q_1(10-11)$ and $Q_2(10-11)$, the q-o-q growth of India's exports of goods and services did, to be sure, decline from a whopping 26.2 per cent to a much moderate 13.8 per cent. But even so, at

13.8 per cent, the export growth was higher than the quarter's GDP growth by no less than 4.9 percentage points (pps). The role of external stimulus in moderating the growth-debilitating impact of domestic factors may be appreciated from the fact that though the share of exports in GDP was 21 per cent, their direct, unadjusted[15] contribution to the quarter's GDP growth was as much as 30 per cent. In fact, a quantum jump of export growth to 57.2 per cent prevented a further slide in GDP growth in the next quarter $Q_3(10-11)$; but in $Q_4(10-11)$, despite a 15.8 per cent growth, and 3.5 percentage points of unadjusted contribution to growth of aggregate demand, the negative impact of factors originating in the domestic economy could not be neutralised. Curiously enough, the domestic factor triggering the slowdown was not a downturn in GFCF, the usual suspect behind cyclical fluctuations: only from $Q_2(11-12)$, four quarters after the onset of the slowdown, did growth of fixed investment start declining.

The proximate source of the slowdown was decelerating growth of consumption, both public and private. The direct, unadjusted contribution of government consumption to q-o-q GDP growth declined from 2.8 pps in $Q_1(10-11)$ to 0.36 pps in $Q_2(10-11)$ and further to 0.32 pps in the next quarter. Much more important in effecting the downturn was the slump in the growth of household consumption from 9.4 per cent in $Q_1(10-11)$ to 6.7 per cent and 3.9 per cent in $Q_2(10-11)$ and $Q_3(10-11)$, respectively. The direct, unadjusted contribution of household consumption to q-o-q GDP growth in the first three quarters of 2010-11 amounted respectively to 5.93, 3.9 and 2.7 pps. However, unlike GFCE, household expenditure on consumption is mostly induced and hence, as discussed earlier, we need to consider the change only in its autonomous component. After allowing for the income-induced change, growth in autonomous household consumption in $Q_1(10-11)$, $Q_2(10-11)$ and $Q_3(10-11)$ is found to be −0.68 pps, −1.68 pps and −4.56 pps, respectively; the corresponding contributions of the components to q-o-q GDP growth were −0.36 pps, −0.96 pps and −2.26 pps, respectively.

The downward shift in the household consumption function, like the slowdown in GFCE, was policy-related. The Reserve Bank's monetary tightening from February 2010 and decline in the pace of public consumption must have had a negative impact on households' expectations relating to economic outlook. Of much greater significance was the withdrawal in the 2010–11 budget (presented in February 2010), of all indirect tax concessions granted after the outbreak of the Global Financial Crisis in September 2008. There can thus be little doubt that it was the consumption-reducing consequence of a fiscal and monetary policy that set the slowdown in motion.

The decline in the growth rate of consumption was however transitory. GFCE staged some, albeit minor, recovery after $Q_4(10-11)$. Given the one-off rise in indirect tax rates, the tax-GDP ratio adjusted to the new, higher rates fairly quickly so that private purchases of goods and services, which constituted by far the major part of aggregate demand, came to be driven mostly by GDP growth. The policy induced fall in consumption growth, which tapered off in no more than 2–3 quarters. Hence, for explaining the economy's lacklustre growth beyond 2010–11, we need to look elsewhere. This is what we do in the next section while discussing the medium-term dynamics of the growth cycle over our reference period.

Medium-Term Growth Dynamics

For analysing the medium-term growth dynamics it seems useful to consider first the relative roles of autonomous components of GDP in driving the macro economy during the two phases of the growth cycle: 2003–11 and 2011–15. Between the two phases the average yearly GDP growth declined from 8.3 per cent to 5.6 per cent. A simple way of assessing the role of the components in effecting the near 3 pps fall in growth is to compare their average yearly changes and contributions to GDP growth in the two periods. Table 1.1 suggests that practically all the autonomous components had some role in accounting for how the booming phase of the economy gave way to a period of decelerating and sluggish growth. The only exception was GFCE: curiously enough, though the cutback in government consumption constituted a trigger of the downturn, yet between the two phases, growth of GFCE and its contribution to GDP growth were on the average larger in the second phase. However, the 0.15 pps rise in the contribution of this component was far too small to make much of a difference to the slump in GDP growth over 2011–15.

Consider first the autonomous components governed primarily by the external economic environment. For the Indian economy, the most important of these components are exports and net oil-cum-fertiliser (NOF) imports.[16] Between 2003–11 and 2011–15, the average growth and contribution to yearly increase in GDP growth of exports of goods and services declined from 14.82 per cent and 2.63 pps to 10.96 per cent and 2.53 pps, respectively. Much more important was the growth debilitating effect of net oil-cum-fertiliser imports: with a jump in their growth from 14.66 per cent to 19.41 per cent, the contribution of this component declined from –0.50 to –0.86 pps. But even so the (0.10 + 0.36) or 0.46 pps fall effected by external factors, though not negligible, leaves the overwhelming part of the fall of GDP growth between the two periods unaccounted for. Like most macroeconomic fluctuations, India's growth cycle was also driven primarily by investment, the most volatile component of aggregate demand. Before considering the nature and sources of variations of this variable, we deem it necessary to take stock of changes, between the two phases, of other factors (listed as memo items in Table 1.1) that affected directly or indirectly the autonomous components of GDP in general and investment in particular.

Table 1.1: Macroeconomic indicators over 2003–11 and 2011–15

		2003–11	2011–15
1) GDP at market prices	Average yearly growth	8.39%	5.61%
2) Govt consumption	Average yearly growth	7.38%	8.23%
2.1) Govt consumption	Contribution to GDP growth	0.80 pps	0.95 pps
3) Gross investment	Average yearly growth	14.21%	2.97%
3.1) Gross investment	Contribution to GDP growth	4.03 pps	1.02 pps
4) Public investment	Average yearly growth	12.82%	4.46%
4.1) Public investment	Contribution to GDP growth	0.99 pps	0.34 pps
5) Private investment	Average yearly growth	15.32%	3.10%
5.1) Private investment	Contribution to GDP growth	3.42 pps	0.81 pps
6) Private corporate investment	Average yearly growth	25.12%	7.83%
6.1) Private corporate investment	Contribution to GDP growth	2.19 pps	0.96 pps
7) GFCF	Average yearly growth	12.87%	4.66%
7.1) GFCF	Contribution to GDP growth	3.69 pps	1.45 pps
8) Exports	Average yearly growth	14.82%	10.96%
8.1) Exports	Contribution to GDP growth	2.63 pps	2.53 pps
9) Net oil + fertiliser imports	Average yearly growth	14.66%	19.41%
9.1) Net oil + fertiliser imports	Contribution to GDP growth	–0.50 pps	–0.86 pps
MEMO ITEMS			
1) Agriculture	Average yearly growth (of value added)	4.27%	3.53%
1.1) Agriculture	Contribution to GDP (at factor cost) growth	0.81 pps	0.53 pps
2) Oil price per barrel	Average	US$ 65.36	US$ 85.75
3) Exchange rate	Re/Dollar (average)	44.96	54.43
4) CPI inflation	Average	7.12%	15.00%
5) WPI food inflation	Average	8.24%	9.68%
6) WPI fuel inflation	Average	7.27%	10.12%
7) WPI inflation	Average	6.10%	6.96%

Source: Author

Agriculture, Oil Prices and Inflationary Pressure

Since even now agriculture plays a major role in governing performance of the Indian economy, it is necessary to examine, in light of our previous discussion, if or how changes in agricultural output can account for the difference in GDP growth between the two phases of the growth cycle. A simple way of assessing its role is to consider the differences between the two periods in the average growth of value added in agriculture and its contribution to growth of GDP at factor costs. On this criterion the role was non-negligible: while the yearly average growth of income originating in agriculture and its contribution to GDP growth were 4.27 per cent and 0.81 pp respectively in 2003–11, over 2011–15 their respective values were 3.53 per cent and 0.53 pp. The near 0.3 pp fall in GDP growth effected by the slowdown in agriculture was quite significant remembering that the share of the farm sector in GDP was only around 15 per cent. But this constitutes an underestimate of the growth-dampening effect of agriculture inasmuch as it (the estimate) takes no account of the several routes through which agriculture impacts the rest of the economy. To recapitulate, the adverse consequences operate through cutbacks in demand for non-agricultural sectors' products both directly and indirectly via spiralling food prices and CPI inflation.

The role of the oil shock in fuelling CPI inflation was more important than the slowdown of agricultural growth. Between 2003–11 and 2011–15 the average crude oil prices went up from US$ 65.36 to US$ 85.75 per barrel. This along with the fall in the Re/US$ exchange rate from Rs 44.96 to Rs 54.43 implies a (30+23) or 53 per cent rise in petroleum prices in rupee terms between the two periods. Large subsidies on petro-products moderated the pass-through of the rise in international prices. But even so fuel price inflation between the two periods rose from 7.27 per cent to 10.12 per cent. The effect of the near 3 pps rise in fuel price inflation was similar to that of the northward movement of food price inflation: because of inelastic demand for fuel and the CPI-induced rise in policy rates, the consequence was contractionary for the non-agricultural sector.

The economic cost of fuel subsidy was not negligible either. Given the priority accorded to limiting fiscal deficit, large budgetary outgoes on petroleum subsidy prevented the government from raising expenditure on investment, which apart from having a larger demand generation impact in the short-run, could have addressed the structural imbalances limiting the country's both short- and medium-term growth potential, something we shall turn to in a short while.

The Prime Mover

Even a cursory glance at Table 1.1 confirms the overarching role of investment in effecting the fall in GDP growth between the two periods of our study. With more than an 8 pps fall in the pace of gross capital formation (GFCF), the difference in the contribution of this component to GDP growth was 2.24 pps, slightly less than 2.8 pps fall in GDP growth between the two phases. The main culprit in this context was private, especially private corporate investment. While public investment declined[17] from 12.82 per cent to 4.46 per cent; the fall in private and private corporate investment were from 15.3 per cent and 25.12 per cent to 3.1 per cent and 7.8 per cent respectively. The significance of the fall in growth rates of private and private corporate investment in effecting the slowdown may be appreciated from the fact that, out of the gross investment-induced 3.0 pps fall in GDP growth, 2.61 pps were directly accounted for by the former and 1.23 pps by the latter. Thus while private investment's share in total investment was 75 per cent, its share in the investment-induced fall in GDP growth was as much as 87 per cent. On this criterion the slowdown due to private corporate investment was steeper: while its share in aggregate capital formation was 33 per cent, 49 per cent of the fall in GDP growth was directly affected by the component.

For an explanation of the relative performance of the economy during the two phases, we thus need to examine the factors behind the boom and bust of private sector capital formation. An important mechanism behind investment-led economic fluctuations is real-financial sector feedback loop. Whatever the trigger of a step-up in investment, aggregate demand rises by a multiple of the incremental capital formation. The immediate consequence is rise in capacity utilisation and the rate of profit since while investment raises capacity output only in the medium run, the overwhelming part of the additional demand for goods and services is generated within a quarter or so. This could lead to a cumulative process of rising investment fuelled by improvement in investors' expectations. Higher profits and capacity utilisation make financing of investments easier: decline in default rates and NPAs (non-performing assets), improved credit ratings, rising share prices—all contribute to enlarging the flow of finances from both domestic and external sources for funding new investment projects. The cumulative process can result in an 'irrational exuberance', leading to unsustainable rates of capital accumulation and pave the way for a recession. The process is reversed during the downward phase of the cycle except that left on its own, the economy could take a considerable time before staging a recovery (Keynes 1936). Fortunately, thanks to Keynesian lessons and increasing weight of public opinion, vigorous government intervention has made recessions significantly shorter since World War II.

Structural Imbalance

A prolonged boom followed by a sharp slowdown and painfully sluggish recovery despite expansionary monetary and fiscal policy is not often due to unsustainable high GFCF during the upward phase of the cycle: in the absence of any structural constraints, aggregate demand-boosting measures, as advocated by Keynes, should be able to effect a recovery.

However, weaknesses of a structural nature seriously impair the efficacy of Keynesian remedies in many economies, especially EMEs (emerging market economies). Some of the common constraints consist of large debt accumulated during the boom, a major part of which is denominated in foreign currency; balance of payments (BOP) vulnerability due to heavy reliance on crucial imports like petroleum and on exports of goods whose prices in the international market are highly volatile; and serious shortage of infrastructural facilities that prevent capacity utilisation in or expansion of manufacturing and services.

So far as the Indian economy is concerned, we have already noted the role of crude oil price movements in helping and hindering GDP growth over the period of our study. The most important structural factor for the economy is the productive capacity of agriculture in relation to that of other sectors. It is important to recognise that the poor performance of agriculture that slowed down economic growth during the second phase was the result of a structural imbalance between agriculture and the rest of the economy built up during the booming phase. Over the 11 year period, 2000–11, the average growth of GFCF in agriculture was 6.86 per cent, more than 3.7 pps less than that of aggregate GFCF. During this period, agriculture's share in GFCF was less than half of its share in GDP (at factor cost). From 2002–03 onward the farm sector's share of investment showed a persistently negative trend. Such unbalanced capital accumulation over so long a period, structuralist macroeconomics suggests, cannot but put pressure on relative prices of agricultural goods and act as a constraint on growth of industries and services. The phase of booming aggregate investment was also characterised by rising inequality of earnings, with the share of employment in the unorganised sector in total employment crossing 90 per cent, and income gains from growth accruing mostly to the middle- and upper-income groups. The resulting rise in highly land-intensive goods like meat, milk and poultry pushed up prices of food grains which together with the subdued income growth of workers in the unorganised sector constituted a non-negligible source of emergence of demand deficiency and growth slowdown in the non-agricultural sector.

Infrastructure Fetishism

By far the most important imbalance developed during the investment boom relates to the relative rates of capacity creation in infrastructure and other areas. It is universally acknowledged that poor infrastructural facilities constitute the most important obstacle in EMEs to full utilisation of non-infrastructural capital stocks and private sector demand for their accumulation. Since in view of their lumpiness, high durability, long gestation lag and large (positive) externality, private investors seldom find it attractive to invest in roads, railways, electricity and other forms of infrastructure, in India, as in other EMEs; the government has been long trying to expand infrastructural facilities both on its own and by providing a whole host of concessions to private investors, especially under the system of PPP. The most important of these concessions consisted of upfront grants, waiving tax on profits for a stipulated period, permission for setting prices of infrastructural products to ensure adequate returns[18] for investors and above all, massive financial support, that is, while domestic financial institutions were prompted to extend loans on easy terms, investors were allowed to issue tax-free bonds as also to borrow substantial sums from the international capital market. Under the benign external environment, it did not take long for these initiatives to bear fruit.

The surge in infrastructural investment started in the late 1990s, gathering momentum from 2004–05 and exceeding other types of investment by a wide margin. In fact, even after the slowdown had set in, infrastructural investment posted a huge growth[19] of 24.33 per cent in 2011–12, while the pace of non-infrastructural capital formation nose-dived to 2.3 per cent. The result was that during 2006–13 the average growth of investment in infrastructure (at 13.0 per cent at constant prices) surpassed that of other forms of capital formation by a whopping 5.0 pps. Indeed, the share of infrastructure in aggregate investment showed a rising trend from the beginning of the millennium. The consequent imbalance in the economy's capital structure was the most important factor behind the precipitous fall in private investment during the second phase of the growth cycle. For an appreciation of how a universally recommended policy can turn counter-productive, a few words on its underlying causal connections seem to be in order. Note first that the overwhelming part of infrastructural facilities, for example, highways, power generation, airports and railways, cater primarily to the domestic market. Hence demand for their output depends on incomes generated in the non-infrastructural sector.

When this sector's productive capacity is small relatively to that of infrastructure, its capacity remains underutilised, investors suffer from mounting losses, expectations sour, new investments in infrastructure turn into a trickle and projects under implementation are stalled or abandoned, triggering a mutually reinforcing downturn in both sectors of the economy. The economic woes resulting from the structural imbalance tend to be long-drawn since infrastructural capital stocks last for decades and there is little incentive for private, non-infrastructural investment under the prevailing economic scenario. The similarity between the housing boom followed by prolonged recession in Ireland, Spain, Portugal and the US, and India's infrastructure-driven cycle is palpable: both types of investments are long-lasting and their viability depends crucially on income generated in other sectors of the domestic economy. Our analysis suggests why, given the large imbalance in composition of capital stock, Keynesian policies would not be of much avail in the short run in effecting a recovery, remembering that the remedy lies in raising non-infrastructural productive capacity at a rapid rate for removing the imbalance. However, the revival of private investment, which accounts for the lion's share of aggregate capital formation in India, is highly problematic because of fragility of the financial system wrought by the investment boom.

Financial Sector Imbalance

Most investment booms are accompanied with financial excesses and India's was no exception. Demand-driven rise in capacity utilisation, profits (current as well as expected) and share prices pave the way for large-scale debt financing of investment at interest rates, which cool-headed calculations would consider too costly. The overwhelming part of such loans, especially in countries like India where the private debt market is extremely shallow and grossly under-developed, is extended by banks through provision of term loans or acquisition of bonds issued by investing companies. The quantum jump in debt financing of capital accumulation during India's investment boom is attested by the fact that the equity-weighted mean of the debt-equity ratio of Indian non-financial companies more than doubled between 2001 and 2012, from 40 per cent to 83 per cent (Lindner and Jung 2014). In fact, companies with a debt-equity ratio of more than 5 accounted for 30 per cent of total debt by end 2012–13. No wonder, the slowdown sent crashing the interest-coverage ratios[20] (ICRs) of debt-ridden firms. As of March 2013, debt of loss-making firms exceeded 26 per cent of the total debt outstanding. The consequence of such historically high share of firms with weak financial indicators was large-scale debt default in the wake of the economic slowdown. Between March 2011 and September 2015, stressed assets (comprising gross NPAs and restructured loans) of banks as a proportion of their total advances shot up from 6.0 to 11.3 per cent (IMF 2015). For public sector banks the ratio was much higher (14.1 per cent). Throughout the slowdown, large provisioning on account of debt default took a heavy toll on banks' profits, reduced their capital adequacy ratio, forced them to reduce loans, and park their funds in SLR (Statutory Liquidity Ratio) securities, significantly in excess (often by 5 pps or more) of the minimum stipulated ratio. This constituted the crucial real-financial feedback loop behind the dizzying fall in private investment, which the (belated) fiscal stimulus and monetary easing were incapable of arresting.

Debt financing was particularly pronounced in investment in infrastructure. Its sources of finance in the domestic market consisted of commercial banks and non-bank financial intermediaries (that do not take deposits), including special purpose vehicles (SPVs) set up for funding infrastructure projects. Since the entities were extended substantial finance by commercial banks, their exposure to infrastructural firms was much larger than loans given directly to these firms. Before the late 1990s, banks' exposure to infrastructural activities was relatively minor. Since then, bank lending to the sector went up by leaps and bounds so that between 2000–01 and 2010–11, the outstanding bank credit to infrastructural firms as a ratio of total advances shot up from 2.2 per cent to 13.3 per cent and hit 14.1 per cent by end 2014–15.

The other source of financial imbalance wrought by investment in infrastructure was heavy reliance on external commercial borrowing. This is reflected in the fact that (*i*) ECBs (external commercial borrowing) as a proportion of total debt of a large number of companies in this sector was 20 per cent or more; and (*ii*) the outstanding stock of ECBs, the lion's share of whose rise was due to the rapid pace of infrastructural investment, surged from US$ 22.0 billion in 2003–04 to US$ 120.14 billion in 2011–12 and reached a mountainous US$ 181.83 billion in 2014–15. Since revenues in infrastructure came almost entirely from domestic sales, debts of such magnitude denominated in foreign currency constituted an important component of the real-financial sector imbalance effected by the investment boom for expansion of infrastructural facilities. Heavy reliance on ECBs,[21] excessively skewed composition of capital stocks, and large long-term bank loans to infrastructure firms, with inordinately low ratios of equity to debt constituted a potent mix that made both the firms and banks highly vulnerable to shocks, domestic and external.

The domestic shock which sank infrastructure companies and damaged the financial system consisted of fiscal and monetary tightening from early 2010, which coming on top of the large, accumulated imbalance in sectoral production potential, set in motion a process of falling capacity utilisation, profits and interest cover ratios (ICR), and forced the firms to renege on their debt obligations. Matters were not helped by the sharp rise in oil prices and more than 33 per cent depreciation of the rupee. The combined effect of the domestic and external shocks was to reduce aggregate demand, push infrastructure firms to the brink of bankruptcy, sharply raise stressed assets of banks, which resulted in an average yearly decline in bank credit by 12 per cent (in real terms) over 2011–15. The main sources of stressed assets are also obvious: according to the RBI (2013), as of March 2011, when infrastructure's share in total bank credit was 13.3 per cent, the ratio of stressed loans to this sector to total stressed asset was 8.4 per cent. By September 2013, infrastructure's share in bank advances crept up to 14.7 per cent, but its share in stressed assets rose to 30.5 per cent. Thus, our analysis and evidence suggest that the role played by investment in infrastructure, in the development of real-financial imbalances and in the sharp slowdown of private investment since 2010 can hardly be in doubt.

Summary and Conclusions

First, discussion of India's GDP growth in official reports and in the large majority of unofficial studies is marred by weak theoretical foundation. This is reflected in (*i*) attempts at explanation of the behaviour of the economy in terms of accounting identities; and (*ii*) use of year-on-year, rather than quarter-on-quarter variations in GDP and its components for the purpose of empirical analysis. While the weak theoretical underpinning stands in the way of identifying (*i*) the causal connections among the autonomous and induced components of GDP and (*ii*) the factors driving the autonomous components, the focus on year-on-year variations of macro variables leads to misspecification of turning points and phases of the growth cycle. Thus on the basis of the quarter-on-quarter growth of deseasonalised, quarterly GDP estimates, the growth slowdown in our reference period is found to have set in from $Q_2(10-11)$, not from $Q_1(11-12)$, as suggested by the y-on-y growth data. Again, contrary to the popular perception, the proximate sources of slowdown were not external but domestic and policy-related. These consisted of deceleration of government consumption, the negative impact of increases in indirect taxes on household purchases of goods and services, lagged effects of cutbacks in public investment and monetary tightening on private capital expenditure.

Second, the autonomous factors behind the persistence of slowdown were primarily domestic: between the two phases of the fall in GDP, growth due to external shocks amounted to 0.5 pps and that too is almost wholly accounted for by the sharp rise in international oil prices, not decelerating exports. Among the domestic depressants, agriculture's role, both directly (with its anemic output growth dampening demand for non-agricultural products) and indirectly (through the food inflation–induced fall in consumption of industrial goods and services) was by no means negligible. However, the most important source of the protracted slowdown was the precipitous fall in private, especially private corporate investment: between the two periods the fall in growth in these two components was from 15.3 per cent and 25.1 per cent to 3.1 per cent and 7.8 per cent, respectively (see Table 1.1). In fact, a huge 2.78 pps fall in the average yearly growth of GDP, more than its average fall between the two phases, was due directly to the decline in private corporate investment.

Third, the private investment boom and bust in India were similar to the housing boom and bust culminating in the Great Recession, in more ways than one. In both cases the investment boom was accompanied with real as well as financial sector imbalances. So far as the housing boom is concerned, the real sector imbalance resulted from the fact that (*i*) a sharp rise in stock of housing in relation to productive capacity in other sectors makes the house rent too low to cover the cost of investment; (*ii*) demand for housing comes almost wholly from the domestic economy; and (*iii*) excessively high durability of houses makes correcting for the imbalance in the composition of capital stock long drawn. The financial sector fragility developed during the surge in residential construction was due to exceptionally high ratio (often 80–90 per cent) of mortgage loans to the construction costs on the one hand, and large exposure (directly and indirectly) of financial entities to the housing sector on the other. All these were also the hallmarks of real-financial sector imbalances accompanying India's infrastructural investment boom. The only exception was the abnormally high ratio of foreign-currency denominated loans as a ratio of total debt of infrastructure companies—something which made the situation worse than in the US. Be that as it may, the fact remains that one needs to look further than the structural imbalances created during the boom in infrastructural investment for locating the source of the sharp decline of private investment in India and the main reason for the ineffectiveness of fiscal expansion and monetary easing in reversing its downturn.

Fourth, our analysis brings into sharp relief a few policy lessons for macro management in countries like India: (*i*) While tracing the behaviour of the economy, policy makers need to look more at the q-o-q rather than the y-o-y changes in deseasonalised, quarterly GDP, its components and other relevant variables like prices and financial flows—data that are conspicuous by their absence in India's official statistics; (*ii*) the policy inputs should include, among other things, not only the trajectory of output growth, but also that of indicators of real and financial imbalances. In this context, it is necessary to construct indices of the imbalances keeping the major structural features of the economy in view. (*iii*) Related to the second point, the importance of monitoring the interaction between agriculture and other sectors of the economy, à la the structuralist macroeconomic framework, can hardly be overemphasised. An important source of policy failure in preventing/reversing the economic slide was inadequate appreciation of (*i*) the short- and medium-run interdependence of agriculture and rest of the economy; and (*ii*) widely different policy implications of CPI inflation driven by food or fuel prices and that resulting from northward movement of prices of industrial products and services. Finally, the policy makers should keep an open mind, not take conventional wisdom as an article of faith and be always on the lookout for new, hitherto unexpected sources of vulnerability of the macro economy; otherwise, they might, like the proverbial Field Marshal, be fighting the last, not the current war.

NOTES

[1] Data- and policy-related problems pose major obstacles to extending the analysis to 2017–18. The change in the concepts and estimation of macroeconomic variables under the new series (with 2011–12 as the base year) has made linking the old and new series for examining the temporal behaviour of the economy highly problematic. What is more important is that, over the period for which data under both the old and new series are available, not only do the two sets of estimates differ widely, but those under the old series are much more consistent with estimates like the index of industrial production and capacity utilisation as per RBI surveys. Two major policy initiatives, demonetisation and GST, have also made the estimation of India's 2016–18 growth trajectory extremely difficult for an individual researcher.

[2] Remembering that, with declining spending in successive rounds of the multiplier, the major part of the total income generated by some autonomous expenditure takes place in the first few rounds.

[3] The lagged effects are due to a) tail of the multiplier process; and b) impact of expectations regarding future earnings, inflation or interest rates; governed primarily by the macroeconomic behaviour in current and recent quarters, not by what happened one year back: the longer the lag, the lesser the likelihood of such happenings having a material consequence for current levels of demand.

[4] $t_0 t_1 = t_2 t_3 = 4$ quarters

[5] Or what may somewhat loosely be called dependent and independent variables from the viewpoint of generation of quarterly output or expenditure.

[6] In mainstream macroeconomics, relative prices of products are presumed to be fixed so that changes in the composition of output are driven by income elasticity of demand. However, when output of a sector is used as inputs in production of other goods and services, value added in different sectors is governed by both the composition of final demand and coefficients of the economy's input-output matrix. In case spending propensities differ across sectors, a change in the composition of final demand effects a change in aggregate demand (and hence GDP) as well.

[7] Prices of which are closely related with that of crude oil.

[8] Recovery from protracted slowdown set in only from 2017.

[9] For $Q_1(03-04)$, $Q_1(11-12)$, and so on, the numbers in the brackets refer to years such as 2003–04 and 2011–12, respectively.

[10] At a later stage, while examining the behaviour of the economy over the reference period, we take account of both demand- and supply-side factors as well as their interactions on the basis of estimates of y-o-y growth of yearly GDP (at market prices and factor costs) and its components.

[11] Strictly speaking, the autonomous component of demand from external sources is exports minus export-related imports. However, quarterly data for such imports (let alone their deseasonalised

estimates), are not available. Since their share in total exports of goods and services is of a minor order, neglect of export-related imports does not significantly affect the results.

[12] Initially taken to be the sum of the three components

[13] Investment in inventories is governed primarily by production and hence needs to be treated as 'induced'. Anyway, in the absence of estimates of deseasonalised quarterly investment in inventories, we cannot take account of this part of investment in our present analysis.

[14] Thus, when an increase (or decrease) in income tax affects a fall (or increase) in consumption, the decline (or increase) constitutes an autonomous change in aggregate demand and triggers a negative (or positive) multiplier process.

[15] That is, not adjusted for the share of exports in total autonomous components of aggregate demand. Some rough and ready estimates suggest the adjusted contribution was around 6.5 percentage points instead of 4.4 percentage points.

[16] Though a large importer of crude oil, India is also an exporter of oil products in the international market.

[17] Deceleration of public investment constitutes a trigger of the slowdown, but within a short while there was some revival of this component of aggregate demand.

[18] That is, producers were permitted to exercise monopoly power to some extent under the supervision of regulatory authorities.

[19] Because of a large number of projects already under implementation.

[20] ICR refers to the ratio of gross profits to the interest obligation.

[21] As mentioned above, the ratio of ECBs to total debt was 20 per cent or more for many an infrastructure firm.

REFERENCES

IMF (International Monetary Fund). 2015. *India: Selected Issues*, March.

Keynes, J. M. 1936. *The General Theory of Employment, Interest and Money*. London: Macmillan.

Lindner, P. and Sung Eun Jung. 2014. 'Corporate Vulnerabilities in India and Banks' Loan Performance', IMF Working Paper No. WP/14/232, December. Available at https://www.imf.org/external/pubs/ft/wp/2014/wp14232.pdf (accessed September 2022).

Rakshit, M. 1982. *The Labour Surplus Economy*. Delhi: Macmillan and New Jersey: Humanities Press.

———. 2007. 'Inflation in a Developing Economy: Theory and Policy'. *ICRA Bulletin: Money & Finance* 3(2): 89–138; reprinted in M. Rakshit. 2009. *Macroeconomics of Post-Reform India*. New Delhi: Oxford University Press.

———. (ed.). 1989. *Studies in the Macroeconomics of Developing Countries*. New Delhi: Oxford University Press.

Reserve Bank of India. 2013. *Financial Stability Report*, December. Available at https://www.rbi.org.in/ (accessed March 2023).

Taylor, L. 1983. *Structuralist Macroeconomics*. New York: Basic Books.

2

THE VOLATILITY OF INDIA'S CATCH-UP GROWTH

A Discussion

Ashima Goyal

Introduction

India's post-liberalisation reform growth rates have been higher but more volatile, when seen alongside the transition periods of other comparable countries. It left behind the steady Hindu rate of growth of 4 per cent for a higher growth[1] of about 7 per cent in the 12 years over 2005–06 to 2017–18, but the lowest rate of growth in this period was 3.1 and the highest 8.5.

China meanwhile, had fast and sustained growth after its GDP per capita in purchasing power parity (PPP) terms crossed US$ 1747 in 1992. The experience of Japan and the US was similar. The volatility of growth rates reduced. After they cross a minimum threshold, dispersed reinforcing growth foci normally allow low-income countries to grow rapidly. India crossed PPP US$ 1800 in 1999. Although its growth since then has been higher, it has continued to be volatile. Why? This chapter argues that the reasons behind this were reform inadequacies which aggravated supply shocks. Macro policy tended to over-react to shocks rather than smoothen them; whereas, sometimes policies were not appropriate for the context.

Catch-up growth[2] is normally faster than industrial country growth but it only defines a potential or trend growth rate. Savings generally rise with growth as incomes grow, firms get cash-rich and tax revenues boom. China's savings rate reached 50 per cent of its GDP. India's savings rate reached 30 per cent of its GDP in the late 2000s, and together with an incremental capital output ratio of four, and a sustainable current account deficit (CAD) of 2 per cent in the Balance of Payments, peak savings defined a potential growth rate of 9 per cent. The savings rate fell below 30, after a period of lower investment and growth but there are signs of rising productivity, which reduces capital required for growth. Entrants to the labour force and transition to higher productivity jobs can provide the required labour inputs. But counter-cyclical macroeconomic policy has to maintain the actual rate of growth in the face of shocks, even while reforms continue to sustain the potential rate. In India's case, this did not happen.

Openness, despite its contribution to diversification and catch-up growth was also a source of shocks—the reform years saw major oil and food price shocks, the East Asian crisis, the Global Financial Crisis (GFC) (which, more correctly, began as a North-Atlantic financial crisis), global slowdown and unconventional monetary policy, the pandemic and the flare-up in Ukraine. Too much macroeconomic stimulus after the GFC was followed by a reaction of too much tightening. The conservative response of fiscal and monetary policy meant that the optimum utilisation of space available for stimulus was missing. The focus remained on structural reforms even in macroeconomic policy despite an extended industrial slowdown after 2011. Industry growth was 3 per cent lower in the period after 2011 compared to that before. Reforms themselves neglected critical bottlenecks. It is often argued that, first, radical reform such as demonetisation reduced growth. Second, essential land and labour reforms were missing. The first is inadequate because a one-off event cannot explain performance over time. Moreover, the slowdown preceded demonetisation. As for the second, it is not very productive to hold to an unachievable reform ideal, while missing out on feasible reforms, many of which are in process.

It can be asked why sustained higher growth is required since India's growth is among the highest in the world. It will become a 10-trillion-dollar economy in 2030 from its 2016 level of US$ 2.26 trillion if real growth rate is 7 per cent per annum, assuming an inflation rate of 4 per cent. If real growth rate is 9 per cent, however, GDP will be US$ 14 trillion.[3] The faster rate of growth will therefore give it US$ 4 trillion more of GDP, creating more employment and raise per capita GDP. But India had only brief growth peaks above 8 per cent. In 2019–20 growth crashed to 3.7 per cent and due to the Covid-19 shock, growth was –6 per cent in the next year before recovering to 9.1 per cent in 2021–22.

India's demographic dividend is both an opportunity and a challenge to create the conditions for sustainable high growth. By 2020, its estimated average age of 29 and dependency ratio of 0.4 will be the lowest in the world. But finding jobs for 8–12 million young people entering the labour force each year, and millions shifting out of low productivity agricultural jobs is a daunting task. There is a controversy around measuring employment but no estimate is anywhere near these numbers. The inability to deliver as many good jobs as required is partly responsible for India's labour participation rate[4] being in the 40s (as a percentage of population aged above 15 years), one of the lowest in the world with the world average being above 60[5].

Women have dropped out of the labour force in large numbers, although this is partly due to choosing to pursue higher levels of education and rising job aspirations.

According to World Bank estimates, about 10 per cent of Indian population, or 140 million people, lived below $2.15 per day in 2019 in terms of 2017 purchasing power parity. Of course distribution of income also matters, but higher growth has been a major factor in bringing down Indian poverty ratios, which were above 50 per cent in the 1970s.[6] The inability to sustain high growth rates is therefore worrying.

A stone thrown into a shallow pond creates large ripples but it would hardly disturb a deep lake. A diverse system has the capacity to absorb shocks, and reduces financial risks. Holding many types of assets means a loss in one can be offset by gains in others and therefore has minimal effect on the total asset portfolio. Despite rising external risks, the Indian economy as a whole is showing signs of having reached such a level of diversity. This was inadequate earlier despite crossing the PPP threshold because of agricultural bottlenecks and vulnerability to oil price shocks, which are now reducing. Reforms are lowering costs through the economy. Macroeconomic tightening was used instead of the required sectoral response to deal with the constraints, which partly explains why India's catch-up growth has shown so many ups and downs. Indian problems are often attributed to insufficient reforms but standard liberalising reforms can be inappropriate for India's structure. This chapter will first demonstrate this. Next it will examine sources of increasing resilience as well as continuing risks, and outline some feasible context-sensitive reforms.

The chapter is structured as follows: the next section shows why standard stabilisation policies may not be appropriate in the Indian context; the two subsequent sections discuss sources of improved diversification, and turns to external shocks and potential defences against them, respectively, before the final section which concludes.

Implications for Reform and for Macroeconomic Policies

India is often advised to reform in order to achieve sustained growth. But what exactly is the type of reform required? The standard Washington Consensus-based advice on reforms for emerging markets (EMs) used to be 'stabilise, privatise and liberalise'. This consensus was hammered out in various programmes designed for Latin America but even there it did not work well, imposing large growth costs and often ending in crisis. Stabilisation is required when a country is spending more than it is producing, and is unable to borrow to sustain it. There is excess demand, which has to be reduced. Reducing public intervention gives markets a greater role in price discovery. Getting prices right improves resource allocation. Liberalising entry of foreign capital may expand the resource base as well as improve efficiency.

As application of these reform programmes proved disappointing, it became clear that financial liberalisation should be gradual and be accompanied by deepening of domestic markets, strengthening of institutions and improvements in regulation. Crisis proofing was required. The 1990s crises in Mexico, Brazil, East Asia, Argentina and Russia centred around high short-term private debt and outflows under full capital account convertibility. The focus only on demand and prices, in the privatise–liberalise mantra, neglected deeper drivers of productivity and of performance.

A new group convened for a rethink. Williamson (2003) summarised modifications to the Washington Consensus. One of the main messages was that institutions and incentives matter. For example, just saying 'reduce fiscal deficit' is not enough. It is necessary to create incentives to make that happen.

Compared to the above advice based on the experience of countries that had not done well, a commission chaired by Spence (World Bank 2008) sought to extract lessons from countries that had managed to lift growth rates sustainably. It examined 13 economies that, in the period after 1950, grew at above 7 per cent for more than 25 years. Nine of these were from Asia. Their common characteristics included openness, macroeconomic stability, high savings and investment rates, and market allocation of resources. Governments were capable—pragmatic and flexible—rather than ideological. While willing to intervene in markets to promote exports through industrial policies, and to manage exchange rates (with the use of selected capital controls and reserve accumulation), they were flexible enough not to get locked into distorting policies, to anticipate and to change policies as required for growth. Labour market reform, competition, resource mobility and urbanisation were all supported. Public investment in infrastructure was raised to 5 to 7 per cent of GDP or more. Specific contextual interventions were made and microeconomic incentives were created. External drivers alone did not create growth. And openness did not imply blind application of market-friendly reforms.

Despite this learning that the Bretton Woods institutions went through, their advice to India continued with the dated message: stabilise, liberalise, privatise (see World Bank 2018).

Stabilise: Despite pointing out that the rate of investment was subdued and needed to accelerate, with low market demand as a possible cause, the World Bank insisted there was limited room for countercyclical measures because of structural constraints. It was important to maintain hard-won macroeconomic stability (ignoring the possibility that growth sacrifice could be reduced). Despite quarterly growth falling to 4.5 per cent in 2019, the IMF in its country review advised against any departure from fiscal consolidation.

Privatise: They saw the genesis of bank balance sheet stress in the period of exuberant bank credit growth over 2004–08, and ever-greening of loans after the GFC (ignoring the role of prolonged high interest rates, asset–liability mismatch and external shocks on infrastructure loans, of low demand and low growth in raising debt ratios). To revive banks and credit growth, besides recapitalisation, they recommended a consolidation of public sector banks, making their incentives more market-based, giving private banks a level playing field, and allowing more competitive entry (ignoring that private banks were not lending to industry, credit to which became negative).

Liberalise: For raising exports they wanted improvements in the competitiveness of Indian firms, largely through reforms to land, labour and financial markets. They saw continued integration into the global economy as essential for accelerating the growth rate (ignoring the necessity of building resilience against continuing external shocks and of possible political constraints on land and labour reforms).

Apart from ideology, this blinkered view may arise from an inadequate appreciation of how the Indian context differs from other nations that have undergone reform. The simple analytical framework below will be used to make a comparison across nations, and bring out nuances in the differences in country growth paths.

AN ANALYTICAL FRAMEWORK FOR STRUCTURAL ADJUSTMENT

Drawn in the space of traded (Q_T) and non-traded goods (Q_N), the tangent of the price to the production possibility frontier in Figure 2.1 gives the point of optimal production and its tangency to the indifference curve gives the point of optimal consumption.[7] It can be used to demonstrate the process of stabilisation and of structural adjustment. An EM needing adjustment could be consuming at point *a* but producing at point *b*. The production of non-traded goods equals its consumption, but there is excess consumption of traded goods financed through a current account deficit (CAD). If the latter is unsustainable, stabilisation is required to reduce absorption (demand), thus shifting the budget line in parallel inwards so that it becomes tangent to the production possibility frontier and the nation is not consuming more than it is producing.

But typically, excess demand for tradable goods would continue even after stabilisation to *b* unless prices also adjust.

The slope of the price line has to change to switch production towards tradable goods and reduce their consumption as they become relatively more expensive. Depreciation of the currency flattens the price line to reach a final equilibrium c where there is no excess consumption and the CAD is zero. Although consumption of both non-traded and traded goods falls compared to a, production and therefore consumption of traded goods rises relative to non-traded goods at c compared to b as they become relatively more expensive. Since at the new price line, traded goods prices have risen relative to non-traded goods, the overall consumption possibilities given by the new price line has less of Q_T compared to Q_N. These are the adjustments required in the case of excess demand and full employment of resources. While consumption of both types of goods falls, there is a rise in the relative domestic production of traded goods.

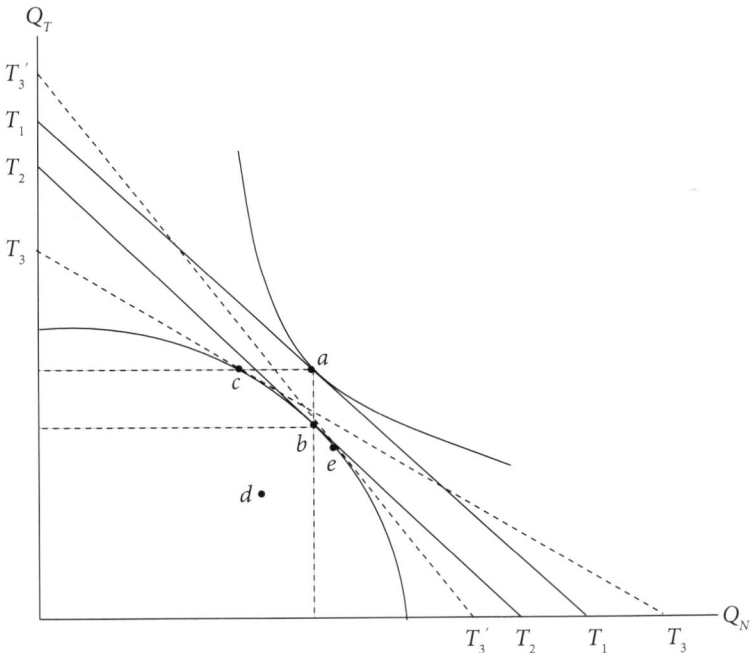

Fig. 2.1: Country structure and growth paths

Source: Author's diagram

If poor organisation and unemployment wastes domestic resources, however, initial production could be at any point inside the production possibility frontier such as d. Consumption could also be at d or could be higher so that there still is a CAD. Consumption could increase as production shifts out to the frontier, or the expansion of domestic supply could remove excess demand and reduce any CAD. This illustrates the process of structural adjustment. Improvements in factor use and productivity can also shift out the frontier over time.

While some Latin American economies, where inflation was running at above 1000 per cent, certainly required a reduction in demand, labour intensive economies such as China and India are better characterised as being at d, with underutilised resources. As long as reform facilitates utilisation of these resources, a contraction of demand may not be necessary. In China, undervaluation of the currency aided a labour-absorbing expansion in production of traded goods and of exports from d to a point such as c.

It is also possible that the optimal move may be from d to e requiring a real appreciation. This may be necessary to keep traded goods such as oil and food, which have a large weight in consumption and therefore second-round effects on inflation, cheaper. Production shifts relatively more towards non-traded goods as relative non-traded goods prices rise.[8] If the path chosen is from d to e, maintaining domestic demand is even more important, since foreign demand plays less of a role in absorbing labour. The choice between c or e would depend on domestic structure that affects inflationary processes. If traded goods have to be kept relatively cheaper to restrain inflation, the choice is e.

COUNTRY STRUCTURE AND REFORM STRATEGIES

A systematic comparison between the structure of Latin American and Asian growth (Table 2.1) helps to show that the relevant framework of analysis differs as argued above. Low macroeconomic volatilities and inflation, low government deficits and debt and higher domestic savings suggest excess demand may not be such a major issue in Asian economies. A more gradual approach to capital account convertibility (CAC) also reduced finance-led overshooting and volatility. Export of secondary rather than primary goods, pragmatic governments focused on providing public goods such as infrastructure and education rather than on redistribution, suggest smooth expansion of the supply-side to absorb surplus labour from a position such as d in Figure 2.1.

A majority of EMs that sustained high growth were from Asia. China's transition is the most recent. India and China have many similarities. Both have one billion plus population, both had similar low per-capita incomes when they followed a strategy of closed government-led import substitution, but India's opening out came about 10 years after that of China. Post liberalisation, both countries followed pragmatic policies that differed from standard reform prescriptions. A gradual growth-oriented approach gave the flexibility to respond to outcomes—like the conscious Chinese strategy of 'crossing the river while feeling the stones'. For example, the Chinese public sector could shrink as the private grew, thus avoiding the wrenching social tensions of the sudden Russian privatisation.

In terms of Figure 2.1, however, a systematic difference between Chinese and Indian growth strategies was that India neglected hard domestic reforms such as improving governance, infrastructure, health, education, and making India one market, that would help it shift out from a point such as d, and use resources more effectively. The provision of public primary health and education facilities remained below Asian levels. Reasons include India's heterogeneity as despite full political inclusion in a democracy, politicians could ignore economic inclusion and yet win elections. Also, the federal structure divided responsibility in many areas between the states and the Centre.

Table 2.1: Comparing Latin America and Asia

	Latin America	Asia
Fiscal and monetary policy	Budget deficit Credibility low	Budget surplus Credibility high
Macroeconomic outcomes	High volatilities: C, I, terms of trade, inflation	Low volatilities
Open economy	Primary goods trade CAC first S nominal anchor	Secondary goods trade CAC later; large FX reserves S competitive
Finance	Close to US Dollarisation GNS low	Relationship lending High debt-equity ratios GNS high
Supply behaviour	M substitution G dominates supply G: Redistribution Inequality high W bargaining Liberalising reforms Corruption Land surplus	Export competition G helps private sector G: Infrastructure, education Inequality low w flexible—food prices affect w Productivity, regulations Connections Labour surplus

Notes: C: Consumption; I: Investment; G: Government; CAC: Capital account convertibility; S: Nominal exchange rate; GNS: Gross national savings; M: Imports; W: Nominal wage rate; w: Real wage rate, FX: Foreign exchange
Source: Author's analysis

Low returns on past government investments and populist schemes left the government with positive deficits and a debt-GDP ratio which was higher than the Asian average. For example, after the oil shocks in the 1970s increased costs, user charges were not raised for many public services. A deterioration in quality of services followed. The fiscal consolidation necessary to reassure mobile capital in a more open economy was achieved through a reduction in public investment. The government borrowed even for consumption—there were revenue as well as fiscal deficits. The neglect of investment in infrastructure further raised costs and created bottlenecks for private endeavour.

A big advantage for China was that it had started its catch-up growth in 1978 with reforms that raised agricultural productivity. Low relative food prices are essential for sustained low-inflation growth in populous countries where food has a large share in the consumption basket. Other major commodity imports such as oil, an essential intermediate good, also contribute to inflation. China used to export oil but became a net oil importer in 1993.[9] By 2006 it imported 47 per cent of its consumption, and had begun building a large strategic oil reserve as domestic production was now only two-thirds of its needs. In 2013 it became the largest oil importing country. Even so, by the time it became a big oil importer its exports had grown enough to finance imports without materially reducing its current account surplus.

India is the third largest oil importer. It is dependent on a wide range of primary energy imports. In 2009–10, crude oil imports amounted to 80 per cent of its domestic consumption and 31 per cent of its total imports compared to 14 per cent for China. Figure 2.2 shows China started its reforms process with a very low share of oil imports, but in India this was high in the beginning of the 90s reforms. This dependence on commodity imports created limits on depreciation. A rise in oil price raised the CAD, but depreciation in response further raised the import bill and was inflationary.

This structure and hysteresis constrains and explains further choices. China chose real depreciation and invited foreign direct investment (FDI), which contributed to a sharp rise in exports. A cheap currency increased foreign demand while FDI developed supply capabilities and created employment in labour-intensive low-skill production. Since China had little domestic industry or trade unions, FDI could drive its opening and allow it to focus on manufacturing exports. India had more private domestic industry. Permissions for FDI, therefore, were slower in coming. Rigid labour and other laws together with poor infrastructure made expansion of manufacturing difficult at scale. India had faster growth in services than in manufacturing, partly because these constraints affected services less.

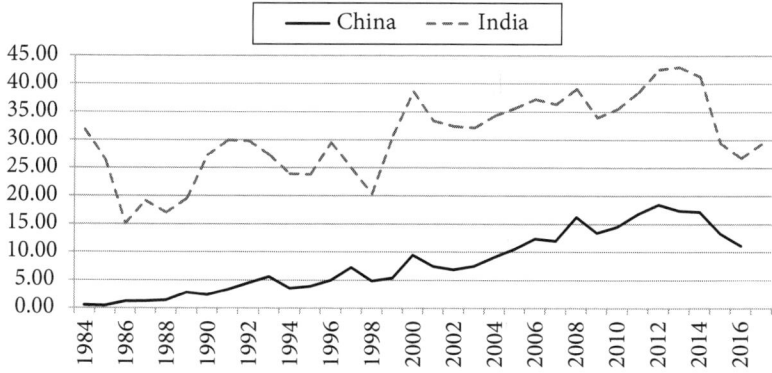

Fig. 2.2: Fuel imports (% of merchandise imports)
Source: Calculated from World Bank (n.d.)

Both countries continued with some capital account controls. But liberalisation of foreign portfolio inflows (FPI) was relatively faster in India. These contributed to financing the CAD and to development and reform of capital markets and financial services, in which its skilled manpower gave India a comparative advantage. It also led to real appreciation, which was excessive in some periods despite reserve accumulation. The path of Indian capital account convertibility (CAC) favoured equity over debt flows—equity flows are volatile but are at least risk-sharing, so the rupee value of outflows during adverse shocks is lower. Indian opening out was also calibrated, but it did relatively too much of external liberalisation and financial reform since it was easier to do compared to harder domestic reform. For example, lifting caps on debt flows without reducing interest rates led to too much of inflows and real appreciation in 2017.

Chinese domestic savings were high and rose further with growth. The government successfully leveraged these for large infrastructure spending from the 1990s, partly through low interest rates paid on deposits in the absence of alternative avenues for savings. Growth in Chinese shadow banking contributed to its post-GFC credit boom. This, together with a large fiscal stimulus, maintained Chinese growth during and after the GFC. Despite misgivings there was adjustment, there was no crisis until the date of writing.

Unlike China, the government in India was not able to make long-term funds available to finance and implement an adequate expansion in infrastructure. Budgetary constraints led the government to invite private participation in infrastructure building. India had a private infrastructure-finance–led bank credit boom prior to the GFC, but then a long squeeze with negative credit growth for industry as non-performing assets (NPAs) grew in public sector banks (PSBs) because of asset–liability mismatch, external shocks, macroeconomic tightening, and a failure of the administrative apparatus to gear up to providing clearances on the new scale required. Politically directed bank lending to infrastructure in the 2000s led to allegations of corruption. Despite rising NPAs and falling credit growth, bankruptcy and governance reform was required to reduce borrower and lender moral hazard before PSBs could be recapitalised. An asset quality review without recapitalisation increased provisioning requirement and further reduced credit growth.

Public–private participation contracts resulted in renegotiation. They were held up in arbitration and payments due, often from government, were delayed. Private participation is difficult without a drastic improvement in procedures, since commercial viability is essential for survival. NBFCs (non-bank financial institutions) that developed as part substitutes for PSBs that were not lending were not given adequate and timely liquidity support in 2018 as problems appeared. As a result, credit growth crashed in 2019 bringing down consumption, investment and output growth with it. Private investment had actually slowed since 2011 with only transient recoveries.

Financing 30-year-long-gestation infrastructure assets with short-term deposits (of public sector banks) or three-month commercial paper infrastructure (of non-banking financial institutions) was inherently not viable. This financing conundrum is yet to be resolved. Infrastructure needs long-term patient money. A combination of better earmarked user charges with the government carrying the initial risks and resolving delays, and more private participation used in toll collection and maintenance in the later stages, shows promise. The government is also able to raise money for new projects by transferring ready projects to the private sector to operate. The long-term objective is to shift financing from banks to more transparent markets.

Table 2.2: Comparing China and India

	China	India
Productivity: Shift from d	Health, Education: Reached c	Constraints in reaching e: States: Division of responsibility; heterogeneity
Infrastructure	G support	More dependence on PPP
Commodities—oil, agriculture	Agricultural reform first; oil imports rose long after exports	Agriculture as a bottleneck: Signs of supply response 30 years after reforms began
Exchange rate	Depreciation	Appreciation
Capital flows	FDI: Production	FPI: Markets and financing
Exports	Rapid growth	Sectoral exports: required for intermediate imports like oil
Specialisation	Manufacturing	Services
BOP	CAS	CAD
S–I	I led S; S leveraged for infrastructure	C rise; I slowdown
Credit growth	Boom	Slowdown
Macroeconomic policies	Counter-cyclical	Pro-cyclical (more risk-averse)
Monetary–Fiscal	Coordination	From fiscal towards monetary dominance
Middle income trap	High per-capita Y: Political repression	Freedoms: Innovation

Notes: CAS: Current account surplus; CAD: Current account deficit; C: Consumption; I: Investment; G: Government; S: Savings; Y: Income; PPP: Purchasing power parity; FDI: Foreign direct investment; FPI: Foreign portfolio investment; d,c,e: Points in Figure 2.1

Source: Author's analysis

Indian domestic savings are high, although less than Chinese savings. Gross savings peaked at 36.8 per cent of GDP in the high-growth period but fell to 29.87 in 2019–20 despite higher real interest rates.[10] Financial intermediation of household savings also remains poor although there was some increase in both the share of financial savings and liabilities. High private savings compensate partly for government dissaving, but consumption is a much higher share of GDP than it is in China. It is also rising. The path from a point such as d towards e, without adequate domestic demand support encouraged imports and consumption over production and exports. Some real appreciation was required, but despite some relaxation of key sectoral bottlenecks such as in agriculture and oil prices by 2015, there was too much pro-cyclical macroeconomic tightening as well as too much real appreciation. It would have been appropriate if the economy was at a point such as a in Figure 2.1 but not for an economy ready to move up from a point such as d; the squeeze in domestic demand reduced investment, manufacturing capacity, exports and future expansion of the production possibility frontier.

The policy tightening was itself an over-reaction to too much stimulus as part of the international coordinated stimulus after the GFC. Outflows due to global risk-off and domestic vulnerabilities from large double deficits in 2011 led to fears that India was going the Latin American way. High inflation increased demand for gold imports and widened the CAD to unsustainable levels as savings in financial assets fell. A standard stabilisation was imposed with a sharp rise in real interest rates. Inflation targeting adopted was flexible but was implemented strictly. Although inflation and macroeconomic vulnerabilities reduced, especially with the fall in oil prices in 2014, they reappeared, although more mildly, when oil prices rose in 2018, while industrial growth remained on average 3 per cent lower after 2011 compared to the previous six years. Therefore, over-strictness also creates vulnerabilities.

There is more monetary–fiscal coordination in the Chinese system where the government dominates. In India the earlier fiscal dominance has shifted towards monetary dominance with the adoption of inflation targeting and the constitution of an independent MPC (Monetary Policy Committee) combined with pressure from foreign investors (Goyal 2018). More coordination may deliver better results in an economy like India's where government polices affect inflation more and interest rates have a greater effect on demand than on inflation. Macroeconomic policy can use the space available to stimulate demand, consistent with the current rule-bound framework, to the extent supply-side measures lower costs and allow better resource utilisation, thus shifting the economy towards the production possibility frontier in Figure 2.1.

Innovations in internet and communication technology and the outsourcing wave allowed Indian firms to expand service exports that helped counter the large merchandise trade deficit. In terms of Figure 2.1 this was a better utilisation of domestic resources. An export expansion in one sector helped finance imports in another. India needs to develop more such export-intensive sectors. Since import dependence on intermediate goods rules out an undervalued currency, other strategies, such as more domestic competition and reduction in business costs, have to be used to stimulate exports. The government is attempting such policies.

Given pervasive state interventions, China found it difficult to switch to a market- and domestic consumption-led system from an export-led system in the period after the GFC, although there was a steady fall in its current account surplus and a real appreciation of its currency. In the current climate of trade wars, innovation and creativity in the service sector, and in manufacturing which is becoming more like a service, may be a more feasible growth path for India. India's diversity and democracy gives it an advantage in innovation. But the latter needs to be supported by relieving critical bottlenecks and reducing business costs.

Sources of Diversity

Although India persisted with inappropriate import-substitution for a long time, certain strengths were built up. For example, its skilled English-speaking educated labour allowed it to catch the outsourcing wave. The planning process did create a diverse economy—a major current strength that was enhanced by reforms. They added export demand to domestic demand, as some manufacturing became globally competitive. Networks of markets and associations became dense, reducing transaction costs, as learning occurred and quality improved. These changes add up to a critical mass. A rise in GDP levels creates diversity with it.

The absence of a market collapse in 2018 despite stranded assets, failure of a number of firms in a tight liquidity environment and continuing external stresses points towards growing resilience. Among other positive trends are: allocation of labour, which is improving in areas where it is difficult to measure it. This partly explains why productivity growth continues to be positive in India despite a worldwide productivity slowdown. Moreover, productivity in the informal sector is growing at a higher rate compared to the formal sector. As a result, capital-output ratios reduce, allowing higher growth with lower savings and investment. The informal sector combines services of old and new types, and sometimes the old type converts into the new, for example, as internet agencies provide drivers, maids and plumbers. Better training, certification and matching improve productivity and salaries as well as jobs. New technologies that leverage youthful skills and reduce prices to target low-income masses give India a special advantage. Reforms that build on these trends will be feasible, even as they have to continue to relieve critical bottlenecks.

AGRICULTURE

Prominent among growth drivers is a slackening of critical constraints in agriculture. A rise in agricultural productivity has to precede a growth surge for it to be sustainable in a populous country. This happened in China, while a jump in food inflation was also responsible for halting India's high-growth phase in the 2000s.

Bottlenecks emerged after the high-growth period in the late 2000s since agriculture reforms were inadequate. As a consequence, double-digit food inflation raised wages and general inflation. The dominant share of employment continued to be in low productivity rural and informal sectors where wages are sensitive to food inflation. Wages, salaries and subsidies were a large share of government spending. This also raised demand for non-traded goods and sustained food inflation.

By 2015, however, India seems to have entered a period of agricultural surpluses. Farmer distress is sometimes due to over-production in relation to demand. For example, in 2018 it kept prices soft despite attempts to raise minimum support prices (MSPs). But unseasonal rains have caused vegetable price peaks in recent years. These may point to climate change risks.

Low food prices benefit low surplus marginal farmers, who are net purchasers of food, as well as other consumers. Rural incomes will ultimately rise from diversification to non-agricultural activities. Reducing the number of active farmers is essential to raising their incomes. There are signs this is happening.

Non-agricultural rural employment is providing valuable support for rural incomes. The rural share of India's workforce may still be 70 per cent but NSS surveys show agriculture accounted for only 59.4 per cent of rural male employment in 2011-12. According to NABARD (2018), only 19 per cent of rural household income came from cultivation. FMCG (fast-moving consumer goods) companies reporting growing rural sales also suggests that rural incomes are rising. To some extent business is also migrating to states and rural areas where the labour is. Unfortunately, the new rural non-agricultural employment is capital intensive, pointing towards a skills shortage that forces capital to substitute for labour.

There is evidence of rising productivity and diversification to horticulture, aquaculture, etc. Sustained improvements in rural roads, electricity production and use of MGNREGA (Mahatma Gandhi National Rural Employment Guarantee Act) funds to strengthen irrigation and other infrastructure raised productivity and allowed farmers to grow high value added crops.[11] States have a major role to play since agriculture is also a state subject. Change is, however, uneven across states.

Even so, data from ministries' websites[12] show rural roads have been growing steadily since 2001 at an average per annum growth of 1.9 per cent for total roads and 8.5 per cent for surfaced roads. Over 2014–15 states with growth above the average in surfaced roads were Rajasthan, Chhattisgarh, Goa, Haryana, Himachal Pradesh, Jammu and Kashmir, Jharkhand, Madhya Pradesh, Manipur, Sikkim, Tamil Nadu, Uttar Pradesh and Uttarakhand.

Water bodies showed an average 41 per cent rate of growth between 1997 and 2017; states with a high share of completed water works in 2017–18 were Andhra Pradesh, Jharkhand, Tamil Nadu, Telangana, West Bengal and Uttar Pradesh. Above-average performing states with completed water works under MGNREGA were Rajasthan, Chhattisgarh, Jharkhand, TN, MP and UP.

Over 2009–10 to 2016–17 cold storage capacity grew above 50 per cent per annum; units increased from 5381 to 7645. States with above the average share of 3 per cent were Andhra Pradesh, Telangana, Bihar, Gujarat, Haryana, Madhya Pradesh, Maharashtra, West Bengal, Punjab and Uttar Pradesh. Odisha, Rajasthan and Uttarakhand had a low share but the rates of growth were above average.

There is a progressive element of competitive catching up that ranking of states encourages. Indirect indicators also point to improvements. It is widely reported that youth do not want to farm, and farmers cannot get hired labour—but then they must turn to income-raising mechanisation. Out-migration from agriculture is an essential feature of development.

However, much improvement is required further. Granular market-facilitating changes, for example, in good quality grading and sorting, are essential for integrating e-markets; removing irritants like export bans, stock limits and the Essential Commodity Act is necessary for improving private sector participation in storage, processing and value chains; improved land records, tenancy laws and producer organisations are required for overcoming fragmentation in production.

The 2018 export policy that promises uninterrupted exports of organic and processed foods needs to be extended to other food crops as an effective way of giving farmers higher price realisation. However, they would still need insurance against global price volatility. As a consequence of strong farm lobbies, MSPs normally rise with international prices, so farmers have benefitted from international price rise. But international food prices softened after the sharp rise in 2007.

If the aim is to cover most crops, it is better to switch from MSP to income transfers to small farmers. This could be linked to crops cultivated using satellite data. But they should be limited so that they do not reduce incentives to work. A Telangana-type 'Rythu Bandhu' transfer needs to be preceded by a cleaning up of land records. Non–price-distorting transfers are also WTO compatible, offering a way out of many recent WTO appeals against Indian agricultural subsidies (*The Economic Times* 2022). An India approaching middle-income status needs to switch to the advanced economy transfer-based way of subsidising agriculture.

INDUSTRY

Government has been acting on reducing costs of doing business in India. Some of the more traditional growth drivers are also there. As sectoral capacity limits began to bite there has been some expansion in investment, and finally some growth in credit to industry since 2018. The infrastructure-led investment boom of the 2000s will not recur soon, however. Government spending on road building and labour-intensive low-cost housing partly explains a revival in steel and cement in 2017. The share of low-income housing in housing loans has risen steeply. Some fine-tuning in the schemes is required, however, to better estimate demand from different income levels. When world trade slows down, investing in non-tradables is good policy. Figure 2.1 suggests non-tradable goods prices can be expected to rise relatively on India's growth path. India's experience corroborates this.

Ongoing structural reforms will begin to deliver efficiency and scale economies for all industry. For example, the GST will remove cost-increasing distortions such as multiple company warehouses across states. Real estate regulation has stabilised, allowing its positive effects to kick-in. With the first few resolutions under NCLT (National Company Law Tribunal) and a revival in growth there are finally signs of a turnaround in NPAs. Indian industry has long suffered from the absence of easy exit. The IBC (Insolvency and Bankruptcy Code) and stricter RBI guidelines on provisioning and resolution are leading to a change in credit markets. Borrowers are repaying loans since they stand to lose their assets. Lenders are monitoring more carefully since they have to make provisions as soon as repayment stops.

Backdated GDP series (2011–12 base) confirm a sharp slowdown in the secondary sector after 2011. Some growth recovery in 2015–16 despite lower investment points to improvements in productivity. The use of a much larger MCA21 (Ministry of Corporate Affairs e-Governance initiative) database of 5 lakh firms better captures the complexity of the Indian economy. The number of registered firms is expanding very fast. GSTN (Goods and Services Tax Network) has 10 million firms, since it creates incentives for small firms to register so that they can claim input tax credit for their purchases from large firms. The formalisation and data trails created in turn allow them access to cheaper credit.

At the same time, tighter regulation and corporate governance norms are cleaning out shell companies. It is often argued that short-term costs associated with anti-corruption reforms were responsible for the slowdown in growth. Some reforms did impose short-term costs but the slowdown started in 2011 before these reforms. A brief investment revival in 2015 had petered out in early 2016 under a sharp rise in real interest rates. These rose since repo rates were not cut although oil prices crashed in 2014. The fall in investment, therefore, had occurred even before demonetisation, one of the costlier actions against corruption, which started in November 2016.

Export revivals in early 2018 and in 2021, as well as survey responses, suggest that the problems small exporters had been facing from GST have tapered off. But, as the analysis in Figure 2.1 suggests, it is necessary for India to expand exports from more sectors. Consider textiles, a labour-intensive sector with good export potential. Since quotas were phased out under WTO in 2005, Indian textile exports grew at 6.8 per cent per annum and were at US$ 17.1 billion in 2017, when India held the fifth rank among global exporters. But its share was only 4.27 per cent in 2016 compared to the first-ranked China's 39 per cent (Mukherjee et al. 2018). Developed country textile tariffs are high, and competitors like Turkey, Vietnam and Korea benefitted from free trade agreements with the major importing regions, namely the US, the EU and the UAE. The EU gives tariff reductions to help developing countries. India gains from its standard generalised system of preferences with 20 per cent lower tariffs, but a less developed country such as Bangladesh gets duty-free entry under EU's 'Everything But Arms' (EBA) scheme.

The WTO bans industry-specific subsidies as trade distorting, but developing and least developed countries whose per capita incomes, measured in US dollars at constant 1990 prices, are below $1000 are allowed exemptions. India crossed this per capita income threshold in 2017. Central and state governments provide over 60 different types of subsidies to textile exporters, but results are not that good and there are complaints about delays and distortions. This is the time for the government in consultation with exporters to shift to other supporting policies, some of which can specially benefit textiles. These include export infrastructure, logistics, technology upgrading and skilling. Although India has a labour cost advantage over China, it lacks in skills and technology especially related to synthetic fibres and high value added products. Obstacles to economies of scale also need to be removed.

SERVICES

The services sector has been the engine of growth for the economy. Differing sub-sectors took the lead in different time periods in response to policy changes, for example, bank nationalisation in the 1970s, financial services and outsourcing in the 1990s, telecom and construction booms in the 2000s, etc. As industry slowed after 2011, much of India's growth came from services.

But provision of public services remains poor. This hurts the less well-off the most since they cannot compensate with paid private services as the rich often can. Poor quality of basic public goods such as air and water quality are responsible for poor health and nutrition outcomes. It becomes difficult for marginal groups especially to make use of the new opportunities that growth creates. Then 'active inclusion', defined as inclusion that creates conditions for the many to contribute to and participate in growth (Goyal 2015), does not happen. This absence of true economic inclusion, despite full political inclusion, is the biggest failure of Indian democracy.

Acemoglu and Robinson (2012: 529) argue that a democracy tends to have inclusive institutions. Broad-based demand and freedoms encourage creative destruction and innovation. This multiplies wealth, and therefore creates the best conditions for the success of a nation. Indian democracy started with full adult franchise, which is quite rare in history, and politicians do tend to deliver what voters demand. Structural aspects such as caste heterogeneity and poverty that made it possible for them to create caste- and community-based vote banks, side-stepping public service delivery, may help explain the puzzle. Today with more awareness, the electorate is demanding governance, development and economic opportunity, which bodes well for creating more economic inclusion.

Excessive centralisation also vitiated inclusive delivery. The Indian civil service inherited from the British was already centralised. At independence, the then dominant ideas of the importance of planning and government investment further increased central control.

A multiplicity of agencies arose from superimposing a centralised planning structure on a constitutional structure. There was a tendency to start new programmes and create new bodies without a clean exit from old ones. With multiple agencies there is no clear accountability. Controls create discretion and corruption. Harassment in permissions, licences and certifications hinders private activity. This results in overlaps, conflicts and delays. What kind of reforms can change this?

FEASIBLE REFORMS

Structural reforms are required to transform a high cost economy. But given entrenched political resistance in an unwieldy federal structure, rather than the straightforward privatisation and liberalisation of land and labour markets the World Bank wants, stealthy opportunistic reform that intensifies and uses trends at the margin may be more feasible. Some examples of this are given below.

Governance reforms that have proved difficult to implement so far can be pushed using India's success in climbing up the World Bank's 'Ease of Doing Business' ranking as a trigger. To help India rise further in the ranking can motivate better coordination across government departments.[13] For example, a special logistics cell has been set up to reduce India's costs of exporting. These costs are much higher than its peers partly because of multiple authorities involved. Clear allocation of responsibilities and of accountability among government departments will help, so will the use of appropriate software for coordination. Delays must be recorded and penalised even in public sector banks. Together with changes in the Prevention of Corruption Act (Goyal 2020) so that evidence of disproportionate assets is required before bringing a case against a government servant, decisiveness over time should improve.

Competition among states and good publicity for best practices, as through the smart cities website, is an example of reform by stealth. This can overcome political constraints that block land and labour market reforms. Better data enables further opportunistic reform—digital land-title records can be built and shared. Federal coordination is improving as the fast response time of the inter-State GST Council demonstrates. The next stage of devolution of power and funds to third-tier municipalities and panchayats requires more attention, however.

There are some improvements in public services, for example, the use of private contractors in city cleaning and garbage collection, but a steady deepening of democracy is also helping counter the under-provision of public goods we continue to suffer from. Horizontal social networks are complementing the vertical state hierarchy or substituting for it. Example of this was the Kerala floods relief effort in 2018 where civil society rose to the occasion valiantly. Social media is facilitating spontaneous organisation in response to calamities or to orchestrate a viable response to long-term problems. The law on corporate social responsibility is forcing firms to contribute. They are financing many NGOs active in local capacity-building and governance.

Technology is also improving public services. For example, e-metering and pre-paid mobile cards can considerably reduce electricity pilferage and the human interface that delivers free electricity at the cost of a reduction in its quality and viability.

Even the poor are willing to pay for uninterrupted electricity supply.

Full inclusion in a country of more than a billion people increases the market size for mass consumer goods and induces innovation. New technologies can reduce prices of mass goods in a virtuous cycle. An example is how NBFCs are able to lend to small and medium enterprises based on cash flow data instead of the collateral banks demand. This is part of the ongoing formalisation in the economy.

Diversity and demography, together with migration to new and hopefully better planned cities all support innovation. India's urbanisation is also proceeding faster than measured or recorded. Rapid growth in so-called census towns again suggests a rapid pace of non-rural employment growth. States have to give the final urban status to the census towns but they delay because of tax and municipal service provision issues. Towns themselves do not want to lose rural development funds. One reason public services are so poor is that facilities tend to be cut to match funds available rather than raising funds to provide a uniform level of services. Tax regime changes in octroi and GST could be used for a proper devolution of funds that removes such dis-incentives. Land-value appreciation with development can be more systematically used to finance facilities; user charges can be tied to more accountable provision and quality of public services, as part of wider fiscal consolidation and tax reform.

A recent worldwide puzzle is the slowdown in productivity growth after the Global Financial Crisis. But India has somehow avoided it. Unorganised sector compound annual productivity growth (7.2 per cent) over 2011–16 exceeded that in the organised sector (3.2 per cent) (MOSPI 2018). There is a long way to catch-up, however, from our current levels of about 45 compared to the US frontier indexed at 100. But the story of ICT (Information and Communications Technology) in India from the body-shopping associated with Y2K at the turn of the century to the creation of value-added products at Koramangala in Bangalore (*The Scalers* 2020) demonstrates the possibility of catch-up.

The rapid spread of smartphone use and mobile internet is sparking many kinds of inclusive innovation—for example, taxi services and ride sharing. This unleashing of natural creativity and innovation is not only raising growth today but may help India avoid the middle-income trap while sustaining services-led employment and growth.

Employment: Jump to the Future

Productive employment is increasing and can increase further if one looks beyond the traditional labour-intensive manufacturing where India lags since technology and the structure of employment is also changing. Measures that will enable the country to jump to the future can be divided into short-, medium- and long-term. Progress is occurring under each of these.

Shorter-term measures address current skill shortages. They can be flexibly adapted to the nature of the workforce and to industry requirements. While a three-month training equips first generation literate rural school leavers for retail malls, three-month nanodegrees can re-train and equip industry workers with new skills linked to clear standards set in industry. Short-term training can provide quality ladders, allowing workers to improve from whatever their level is and industry to find the required skills. It can compensate for the fall in quality of school education that accompanied universal enrollment.

But for this to happen two major bottlenecks have to be removed. First, the completion certificate government programmes require is difficult to get from informal sectors—this seriously reduces the programmes' contribution in general and to up-skilling the informal sector in particular. There is a fear that government funds will be misused without formal certification. Flexible big data and Aadhaar and mobile-based verifications should be designed and accepted. Second, industry training programmes are less effective because industry bodies do not agree on common standards. Standards tend to vary with their foreign collaborator needs. Regulators must ensure standardisation so that in-house technical industrial training in one industry is relevant in another. As more formalisation of the economy raises the tax base, the government will be able to spend more on training, which is specially required for the MSME (Micro, Small and Medium Enterprises) sector.

For *medium–term* employment expansion, India could refocus its attempts to develop labour-intensive manufacturing on a few sectors with potential. Estimates for the 2000s show employment elasticity in Indian manufacturing was only 0.09 compared to a world average of 0.3 (Misra and Suresh 2014). This is unacceptable for a populous country. For change to occur, labour laws that induce industry to substitute towards capital need to be modified. Simplification and codification in four brackets undertaken is a good step, as is encouraging competition among states to reform. Second, relatively low-skill labour-intensive industries could be encouraged. These include textiles, electronics, chemicals and food processing and are sectors where export potential exists. The government has given incentives such as tax deductions and provident fund contributions for new employees and skilling support as well as allowed fixed term employment in some labour-intensive sectors. Issues around textile exports have already been examined earlier in the section on industry.

Apart from manufacturing, construction has a higher employment elasticity of 0.19. Stimulus to low-income housing and revival of construction in general will improve job creation. Service industry will continue to be a major employer. Health and education services are severely under-provided in India. Their expansion at all levels will improve the capability of the workforce even while providing jobs. There are attempts to reform the Indian Medical Council that creates entry barriers and chokes the expansion in the supply of doctors and nurses. New teaching facilities can be judged on the basis of accreditation and outcomes rather than infrastructure and competition can be encouraged. Primary health centres with Centre-state and private partnership under Ayushman Bharat are a good initiative.

In the *long-term*, the quality of primary education needs to improve. At present, schools are not even teaching the basics effectively when they should be preparing students for flexible lifelong learning, giving them a thorough grounding in code languages, and the ability to pick up and work with the new technologies that are coming. This requires government schools to be freed from state control and allowed to compete and to innovate in response to community needs while being subject to community discipline. The Right to Education (RTE) Act needs to be modified and based on outcomes, not on inputs such as infrastructure.

It is feared that automation will destroy jobs, especially low-skill ones. For example, robots are being developed to cut cloth so that textile production may also be automated. Answering robots are already replacing workers in call centres. But historically, although technological change made some occupations obsolete, it also created new jobs and raised income levels. Mechanical jobs get taken away but new complex tasks are created. Rising quality and levels of education are essential for mastery and creation of new highly productive jobs that should define the India of tomorrow. Availability of social insurance would encourage risk-taking.

India's informal employment structure is well-suited to align with worldwide changes towards the so-called 'gig-economy', where skills are made available to multiple employers through the internet, in lieu of formal 9-to-5 jobs. For example, internet agencies standardise and better match a range of services, thus improving their quality and salaries. India, however, is yet to position itself for this by creating skill ladders for different levels of training and capability.

Diversity and External Shocks

India's opening out has coincided with a large number of external shocks and these risks are ongoing. Quantitative easing (QE) and near-zero interest rates in AEs (advanced economies) after the GFC led to capital flow surges into EMs in search of yield. Global more than domestic factors were responsible for these risk-on inflows. Risk-off periods of outflows normally coincided with US financial tightening.[14] In 2018 US political actions such as sanctions against Iran provoked a rise in oil prices while its large tax-cut-based fiscal stimulus raised growth, interest rates and strengthened the dollar, provoking outflows from EMs. The CAD widened and there was rupee volatility. An EM such as India, whose CAD rises with oil prices, is particularly vulnerable.

The IMF recommends a flexible exchange rate, reduction in government deficits and a last resort to cautious and temporary capital flow management measures as ways for EMs to deal with these risks. But a floating exchange rate can be too volatile or appreciate too much, while productive government expenditure is replaced by FPI (Foreign Portfolio Investment)-funded real estate bubbles.

A global risk often flagged is large EM corporate dollar debt taken in the period of low interest rates.[15] In India, however, caps on corporate foreign borrowing kept corporate dollar debt low. Its gradual and sequenced approach to capital account convertibility was responsible for this mitigation of external shocks.[16] Therefore, continuing with careful and gradual liberalisation is one way for India to manage external risks. There were large fluctuations in foreign portfolio flows and a rise in the share of debt flows as caps on these were relaxed, while Indian interest rates remained too high relative to world rates. As debt inflows flocked in, there was real appreciation and export growth stagnated in 2017 despite a rise in world trade. Debt inflows, however, gained from the appreciation. Excess inflows were accumulated as reserves. Since buying dollars increases the money supply, the RBI has to sell Indian government securities to sterilise the increase. This swap replaces foreign for domestic securities in the RBI's balance sheet. It tends to raise the yields on government securities or the rate at which the government can borrow.

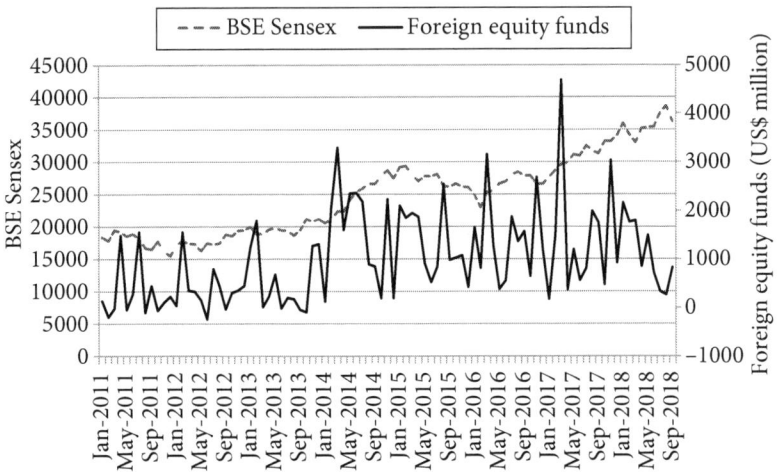

Fig. 2.3: Monthly foreign equity flows and the BSE Sensex
Source: Calculated from RBI database, see www.rbi.org.in

Foreign equity flows are also volatile but despite exit of foreign investors, stock price volatility was much reduced after 2011 as Indian households adopted the mutual fund investment route. Domestic retail entry into stock markets also rose sharply in the Covid-19 period. Figure 2.3 shows a steady rise in stock indices despite volatility in foreign equity flows. There was sufficient diversity in views about the economy for different types of investors to come in and buy on dips. A similar expansion of domestic retail debt markets should be a pre-condition for further liberalisation of foreign debt inflows. The pace of capital account liberalisation, which has reduced external risks for India, must therefore continue to be slow, with a prudential use of capital flow management tools.

Oil price shocks are a major risk for an economy dependent on large oil-imports. Political tensions did raise global oil prices above US$ 80 in 2018 but the long-term trend is toward softening, as OPEC (Organization of the Petroleum Exporting Countries) shows signs of fissures, shale oil provides an alternative and there are trends towards substituting away from oil towards renewable fuels. By November 2018, the Indian oil basket was at US$ 65. A middling oil price range between US$ 60–70 suits both oil importing and exporting countries, while maintaining future oil supplies and reducing future volatility. The political economy of oil pricing is likely to maintain this range but the flare-up in Ukraine in 2022 led to major upsets, which are unlikely, however, to persist.

India's oil intensity has been falling since 2005, because of the larger share of less-energy-intensive services output, and the thrust on renewables. Domestic oil prices are more market-determined since 2012. That they rise more with international prices contributes to substitution away from crude oil consumption. Long-run security can improve as these trends towards reducing oil intensity continue. Renewable energy can itself be a growth area. Specific competitive sectors must still be encouraged, however, for the export expansion required to cover the oil import bill. India does gain as world export demand rises. Even if oil prices rise, its exports of refined crude as well as non-resident remittances rise. This is another example of resilience from its growing diversity.

The US reached the peak of its post GFC recovery in 2019. Since global growth was slowing, US monetary policy turned dovish. Covid-19 intensified this. But sharp tightening followed in 2022 in a delayed reaction to rising inflation. These US over-reactions increased risks to EMs. India's large domestic economy and well-used macroeconomic policy space was able to insulate it somewhat. There are opportunities to expand exports and attract more FDI as countries diversify from China.

A CAD implies investment exceeds domestic savings. Financial savings largely fund investments involving goods that are tradable, while physical savings are invested more in non-traded goods, such as in real estate. Estimates of physical savings in the household sector are identical to those of investment in the unorganised sector. It follows, then, that if organised sector investment exceeds financial savings, it will have to be financed by foreign savings that is, by running a CAD.

Although household savings ratios reduced, the share of financial savings increased. The ratio of gross savings to GDP fell to about 30 per cent in the mid-2010s as growth slowed. But it was household physical savings that fell, while household financial savings recovered from a low of 8 per cent in 2011–12. Savings of non-financial corporations, which are held in financial assets, rose. This implies more of domestic savings are available to finance imports, thus reducing the CAD and dependence on volatile foreign capital inflows.

During external stresses, however, domestic demand cannot be neglected, and is an important smoothing mechanism. Low growth lasted for only one year after the 2008 GFC but persisted after 2011 because macroeconomic policy was countercyclical after 2008 but not after 2011. Smart and context-sensitive macroeconomic policy can act counter-cyclically with a complementary combination of supply-side actions, feasible reforms and capital flow management. There is space for such action consistent with flexible inflation targeting implemented by an independent monetary policy committee. Financial sector regulation also needs to be counter-cyclical. Depth of and diversity in the financial sector is now sufficient to allow moderation of external shocks. Such appropriate policy enabled India's relatively better performance under the many shocks that followed the pandemic.

Conclusion

Indian catch-up growth was volatile because of aggravation of shocks due to unaddressed critical bottlenecks while pro-cyclical macroeconomic policy and regulation compressed aggregate demand. Policies were also sometimes not appropriate for the context. Increasing diversity has built sufficient resilience, however, for policy to be able to smooth shocks.

Inappropriate policies came from incorrect macroeconomic stabilisation understanding. In a populous country with underemployed labour, sectoral bottlenecks and price shocks result in inflation. For example, a CAD does not necessarily indicate excess demand, but points to an inability to adequately expand export sectors. India's CAD tended to be smallest in periods of highest growth, suggesting it did not come from excess demand but from oil shocks that reduced growth.[17] The large share of intermediate goods imports implies that an undervalued exchange rate would add to cost pressures and end in real appreciation. Therefore, the Indian growth path requires a constant or mildly appreciating real exchange rate with focused sectoral and general supply-side measures to improve exports, unlike the Chinese depreciated real exchange rate that helped its export push. A policy demand squeeze can be counter-productive and self-fulfilling if it reduces export capacity. As appreciation tends to reduce foreign demand for Indian goods, if domestic demand is not maintained to compensate, it can hurt domestic production creating the over-dependence on imports seen in India since 2017.

Apart from critical bottlenecks in agriculture and energy, India has to grow out of poor public services such as health, nutrition, quality of education, congestion and pollution; failures in land, labour and financial markets; failures of market integration and of fiscal federalism that result in heterogeneous quality of life in the Indian states. These are the structural reforms that can transform a high-cost economy and shift it to fuller and better utilisation of resources. There is progress.

But straightforward liberalising of land and labour reform that external agencies recommend generates intense opposition from large domestic interest groups. Therefore, feasible reform that intensifies and uses trends at the margin may work better. This includes use of technology to improve public services and land records; generate competition, coordination and convergence across states including in land, labour and farm laws; and psychological triggers such as India's move up the 'Ease of Doing Business' ranking to improve coordination across multiple government agencies. Such reforms would be pragmatic, like those undertaken by the countries that managed to sustain high growth.

If land and labour reforms remain inadequate even 30 years after liberalising reforms began, there are probably intractable political hurdles complicated by India's vocal democracy, federal structure and division of responsibilities. The reform mantra of stabilisation, liberalisation and privatisation by itself would also hurt domestic industry and investment, making the economy too consumption- and import-dependent. The 2010s showed such trends, which need to be reversed to achieve a more balanced path.

Change has acquired a critical mass, especially because of relief in major bottlenecks in recent years. With appropriate reforms that build on these changes, sustained high growth is surely possible.

NOTES

Acknowledgements: This chapter has evolved from a paper which was presented at a conference in IIM Calcutta. Extracts from here were presented as the keynote address at a conference at Vidyalankar Institute, Mumbai and as the inaugural lecture for an Indian Statistical Service Training Programme at IGIDR, Mumbai. I thank the participants for their enthusiastic questions and feedback, and B. K. Bhoi, Niranjan Rajadhyaksha, Partha Ray, Abhirup Sarkar and Anindya Sen for their comments, and Reshma Aguiar and Shreeja Joy Velu for secretarial assistance.

[1] Calculated with the back series from 2005–06 at the base 2011–12 released by the Central Statistics Office (CSO) on 28 November 2018.

Available at https://www.mospi.gov.in/documents/213904/416359// Press-Note-28Nov20181600851107922.pdf/d46e1369-0285-a99f-749d-004abe264355 (accessed March 2023).

[2] This is clear from country comparisons using data from https://datatopics.worldbank.org/world-development-indicators/. It is well known that China grew above 10 per cent for more than two decades.

[3] Author calculation. Dividing 0.7 by the rate of growth gives a rough estimate of the time required to double income. Therefore doubling time at 5 per cent growth rate is 14 years ($0.7/.05 = 14$), at 7 per cent it shrinks to 10 years and further to 7.8 years if the growth rate rises to a 9 per cent.

[4] See https://tradingeconomics.com/india/labor-force-participation-rate (accessed March 2023).

[5] See https://data.worldbank.org/indicator/SL.TLF.CACT.ZS (accessed March 2023).

[6] See https://pip.worldbank.org/country-profiles/IND (accessed March 2023). Examination of trends in poverty, as defined by the Tendulkar Committee, and based on NSS Consumer Expenditure data for the period 1983 to 2011–12, show that in the low-growth pre-reform period, 1983 to 1993–94, poverty declined at 0.8 pps per annum, with the number of persons below the poverty line almost constant at 320 million. Post-reform poverty declined faster at 1.3 pps per annum, from 45.3 per cent in 1993–94 to 21.9 per cent in 2011–12. Over 1993–94 to 2004–05 it fell at 0.75 pps per annum, but fell faster at 2.2 pps per annum over the high-growth period 2004–05 to 2011–12. Around 135 million people were lifted above the poverty line in the post-reform period (Rangarajan and Dev 2018).

[7] See Corbo and Fischer (1995) for such an application of the Salter–Swan model.

[8] On this path non-traded goods prices rise relatively as in the Balassa–Samuelson effect but it is not necessarily due to higher productivity and wages in the traded goods sector (Goyal 2014), since there is no full-employment as is assumed in the Balassa–Samuelson model.

⁹See Zhang (2018) and https://en.wikipedia.org/wiki/Petroleum_industry_in_China and https://en.wikipedia.org/wiki/Energy_policy_of_India.

[10] See Table 223: Select Macro-Economic Aggregates—Growth, Saving and Investment Rates (At Current Prices), available at https://www.rbi.org.in/Scripts/PublicationsView.aspx?id=15348 (accessed March 2023); also see Table 218: Select Macro-Economic Aggregates—Growth, Saving and Investment Rates (At Current Prices), available at https://www.rbi.org.in/Scripts/PublicationsView.aspx?id=21315 (accessed March 2023).

[11] For example, the share of fruits and vegetables in gross cropped area rose from 1.9 over 1960–61 to 1968–69 to 6.5 over 2004–05 to 2014–15. The share in value of production rose from 10.6 to 18.8 (Dev 2018).

[12] Some of these sites are http://www.mospi.gov.in/, https://www.indiabudget.gov.in/economicsurvey/, https://www.india.gov.in/. I also thank the Economic Advisory Council to the Prime Minister (EAC PM) secretariat for providing some data.

[13] In 2017, India climbed to 100 on this index and in 2018 reached 77—showing that speedy improvement is possible, and that the index does focus on efforts of government departments. There is an argument that focusing on this ranking which is based on a narrow database can lead to a neglect of other necessary reform. It is good, however, to begin somewhere and get results. NITI Aayog could create its own more inclusive rankings.

[14] IMF estimates of inflows to EMs over July 2009–June 2014 were US$ 2 trillion. In 2017 US$ 160 billion came in. In the nine largest EMs, outflows over 2008–09 were US$ 0.5 trillion; in 2014–15 US$ 1 trillion flowed out.

[15] A 2017 estimate from the Institute of International Finance was that non-financial corporate debt grew from US$ 5 trillion in 2005 to US$ 21 trillion in 2016.

[16] In India, foreign holders accounted for less than 5 per cent of debt, compared to 38 per cent in Indonesia during the taper tantrum.

[17] Goyal and Kumar (2018), in a careful empirical estimation, find the CAD to be counter-cyclical in India. A fiscal deficit shock raises the CAD, but high-impact growth shocks and large variance oil shocks lead to overall divergence of the deficits. There is some evidence of the impact of aggregate demand on outcomes, but it is moderated by supply shocks and compositional effects.

REFERENCES

Acemoglu, D. and J. Robinson. 2012. *Why Nations Fail: The Origins of Power, Prosperity and Poverty*. New York: Crown Business.

Corbo, V. and S. Fischer. 1995. 'Structural Adjustment, Stabilisation and Policy Reform: Domestic and International Finance'. In J. Behrman and T. N. Srinivasan (eds), *Handbook of Development Economics*, Vol. 3: 2845–2924. North-Holland, Amsterdam: Elsevier.

Dev, M. 2018. 'Transformation of Indian Agriculture: Growth, Inclusiveness and Sustainability'. Presidential Address at the 78th Annual Conference of the Indian Society of Agricultural Economics, November 1–3, New Delhi.

Goyal, A. 2014. 'Purchasing Power Parity, Wages and Inflation in Emerging Markets'. *Foreign Trade Review* 49(4).

———. 2015. 'Sustaining Indian Growth: Interests Versus Institutions'. *India Review* 14(3): 330–351, July–September.

———. 2018. 'The Indian Fiscal-Monetary Framework: Dominance or Coordination?' *International Journal of Development and Conflict* 8(1): 01–13.

———. 2020. 'Indian Banks and the Prevention of Corruption Act: Freedom and Discipline'. In S. Mahendra Dev (ed.), *India Development Report 2022*. Delhi: OUP. Earlier version available as *IGIDR working paper* no. WP-2018-021. Available at http://www.igidr.ac.in/pdf/publication/WP-2018-021.pdf (accessed June 2023).

Goyal, A. and A. Kumar. 2018. 'The Effect of Oil Shocks and Cyclicality in Hiding Indian Twin Deficits'. *Journal of Economic Studies* 45(1): 27–45.

Misra, S. and Anoop K. Suresh. 2014. 'Estimating Employment Elasticity of Growth for the Indian Economy,' RBI Working Paper Series No. 6. Available at https://www.rbi.org.in/SCRIPTS/PublicationsView.aspx?id=15763 (accessed March 2023).

MOSPI. 2018. *Economic Characteristics of Unincorporated Non-agricultural Enterprises (Excluding Construction) in India for July 2015–June 2016*, NSS 73rd Round, Report No. 582. Ministry of Statistics and Programme Implementation, Government of India. Available at https://www.mofpi.gov.in/sites/default/files/2015_16_nsso_73rd_round.pdf (accessed March 2023).

Mukherjee, A., A. Paul, A. P. Sarma and S. Sinha. 2018. 'Trade, Trade Agreements and Subsidies: The Case of the Indian Apparel Industry', ICRIER Working Paper no. 365. Available at http://icrier.org/publications/working-papers/ (accessed October 2022).

NABARD (National Bank For Agriculture And Rural Development). 2018. *All India Rural Financial Inclusion Survey 2016–17*. Available at https://www.nabard.org/auth/writereaddata/tender/1608180417NABARD-Repo-16_Web_P.pdf (accessed October 2022).

Rangarajan, C. and M. Dev. 2018. 'How the Data Sets Stack Up', *The Hindu*, 4 April. Available at http://www.thehindu.com/opinion/lead/how-the-data-sets-stack-up/article23427619.ece (accessed September 2022).

The Economic Times. 2022. 'India appeals against WTO dispute panel ruling on sugar export subsidies at appellate body', 02 January. Available at https://economictimes.indiatimes.com/news/economy/foreign-trade/india-appeals-against-wto-dispute-panel-ruling-on-sugar-export-subsidies-at-appellate-body/articleshow/88644928.cms?from=mdr (accessed March 2023).

The Scalers. 2020. 'How Bangalore became Asia's Silicon Valley', 24 June. Available at https://thescalers.com/how-bangalore-became-asias-silicon-valley/ (accessed March 2023).

Williamson, J. 2003. 'The Washington Consensus and Beyond'. *Economic and Political Weekly* 38(15): 1475–1481.

World Bank. n.d. 'Fuel imports (% of merchandise imports)'. Available at https://data.worldbank.org/indicator/TM.VAL.FUEL.ZS.UN (accessed March 2023).

———. 2008. 'The Growth Report: Strategies for Sustained Growth and Inclusive Development, Commission on Growth and Development'. Washington, D. C.: World Bank. Available at https://openknowledge.worldbank.org/handle/10986/6507 (accessed September 2022).

———. 2018. 'India Development Update – India's Growth Story'. Washington, D. C.: World Bank Group. Available at http://documents.worldbank.org/curated/en/814101517840592525/ (accessed September 2022).

Zhang, Z. X. 2018. 'Energy Price Reform in China'. In Ross Garnaut, Ligang Song and Cai Fang (eds), *China's 40 Years of Reform and Development: 1978–2018*, China Update Series. Canberra: ANU Press.

3
MEASURING THE TREND OF ECONOMIC WELL-BEING IN INDIA IN RECENT DECADES

Asis Kumar Banerjee

Introduction

This chapter seeks to investigate the trend of well-being of the Indian economy in recent decades. Well-being is a multidimensional notion. Even *economic* well-being may have multiple determinants. In this chapter, however, we do not aspire to address the issue in its totality. The focus will only be on well-being, as measured by income (or expenditure, which is traditionally used in India as the proxy for income in view of the paucity of income data).[1]

We shall ensure that our measure of well-being is *inequality-sensitive*. The importance of the problem of inequality in the distribution of income or expenditure is now widely recognised.

In the Indian context, the emphasis placed in the policy discourse on 'inclusive growth' is a sign of such recognition. Expectedly, therefore, recent years have witnessed a considerable amount of research on inequality in the Indian economy and its trend over time (See, for instance, Himanshu [2018] and the references cited therein on different types of inequality in India.) As stated above, we shall be concerned with well-being as measured by expenditure. So far as inequality is concerned, we shall focus on the inequality in the distribution of expenditure.

It needs to be emphasised, however, that while inequality should receive its due attention, it cannot be considered to be the sole determinant of well-being. Both the average value and the inequality of expenditure (or, in other words, both the 'efficiency' and the 'equity' aspects of well-being) are important. Indeed, even a poor economy can be perfectly egalitarian if poverty is equally distributed.

From this point of view, the relatively limited attention given so far to studying the trend of well-being in the Indian economy must be considered to be a gap in available literature. This chapter is an initial step taken towards filling this gap.

How to measure well-being (as determined by expenditure) is, therefore, the central issue in this chapter. One such measure that has been used for this purpose is given by the formula $\mu(1 - G)$ where μ denotes the arithmetic mean and G the Gini coefficient of the distribution of expenditure. However, this particular formula represents one specific measure of well-being and there is no guarantee that conclusions (regarding the time trend of well-being) reached on the basis of this measure would agree with those obtained from other plausible measures.

A better approach to the problem of inequality-sensitive measurement of well-being seems to be the normative one developed by Atkinson (1970), Dasgupta, Sen and Starrett (1973) and, especially, Shorrocks (1983) (Also see 'Technical Note' in NSSO 2006: 32–36). In this approach, instead of working with a particular measure of well-being, we start with some normative conditions which any reasonable measure of well-being can be expected to satisfy. We then try to obtain some criteria (stated in terms of the observed data) that we can apply for the purpose of comparing the well-being levels of any two economies (or of the same economy at any two points of time). The conclusions of the exercise would then be valid for *all* measures of well-being satisfying the normative conditions.

In this chapter we shall largely follow this approach. In this type of theory the notions of Lorenz dominance and generalised Lorenz dominance of one income (or expenditure) distribution over another play important roles. Let x and y be two vectors describing the expenditure levels of all the individuals in an economy in years 1 and 2 respectively. Under one set of normative conditions, the resulting criterion of well-being comparison would say that well-being in Year 1 is not less than that in Year 2 if and only if [$\mu(x) \geq \mu(y)$ and x weakly Lorenz dominates y]. Under a somewhat different set of normative conditions the criterion would say that this is the case if and only if x generalised Lorenz dominates y. For reasons explained in the second section below, we shall, in this chapter, prefer the first of these two criteria, although, for the sake of completeness, we shall also mention the results of applying the second.

The strong point of this approach is that in the cases where the criteria apply, they lead to robust conclusions regarding the ranking of the levels of well-being in the two years since the conclusions do not depend on the arbitrary choice of any particular measure of well-being. In some cases, however, this approach may lead to ambiguous conclusions. For instance, in the case of the first of the two criteria mentioned above, there are two sources of ambiguity. First, it is possible that, of the two vectors, x and y, neither Lorenz dominates the other. This will be the case if the Lorenz curves of x and y intersect. Irrespective of the mean values of x and y, we shall then be unable to compare the levels of well-being in the two years by this criterion. Second, even if the Lorenz curves do not intersect, there may be a conflict between the 'efficiency' and the 'equity' aspects of the comparison. For instance, if $\mu(x) > \mu(y)$ but y Lorenz dominates x, we shall, again, be unable to rank the levels of well-being in the two years.[2]

In this chapter we propose to get around the problem posed by the possibility of intersections of Lorenz curves by applying the concept of fuzzy Lorenz dominance. For any x and y, even when the Lorenz curves of x and y intersect, it is possible to define a real number say, $R(x, y)$, that indicates the 'extent to which x Lorenz dominates y'. If the number is 1, this is interpreted to mean that the statement that x Lorenz dominates y is definitely true. If it is 0, then the statement is definitely false. If the Lorenz curves intersect, the number is between 0 and 1. We shall formulate a specific fuzzy Lorenz dominance relation R. From this fuzzy relation we easily obtain a simple and transparent crisp (i.e., non-fuzzy) dominance relation (sometimes called the crisp approximation of the fuzzy relation R): in all cases (i.e., irrespective of whether the Lorenz curves intersect or not) we say that x (weakly) dominates y if and only if $R(x, y) \geq R(y, x)$. Since R is a real number, either $R(x, y) \geq R(y, x)$ or $R(y, x) \geq R(x, y)$. Thus, it will always be the case that either x Lorenz dominates y or y Lorenz dominates x in this extended (fuzzy) sense. Note, however, that this extension of the crisp theory would remove only the first of the two sources of ambiguity of well-being comparison noted above. The second would remain.

We shall use the extended version of the normative theory of well-being comparisons for the purpose of deciphering the time trend of well-being in India in recent decades, using the NSSO quinquennial consumer expenditure surveys as the data source. The main finding in this regard is that while there was an increase in well-being between the survey years 1983 and 1993–94 as well as between 2004–05 and 2011–12, it is not possible to rank the levels of well-being in 1993–94 and 2004–05.

In the following section, we briefly present the theoretical framework used in this chapter for the purpose of well-being comparisons. The next section contains the empirical findings. The fourth and final section concludes the discussion.

The Theoretical Framework: Measures of Well-Being

Let W be a real-valued function on the set X of all expenditure vectors. W will be interpreted as the measure of well-being in the economy. For our purposes it will suffice to define the function ordinally: if x and y are any two expenditure vectors (i.e., vectors specifying the expenditure levels of all the individuals [or households] in the economy) in say, Year 1 and Year 2 respectively, all we wish to do is to decide whether $W(x)$ is no less than $W(y)$.

Now, if the function W is known to start with, the task would be trivial. The challenge of making well-being comparisons consists in the fact that W is not known to the researcher. The task would also remain simple if inequality was of no concern. It would then be natural to assume that well-being of the economy is determined exclusively by its per capita expenditure, that is, for all x in X, $W(x) = \mu(x)$ where μ stands for arithmetic mean.

In general, however, we desire W to be *inequality-sensitive*. We require that, for all x and y in X such that $\mu(x) = \mu(y)$ but with greater inequality in x than in y, we should have: $W(x) < W(y)$. One way of formalising the idea is to use the notion of Lorenz dominance. For any x in X, let $L(x, k/n) = \sum_{i=1}^{k} x_i / \{n\mu(x)\}$ for all $k = 1, 2, ..., n$. The Lorenz curve of x is the curve obtained by letting $L(x, 0) = 0$ and joining adjacent points of the form $(k/n, L(x, k/n))$ with line segments. Equivalently, for any given vector x let $L_x(p)$ denote the proportion of the total available amount of the attribute going to the bottom (i.e., the poorest) p proportion of the population. The Lorenz curve of x is obtained by plotting $L_x(p)$ against p. Needless to say, p ranges from 0 to 1 and, for any x, $L_x(0) = 0$ and $L_x(1) = 1$. For any two expenditure vectors

x and y in X, x is said to Lorenz dominate y if and only if the Lorenz curve of x is not below that of y for any $k = 1, 2, ..., n$.

The idea of inequality sensitivity of W is then formalised by the requirement that, for any x and y in X, if $\mu(x) = \mu(y)$ and if x Lorenz dominates y, then $W(x) \geq W(y)$. We shall call this property Lorenz Consistency (LC).

The notion of Lorenz dominance is closely related to ranking of expenditure vectors in terms of inequality. If x and y have the same mean (which is the case here), $I(x) \leq I(y)$ for all inequality indices I, if and only if x Lorenz dominates y (See Foster 1985). In other words, if x Lorenz dominates y, then x is unambiguously no more unequal than y, irrespective of which specific inequality index I we choose to use for measuring inequality. The converse is also true.

We shall also make the reasonable assumptions that W satisfies the conditions of Anonymity (ANON) and Population Replication Invariance (PRI).[3]

Within the class of well-being functions satisfying the three above-mentioned assumptions, we distinguish between two broad types. One type of measure will be called monotonic. (It has also been called Paretian in the literature.) W satisfies monotonicity (MON) if, for any x and y in X, $[x \geq y$ and $x \neq y]$ implies $W(x) > W(y)$. Obviously, this is a Pareto-type condition, saying that if, in going from y to x, nobody's expenditure falls but there is at least one individual whose expenditure rises, then there is an increase in the level of well-being in the economy.

Objections have been raised against the condition of monotonicity. The most important of these in our context is that it may turn out to be inegalitarian in an intuitive sense. Consider the hypothetical situation y where 99.9 per cent of the total expenditure in the economy is undertaken by only one individual, with *all* of the other individuals together accounting for the rest. Let x be the situation in which the privileged person's expenditure increases even further while that of everybody else remains unchanged. If W is monotonic, it will follow that

$W(x) > W(y)$. But many would feel uncomfortable with this conclusion.

From this point of view, a somewhat different property has been proposed. W is said to satisfy scale monotonicity (SMON) if, for all x and y in X such that $x = ky$ for some scalar $k \geq 1$, $W(x) \geq W(y)$. In other words, if everybody's expenditure remains unchanged or increases in the same proportion (so that there is an increase in per capita expenditure but there is no change in relative inequality) then well-being does not decrease. In our work below, we shall in most cases assume that W satisfies SMON although occasionally we shall also refer to well-being functions satisfying MON.

In the above discussion we have used the notion of Lorenz dominance. There is a related notion called generalised Lorenz dominance. The generalised Lorenz curve of x is obtained by simply scaling up the Lorenz curve of x by $\mu(x)$. At each point on the horizontal axis in the familiar Lorenz diagram, the height of the Lorenz curve is multiplied by $\mu(x)$ to obtain the height of the generalised Lorenz curve. Now, generalised Lorenz dominance is defined in the same way as ordinary Lorenz dominance: x generalised Lorenz dominates y if the generalised Lorenz curve of x does not lie below that of y at any point.

The following two results are due to Shorrocks (1983):

Proposition 1: For all x and y in X, [$W(x) \geq W(y)$ for all functions $W:X \to \Re$ satisfying ANON, PRI, LC and SMON] if and only if [(i) $\mu(x) \geq \mu(y)$ and (ii) x Lorenz dominates y].

Proposition 2: For all x and y in X, [$W(x) \geq W(y)$ for all functions $W:X \to \Re$ satisfying ANON, PRI, LC and MON] if and only if x generalised Lorenz dominates y.

Since ANON and PRI are standard conditions on the well-being function, in our discussion below we shall often desist from referring to these two conditions explicitly and use the term 'scale monotonic Lorenz consistent well-being function' to mean a well-being function that satisfies SMON and LC in addition to the two other conditions. Similarly, for convenience a 'monotonic Lorenz consistent well-being function' would often be taken to mean a well-being function that satisfies MON and LC in addition to ANON and PRI.

The two propositions stated above permit the empirical researcher in some cases to make well-being comparisons without knowing the well-being function W precisely. For instance, Proposition 1 above implies that if it is seen that [(i) $\mu(x) \geq \mu(y)$ and (ii) x Lorenz dominates y], then it follows that well-being in x is greater than that in y when well-being is measured by any function W, satisfying the properties stated in that proposition. There is no need to know the function W specifically. A similar remark applies to Proposition 2.

Unfortunately, this is not always the case. Consider Proposition 1. There are two sources from which non-comparability may arise. The first of these is the possibility that the Lorenz curves of x and y intersect. If that happens, x does not Lorenz dominate y. So the proposition now says that it is *not* the case that $W(x) \geq W(y)$ for all W functions having the stated properties. Moreover, neither does y Lorenz dominate x and therefore, nor is it the case that for all such W, $W(y) \geq W(x)$. In other words, for some admissible W, $W(y) > W(x)$, while for some other W, $W(x) \geq W(y)$. We cannot now compare x and y without knowing W. Second, there is also the possibility that even if the Lorenz curves do not intersect, the inequality ranking obtained from the Lorenz curves may contradict the ranking of the average value of x and y. For instance, suppose that x Lorenz dominates y. Even then, if $\mu(x) < \mu(y)$, it is again seen from Proposition 1 that we cannot compare x and y definitively in terms of the levels of well-being without knowing W. Similar will be the case if y Lorenz dominates x but $\mu(x) > \mu(y)$.

In theory, non-comparability may arise in the case of monotonic W functions also because generalised Lorenz curves may also intersect. In practice, however, the problem arises less frequently for such W functions because if $\mu(x) > \mu(y)$, chances are that x will generalised Lorenz dominate y.[4]

As stated before, however, we shall work mainly with W functions satisfying SMON. For us, therefore, the possibility of comparability failures is non-trivial. As a partial solution of the problem we now introduce the notion of a fuzzy Lorenz dominance relation. This will remove the first of the two sources of non-comparability of expenditure vectors stated above (though not the second).

Let R be a fuzzy binary relation i.e., it is a real-valued function on $X \times X$. For all x and y in X, $R(x, y)$ denotes the extent to which the statement 'x Lorenz dominates y' is true. R is assumed to be a real number between 0 and 1. If $R(x, y) = 1$, that would mean that the statement is definitely true; if it is 0, then the statement is definitely false. But we allow $R(x, y)$ to take intermediate values. We shall call R a fuzzy Lorenz dominance relation.

If the extent to which x Lorenz dominates y is greater than or equal to the extent to which y Lorenz dominates x, (i.e., if $R(x, y) \geq R(y, x)$), we shall say that x fuzzy Lorenz dominates y. We shall consider this to mean that although the Lorenz curves of x and y may intersect, x is judged to be less unequally distributed than y in an extended (viz., fuzzy) sense. We, therefore, obtain the crisp (i.e., non-fuzzy) dominance relation S defined as follows: For all x and y in X, $x \, S \, y$ if and only if $R(x, y) \geq R(y, x)$. S is sometimes called the crisp approximation of the fuzzy relation R.

Note that since R is a real number, we shall always have either $R(x, y) \geq R(y, x)$ or $R(y, x) \geq R(x, y)$. Hence, either x fuzzy Lorenz dominates y or y fuzzy Lorenz dominates x. Thus, S is a complete (crisp) relation. It may seem that the problem of incompleteness of the crisp Lorenz dominance relation has been solved trivially, by a sleight of hand so to speak. The acceptability of the solution, however, will depend on whether R can be judged to be an intuitively reasonable fuzzy Lorenz dominance relation.

One obvious condition of reasonability is that R should be consistent with the crisp (i.e., non-fuzzy) notion of Lorenz dominance, that is, for all x and y in X, it must be the case that if it so happens that x Lorenz dominates y (in the crisp sense), then $[R(x, y) = 1$ and $R(y, x) = 0]$.

We also require R to satisfy the fuzzy versions of the usual consistency conditions (reflexivity, completeness and transitivity) of the theory of crisp relations. A fuzzy relation R is said to be *reflexive* if $R(x, y) = 1 = R(y, x)$ whenever $x = y$. It is *complete* if $R(x, y) + R(y, x) \geq 1$ for all x and y. Note that if R is a complete crisp relation, then either $R(x, y) = 1$ or $R(y, x) = 1$ (or both of the equalities are true). Hence, in this case $R(x, y) + R(y, x)$ cannot be less than 1. The fuzzy completeness condition stated above demands that this weak inequality is also valid when R takes values between 0 and 1.

However, there does not seem to be an agreed definition of *transitivity* of a fuzzy relation. Many different definitions (all of which are consistent with the notion of transitivity in crisp theory) have been proposed. In this chapter we shall use the following notion of f-transitivity which seems to be intuitively fairly transparent (Ok 1996). R is *f-transitive* if, for all x, y and z in X, $[R(x, y) \geq R(y, x), R(y, z) \geq R(z, y)]$ implies $R(x, z) \geq R(z, x)$. A fuzzy Lorenz dominance f-ordering is defined to be a fuzzy relation that is (i) consistent with crisp Lorenz dominance and (ii) reflexive, complete and f-transitive.

Let R be a fuzzy Lorenz dominance f-ordering. We can now formulate the following modifications of Proposition 1 stated before. Introduce the following condition on W: for all x and y in X, $W(x) \geq W(y)$ if $[\mu(x) = \mu(y)$ and $R(x, y) \geq R(y, x)]$. We shall call this condition Fuzzy Lorenz Consistency (FLC).

Proposition 1': For all x and y in X, $[W(x) \geq W(y)$ for all functions $W: X \rightarrow \Re$ satisfying FLC, ANON, PRI and SMON] if and only if [(i) $\mu(x) \geq \mu(y)$ and (ii) x fuzzy Lorenz dominates y].

The proof of Proposition 1' is fairly analogous to that of Proposition 1. It is also possible to formulate fuzzy versions of Proposition 2 in an analogous way by defining the notion of fuzzy generalised Lorenz dominance. However, we shall not need to use these formulations for our purposes in this chapter.

Again, in the discussion below, we shall often suppress any direct reference to the standard conditions of ANON and PRI and take the term 'scale monotonic fuzzy Lorenz consistent well-being function' to mean a well-being function that satisfies SMON and FLC in addition to ANON and PRI.

In order to apply Proposition 1' to the task of well-being comparisons, however, we have to specify a fuzzy Lorenz dominance f-ordering R (and its crisp approximation S) which can be empirically applied. For that purpose, to start with let us assume that the number of individuals is n for all expenditure vectors and that all such vectors are arranged in non-decreasing order.

In this framework one possible measure of the extent to which x Lorenz dominates y would be a measure of the set $\{p \in [0, 1]: L_x(p) > L_y(p)\}$. This will be denoted by N_{xy}. For example, if $L_x(p)$ and $L_y(p)$ intersect at a point where $p = 0.6$ and if $L_x(p) > L_y(p)$ for p in $(0, 0.6)$ while $L_x(p) < L_y(p)$ for p in $(0.6, 1)$, then we shall say that $N_{xy} = 0.6$ and $N_{yx} = 0.4$ so that $N_{xy} > N_{yx}$.

We now suggest the fuzzy binary relation R^* on X such that, for all x and y in X,

$R^*(x, y) = 1$ if $x = y$ and
$= N_{xy} / (N_{xy} + N_{yx})$ otherwise.

It can be shown that R^* is a fuzzy Lorenz dominance f-ordering. The fuzzy dominance relation S^* derived from R^* is as follows: For all x and y in X, $x\ S^*\ y$ if and only if $R^*(x, y) \geq R^*(y, x)$, i.e., if and only if $N_{xy} \geq N_{yx}$. It can be checked that S^* is an ordering.

The assumptions (made above) that the entries in all expenditure vectors are arranged in non-decreasing order and that any pair of distributions have the same population size are dispensable. Any permutation of x will have the same Lorenz curve as x. Hence, for any x and y, both N_{xy} and N_{yx} are invariant with respect to how the entries in *x* and *y* are arranged. Similarly, any replication of *x* has the same Lorenz curve as *x*. Therefore, if *x* and *y* have different population sizes (but the same mean), by choosing an appropriate replication *x'* of *x* and an appropriate replication *y'* of *y*, we can ensure that *x'* and *y'* will have the same population size.[5] But *x'* and *y'* will have the same Lorenz curves as *x* and *y* respectively. Thus, we might as well assume to start with that *x* and *y* are of the same population size.

There are other suggested fuzzy dominance relations in the literature. However, most of these are oriented towards specific inequality indices. For instance, the following fuzzy relation is a slightly modified form of a relation suggested in Basu (1987). For all *x* and *y* in X, let $E_{xy} = \sum_{j=1}^{n} \max \left(\sum_{i=1}^{j} (x_i - y_i), 0 \right)$.

In the familiar Lorenz diagram E_{xy} is the area of the dominance of Lorenz curve of *x* over that of *y*. Consider now the fuzzy relation *R'* defined as follows:

$R'(x, y) = 1$ if $x = y$ and
$= E_{xy} / (E_{xy} + E_{yx})$ otherwise.

It can be checked that *R'* is a fuzzy Lorenz dominance *f*-ordering. The crisp approximation of *R'* (say, *S'*) can then be defined in the usual way: for all *x* and *y* in X, *x S' y* if and only if $R'(x, y) \geq R'(y, x)$, i.e., if and only if $E_{xy} \geq E_{yx}$.

The crisp relation *S'* is an ordering. However, it is essentially the Gini ordering since $E_{xy} \geq E_{yx}$ if and only if $G(x) < G(y)$ where G is the Gini inequality index. Thus, this ranking relation is oriented toward a specific inequality index. (This is not surprising since Basu [1987] made it clear that the objective of that paper was fuzzification of the 'Gini-Lorenz' framework of inequality measurement.) A basic purpose of deriving inequality rankings on the basis of Lorenz dominance however, is to avoid reliance on particular inequality indices. *S** is not oriented in this sense toward any of the inequality indices that are widely used in empirical work. In the present context, that is its strong point. For this reason, in our empirical application we shall use the fuzzy inequality dominance relation S^*.

The Trend of Economic Well-Being in India

For the purpose of determining whether there has been an increase in economic well-being in India between any two given years, as per the criterion developed in the preceding section, we need information on average expenditure and the Lorenz curve of the distribution of expenditure in each of the two years.

The expenditure surveys conducted by the National Sample Survey Office (NSSO) generate data on the monthly per capita expenditure (MPCE) of households (i.e., household expenditure on consumption divided by the size of the household) for each household in samples drawn from the rural sector and the urban sector separately. From this information we can calculate the all-India average MPCEs and the Lorenz curves of the distribution of MPCE for the country as a whole for the different survey years.[6]

Nowadays almost every round of NSSO survey contains some information on the MPCE distribution in India. For a long time, however, it was the quinquennial large sample consumer expenditure surveys that were the only dependable source of such information. (Sometimes, however, the NSSO conducted thin sample surveys in-between two consecutive quinquennial surveys.) Since we are interested only in the broad trends of change in economic well-being in India in the 1980s, 1990s and 2000s, we shall, for simplicity, concentrate on the data generated by the large sample surveys of the years 1983, 1993–94, 2004–05 and 2011–12.

Quinquennial surveys were also carried out in 1987 and 1999–2000. Inclusion of the 1987 data would make little difference to our findings on the trends reported below.

Dropping the year 1999–2000 from the picture, however, is motivated by deeper problems relating to inter-temporal comparability of the data. The most important of these relates to the recall period that is, the length of the period of time for which the households are requested to recall their expenditure on various items. Traditionally, NSSO has followed the system of a uniform recall period (URP) of 30 days for all goods. In many other countries of the world, however, the practice is to use a shorter recall period for high frequency items of expenditure (such as food items) and a longer one for low frequency items (such as consumer durables).

After the large sample quinquennial survey of 1993–94 (the 50th Round of NSSO surveys), the NSSO experimented with a system of multiple questionnaires. Two different questionnaires were now used in the interviews. One of these used the 30-day URP as before while the other used a mixed recall period (MRP). In the latter type of questionnaire, three different recall periods (of 7, 30 and 365 days) were used for items of different degrees of frequency. In the four thin sample surveys (the 51st through the 54th Rounds) conducted in the four years following 1993–94, both types of questionnaires were used. Which type was to be used for a particular household was decided randomly.

This system, however, proved to be too cumbersome to implement. In the quinquennial survey of 1999–2000 (the 55th Round), the procedure was simplified to some extent. The number of different recall periods was brought down from three to two: 7 and 30 days. Moreover, the procedure of assigning households randomly to one of the two types of questionnaires was discarded. Instead, all households were now asked to report their expenditure on high frequency items for both 7-day and 30-day recall periods and that on low frequency items on the basis of the 30-day period only.

Deaton (2003) pointed out that while there is nothing wrong with the use of multiple recall periods in household expenditure surveys (and, that, on the contrary, it may produce better estimates of the parameters of the expenditure distribution than the single recall period procedure), problems arise if we want to compare these estimates with those generated by the earlier quinquennial surveys.[7] In order to avoid this problem, we drop the 1999–2000 survey from the scope of our study.

In the 61st Round Survey of 2004–05, in addition to the 30-day recall period which was used for collecting information from all households on all items, a recall period of 365 days was used for clothing (and bedding), footwear, education, medical care (institutional) and durable goods. Those estimates that were based on the 30-day recall period data would be comparable with those for 1983, 1993–94 and 2011–12.[8]

In the 68th Round Survey of 2011–12, a questionnaire called Schedule Type 1 was used for half of the sampled households. For the other half, Schedule Type 2 was used. While the items of consumption were identical in the two Schedules, the recall periods differed. The items were divided into three categories. Category I consisted of infrequently purchased items, for instance, footwear and durable goods. Category II included the major food items, for instance, vegetables, fruits, edible oil, fish, meat, poultry, etc. Category III contained other food items, fuel and light, rents, taxes, etc. Schedule Type 1 collected two types of information. One of these was based on the 30-day URP for all the three categories of goods mentioned above. These were called the URP estimates. Additionally, however, on Category I items, information was also collected on the 365-day recall period basis. Estimates that were based on the 365-day recall period for Category I items and the 30-day recall period for Category II and Category III items were called Mixed Recall (or Reference) Period (MRP) estimates. Households interviewed with Schedule Type 2 were requested to use different recall periods for the different categories of items although for a given category there was only one recall period. The recall periods for this type of schedule were: 365 days for Category I, 7 days for Category II and 30 days for Category III. Estimates based on this type of data were called Modified Mixed Reference Period

(MMRP) estimates. For our purposes, clearly, using the URP estimates would ensure comparability across all the three years of our interest excepting for 1999–2000.[9]

To get an idea of the trend of economic well-being in India (as per the theoretical framework laid down in the second section of this chapter) over the period of time indicated above, we need estimates of the average values of MPCE and of the Lorenz curves for the different NSSO survey years. Regarding average MPCE, the NSSO reports give estimates for the rural sector and the urban sector separately. Table 3.1 below displays the average MPCEs in current prices in these two sectors for the different large sample survey years.

Table 3.1: Average MPCE at current prices in the rural and the urban sectors in India in various NSSO survey years (Rs)

Year	Rural	Urban
1983	112.31	165.80
1993–94	281.40	458.04
2004–05	558.78	1052.36
2011–12	1278.94	2399.24

Source: NSSO (2006, 61st Round Survey Report, p. 18, Table P6) and NSSO (2013, 68th Round Survey Report, p. 12, Table T4); see also Banerjee (2020)

Since these are current price figures, they need to be expressed in real terms in order to neutralise effects of inflation. For this purpose we use the NSSO procedure of using Consumer Price Index for Agricultural Labourers (CPI-AL) and the Consumer Price Index for Industrial Workers (CPI-IW) for the rural and the urban sectors respectively. The index of average MPCE at current prices, the price deflator and the index of real average MPCE for the different years for the rural and the urban sectors are shown in Tables 3.2 and 3.3 respectively. All the index numbers use 1983 as the base year.

Table 3.2: Index of average MPCE at current prices, the price deflator and the index of real average MPCE in the rural sector in India in various years (Base: 1983)

Year	Index of average MPCE at current prices	Price deflator	Index of real average MPCE
1983	100	100	100.00
1993–94	255	229	111.35
2004–05	497	406	122.41
2011–12	1139	737	154.55

Note: The price deflator is the Consumer Price Index for Agricultural Labourers (CPI-AL).
Source: Author's calculations based on Table P6 in NSSO (2006) and Table T4 in NSSO (2013); see also Banerjee (2020)

Table 3.3: Index of average MPCE at current prices, the price deflator and the index of real average MPCE in the urban sector in India in various years (Base: 1983)

Year	Index of average MPCE at current prices	Price deflator	Index of real average MPCE
1983	100	100	100.00
1993–94	280	240	116.67
2004–05	635	477	133.12
2011–12	1447	845	1171.12

Note: The price deflator is the Consumer Price Index for Industrial Workers (CPI-IW).
Source: Author's calculations based on Table P6 in NSSO (2006) and Table T4 in NSSO (2013); see also Banerjee (2020)

Next, we have to combine the rural and the urban average MPCEs into all-India figures. While the NSSO reports do not give these country-wide averages, it is easy to see that, if a number of observations on a variable is divided into two groups, the overall mean equals the weighted average of the group means, if we use the group population shares as the weights. Hence, to obtain the all-India average MPCEs for the different years, we compute the rural and the urban population shares. However, since population censuses are carried out only decennially, we have direct observations on the rural and the urban population sizes in India in 1981, 1991, 2001 and 2011 but not for those in the intermediate years. For 2011–12, therefore, we have used the rural and urban population shares as reported in the 2011 Census while for 1983, 1993–94 and 2004–05, we have used the sectoral shares in total population as computed by interpolation. Table 3.4 displays the population shares in the different survey years.[10, 11]

Table 3.4: Rural and urban shares (per cent) in population in India

Year	Rural	Urban
1983	76	24
1993	74	26
2004	71	29
2011	69	31

Source: Author's calculations based on Census of India, 1981, 1991, 2001 and 2011.

We can now calculate the index of real average MPCEs in India for the various survey years (with 1983 as the base year). These are reported in Table 3.5.

Table 3.5: Index numbers of average real MPCE in India in various years (Base: 1983)

Year	Index
1983	100.00
1993–94	112.73
2004–05	125.51
2011–12	160.00

Source: Author's calculations based on Tables 3.2, 3.3 and 3.4; see also Banerjee (2020)

If real average MPCE was our measure of economic well-being, this would have been the end-point of the exercise.[11] However, to apply the well-being criteria developed in the second section of this chapter, we also need to look at the distribution of MPCE in the different years. Table 3.6 below presents the cumulative quintile shares in this distribution for the relevant years. For example, in the year 1983, the bottom 20 per cent of the households (i.e., the first quintile) in the distribution of MPCE incurred 8.4 per cent of the aggregate MPCE in India, the bottom 40 per cent (i.e., the first and the second quintile together) accounted for 20.9 per cent and so on.

Table 3.6: Cumulative quintile shares in the distribution of MPCE in India

Quintile number	Cumulative shares (%)			
	1983	1993–94	2004–05	2011–12
1	8.4	8.7	8.1	8.3
2	20.9	21.1	19.6	20.2
3	37.1	36.9	34.5	35.5
4	58.5	58.0	54.8	56.0
5	100.0	100.0	100.0	100.0

Source: Pal and Ghosh (2006) and www.worldbank.org; see also Banerjee (2020)

The figures in Table 3.6 show that the Lorenz curves of the distribution of MPCE for the years 1983 and 1993–94 intersect since shares of the bottom 20 and 40 per cents of the households in this distribution in 1983 (8.4 per cent and 20.9 per cent, respectively) are lower than the corresponding figures for 1993–94 (8.7 per cent and 21.1 per cent) while the shares of the bottom 60 and 80 per cents (37.1 per cent and 58.5 per cent, respectively) in 1983 are higher than those in 1993–94 (36.9 per cent and 58 per cent).

As explained earlier in the second section, if we want our measure of well-being to satisfy the condition of monotonicity, we need to look at the generalised Lorenz curves of the MPCE distributions. As explained there, the proportional changes over time in the mean value of income (or any proxy such as MPCE) is usually seen to be by far greater than the proportional variation in the measures of inequality, such as the length of the Lorenz curve or the generalised Lorenz curve (or of any part

Measuring the Trend of Economic Well-Being in India in Recent Decades   95

thereof). Informally, it is the direction of change in the mean value of the variable that effectively determines the overall ranking. Since over the entire time period of our interest, average MPCE has continuously grown, the generalised Lorenz curve is expected to have shifted upward from any one survey year to any of the others. This seems to be verified by the data. As a random example, Table 3.7 below describes the coordinates of the generalised Lorenz curves of the MPCE distribution in the years 1983 and 2004–05.

Table 3.7: Coordinates of generalised Lorenz curves of the distribution of MPCE in India in 1983 and 2004–05

(1) Quintile no.	(2) Cumulative share (%), 1983	(3) Index of average real MPCE, 1983	(4) Column (2) × Column (3)	(5) Cumulative share (%), 2004–05	(6) Index of average real MPCE, 2004–05	(7) Column (5) × Column (6)
1	8.4	100	840	8.1	125.51	1016.6
2	20.9	100	2090	19.6	125.51	2459.9
3	37.1	100	3710	34.5	125.51	4330.1
4	58.5	100	5850	54.8	125.51	6877.9
5	100.0	100	10000	100.0	125.51	12551

Source: Tables 3.5 and 3.6; see also Banerjee (2020)

As is seen from Columns (4) and (7) of Table 3.7, the generalised Lorenz curve of the MPCE distribution in 2004–05 lies wholly above that of the distribution in 1983, implying that the level of well-being (as measured by MPCE) in India in 2004–05 was higher than that in 1983. Similar exercises (the details of which are omitted) show that there was, in fact, a steady upward movement of the generalised Lorenz curve throughout the period from 1983 to 2011–12. It follows from Proposition 2 from the second section that well-being measured by *any* function satisfying the conditions mentioned in that proposition must be considered to have steadily increased from any survey year to the next.

The conditions listed in Proposition 2, however, includes the condition of monotonicity. We have discussed earlier the reasons why many economists believe that as a condition on an inequality-sensitive measure of well-being, it should be replaced by the condition of scale monotonicity (SMON). In other words, the relevant list of conditions on the well-being function should be the one stated in Proposition 1.

It so happens, however, that one particular well-being function that satisfies all the conditions of Proposition 1 (including SMON) is related to the generalised Lorenz curve. It is also perhaps the most widely used measure of well-being in empirical work. This is the function W for which, for any vector x describing the expenditure levels of the individuals, the level of well-being in the economy is $W(x) = \mu(x)(1 - G(x))$ where G is the Gini coefficient. On the face of it, this well-being function seems to be entirely reasonable since it pays attention to both the 'efficiency' and the 'equity' aspects of well-being. It is known that if the generalised Lorenz curve of x is drawn in a box diagram in which the horizontal axis represents the interval $[0, 1]$, $\mu(x)(1 - G(x))$ is proportional to the area between the curve and the horizontal axis (just as, for the ordinary Lorenz curve, it is $(1 - G(x))$ which is proportional to the similarly defined area).

It is no wonder, therefore, that if there is a steady upward shift of the generalised Lorenz curve, there would be a steady increase in the level of well-being measured in this particular way. That this indeed is the case is verified in Table 3.8 below.

For the purposes of this chapter, however, the crucial question is how robust this finding is. Thus, we are interested in knowing whether it is true not only for this particular well-being function but also for *all* functions satisfying the conditions of SMON, ANON, PRI and LC. We first attempt to answer the question by applying Proposition 1 which, it may be recalled, gives a necessary and sufficient condition under which, for any two expenditure vectors x and y, $W(x)$ is not less than $W(y)$ for all W functions satisfying the four conditions mentioned above.

Table 3.8: Value of the well-being measure $W = \mu(1 - G)$ in India in various NSSO survey years

Year	$W = \mu(1 - G)$
1983	67.50
1993–94	77.78
2004–05	80.33
2011–12	105.60

Note: μ = index of average MPCE (Base year: 1983); G = Gini coefficient of the MPCE distribution.
Source: For μ: Table 3.5; for values of G: Bhalla (2003), Banerjee et al. (2012) and Ghosh (2016).

If the answer to the question is in the affirmative, we can take x to be at least as good as y in an overall assessment of well-being. The result of this exercise is reported in Table 3.9 below. For each of the three time periods, 1983 to 1993–94, 1993–94 to 2004–05 and 2004–05 to 2011–12, we ask whether well-being (as per all scale monotonic Lorenz consistent well-being functions) at the end point is at least as great as that at the starting point. Recall that as per Proposition 1, the answer is 'yes' if and only if, (a) average MPCE has not decreased over the relevant time period and (b) the Lorenz curve at the end point of the time period is not below that at the beginning of the period. Whether (a) and (b) are satisfied can be checked from Table 3.5 and 3.6 respectively.

We now ask whether the criterion of fuzzy dominance that we developed earlier can add anything to the above analysis. For that purpose we have to apply Proposition 1′ discussed in the second section. However, from Table 3.6 it is seen that, of the three time periods considered in Table 3.9, it is only the first (1983 to 1993–94) that is beset with the problem of intersecting Lorenz curves. In both of the other two periods there were unambiguous upward or downward movements of the Lorenz curve: between 1993–94 and 2004–05 it shifted downward and between 2004–05 and 2011–12 it shifted upward. It follows that for the last two of the three periods of time of our interest,

98 Asis Kumar Banerjee

the result of the well-being comparison exercise on the basis of Proposition 1' would be the same as that on the basis of Proposition 1.

Table 3.9: Qualitative trend of economic well-being in India as per any scale monotonic Lorenz consistent well-being function

Time period	Direction of movement
1983 to 1993–94	?
1993–94 to 2004–05	?
2004–05 to 2011–12	+

Note: A plus sign indicates that well-being (as measured by *all* scale monotonic Lorenz consistent well-being functions) at the end of the stated time period is at least as great as that at the beginning. A question mark indicates that it is not possible to rank the levels of well-being at the two time points. For instance, between 1983 and 1993–94 average MPCE increased. But the MPCE distribution for 1993–94 does not Lorenz dominate that for 1983. Hence, (as per Proposition 1) it is not possible to rank the levels of well-being in these two years. On the other hand, the question mark against the time period from 1993–94 to 2004–05 is due to the fact that while average MPCE increased over this period, the Lorenz curve shifted downward. The period from 2004–05, however, is assigned a plus sign since over this period there was an increase in average MPCE as well as an upward shift in the Lorenz curve.
Source: Tables 3.5 and 3.6.

To see the implications of Proposition 1' for the 1983 to 1993–94 period, let x and y denote the MPCE distributions at the end-point and at the starting point. To check whether x represents at least as high a level of well-being as y as per *all* scale monotonic and fuzzy Lorenz consistent well-being functions, we have to check whether [(i) $\mu(x) \geq \mu(y)$ and (ii) x weakly fuzzy Lorenz dominates y]. As explained in the second section, the fuzzy Lorenz dominance relation that we shall use is the fuzzy relation R^* and its crisp approximation S^* as defined there. To recall, $x\, S^*\, y$ if and only if $N_{xy} \geq N_{yx}$.

Now, computations based on the columns referring to the years 1983 and 1993–94 in Table 3.6 reveal that the Lorenz curves for these two years intersect at the point (50, 29) and that the curve for 1983 lies below that of 1993–94 on the left-hand side of the intersection point while on the right-hand side of the point it lies above. Thus, $N_{xy} = 50 = N_{yx}$. Hence, $R^*(x, y) = R^*(y, x)$. In other words, we have both $x\ S^*\ y$ and $y\ S^*\ x$. Therefore, $x\ I^*\ y$ if I^* denotes the symmetric component of S^*.

Moreover, since average MPCE increased between 1983 and 1993–94, it would follow from Proposition 1' that it is now possible to rank the levels of well-being in these two years: economic well-being in x was at least as high as that in y but the converse was not true. In other words, well-being increased between 1983 and 1993–94. Hence, the question mark in the first row of Table 3.9 is now replaced by a plus sign. This illustrates the usefulness of the fuzzy Lorenz consistency approach developed earlier.

However, since between 1993–94 and 2004–05, average MPCE increased but the Lorenz curve shifted downward, the question mark in the second row of that table remains unchanged. The amended picture is presented in Table 3.10 below.

Table 3.10: Qualitative trend of economic well-being in India as per any scale monotonic fuzzy Lorenz consistent well-being function

Time period	Direction of movement
1983 to 1993–94	+
1993–94 to 2004–05	?
2004–05 to 2011–12	+

Note: The plus signs and the question mark have the same connotations as in Table 3.9.
Source: Calculations based on Tables 3.5 and 3.6.

Conclusion

To summarise, the picture of a relentless increase in the level of economic well-being in India throughout the period from 1983 to 2011–12 that emerges from Tables 3.7 and 3.8 is conditional on the use of either monotonic well-being functions (in case of Table 3.7), or on that of the specific well-being function $W = \mu(1 - G)$ (in case of Table 3.8). However, monotonicity in the present context is essentially a Pareto-type condition. As explained in the second section on the theoretical framework, it is open to the criticism that in certain situations it may turn out to be inegalitarian. (For a more detailed discussion of this issue see Fleurbaey and Trannoy [2003].) On the other hand, the $\mu(1 - G)$ formula does satisfy the conditions of scale monotonicity, Anonymity, Population Replication Invariance and Lorenz Consistency. However, the important question is whether the conclusion based on this particular well-being function would be valid for the class of *all* functions satisfying these conditions. Table 3.9 shows that the answer is in the negative. Since the choice of any particular member of the class must be arbitrary, the finding of a steady increase in well-being throughout the period of our interest does not seem to be a robust one. It is seen from Table 3.9 that if we stick to the conventional (crisp, i.e., non-fuzzy) form of the Lorenz Consistency condition, there was improvement in well-being between 2004–05 and 2011–12. But the directions of change in well-being in the other two time periods shown in that table are indeterminate. In this chapter, however, we have argued for the introduction of fuzzy Lorenz dominance relations and for replacing the condition of Lorenz Consistency by that of Fuzzy Lorenz Consistency. Table 3.10 shows that if we do so, the 'zone of ignorance' is reduced but it does not vanish. We can now conclude that there was also an improvement in the level of well-being between 1983 and 1993–94. The direction of movement in well-being during the period 1993–94 to 2004–05, however, continues to be ambiguous. For reasons explained in the chapter we believe that these conclusions can be considered to have some degree of robustness.

We conclude by noting one direction of further research in this area. It is now widely recognised that well-being is a multidimensional concept, depending, as it does, on not only income or expenditure but also on a number of other variables such as education, health and so on. The time trend of multidimensional well-being in India is an important topic for investigation. Because of the multidimensionality issues, however, it is also likely to be an even more challenging topic than the one this chapter grapples with.

NOTES

[1] Very recently, a start has been made in collecting personal income data in India. See the reports of the India Human Development Surveys conducted by the University of Maryland and the National Council of Applied Economic Research in 2004–05 and 2011–12 at the website https://ihds.umd.edu. The NSSO is also reported to be planning to collect personal income data in its future surveys. However, the currently available data on income are insufficient for the purpose of analysing time trends of economic well-being in India.

[2] Similarly, in theory, generalised Lorenz curves may also intersect. When they do so, the second criterion too, would lead to a comparison failure. In practice, however, in a *growing* economy, for reasons that we shall note in the second section above, generalised Lorenz curves for different years seldom intersect.

[3] Anonymity requires that if x is a permutation of y, then $W(x) = W(y)$. It means that in measuring the well-being of an economy the individuals can be taken in any order. Population Replication Invariance says that if y is an m-fold replication of x for any positive integer m, i.e., if y is obtained by writing x m times, $y = (x, x, ..., x)$, then $W(x) = W(y)$. This condition implies that well-being is measured in per capita terms. In our context it reminds us that if between any two years the population size of a country increases without any change either in per capita expenditure or in the inequality of the distribution of expenditure, then we should *not* say that there has been an increase in well-being.

[4] The reason is that in any economy, average expenditure (or income) usually changes faster than the degree of inequality. Hence, between any two time points (especially, if these are a few years apart) average expenditure differs relatively significantly but the Lorenz curves do not differ that much. Recall that the generalised Lorenz curve is the Lorenz curve scaled up by the average value of expenditure. Hence, the effect of the change in average expenditure dominates. For this reason even when Lorenz curves intersect, the generalised Lorenz curves frequently do not.

[5] For instance, if x is of population size 3 and y is of size 4, we can replicate x 4 times to obtain x' and replicate y 3 times to obtain y'.

[6] Calculation of the all-India Lorenz curves often requires going to the unit-level data generated by the surveys because the published official reports often give only the curves (or, at least, the information necessary for calculating them) for the rural and the urban sectors separately. The all-India average MPCE for any year can however, be calculated relatively easily from the sectoral averages given in the reports by taking their population-share-weighted arithmetic mean.

[7] It may seem that since data were collected from each household on both high- and low-frequency items with the 30-day recall period, these could easily be used to deduce total expenditure with this recall period and the resulting estimates can be compared with those for the other large sample survey years. The additional data on high-frequency items with the 7-day recall period can just be ignored for the purpose of this exercise. However, one major problem here is that when the respondents are asked to report on expenditure on any item, they are effectively prodded to reconcile their rates of consumption across the two periods. This affects data quality. Deaton (2003) notes that there is some evidence that is consistent with this type of reconciliation.

[8] In the survey report, MPCE meant the MPCE based on the 30-day recall period although it was also sometimes called 'MPCE(U30)' or 'unadjusted MPCE'. In contrast, the MPCE that used the 365-day-recall-period data on the five low-frequency items mentioned in the text was called 'MPCE(M)' or 'adjusted

MPCE". It is conceivable that the problem of the type mentioned in Note 7 above might persist here to some extent. However, the problem would be much less pronounced here because the items involved are now the *infrequently* purchased items (unlike in the 1999–2000 survey when it was the frequently purchased items on which such dual information was elicited). It may reasonably be assumed that the problem of reconciliation would be less severe here.

[9] Again, theoretically, here there is the possibility of persistence of the Deaton-type problem (2003) since, although the two types of Schedules were used on two different sets of households, the households interviewed with Schedule Type 1 were asked for information regarding a subset (Category I) of the items on the basis of both the 30-day and the 365-day recall periods. However, since these were the relatively low-frequency items, remarks similar to those in Note 8 apply. It can be assumed that the problem is of negligible proportions.

[10] For the survey years 1983, 1993–94, 2004–05 and 2011–12 the rural and the urban population shares have been identified with those for the years 1983, 1993, 2004 and 2011, respectively.

[11] The figures in Table 3.4 were arrived at on the basis of linear interpolation. For instance, for calculating the rural population share in 1983, it was assumed that the growth path of the rural population in India was the straight line joining the rural populations in the Census years 1981 and 1991. Similar remarks apply to the urban population and to the years 1993 and 2004 which fell in-between two Census years. We are aware of the limitations of the linearity assumption in an interpolation model. However, the very slow changes in the sectoral population shares in India revealed by the figures in Table 3.4 lead us to believe that more complex interpolation models are unlikely to change our findings significantly. Some experiments with alternative interpolation models (based, for instance, on the exponential formula or the logistic curve), the results of which are not reported here, confirmed the suspicion. Recall that what we are actually concerned with is the directions of change in the all-India average

MPCE between various pairs of NSSO survey years. In no case was the finding in this regard affected by the choice among the alternative population interpolation procedures mentioned above.

REFERENCES

Atkinson, A. B. 1970. 'On the Measurement of Inequality'. *Journal of Economic Theory* 2(3): 244–263.

Banerjee, Asis Kumar. 2020. *Measuring Development: An Inequality Dominance Approach*, Themes in Economics. Singapore: Springer.

Banerjee, L., A. Deshpande, Y. Ming, S. Ruparelia, V. Vakulabharanam and W. Zhong. 2012. 'Growth, Reforms and Inequality: Comparing India and China'. In A. K. Bagchi and A. P. D'Costa (eds), *Transformation and Development: The Political Economy of Transition in India and China*. New Delhi: Oxford University Press.

Basu, K. 1987. 'Axioms for a Fuzzy Measure of Inequality'. *Mathematical Social Sciences* 14(3): 275–288.

Bhalla, S. S. 2003. 'Recounting the Poor: Poverty in India, 1983–1999'. *Economic and Political Weekly* 38(4): 338–349.

Dasgupta, P., A. K. Sen and D. Starrett. 1973. 'Notes on the Measurement of Inequality'. *Journal of Economic Theory* 6(2): 180–187.

Deaton, A. 2003. 'Adjusted Indian Poverty Estimates for 1999–2000'. *Economic and Political Weekly* 38(4): 322–326.

Fleurbaey, M. and A. Trannoy. 2003. 'The impossibility of a Paretian egalitarian'. *Social Choice and Welfare* 21: 243–263.

Foster, J. E. 1985. 'Inequality Measurement'. In H. P. Young (ed.), *Fair Allocation*. Providence, RI: American Mathematical Society, 31–68.

Ghosh, J. 2016. 'Inequality in India: Drivers and Consequences'. In ISSC, IDS and UNESCO, *World Social Science Report 2016*. Paris: UNESCO Publishing.

Himanshu. 2018. *India Inequality Report 2018: Widening Gaps*. New Delhi: Oxfam India.

NSSO. 2006. 'Level and Pattern of Consumer Expenditure, 2004–05', NSS 61st Round. National Sample Survey Organisation, Ministry of Statistics and Programme Implementation, Government of India.

———. 2013. 'Key Indicators of Household Consumer Expenditure in India', NSS 68th Round. National Sample Survey Office, Ministry of Statistics and Programme Implementation, Government of India.

Ok, Efe A. 1996. 'Fuzzy Measurement of Income Inequality: Some Possibility Results on the Fuzzification of the Lorenz Ordering'. *Economic Theory* 7(3): 513–530.

Pal, P. and J. Ghosh. 2006. 'Inequality in India: A Survey of Recent Trends'. In Jomo K. S. and J. Baudot (eds), *Flat World, Big Gaps: Economic Liberalization, Globalization, Poverty & Inequality*. New York: UN Publications.

Shorrocks, A. F. 1983. 'Ranking Income Distributions'. *Economica* 50: 3–17.

4
DO STOCK MARKETS SIGNAL REAL ECONOMIC PERFORMANCE?
A Theoretical and Empirical Note

Abhirup Sarkar and *Agnirup Sarkar*

Introduction

Financial development in an economy has long been recognised as an important determinant of economic development. There is an old literature, both theoretical and empirical, which emphasises financial intermediation in general, and stock market developments in particular, as major factors behind *long-run* growth. The theoretical literature goes as far back as Schumpeter (1912) and Hicks (1969) and culminates in more recent works of Jacklin (1987), Gorton and Pennacchi (1990), Greenwood and Jovanovic (1990), Bencivenga and

Smith (1991), Levine (1991), Japelli and Pagano (1994) and Bencivenga, Smith and Starr (1995), among others. In this literature, there are primarily two ways in which stock markets help growth and development. First, they act as an efficient bridge between savers and investors, thereby channelising funds for investment, capital accumulation and growth. Second, a vibrant secondary market in stocks makes stocks more liquid and thereby, increases the incentive for agents to invest into the primary market.

The financial intermediation and growth nexus is supported by a host of empirical work which includes King and Levine (1993a, b), Levine and Zervos (1996, 1998) and others. While King and Levine (ibid.) are concerned with financial intermediation in general, Levine and Zervos (ibid.) are concerned particularly with the stock market. These empirical studies consider the state of financial development at some initial period and look at its effect on future average long-run growth. For example, King and Levine (1993a) consider a set of 88 countries. They regress real per capita GDP growth on four measures of financial development: total liquid liabilities of the financial system divided by GDP; total bank credit as a proportion of bank plus central bank credit; ratio of credit allocated to private enterprises to total credit; and credit to private enterprises divided by GDP. All the four regressors are significant at 1 per cent level. Similarly, they show that these variables measuring financial development are significant determinants of capital formation and productivity growth as well.

Levine and Zervos (1996) look at the relationship specifically between stock market development and real per capita GDP growth for a broad cross-section of 49 countries over the period 1976–93. Two variables, *value traded ratio* (value of domestic equity transactions in domestic stock exchanges divided by GDP) and *turnover ratio* (value of domestic equity transactions in domestic stock exchanges divided by domestic market capitalisation) are considered to represent stock market development. It is shown that both variables significantly influence future per capita growth.

Curiously enough, while most of the existing research focuses on how financial development in general, and stock market development in particular, affect *future average long-run* growth; public interest is predominantly in the *contemporaneous* relation between the stock market and the real economy. A section of the media treats the stock market as a mirror which faithfully reflects the instantaneous performance of the economy. This view is shared by a section of the public who interprets ups and downs in the stock market as signals of short-run booms and busts. The purpose of the present chapter is to evaluate this public perception both theoretically and empirically. In particular, we ask whether in the *short run,* a rise in income is reflected by a rise in stock market performance so that by observing a boom in the stock market, we may infer that the economy is going through good times. Indeed, stock prices are much more frequently observable than real income. Therefore, if stock prices mirror real economic performance, it will be easier to keep track of the real economy through the stock market. But if this is not so, then the message is that an asset price bubble can occur without a real boom in the economy. In addition, we will also look at the *long-run co-movements,* if any, of the stock market and the growth of real income. This will tell us whether there is a long-run contemporaneous relationship between the two variables.

In what follows, we measure performance of the stock market by the market capitalisation ratio.[1] Suppose, the relationship between the market capitalisation ratio and real income is positive. Then a rise in the value of stocks must imply that real income has indeed gone up. To see this more clearly, let the market capitalisation ratio $MK = V/Y$, where V is the value of stocks and Y is real income. Also, $\widehat{MK} = \theta \hat{Y}, \theta > 0$, signifying the assumed positive relationship between the two variables, where a 'hat' on a variable indicates proportionate change. Since $\widehat{MK} = \hat{V} - \hat{Y}$, it follows that $\hat{V} = (1 + \theta)\hat{Y}$. The last equality implies that if we observe a rise in the value of stocks, we may infer that there has been a rise in real income. We can only make this inference provided θ is positive. If, on the other hand, θ is negative or ambiguous, we cannot make such an inference. In other words, in the former case, the stock market can be taken as a mirror of the real economy while in the latter cases, it cannot.

For our theoretical analysis, we use the Lucas (1978) asset pricing model. In this consumption-based asset pricing model, stocks are the only instrument in terms of which agents can save. An exogenous increase in income has two effects on savings and hence on the demand for stocks. Due to a standard income effect, current as well as future consumption should both increase, which means that current savings should also go up. But the proportionate increase in savings may be less than that of income and if so, the increase in the demand for stocks will be less in proportion to the increase in income. As a consequence, the market capitalisation ratio will have a tendency to fall. On the other hand, if agents are sufficiently risk averse and perceive that the current increase in income will be followed by a severe fall in income in the future, then due to the inter-temporal substitution effect, they will save more and as we shall see below, this can actually lead to a rise in the market capitalisation ratio. So the net effect will depend upon the degree of risk aversion and the information that the current increase in income provides about the future income stream. In general, therefore, the net effect will be ambiguous. We obtain similar ambiguous results about the relationship between the long-run stationary state values of per capita income and the market capitalisation ratio. Finally, the ambiguity result persists when we introduce the possibility of growth. In short, our theoretical analysis suggests that nothing specific can be inferred about the real state of the economy from a boom or a bust in the stock market.

Our theoretical conclusions are supported by our empirical analysis. We represent stock market development by the market capitalisation ratio. We consider time series data of market capitalisation ratio and per capita income for 33 countries for the time period 1988–2018.

We could obtain a long-run relationship between these two variables only for five of these countries, and a statistically significant short-run relationship between market capitalisation ratio and per capita income with the latter as the independent variable, for six countries. For India, though the data reveal a long-run relationship between the stock market and per capita income, no short-run relationship could be obtained between the two.

Our theoretical results are presented in the following section. In the third section, we report our empirical findings, whereas the fourth section concludes the chapter.

A Theoretical Framework

Consider an economy inhabited by a large number of identical and infinitely lived agents who allocate their resources each period between consumption (C_t) and saving, in the form of stocks. A share of stock pays a dividend $y_t > 0$ in period t and commands an ex-dividend price p_t at the end of the period. The dividend is the only source of income in the economy and is exogenous. It is given in terms of a *non-storable* consumption good. Let K_t be the number of shares purchased by the representative agent at the end of period t and $\beta < 1$ be the discount factor.

Budget constraint at t of a representative agent is

$$C_t + p_t (K_t - K_{t-1}) = y_t K_{t-1} \qquad (1)$$

The agent's objective is to maximise the discounted sum of her lifetime expected utility subject to her budget constraint, that is,

$$\text{maximise } E_t \{\sum_{j=0}^{\infty} \beta^j U(C_{t+j})\} \qquad (2)$$

subject to the budget constraint (1). The choice variables are C_t and K_t.

A number of observations are in order on the nature of this economy and its equilibrium. First, there is a single market in this economy where consumption goods can be traded for stocks. However, since agents are all identical, there is no trade in equilibrium. Second, since consumption goods are non-storable, in equilibrium, total output must equal total consumption in each period. But because there is no trade in equilibrium, each agent must consume her entire dividend income, i.e., $C_t = y_t K_{t-1}$. Third, to simplify the analysis we assume that the total number of shares in the economy is constant over time and is exactly equal to the number of consumers which also remains constant over time.[2] Since consumers are all identical, each has one unit of stock so that $K_t = K_{t-1} = 1$ and $C_t = y_t$, $\forall t$. To make the model tractable, we assume further that

Assumption 1: $U(C) = \dfrac{C^{1-\alpha}}{1-\alpha}$, $\alpha > 0$ where α is the risk aversion parameter.

Substituting the value of C_t from the budget constraint in (2) and using Assumption 1, the consumer's problem becomes

$$\text{maximise } E_t \left\{ \sum_{j=0}^{\infty} \beta^j \frac{[y_t K_{t-1} - p_t(K_t - K_{t-1})]^{1-\alpha}}{1-\alpha} \right\}$$

Given that $C_t = y_t \forall t$, the first order condition with respect to K_t can be written as

$$p_t y_t^{-\alpha} = \beta E_t \left\{ (p_{t+1} + y_{t+1}) y_{t+1}^{-\alpha} \right\} \qquad (3)$$

Defining market capitalisation $m_t \equiv \dfrac{p_t}{y_t}$ and dividing both sides of (3) by $y_t^{1-\alpha}$ we get

$$m_t = \beta E_t \left\{ (m_{t+1} + 1) \left(\frac{y_{t+1}}{y_t} \right)^{1-\alpha} \right\} \qquad (4)$$

Using the above Euler equation, we need to understand the relationship between market capitalisation and per capita income. But before doing that, let us add some more structure to the model through the following assumption:

Assumption 2: Dividends y_t follow a stationary Markov chain with S possible states and transition matrix Q whose typical element $q_{ss'}$ represents the conditional probability that state s' is reached in period $t+1$, given that state s has been reached in period t.[3]

Let y_t take the value y_s if state s occurs at period t. We assume that uncertainty about the state is resolved at the beginning of every period.

A Special Case

Suppose $\alpha = 1$, i.e., $U(C) = \ln C$. Then equation (4) becomes

$$m_t = \beta E_t(m_{t+1}) + \beta \tag{5}$$

Suppose state s is reached in period t. Then from (5) we get

$$m_s = \beta[\sum_{s'=1}^{S} q_{ss'} m_{s'} + 1], \text{ where } s = 1, 2, ..., S; s' = 1, 2, ..., S. \tag{6}$$

Here S unknowns $m_1, m_2, ..., m_S$ are to be solved from S linear equations given in (6). Let us guess that the solution is $m_s = m \; \forall s$. Then noting that $\sum_{s'=1}^{S} q_{ss'} = 1$ from (6) we get

$$m = \beta m + \beta$$

i.e., $m = \dfrac{\beta}{1 - \beta}$ \hfill (7)

We know that a system of independent linear equations can either have no solution or a unique solution. Clearly, (7) gives the unique solution to the market capitalisation ratios. Therefore, in the special case of log utility, the market capitalisation ratio remains constant across all states. We write down our finding in the form of a proposition:

Proposition 1: For a log utility function, the market capitalisation ratio remains constant over time.[4]

THE GENERAL CASE

Let us now consider the more general case where the only restriction is that $\alpha > 0$, $\alpha \neq 1$. In this case equation (4) can be written as

$$m_t = \beta \left[E_t \left\{ m_{t+1} \left(\frac{y_{t+1}}{t_t} \right)^{1-\alpha} \right\} + E_t \left\{ \left(\frac{y_{t+1}}{y_t} \right)^{1-\alpha} \right\} \right] \quad (8)$$

Let $\left(\frac{y_{s'}}{y_s} \right)^{1-\alpha} \equiv g_{ss'}$. Then if at period t the economy is at state s, equation (9) can be written as

$$m_s = \beta \{ E_s [m_{s'} g_{ss'}] + E_s [g_{ss'}] \}$$
$$= \beta \sum_{s'=1}^{S} q_{ss'} g_{ss'} m_{s'} + \beta \sum_{s'=1}^{S} q_{ss'} g_{ss'} \quad (9)$$

where $s' = 1, 2, ..., S$.
The second step in (9) follows from the fact that $\text{Prob}[m_{s'} g_{ss''}] = 0 \forall s', s'', s' \neq s''$. In other words, the probability that in the next period the value of market capitalisation becomes $m_{s'}$ and the value of dividend becomes $y_{s''}$ is zero for all $s' \neq s''$.

Equation (9) gives a system of S linear equations with S unknowns. Once more we can solve

$$m_s = \varphi_s(q_{ss'}, g_{ss'}, \beta) \quad (10)$$

where $s = 1, 2, ..., S$; $s' = 1, 2, ..., S$.

Solutions to (10) are obtained as follows. Let M be the column vector of market capitalisation with m_i as its ith element and let B be a column vector with $\beta \sum_{s=1}^{S} q_{is} g_{is}$ as its ith element. Finally let $\tilde{Q} = [\beta q_{is} g_{is}]$ be an $S \times S$ matrix, where $i = 1, 2, ..., S$; $s = 1, 2, ..., S$. The system of equations (9) may be written as

$$M = \tilde{Q}M + B \qquad (11)$$

From (11), solutions of market capitalisation are obtained as

$$M = (I - \tilde{Q})^{-1} B \qquad (12)$$

The solution is too general to yield a monotonic relation between market capitalisation and per capita income. We have to look at special cases.

A Two-State Economy

Let us first consider the simple case where the number of states is 2. In this case, noting that $g_{11} = g_{22} = 1$, the solution can be written as

$$m_1 = \frac{\beta}{\Delta}[q_{11} - \beta q_{11} q_{22} + q_{12} g_{12} + \beta q_{12} q_{21}] \qquad (13)$$

$$m_2 = \frac{\beta}{\Delta}[q_{22} - \beta q_{11} q_{22} + q_{21} g_{21} + \beta q_{12} q_{21}] \qquad (14)$$

where $\Delta = (1 - \beta q_{11})(1 - \beta q_{22}) - \beta^2 q_{12} q_{21}$. It is shown in Appendix A that $\Delta > 0$. In this simple 2×2 case, the relationship between the market capitalisation ratio and per capita income is indeed monotonic as stated in the following proposition.

Proposition 2: Suppose there are two states of nature. The higher state is associated with a higher (or lower) value of market capitalisation if and only if the risk aversion parameter is greater (or less) than unity.

Proof:
Let us assume, without any loss of generality, that $y_1 > y_2$. Comparison of (13) with (14) immediately tells us that $m_1 > m_2$ if and only if

$$q_{11} + q_{12} g_{12} > q_{22} + q_{21} g_{21} \qquad (15)$$

Noting that $q_{11} = 1 - q_{12}$ and $q_{22} = 1 - q_{21}$ we may rewrite (15) as

$$q_{12}(g_{12} - 1) > q_{21}(g_{21} - 1) \qquad (16)$$

Since $g_{12} = \left(\dfrac{y_2}{y_1}\right)^{1-\alpha} = \dfrac{1}{g_{21}}$, if the left-hand side of (16) is positive, the right-hand side is negative and vice versa. Now, $\left(\dfrac{y_2}{y_1}\right) < 1$. Therefore, $g_{12} = \left(\dfrac{y_2}{y_1}\right)^{1-\alpha} > 1$ if $\alpha > 1$. (Negative exponent on an expression less than unity makes it greater than unity). Therefore $m_1 > m_2$ if $\alpha > 1$. Using the same logic we can show that $m_1 < m_2$ if $\alpha < 1$. This proves Proposition 2.

It may be recalled that α is the risk aversion parameter. Our analysis shows that if risk aversion is high enough (that is, greater than 1) then the high state will be associated with high value of market capitalisation. Exactly the opposite will happen if α < 1. The intuition behind this result is not hard to find. Higher risk aversion means that the agents have a high aversion towards fluctuating income. As a result, they will have a higher tendency to smooth out consumption over time. When a good state is realised, since there are only two states, income can either go down or remain constant in future. Therefore, in a good state consumers will save more, which, in turn, would increase the demand for stock-holding and the price of stocks. In other words, if risk aversion is high, inter-temporal substitution effect will dominate the income effect. On the other hand, if risk aversion is low, the income effect emanating from a higher state will dominate and current consumption rather than savings will go up with a rise in income. It may be mentioned that for the logarithmic utility function, the income effect will exactly counter-balance the inter-temporal substitution effect so that stock prices will remain unchanged.

For $S > 2$ the relationship between market capitalisation and per capita income is complicated and in general, ambiguous. We may explain why this is so with the help of an example. Suppose the agents are highly risk averse, that is, the risk aversion parameter is greater than unity. Suppose there are three states with incomes $y_1 > y_2 > y_3$. When the economy is in state 1, the state with the highest income, suppose it has a 99 per cent probability of going to state 2 next period and y_2 is very close to y_1. As a result, the *expected fall* in income is not very high. This in turn means that the demand for savings and stocks will not be very high either, leading to a relatively low value of m_1. Next, suppose that if the economy is at state 2, it goes to state 3 next period with 99 per cent probability, but the difference between y_2 and y_3 is very large. In this case, the expected fall in income will be large and the value of m_2 will also be large. Hence, in spite of high risk aversion, there will be an inverse relationship between the two variables. This relationship can get reversed if the expected fall in income from state 1 is large and that from state 2 is small. Hence the relationship between market capitalisation and per capita income will be non-monotonic in general. I record this finding in the following proposition.

Proposition 3: When the number of states is greater than two, the relationship between market capitalisation and per capita income is in general non-monotonic. However, in our model, though generally we cannot expect a specific monotonic relationship, it cannot be strictly ruled out either in stray cases.

Long-Run Relationships

Next, we look at the relationship between per capita income and the long-run expected values of the market capitalisation ratio. Let $\pi_1, \pi_2, ..., \pi_S$ be the unconditional probabilities of occurrence of the states. We have

$$\pi_S = \sum_{S'=1}^{S} \pi_{S'} q_{S'S} \qquad (17)$$

Note that the right-hand side of equation (17) gives us the probability of going to state s from any state including state s itself. Therefore, the interpretation of π_S is that it is the proportion of times the economy is in state s in the long run. We may then define the long-run expected values of market capitalisation ratio and income as $\bar{m} = \frac{1}{S}\sum \pi_S m_S$ and $\bar{y} = \frac{1}{S}\sum \pi_S y_S$ respectively. Market capitalisation and per capita income fluctuate around their long-run values but most likely remain uncorrelated to each other. Even for the two-state case, a monotonic relationship cannot, in general, be established between the two long-run values.

In the two-state case, the unconditional probabilities can be solved from (17) as

$$\pi_1 = \frac{q_{21}}{q_{21} + q_{12}} \text{ and } \pi_2 = \frac{q_{12}}{q_{21} + q_{12}} \qquad (17A)$$

Again, in the two-state case,

$$\bar{m} = \frac{\beta}{\Delta}[\pi_1\{q_{11} - \beta q_{11} q_{22} + q_{12} g_{12} + \beta q_{12} q_{21}\} +$$

$$\pi_2\{q_{22} - \beta q_{11} q_{22} + q_{21} g_{21} + \beta q_{12} q_{21}\}] \qquad (18)$$

Now suppose that there are changes in y_1 and y_2 with transition probabilities remaining the same. Using (17A) and (18), we get, after some simplification

$$d\bar{m} = \frac{\beta}{\Delta} \frac{q_{21} q_{12}}{q_{21}+q_{12}} [dg_{12} + dg_{21}]$$

$$= \frac{\beta}{\Delta} \frac{q_{21} q_{12}}{q_{21}+q_{12}} (1-\alpha)(\widehat{y_2} - \widehat{y_1}) \left[\left(\frac{y_1}{y_2}\right)^{\alpha-1} - \left(\frac{y_2}{y_1}\right)^{\alpha-1} \right] \quad (19)$$

In equation (19), a '^' on a variable denotes proportionate change. Now, suppose $\alpha > 1$. Then, since $y_1 > y_2$, the term in square brackets in the second line in (19) is positive and $d\bar{m} > 0$ if and only if $\widehat{y_2} < \widehat{y_1}$, that is, $\left(\frac{y_1}{y_2}\right)$ has increased. Again, if $\alpha < 1$, the term within square brackets in the second line of (19) is negative. Hence, once again, $d\bar{m} > 0$ if and only if $\widehat{y_2} < \widehat{y_1}$, that is, $\left(\frac{y_1}{y_2}\right)$ has increased. But an increase in $\left(\frac{y_1}{y_2}\right)$ is perfectly consistent with either an increase or a decrease in $\bar{y}$. Therefore, even in the two-state case, we cannot say for sure that there is a monotonically increasing relationship between the long-run values of the market capitalisation ratio and per capita income. We summarise our findings in the following proposition:

Proposition 4: In the two-state case, long-run expected value of the market capitalisation ratio increases if and only if $\left(\frac{y_1}{y_2}\right)$ goes up. Since this is consistent with either a rise or a fall in the long-run expected value of per capita income, in general, no monotonically increasing relationship can be established between the two variables.

We make two observations before going into our empirical analysis. First, the income stream $\{y_t\}$ in our set up is *exogenous*. Though we have taken it to be coming from dividends of stocks, it could have come from all sectors or sources in the economy without affecting our theoretical analysis, provided of course, that the stream of income remains exogenous. This allows us to interpret y_t as the economy-wide per capita income.

Second, in our set up, the only role of an asset is to provide an instrument of savings and therefore, its price depends on the urge to save which again would depend on income effects and inter-temporal substitution effects. This is a common feature of consumption-based asset pricing models. If we had many assets with different risk-return profiles, the consumer would be confronted with a portfolio choice problem, but that additional problem cannot obscure the basic inter-temporal utility maximisation problem which lies at the crux of the analysis.

Growth

We can easily incorporate growth into the model. Suppose there are two possible states that the economy can be in: a state of high growth with a growth rate g_1 and a state of low growth with a growth rate g_2 where $g_1 > g_2$. Let y_t be income at period t. Then $y_{t+1} = (1 + g_s) y_t$ provided the economy attains state s in period $t + 1$, and $s = 1, 2$. Let $q_{ss'}$ be the probability of going to state s' from state s, where $s = 1, 2$ and $s' = 1, 2$. We can directly use equation (9) to write the expressions for market capitalisation in the two states, after noting that in the present context $g_{11} = g_{21} = (1 + g_1)$ and $g_{22} = g_{12} = (1 + g_2)$. Consequently, the market capitalisation ratios in the two states may be solved as

$$m_1 = \frac{\beta}{\Delta'} [q_{11}(1+g_1)^{1-\alpha} - \beta q_{11} q_{22}(1+g_1)^{1-\alpha}(1+g_2)^{1-\alpha} + q_{12}(1+g_2)^{1-\alpha} + \beta q_{12} q_{21}(1+g_1)^{1-\alpha}(1+g_2)^{1-\alpha}] \quad (20)$$

$$m_2 = \frac{\beta}{\Delta'}[q_{22}(1+g_2)^{1-\alpha} - \beta q_{11}q_{22}(1+g_1)^{1-\alpha}(1+g_2)^{1-\alpha} +$$
$$q_{21}(1+g_1)^{1-\alpha} + \beta q_{12}q_{21}(1+g_1)^{1-\alpha}(1+g_2)^{1-\alpha}] \quad (21)$$

$$\Delta' = \{1-\beta q_{11}(1+g_1)^{1-\alpha}\}\{1-\beta q_{22}(1+g_2)^{1-\alpha}\} -$$
$$\beta^2 q_{12}q_{21}(1+g_1)^{1-\alpha}(1+g_2)^{1-\alpha}.$$

For solutions to exist $\Delta' > 0$ must hold. In general, this cannot be guaranteed. However, to continue with the subsequent analysis, I *assume* that $\Delta' > 0$ and solutions exist.

Proposition 5: Suppose $\alpha > 1$. Then with stationary growth, market capitalisation and the current state of the economy are positively (negatively) related iff $q_{11} < q_{21}$ ($q_{11} > q_{21}$). The reverse relationships will prevail with $\alpha < 1$. The proof of Proposition 5 is given in Appendix B.

This condition is not difficult to interpret. If consumers are sufficiently risk averse, they will have a strong tendency to smooth out consumption over time. This will make their intertemporal substitution effect dominate their income effect when the economy is in a high-growth state and the expectation of a high-growth state is low. As a result, they will save more if they attach a lower probability to high growth in the next period, the current period being high growth. This will happen if state 1 is attained at present and $q_{11} < q_{21}$. The direct relationship between the state of the economy and market capitalisation will get reversed if either $q_{11} > q_{21}$ or $\alpha < 1$. If both happen simultaneously, then we will get back the direct relationship again. Therefore, in the present set-up with stationary growth, the relationship between market capitalisation and the current state of the economy will depend not only on the risk aversion parameter but also on whether the prospect of a good state increases or decreases when the economy is in a good state.

For the number of states of growth greater than 2, however, the monotonic relationship between the current state and the current value of market capitalisation would not hold in general.

Market Capitalisation and Per Capita Income: Empirical Relationships

To understand the relationships between market capitalisation as a proportion of GDP (MK) and per capita income (PCY) over time, we looked at the data of 33 countries for the time period 1988–2018. All data used in our analysis are secondary and taken from the *World Development Indicators* of the World Bank. The time period and the choice of countries have been dictated by availability of data. For each country, we find out whether there are long-run and short-run relationships between log (MK) and log (PCY).

Long-Run Relationships

It is well known that the long-run relationship between the two variables can be obtained, provided both the time series are integrated of order 1, i.e., I(1) and they pass a test like Johansen's cointegration test. Again, to test short-run relationships, first we have to ensure that both series are I(0) and then we can run OLS regressions. Therefore, our first step is to check for stationarity of the two series log (MK) and log (PCY) for all the 33 countries.

Only 15 countries out of 33 have both their log MK and log PCY series as I(1) and therefore, are possible candidates for exhibiting long-run relationships between the two variables. These countries are Colombia, Chile, Denmark, Germany, Hong Kong, India, Nigeria, Peru, Philippines, Singapore, Sri Lanka, Sweden, Switzerland, Thailand and US.

Next, we run Johansen's cointegration test for these 15 countries. Only five of these 15 countries pass the Johansen test. These five countries are Denmark, Switzerland, Chile, India and Sri Lanka. In other words, only five out of 33 countries, which include two high-income (Denmark, Switzerland), one middle-income (Chile) and two low-income countries (India and Srilanka), exhibit long-run relations between market capitalisation as a ratio of GDP on the one hand and per capita income on the other.

The remaining consists of about 85 per cent of the 33 countries. For these countries, we did not find any systematic relationship. These empirical findings seem to support the theoretical result we got in the previous section about long-term relationships.

SHORT-RUN RELATIONSHIPS

Next we look for short-run relationships between the two variables. In particular, we look at the short-run effects of a change in the rate of growth on the rate of growth of market capitalisation ratio. We have already noted that out of the 33 countries under study, 15 countries have both log PCY and log MK as I(1). Hence the first differences of these variables are I(0) for these 15 countries. It is, therefore, legitimate to run OLS regressions for these countries making ($\log MK_{t+1} - \log MK_t$) as the dependent variable and ($\log PCY_{t+1} - \log PCY_t$) as the independent variable. Clearly, the dependent variable can be interpreted as growth of market capitalisation ratio and the independent variable as growth of per capita income.

Table 4.1 presents the regression results. Three things are worth noting. First, out of the 15 countries, while three countries exhibited a *negative* relationship between per capita growth and market capitalisation growth, for 12 countries the relationship was *positive*. This vindicates our result that depending on the value of the risk aversion parameter, the relationship could be positive or negative.

Table 4.1: Short-run relationship between log MK and log PCY

Country	Coefficient of Δ Log PCY	t-value
Colombia	−1.065	−0.619
Chile	0.063	1.31*
Denmark	0.023	0.811
Germany	0.045	1.382*
Hong Kong	0.07	2.134***
India	0.036	0.537
Nigeria	−0.193	−2.189***
Peru	0.054	1.185
Philippines	0.042	0.555
Singapore	0.162	0.789
Sri Lanka	0.125	1.502*
Sweden	0.049	0.587
Switzerland	0.044	2.072***
Thailand	0.021	0.403
US	−0.005	−0.465

Note: *significant at 90 per cent, ***significant at 97.5 per cent.
Source: Based on data obtained from World Bank (n.d.)

Second, six out of 15 countries show a statistically significant relationship between per capita growth and stock market growth. Out of the six countries, three countries exhibited significance at 90 per cent and the remaining three at 97.5 per cent. While Nigeria is the only country exhibiting a negative and significant relationship, all the other five countries show a positive relationship between per capita growth and stock market growth. This vindicates our other theoretical result that in general, the short-run relationship between the two variables is ambiguous.

Third, for the countries which have exhibited statistically significant relationship between per capita growth and growth of stock market, the values of the coefficients of the dependent variable are not very high. The highest value is exhibited by Nigeria where a 1 per cent rise in per capita growth leads to a 0.19 per cent decline in the growth of the stock market.

Concluding Remarks

One can think of three different types of relationships between the stock market and the real economy. The first kind underscores the role of the stock market as an institution which facilitates savings to be channelised to investment and hence enhance long-run growth. The second kind of relationship may exist when a change in the performance of the real economy is immediately transmitted to stock prices and market capitalisation. This is a short-run relationship. A third relationship can be observed when an outside factor affects both the long-run performance of the economy as well as that of the stock market inducing a long-run co-movement of the two.

A vast literature, both theoretical and empirical, exists which focuses on the first type of relationship. The present chapter has been concerned with the other two. Our findings are, in general, not very positive. While about 15 per cent of the countries under consideration show some kind of long-run co-movements, about 18 per cent show short-run relationships. However, these relationships can be either positive or negative. This in turn, implies that nothing substantial can be inferred about the short-run or long-run behaviour of the real economy from either short-run fluctuations or long-run trends of the stock market.

NOTES

[1] The market capitalisation ratio is the total market value of stocks divided by GDP. The market value of any particular stock is the average price at which the stock has been traded in the market over a period multiplied by the quantity of that stock. The total value of stocks is the sum of the market values of all individual stocks.

[2] The assumption that the number of agents is exactly equal to the number of shares only simplifies the notation.

[3] A similar model has been used by Mehra and Prescott (1985) where the growth rate of income, rather than its level, follows a stationary Markov chain. We use that framework in the subsection on growth. It should be mentioned, however, that the purpose of Mehra and Prescott (ibid.) is different from that of the present chapter. While the former is concerned with the equity premium puzzle, the latter looks at the relationship between the stock market and the real economy.

[4] This result is reported in Ljungqvist and Sargent (2004). We are reproducing this result to put into perspective the discussion of the more general case where $\alpha \neq 1$.

REFERENCES

Bencivenga, Valerie R. and Bruce D. Smith. 1991. 'Financial Intermediation and Endogenous Growth'. *The Review of Economic Studies* 58(2): 195–209.

Bencivenga, Valerie R., Bruce D. Smith and Ross M. Starr. 1995. 'Equity Markets, Transaction Costs, and Capital Accumulation: An Illustration', Policy Research Working Paper Series 1456. World Bank.

Gorton, Gary and George Pennacchi. 1990. 'Financial Intermediaries and Liquidity Creation'. *Journal of Finance* 45(1): 49–71.

Greenwood, Jeremy and Boyan Jovanovic. 1990. 'Financial Development, Growth, and the Distribution of Income'. *Journal of Political Economy* 98(5): 1076–1107.

Hicks, John. 1969. *A Theory of Economic History*. Oxford: Clarendon Press.

Jacklin, Charles J. 1987. 'Demand Deposits, Trading Restrictions and Risk Sharing'. In Edward Prescott and Neil Wallace (eds), *Contractual Arrangements for Intertemporal Trade*, 26–47. Minneapolis, MN: University of Minnesota Press.

Jappelli, Tullio and Marco Pagano. 1994. 'Saving, Growth and Liquidity Constraints'. *The Quarterly Journal of Economics* 109(1): 83–109.

King, Robert G. and Ross Levine. 1993a. 'Financial Intermediation and Economic Development'. In Colin Mayer and Xavier Vives (eds), *Financial Intermediation in the Construction Of Europe*, 156–189. London: Centre for Economic Policy Research.

———. 1993b. 'Finance and Growth: Schumpeter Might Be Right'. *The Quarterly Journal of Economics* 108(3): 717–737.

Levine, Ross. 1991. 'Stock Markets, Growth, and Tax Policy'. *The Journal of Finance* 46(4): 1445–1465.

Levine, Ross and Sara Zervos. 1996. 'Stock Market Development and Long-Run Growth'. *The World Bank Economic Review* 10(2): 323–339.

———. 1998. 'Stock Markets, Banks, and Economic Growth'. *The American Economic Review* 88(3): 537–558.

Ljungqvist, Lars and Thomas J. Sargent. 2004. *Recursive Macroeconomic Theory*, Second Edition. Cambridge, Massachusetts: MIT Press.

Lucas Jr., Robert E. 1978. 'Asset Prices in an Exchange Economy'. *Econometrica* 46(6): 1429–1445.

Mehra, Rajnish and Edward Prescott. 1985. 'The Equity Premium: A Puzzle'. *Journal of Monetary Economics* 15(2): 145–162.

Schumpeter, Joseph A. 1934 [1912]. *The Theory of Economic Development*, Redvers Opie (trans.). Cambridge, MA: Harvard University Press.

World Bank. n.d. *World Development Indicators*. Available at https://databank.worldbank.org/source/world-development-indicators (accessed November 2022).

APPENDIX A

Proof of $\Delta > 0$

Straightforward calculations yield

$$\Delta = (1-\beta)[1 + \beta(q_{12} - q_{22})]$$

Since $|q_{12} - q_{22}| < 1$ and β is a positive fraction, the term within square brackets is positive and so is Δ.

APPENDIX B

Proof of Proposition 5:

First, suppose that consumers are sufficiently risk-averse, that is $\alpha > 1$. Then, comparing (18) with (19) we have:

$m_1 > m_2$ if

$$[q_{11}(1+g_1)^{1-\alpha} - \beta q_{11} q_{22}(1+g_1)^{1-\alpha}(1+g_2)^{1-\alpha} +$$
$$q_{12}(1+g_2)^{1-\alpha} + \beta q_{12} q_{21}(1+g_1)^{1-\alpha}(1+g_2)^{1-\alpha}] >$$
$$[q_{22}(1+g_2)^{1-\alpha} - \beta q_{11} q_{22}(1+g_1)^{1-\alpha}(1+g_2)^{1-\alpha} +$$
$$q_{21}(1+g_1)^{1-\alpha} + \beta q_{12} q_{21}(1+g_1)^{1-\alpha}(1+g_2)^{1-\alpha}]$$

$$\Rightarrow [q_{11}(1+g_1)^{1-\alpha} + q_{12}(1+g_2)^{1-\alpha}] > [q_{22}(1+g_2)^{1-\alpha} + q_{21}(1+g_1)^{1-\alpha}]$$

$$\Rightarrow [(1-q_{12})(1+g_1)^{1-\alpha} + q_{12}(1+g_2)^{1-\alpha}] >$$
$$[(1-q_{21})(1+g_2)^{1-\alpha} + q_{21}(1+g_1)^{1-\alpha}]$$

$$\Rightarrow [(1+g_1)^{1-\alpha} - q_{12}(1+g_1)^{1-\alpha} - (1+g_2)^{1-\alpha}] >$$
$$(1+g_2)^{1-\alpha} + q_{21}[(1+g_1)^{1-\alpha} - (1+g_2)^{1-\alpha}$$

$$\Rightarrow [(1+g_1)^{1-\alpha} - (1+g_2)^{1-\alpha} -$$
$$q_{12}(1+g_1)^{1-\alpha} - (1+g_2)^{1-\alpha}] >$$
$$q_{21}[(1+g_1)^{1-\alpha} - (1+g_2)^{1-\alpha}]$$
$$\Rightarrow [(1+g_1)^{1-\alpha} - (1+g_2)^{1-\alpha}]\{1 - q_{21} - q_{12}\} > 0 \quad \text{(a)}$$

Now let us check if $[(1+g_1)^{1-\alpha} - (1+g_2)^{1-\alpha}]$ is positive or negative.

We can say that $\ln(1+g_1) > \ln(1+g_2)$

[since $g_1 > g_2$ and we know that $\ln(x) > \ln(y)$ if $x > y$]

$$\Rightarrow (1-\alpha)\ln(1+g_1) < (1-\alpha)\ln(1+g_2)$$

[$\alpha > 1$ is assumed and hence, $(1-\alpha) < 0$ which causes the inequality to get reversed.]

$$\Rightarrow (1+g_1)^{1-\alpha} < (1+g_2)^{1-\alpha}$$
$$\Rightarrow [(1+g_1)^{1-\alpha} - (1+g_2)^{1-\alpha}] < 0 \quad \text{(b)}$$

(a) and (b) together imply that $\{1 - q_{21} - q_{12}\} < 0$.

i.e., $\{1 - q_{21} - (1 - q_{11})\} < 0$, which means:

$$q_{21} > q_{11}$$

Thus, it is proved that $m_1 > m_2$ if and only if $q_{21} > q_{11}$.

The case where $\alpha < 1$ will be similar. This completes the proof of proposition (5).

5
YIELD CURVE AND ECONOMIC ACTIVITY

Abhishek Naresh, Jong Kook Shin and
Chetan Subramanian

Introduction

In the last couple of decades, the Indian economy and financial markets have integrated with the global markets to an extent unprecedented in history. To what extent does this economic integration impact the transmission of monetary policy in an emerging economy such as India? Does the increased economic integration translate into higher global monetary policy spillovers for the Indian economy? Does, for instance, a monetary contraction in the United States lead to a recession in India? Our objective is to investigate these issues both from an empirical and a theoretical standpoint in this chapter. Specifically, we examine the linkages between the US and Indian interest rates along different points on the yield curve and contrast the effectiveness of the US and the Indian yield spreads in predicting economic activity in India.

Modern central banks conduct monetary policy by influencing the short-term interest rates. However, since the real economy is a function of the long-term real interest rate, the effectiveness of such actions will crucially depend on the ability of the policy maker to influence the long-term nominal interest rate. Theoretically, this link between the two rates is established through the expectations hypothesis, according to which the long-term interest rates can be thought of as an average of expected future short-term rates. Thus, an increase in the long-term rate can be interpreted as implying rising future short-term rates. It follows that, in standard monetary business cycle models, domestic monetary policy is effective to the extent that the long-term nominal interest rates are not decoupled from the expected path of the short-term interest rates. The yield spread, i.e., the difference between long-term and short-term interest rates, therefore, becomes a critical indicator of monetary policy stance. It has over the years emerged as an important input in forecasting the evolution of future real economic activity, particularly in advanced economies such as the US. For example, monetary policy tightening, which usually means a rise in short-term interest rates, is typically implemented to slow down economic activities and to reduce inflationary pressures. However, once these pressures subside, if the policy is expected to ease, then lower short-term interest rates will follow. Long-term rates, which reflect expectations of future short-term interest rates, therefore, should rise at a slower pace than the short-term rate after inflationary pressures have subsided. Thus, monetary tightening both slows down the economy and flattens (or even inverts) the yield curve. Consistent with this line of reasoning, the yield curve has inverted in the US before each of the last six recessions.

Surprisingly and in stark contrast to large economies, there is growing evidence to suggest a decoupling of the short-term and long-term interest rates in inflation-targeting small open economies. Recent studies (Bernanke 2013; Dahlquist and Hasseltoft 2013; Kulish and Rees 2011; Swanson and Williams 2014; Wright 2011) have highlighted the fact that long-term nominal rates have exhibited a strong co-movement over the post–World War II period rates in a number of inflation-targeting small open economies (such as Australia, Canada, New Zealand, and the UK) with their US counterparts. The interest rate correlation between the US and small open economies appears to be stronger at longer maturities than at shorter maturities. Figure 5.1 illustrates this phenomenon for India. The correlation between the Indian and the US 10-year government bond yields over the period from January 2001 to November 2019 is significantly greater than the correlation at short-term maturities. Does this correlation between the US and Indian long-term rates make the US yield spread a good

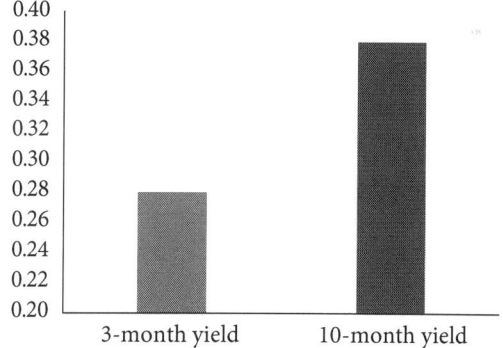

FIG. 5.1: Correlation between the US and Indian bond yield

Note: Data is HP filtered. The light grey bar shows the correlation between 3-month government bond yield of the US and India. The dark grey bar shows the correlation between 10-year government bond yield of the US and India.

Source: Authors' calculations based on data from https://data.bloomberg.com/ and RBI (n.d.)

predictor of Indian business cycles? In this chapter, we examine the effectiveness of the US yield spreads in predicting recessions in the post-reform period in India.

There is an emerging literature that has sought to address the apparent decoupling of the long- and short-term interest rates exhibited in Figure 5.1. One arm of this literature points to the existence of significant term premiums in domestic interest rates which are correlated internationally. This creates a 'wedge' between expectations over the path of future policy rates and long-term interest rates (see Dahlquist and Hasseltoft 2013; Jotikasthira et al. 2015; Wright 2011). On the other hand, Kulish and Rees (2011), offer an alternative explanation that does not rely on the decoupling hypothesis. They use the standard small open economy augmented model to include term structure of interest rates to show that the observed patterns of interest rate correlations would emerge if foreign disturbances are more persistent than domestic ones, a hypothesis for which they find support in Australian data.

In this chapter, we estimate the Kulish-Rees model using Indian data and seek to explain the pattern of the interest rates observed in Figure 5.1. We also use this framework to analyse the effectiveness of both the domestic as well as foreign yield curve in predicting economic activity in India. The rest of the chapter is organised as follows. The second section presents a chronology of business cycles in India and develops an empirical model used to predict recessions in India. This model is set up in the third section. In the fourth section, we estimate the model and carry out a discussion of the results, before our concluding remarks in the last section.

Empirical Section

In this section, we compare the effectiveness of the US and Indian yield spreads in predicting recessions in the post-reform period in India. There is a fairly large empirical literature that has found the yield spread to be useful in predicting recessions in the US. Estrella and Mishkin (1998), for example, analyse several candidates for recession predictors in the US context, and conclude that the yield-curve slope is the single most powerful predictor of recession. Surprisingly, there is very little work on this issue in the context of emerging markets such as India. In carrying out this analysis for India, we begin by laying out the methodology used to date business cycles. Next, we specify the long-term and short-term interest rates which we will use to produce the spread that constitutes our measure of steepness. Finally, we provide an empirical model which uses the yield spread to predict the onset of a recession.

DEFINING RECESSIONS

Our work in this section essentially follows Pandey et al. (2017). We use seasonally adjusted quarterly GDP series from 1996 Q2 to 2014 Q3 from India to arrive at the chronology of business cycles. There are broadly two approaches for measuring business cycles. The classical approach identifies expansion and contraction based on the level of output. By contrast, the 'growth rate cycle' method identifies turning points based on the growth rate of output. Following much of the literature on dating business cycles in India, we use the growth cycle approach as this is deemed the most appropriate for the post-reform period in India. Following Pandey et al. (ibid.), the trend is extracted using the band-pass filter developed by Christiano and Fitzgerald (2003), and the cycles are extracted using the NBER (National Bureau of Economic Research) business cycle periodicity of 2–8 years. The Harding and Pagan (2002) algorithm is then applied to the detrended data to date the periods of peaks and troughs in a business cycle. Using this approach, the specific periods during which the economy slipped into a downturn were (*i*) 1999 Q4 to 2003 Q1; (*ii*) 2007 Q2 to 2009 Q3; and (*iii*) 2011 Q2 to 2012 Q4.

MEASURING THE SPREAD

In choosing the most appropriate rates to measure the yield spread, the literature has largely focused on factors such as the availability of historical data and consistency in the computation of rates over time. (Our discussion in this section largely follows from Dueker [1997].)

For the US, the Treasury rates easily meet these criteria and are therefore the most popular candidates for constructing the yield spreads. In terms of the maturity combination, the 10-year rate is the preferred choice as the series has consistently computed data available over a long period. With regard to the short-term rate, the literature has found that the 3-month Treasury rate, when used together with the 10-year Treasury rate, is effective in predicting US recessions. Since our objective is to examine monetary policy spillovers, we follow the literature in measuring the US yield spread as the difference between the 10-year and the 3-month Treasury rates. For comparison purposes, the Indian yield spread is constructed based on the same combination of maturities using Indian treasury yields.

SLOPE OF THE YIELD CURVE AND RECESSIONS

In this section, we present a chronology of business cycles in the period 1996 Q2 to 2014 Q3 and examine the effectiveness of the US and Indian yield spreads in predicting recessions in India. Are recessions in India preceded by a sharp decline in the slope of the US and Indian yield curves? Figure 5.2 examines the link between the US yield spread and recessions in India. The yield spread is measured as the difference between the yields on 3-month and 10-year US Treasury securities for 1996 Q2 to 2014 Q3. The shaded regions indicate recession periods for India using the methodology discussed earlier.

It is clear from Figure 5.2 that two of the three Indian recessions since 1996 Q2 were preceded by a flattening of the US yield curve or a large decline in the yield on 10-year US

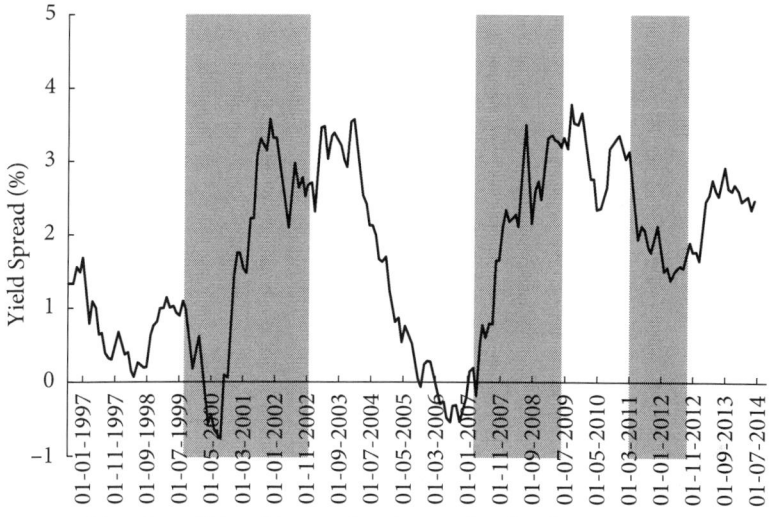

FIG. 5.2: US yield spread and periods of Indian recession

Note: Shaded regions are periods of recession. Yield spread is defined as the difference between 10-year government bond yield and 3-month government bond yield.

Source: Authors' calculations based on data from https://data.bloomberg.com/ and RBI (n.d.)

Treasury securities relative to the yield on 3-month US Treasury securities. The only occasion when the US yield curve flattened without a subsequent slowdown in economic activity was the recession beginning 2011 Q2. Figure 5.3 plots the movement of Indian yield spread and Indian recessions. Unlike the case of the US yield spread, most Indian recessions were not preceded by a flattening in the Indian yield curve. It would, therefore, appear that the US yield curve is more effective in predicting Indian business cycles. In the next section, we examine this hypothesis formally by constructing a model that translates the steepness of the US and Indian yield curves at the present time into the likelihood of a future Indian recession.

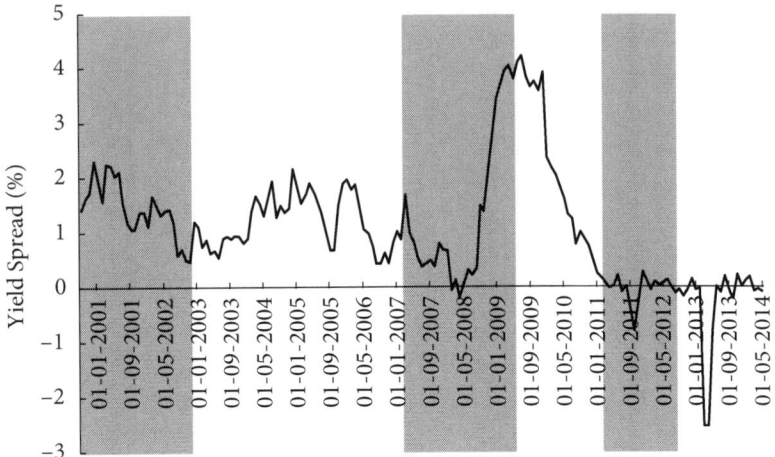

Fig. 5.3: India yield spread and periods of Indian recession

Note: Shaded regions are periods of recession. Yield spread is defined as the difference between 10-year government bond yield and 3-month government bond yield.

Source: Authors' calculations based on data from https://data.bloomberg.com/ and RBI (n.d.)

Predictive Power of the Yield Curve

Papers in the US context that examine the predictive power of the yield curve have typically estimated probit models of the form

$$\text{Prob}(R_t) = \Phi(c_0 + c_1 SPR_{t-k}) \qquad (1)$$

where R_t is a 0/1 indicator variable that equals 1 if and only if there is an NBER-dated recession at time t. SPR_{t-k} is a measure of the slope of the yield curve in period $t - k$, and Φ denotes the standard normal cumulative distribution function. Intuitively, the simple probit model uses the normal distribution to translate the term spread in period $t - k$ into a probability of a recession at some point t in the future.

Here, we follow the same methodology to estimate the probability of an Indian recession 12 months ahead, using

Yield Curve and Economic Activity   137

both Indian and US yield spreads as the explanatory variables. The model is estimated using data from 2001 Q1 to 2014 Q3. Table 5.1 presents the results for the case where the Indian yield spread is the explanatory variable. The insignificant coefficients suggest that the Indian yield spread is not very effective in predicting recessions. Figure 5.4 which plots the probability of a recession 12 months ahead using the Indian yield spread indicates that the estimated probability of a recession did not increase significantly before any of the documented recessions. Next, we examine the case where we use the US yield spread as the independent variable. This model is estimated using data from 1996 Q2 to 2014 Q3. In contrast, Table 5.2 indicates that the US yield spread is an effective predictor of Indian recessions. Furthermore, when we convert the US yield spread into a probability of recession 12 months ahead using the probit model, the estimated probability of recession rose close to 60 per cent before both the 1999 Q4 to 2003 Q1, and 2007 Q2 to 2009 Q3 recessions. Figure 5.5 illustrates this point. The US yield curve, however, failed to predict the 2011–12 recession where the estimated 12-month-ahead probability actually declined before the onset of the recession. One could argue that the quantitative easing programme pursued by the Federal Reserve during this period, where it aggressively intervened at the long-end of the yield curve, broke the conventional monetary policy transmission channel, rendering the yield curve ineffective as a recession predictor.

Table 5.1: Result from probit regression of Indian periods of recession on Indian term spread

Variable	Coefficient	Std. error	z-statistic	Prob.
SC_0	−0.107	0.144	−0.743	0.458
Yield spread (−12)	−0.154	0.095	−1.609	0.107

Note: Dependent variable (R_t) is occurrence of recession
  R_t = 0 if no recession occurs at time t
  R_t = 1 if recession occurs at time t
Source: Authors' calculations based on data from https://data.bloomberg.com/ and RBI (n.d.)

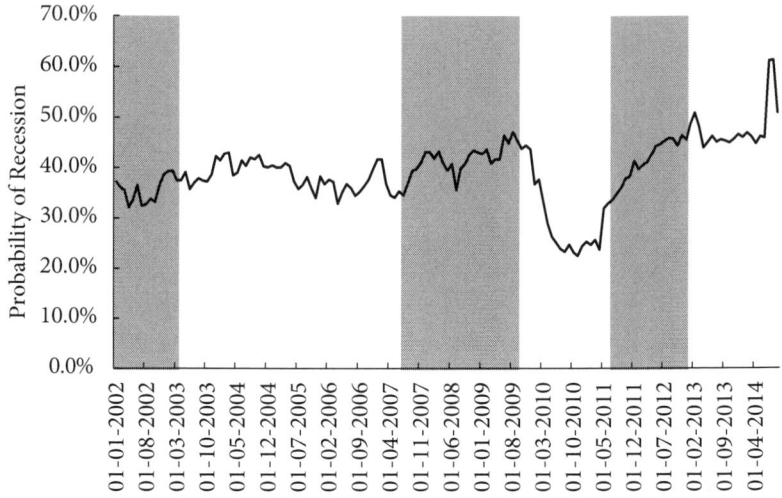

Fig. 5.4: Predictive power for Indian recession using Indian yield spread (12 months in advance)

Note: Shaded regions indicate periods of recession.
Source: Authors' calculations based on data from https://data.bloomberg.com/ and RBI (n.d.)

Table 5.2: Result from probit regression of Indian periods of recession on US term spread

Variable	Coefficient	Std. error	z-statistic	Prob.
C_0	0.284	0.154	1.837	0.0662
Yield spread (−12)	−0.298	0.076	−3.915	0.0001

Note: Dependent variable (R_t) is occurrence of recession
R_t = 0 if no recession occurs at time t
R_t =1 if recession occurs at time t
Source: Authors' calculations based on data from https://data.bloomberg.com/ and RBI (n.d.)

Next, we go a step further and forecast the probabilities of Indian recession post 2015 Q1 using the empirical model with the US yield spread. The probabilities are plotted in Figure 5.6. Interestingly, Figure 5.6 shows that the probability of the next recession steadily rose and reached close to 60 per cent around February of 2020.

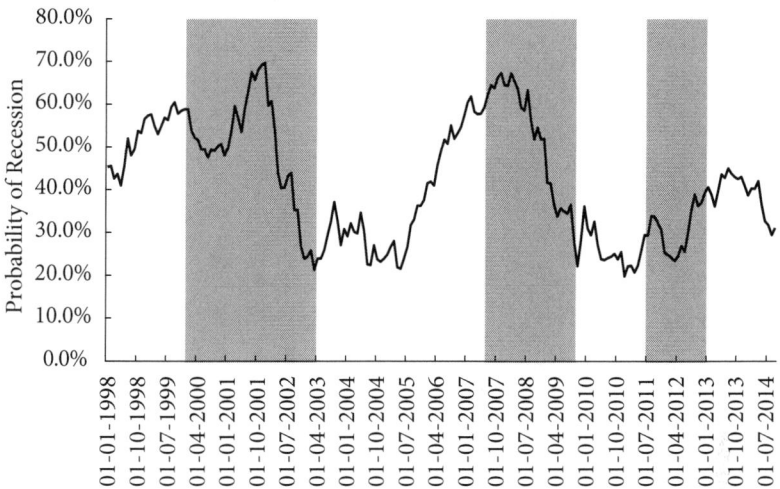

Fig. 5.5: Predictive power for Indian recession using the US yield spread (12 months in advance)

Note: Shaded regions indicate periods of recession.
Source: Authors' calculations based on data from https://data.bloomberg.com/ and RBI (n.d.)

Fig. 5.6: Forecast of Indian recession using the US yield spread (12 months in advance)

Source: Authors' model simulation results

In the next section, we write down a simple model which we use to investigate the pattern of interest rate correlations along different points on the yield curve. The framework also enables us to contrast the effectiveness of the US and Indian yield spreads in forecasting economic activity in India.

The Model

In this section, we reproduce the model of Kulish and Rees (KR from now) (2011) who extend Gali and Monacelli's (GM from now) (2005) workhorse small open economy framework to incorporate a term structure of interest rates. Our objective is to estimate this model using Indian data and examine the conditions under which the workhorse small open economy model is able to match the two empirical stylised facts pointed out about the Indian yield curve in the previous section. In this setup, two asymmetric countries, a small open economy, and a rest-of-the-world foreign economy coexist. The small open economy consists of households that supply labour to firms and consume a composite good. Households have access to complete asset markets. Firms hire labour, produce, and sell differentiated products in monopolistically competitive goods markets. Households maximise the present value of expected utility, and firms maximise profits.

In what follows, lowercase letters denote log deviations from steady state, i.e., $x \equiv \ln(X) - \ln(\bar{X})$ and the superscript * is used to denote variables of the foreign country. As in KR, we focus on the log-linear aggregate equations. We refer the reader to KR and GM for details of the derivations.

Large Economy

The foreign economy block can be summarised by aggregate demand, aggregate supply, monetary policy rule, and an exogenous process for demand and supply shocks. The aggregate demand for the foreign economy is given by

$$y_t^* = E_t y_{t+1}^* - \frac{1}{\sigma}(R_{1,t}^* - E_t \pi_{t+1}^*) + \frac{1}{\sigma}(1 - \rho_g^*)g_t^* \qquad (2)$$

where $R_{1,t}^*$ is the foreign short-term nominal interest rate; π_{t+1}^* is the foreign inflation rate; and σ is the inter-temporal substitution; g_t^* is the demand shock and ρ_g^* its persistence. The term structure of interest rates which follows from the expectations hypothesis is given by

$$R_{m,t}^* = \frac{1}{m} E_t \sum_{j=1}^m R_{1,t+j-1}^* \qquad m = 2, 3, 4 \quad (3)$$

The expectational Phillips equation for the large open economy is given by

$$\pi_t^* = \beta E_t \pi_{t+1}^* + \lambda(\sigma + \varphi) y_t^* - \lambda(\sigma + \rho)\alpha_t^* \qquad (4)$$

where $\lambda \equiv \dfrac{(1-\theta)(1-\beta\theta)}{\theta}$; and θ is a measure of the degree of price stickiness; φ measures the elasticity of labour supply; β is the discount factor and α_t^* is the technology shock.

Monetary policy in the foreign economy is assumed to follow a Taylor rule of the form

$$R_{1,t}^* = \rho_r^* R_{1,t-1}^* + \alpha_\pi^* \pi_t^* + \alpha_y^* y_t^* + \varepsilon_{r,t}^* \qquad (5)$$

where $\varepsilon_{r,t}^*$ is an iid foreign monetary shock with mean zero and standard deviation of $\sigma_{\varepsilon_r}^*$.

The technology shock α_t^* and demand shock g_t^* follow an AR(1) process given by

$$\alpha_t^* = \rho_a^* \alpha_{t-1}^* + \varepsilon_{a,t}^* \qquad (6)$$

$$g_t^* = \rho_g^* g_{t-1}^* + \varepsilon_{g,t}^* \qquad (7)$$

where, $\varepsilon^*_{a,t}$, $\varepsilon^*_{g,t}$ are zero mean iid with standard deviations given by $\sigma^*_{\varepsilon_a}$ and $\sigma^*_{\varepsilon_g}$, respectively.

Small Open Economy

The consumption Euler equation for the small open economy is given by

$$c_t = E_t c_{t+1} - \frac{1}{\sigma}(R_{1,t} - E_t \pi_{t+1}) + \frac{1}{\sigma}(1 - \rho_g) g_t \tag{8}$$

It is easy to see by iterating equation (8) forward that consumption in the economy is a function of the long-term real interest rates. Under the expectations hypothesis, a change in the short-term policy rate impacts the long-term nominal interest rate, which in the presence of price stickiness, influences the long-term real interest rate. The market clearing condition in the goods market is given by

$$y_t = c_t + \frac{\alpha \omega}{\sigma} s_t \tag{9}$$

where $\omega = \sigma \tau + (\sigma \iota - 1)$, τ is the intra-temporal elasticity of substitution between foreign and domestic goods, and ι is the elasticity of substitution across varieties of foreign goods. The parameter α is the share of foreign goods in the consumption basket and therefore serves as a measure of openness. The terms of trade is denoted by s_t, which is defined as the ratio of foreign prices expressed in terms of domestic currency $(e_t + p^*_t)$ and domestic prices $(p_{H,t})$. Given that the law of one price holds, we can write the terms of trade as

$$s_t = e_t + p^*_t - p_{H,t} \tag{10}$$

The log-linearisation of the CPI around a steady state with $P_H = P^*$ yields

$$p_t = p_{H,t} + \alpha s_t \tag{11}$$

It follows that the CPI inflation, π_t, in the economy is given by

$$\pi_t = \pi_{H,t} + \alpha \Delta s_t \tag{12}$$

The price inflation, $\pi_{H,t}$, for domestically produced good is given by the expectational Phillips curve given below

$$\pi_{H,t} = \beta E_t \pi_{H,t+1} + \lambda(\varphi y_t + \sigma c_t + \alpha s_t) - \lambda(1+\varphi) a_t \tag{13}$$

The real exchange rate, $Q_t = \dfrac{E_t P_t^*}{P_t}$, can be expressed in log linear form as $q_t = e_t + p_t^* - p_t$. Using (10), changes in the real exchange rate are given

$$\Delta q_t = (1-\alpha)\Delta s_t \tag{14}$$

Thus, the real exchange rate fluctuates over time with changes in the terms of trade. It follows from (14), that the movement in the nominal exchange rate is given by

$$\Delta e_t = \Delta q_t + \pi_t - \pi_t^* \tag{15}$$

The existence of a complete set of domestic currency state-contingent bonds leads to the following risk-sharing condition in the log-linear form:

$$c_t = y_t^* + \frac{(1-\alpha)}{\sigma} s_t + \frac{1}{\sigma}(g_t - g_t^*) \tag{16}$$

It follows from (16) that domestic consumption is a function of both domestic and foreign disturbances.

The monetary policy in the small open economy is given by

$$R_{1,t} = \rho_r R_{1,t-1} + \alpha_\pi \pi_t + \alpha_y y_t + \varepsilon_{r,t} \qquad (17)$$

where $\varepsilon_{r,t}$ is an iid domestic monetary shock with mean zero and standard deviation σ_{ε_r}. Analogous to the foreign case, the term structure of interest rates follows from the expectations hypothesis and is given by

$$R_{m,t} = \frac{1}{m} E_t \sum_{j=1}^{m} R_{1,t+j-1} \qquad m = 2, 3, 4 \quad (18)$$

The technology shocks a_t and demand shock g_t follow an AR(1) process given by

$$a_t = \rho_a a_{t-1} + \varepsilon_{a,t} \qquad (19)$$

$$g_t = \rho_g g_{t-1} + \varepsilon_{g,t} \qquad (20)$$

where $\varepsilon_{a,t}$, $\varepsilon_{g,t}$ are zero mean iid disturbances with standard deviations given by σ_{ε_a} and σ_{ε_g}.

In such a framework, it is easy to see that any non-random co-movement between foreign and domestic variables must be driven by foreign shocks. Domestic shocks do not affect foreign variables and therefore, do not reduce co-movement between variables. Furthermore, observe that the lower the persistence of the shocks, the lesser is the impact on the long-term interest rate. Intuitively, low persistence of the shock implies smaller changes in the expected short-term interest rates. Since long-term rates are a function of expected short-term rates, they too will change less.

On the other hand, the lower the persistence of the shock, the greater is the change to short-term interest rates. To understand this, consider for instance a temporary increase in productivity. On the supply side, this would cause lower marginal costs and a decline in inflation. On the demand side, since the rise in income is temporary, an increase in consumption would be muted as agents would look to smoothen their consumption. On balance, therefore, inflation would fall, causing an inflation-targeting policy maker to reduce short-term rates aggressively. By contrast, under a permanent productivity change, consumption would rise by more thereby mitigating the need for the policy maker to intervene aggressively with interest rates. To summarise, shocks with low persistence will cause a greater movement in the short-term interest rates, whereas shocks with high persistence will cause greater movements in the long-term interest rates.

Using the above intuition, KR establish that if foreign shocks are more persistent than domestic shocks, the long-term interest rates in the two economies are likely to be more correlated. On the other hand, the low persistence of the domestic shocks results in a larger movement in the short-term domestic interest rate, thereby reducing correlation with the short-term foreign interest rate. Can this explanation be used to explain the pattern of correlations observed in Figure 5.1? In other words, is the persistence of foreign shocks higher than domestic shocks in India? Moreover, can this explain the difference in the predictive power of domestic and foreign yield curves? We examine this hypothesis by estimating equations (2) to (20) using Indian and US data in the next section.

Estimation

In this section, we use Bayesian estimation techniques proposed widely in the literature (see An and Schorfheide 2007) to estimate the KR model described in the previous section. Our main objective here is to estimate and compare the persistence of shocks in the two economies. If foreign shocks are more persistent than the domestic shocks, then the intuition from the model would be able to explain the pattern of correlation in Figure 5.1. Then, we simulate our estimated model and investigate whether the US or the Indian yield spread does a better job in predicting economic activities in India. Once again, our analysis largely follows KR. In our estimation, we treat the US as the large economy and India as the small open economy. Following much of the literature, the discount factor, β, is set at 0.99, which at a quarterly frequency corresponds to a steady-state real rate of interest of 4.1 per cent. The degree of openness, α, is set at 0.4 to match the ratio of the trade balance to GDP.

In estimating the remaining parameters, we follow KR in carrying out the estimation in two stages. In the first stage, the large open economy's parameters are estimated. The parameters being estimated for the large economy are σ, λ, φ, ρ_r^*, α_π^*, α_y^*, ρ_g^*, ρ_a^*, $\sigma_{\varepsilon a}^*$, $\sigma_{\varepsilon g}^*$, $\sigma_{\varepsilon r}^*$. Next, we proceed to estimate the parameters for the Indian economy. For the Indian economy, we estimate ω, ρ_r, α_π, α_y, ρ_g, ρ_a, $\sigma_{\varepsilon a}$, $\sigma_{\varepsilon g}$, $\sigma_{\varepsilon r}$. For the case of the US, we use quarterly HP-filtered data on real US GDP per capita, US CPI-inflation and a US 3-month nominal interest rate for the sample period 2001 Q1 to 2018 Q2. Table 5.3 summarises results from this first step of the estimation. Consistent with KR, we find demand shocks to be highly persistent and the most important source of aggregate fluctuations.

As discussed earlier for the estimation of parameters for India (small open economy), the posterior mode parameter values from the first stage are taken while the rest are estimated. For India, we use quarterly HP-filtered data on real GDP per capita, CPI-inflation and a 3-month nominal interest rate for the sample period 2001 Q1 to 2018 Q2. Table 5.4 summarises results from this second step of the estimation. Our estimation results from this second step are also in line with those found in other studies. Crucial to our understanding of Figure 5.1 is the magnitude to the persistence parameter of the shocks. Comparison between Tables 5.3 and 5.4 reveals that the persistence of the domestic shocks is much lower than that of the foreign shocks.

Table 5.3: Estimated values of US (large economy) parameters from Bayesian estimation

Parameters	Prior mean	Posterior mean	90% probability interval		Prior density	Prior std.
σ^{-1}	1.5	0.9544	0.4605	1.4427	Gamma	0.5
λ	0.3	0.7952	0.4961	1.0857	Normal	0.25
φ	0.9	1.0255	0.6594	1.3772	Gamma	0.2
ρ_r^*	0.9	0.8963	0.8299	0.9665	Beta	0.05
α_π^*	0.5	0.9326	0.7247	1.1336	Normal	0.2
α_y^*	0.25	0.0294	−0.0724	0.133	Normal	0.1
ρ_g^*	0.5	0.8252	0.7668	0.8855	Beta	0.15
ρ_a^*	0.5	0.8287	0.7361	0.9239	Beta	0.15
Standard deviation	Prior mean	Post. mean	90% probability interval		Prior density	Prior std.
$\sigma_{\varepsilon a}^*$	0.015	0.0059	0.0041	0.0077	Uniform	0.0087
$\sigma_{\varepsilon g}^*$	0.02	0.0313	0.0249	0.0398	Uniform	0.0115
$\sigma_{\varepsilon r}^*$	0.015	0.006	0.0047	0.0072	Uniform	0.0087

Source: Author's model simulation results

In Table 5.5, we compare the theoretical standard deviations of output, inflation, and nominal interest rates, which are computed from the simulated estimated model with their empirical counterparts. The standard deviations of output, short-term interest rate, and inflation match well with their empirical values, however, long-term interest rates are underestimated by our model. These results are consistent with the literature. For example, Shiller (1979) and Meese and Rogoff (1983) also document the fact that models of standard business cycles find it difficult to replicate the variation of long-term interest rates.

Table 5.4: Estimated values of Indian (small economy) parameters from Bayesian estimation

Parameters	Prior mean	Post. mean	90% probability interval		Prior density	Prior std.
ω	2	1.3521	1.0881	1.612	Gamma	0.5
ρ_r	0.9	0.8423	0.7495	0.9383	Beta	0.05
α_π	0.5	0.8108	0.6153	1.0026	Normal	0.2
α_y	0.25	0.3475	0.2381	0.4609	Normal	0.1
ρ_g	0.5	0.3619	0.204	0.519	Beta	0.15
ρ_a	0.5	0.6237	0.532	0.7179	Beta	0.15
Standard deviation	Prior mean	Post. mean	90% probability interval		Prior density	Prior std.
$\sigma_{\varepsilon a}$	0.01	0.0139	0.0115	0.0162	Inv. Gamma	0.1
$\sigma_{\varepsilon g}$	0.01	0.0427	0.0344	0.0507	Inv. Gamma	0.1
$\sigma_{\varepsilon r}$	0.01	0.0123	0.0096	0.0149	Inv. Gamma	0.1

Source: Authors' model simulation results

Table 5.5: Standard deviations

Variable	Model posterior	Data (2001 Q1 to 2014 Q3)
y_t	0.0140	0.0156
$\pi_{1,t}$	0.0128	0.0146
$R_{1,t}$	0.0095	0.0093
$R_{40,t}$	0.0008	0.0052

Source: Authors' model simulation results compared to data from https://data.bloomberg.com/ and RBI (n.d.)

Figure 5.7 shows the prior and posterior densities for the AR(1) parameters that govern exogenous persistence. As in KR, the choice of prior distributions is the same for foreign and domestic exogenous processes. The priors are therefore agnostic about the difference in persistence between domestic and foreign shocks. Using the data, we find that the prior distribution shifts. In the case of the foreign AR(1) processes,

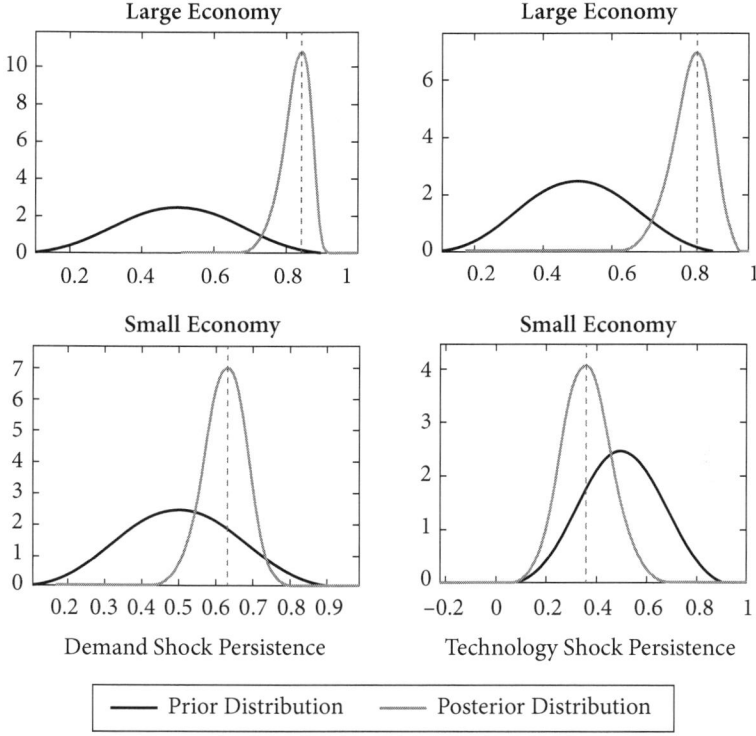

FIG. 5.7: Prior and posterior distributions of large and small economies' technology and demand persistence

Source: Authors' model simulation results

the data shifts in the direction of higher persistence and the distribution is concentrated around it. However, for the domestic AR(1) processes, the concentration is around lower persistence.

Does the pattern of interest rate correlations make the US yield curve a better predictor of economic activity in India? Intuitively, if the domestic long-term interest rate exhibits a higher correlation with the foreign long-term rate and lower correlation with the domestic short-term rate, then the foreign yield spread may be more effective in predicting future domestic economic activity.

Table 5.6: Correlation of Indian GDP growth and lagged and future term spreads (model)

	Lagged term spread						
	t	t−1	t−2	t−3	t−4	t−5	t−6
Using US Spread	0.053	0.070	0.060	0.044	0.040	0.031	0.044
Using Indian Spread	0.059	0.046	0.049	0.039	0.042	0.024	0.005
	Future term spread						
	t	t+1	t+2	t+3	t+4	t+5	t+6
Using US Spread	0.053	0.031	0.033	0.020	0.001	−0.021	−0.029
Using Indian Spread	0.059	0.031	0.009	−0.055	−0.085	−0.085	−0.056

Source: Authors' model simulation results

Table 5.6 presents correlations between (a) the US yield spread and (b) the Indian yield spread (measured as a monthly average of quarterly observations) and the year-over-year percentage change in real gross domestic product (GDP) for India. The table presents the contemporaneous correlation between the variables, as well as correlations at various leads and lags. The top panel of the table reports the lagged and the bottom panel the lead correlations between the variables.

Interestingly, the correlations between GDP growth, and the US term spread, lagged from one to six quarters, are uniformly positive and higher than the correlations between the Indian term spread and GDP growth rate. For lagged correlation, we observe that till the fourth lag period, the US correlations are between 0.07 and 0.04 whereas Indian correlation remains around 0.04 across these periods.

Thus, these correlations indicate that the more steeply sloped the US yield curve, the higher the rate of future Indian GDP growth. Conversely, the less steeply sloped the yield curve, the lower the subsequent rate of Indian GDP growth. The correlations between current GDP growth and future US term spreads shown in the lower panel are negative after the fifth quarter. Thus, a higher GDP growth rate in one quarter is associated with a decline in the slope of the US yield curve in subsequent quarters. The corresponding patterns of correlations are slightly weaker when one considers the Indian yield spread. Our results suggest that the US yield spread seems much more correlated with economic activity in India than the corresponding Indian yield spread. To conclude our results, we suggest that the higher persistence of foreign shocks relative to domestic shocks is able to explain both the pattern of interest rate correlations documented in Figure 5.1 as well as the effectiveness of the US term spread in predicting economic activity in India.

Conclusion

Conventional wisdom suggests that the transmission of monetary policy takes place from the short end to the long end of the domestic yield curve. In this chapter, we document the fact that long-term interest rates in India are highly correlated with their counterparts in the US. Furthermore, we also empirically show that the US yield spread does a better job in forecasting Indian business cycles than the Indian yield spread. Does this imply that domestic monetary policy now plays a reduced role in stabilising business cycles in the Indian economy?

In this chapter, we estimate the workhorse small open economy model augmented to include the term structure of interest rates. We use our estimated model to investigate the co-movement of the US and Indian interest rates along different points of the yield curve. We also simulate the model and compare the relative effectiveness of the US and Indian yield spread in forecasting economic activity in India. Our results suggest that the higher persistence of foreign shocks as compared to domestic shocks is able to explain the pattern of co-movements in the interest rates as well as the superior ability of the US yield spread in predicting economic activity in India. Put differently, the conventional small open economy model that does not assume any decoupling of the short- and long-term interest rates does a good job in explaining both the empirical features documented in this chapter.

REFERENCES

An, Sungbae and Frank Schorfheide. 2007. 'Bayesian Analysis of DSGE Models'. *Econometric Reviews* 26(2–4): 113–172.

Bernanke, B. S. 2013. 'Long-Term Interest Rates', Speech at the Annual Monetary/Macroeconomics Conference: The Past and Future of Monetary Policy. San Francisco, California: Federal Reserve Bank of San Francisco.

Christiano, L. and T. Fitzgerald. 2003. 'The Band Pass Filter'. *International Economic Review* 44(2): 435–65.

Dahlquist, M. and H. Hasseltoft. 2013. 'International Bond Risk Premia'. *Journal of International Economics* 90(1): 17–32.

Dueker, M. J. 1997. 'Strengthening the Case for the Yield Curve as a Predictor of U.S. Recessions'. *Federal Reserve Bank of St. Louis Review* 79: 41–51.

Estrella, A. and G. A. Hardouvelis. 1991. 'The Term Structure as a Predictor of Real Economic Activity'. *Journal of Finance* 46(2): 555–76.

Estrella, A. and F. S. Mishkin. 1998. 'Predicting U.S. Recessions: Financial Variables as Leading Indicators'. *Review of Economics and Statistics* 80(1): 45–61.

Gali, J. and T. Monacelli. 2005. 'Monetary Policy and Exchange Rate Volatility in a Small Open Economy'. *The Review of Economic Studies* 72: 707–34.

Harding, D. and A. Pagan. 2002. 'Dissecting the Cycle: A Methodological Investigation'. *Journal of Monetary Economics* 49(2): 365–81.

Jotikasthira, C., A. Le, and C. Lundblad. 2015. 'Why do Term Structures in Different Currencies Co-move?' *Journal of Financial Economics* 115: 58–83.

Kulish, Mariano and Daniel Rees. 2011. 'The Yield Curve in a Small Open Economy'. *Journal of International Economics* 85(2): 268–79.

Meese, R. and K. Rogoff. 1983. 'Empirical Exchange Rate Models of the Seventies: Do they Fit Out of Sample?'. *Journal of International Economics* 14: 3–24.

Pandey, R., I. Patnaik and A. Shah. 2017. 'Dating Business Cycles in India'. *Indian Growth and Development Review* 10(1): 32–61.

RBI. n.d. 'Handbook of Statistics on Indian Economy'. Available at https://www.rbi.org.in/Scripts/AnnualPublications.aspx?head=Handbook%20of%20Statistics%20on%20Indian%20Economy (accessed March 2023).

Shiller, R. J. 1979. 'The Volatility of Long-Term Interest Rates and Expectations Models of the Term Structure'. *Journal of Political Economy* 87(6): 1190–1219.

Swanson, E. T. and J. C. Williams. 2014. 'Measuring the effect of the zero lower bound on yields and exchange rates in the U.K. and Germany'. *Journal of International Economics* 92, Supplement 1, S2–S21, 36th Annual NBER International Seminar on Macroeconomics. Available at https://www.sciencedirect.com/journal/journal-of-international-economics/vol/92/suppl/S1 (accessed March 2023).

Wright, J. H. 2011. 'Term Premia and Inflation Uncertainty: Empirical Evidence from an International Panel Dataset'. *American Economic Review* 101(4): 1514–34.

6
INFLATION AND STABILISATION POLICIES IN INDIA

Debashree Chakraborty and *Ambar Ghosh*

Introduction

At the outset of this chapter, we would like to briefly delineate the main features of the Nehru-Mahalanobis strategy, the strategy of economic development that India followed in the post-Independence period till the middle of 1991. Under this strategy, planners imposed stringent restrictions on all kinds of economic activities such as production, investment, consumption, export, import, cross-border capital flows, and so on. Through these restrictions, planners determined the allocation of resources, that is, the planners decided which commodities are to be produced and in what quantities. The objective of the planners was to achieve self-reliance and to provide the masses with the necessities of life at affordable prices. With this end in view, the planners utilised India's resources for accomplishing the following tasks: setting up basic and heavy industries, investing on a large scale in irrigation, flood control facilities and agricultural R&D to develop agriculture, and also in the financial sector to set up a nationwide system of banking, insurance companies and special development financial institutions to provide the masses with a safe and remunerative avenue of saving and mobilising these savings to meet the essential social needs of credit as specified by the planners. They also invested substantially in education and health care to provide the masses with these services at negligible prices and, finally, they set up a public distribution system to provide the masses with food and other necessities of life at affordable prices. Restrictions were imposed on all kinds of economic activities to prevent leakage of scarce productive resources into the production of non-essential items of consumption and investment. These restrictions were necessary to maximise the production of those goods, which were necessary to achieve the planned objectives of self-reliance, and providing the masses with the basic necessities of life along with health care and education at negligible or low prices.

India, however, had to give up the Nehru-Mahalanobis strategy and adopt the New Economic Policy (NEP) at the behest of the IMF in July 1991. The NEP consists in removing all controls over the economic activities such as production, investment, consumption, export, import and cross-border capital flows of the Mahalanobis era. The objective is obviously to allow the market forces a free play in the allocation of scarce productive resources. What is the motivation behind this policy? If free-market forces determine allocation of resources, people with purchasing power, i.e., the rich, will secure most of the resources, while the poor will have to make do with very little. In consonance with this policy of favouring the rich, direct tax rates have been slashed drastically under NEP. This has been done in a country, where, according to a recent Oxfam

India (2018) report, only 1 percent of Indians own 73 per cent of India's total wealth. Obviously, this estimate has been made on the basis of declared assets. If undeclared assets were taken into account, the inequality would have been much more extreme. The inequality in the distribution of wealth obviously reflects the inequality in the distribution of income. Since most of the aggregate income of India in every period accrues to a small number of people, drastic reduction in direct tax rates has very substantially reduced the government's command over resources. The scope for mobilising resources by raising indirect tax rates is also extremely limited, as it raises prices and, thereby, adversely affects demand and output through its distribution effects and its impact on trade balance. Hence, following a hike in indirect tax rates, real resources at the command of the government may even fall instead of rising. In addition, NEP has imposed stringent restrictions on the size of the fiscal deficit (which stands for the government's borrowing) as a proportion of GDP. All the fiscal measures mentioned above have severely reduced the government's command over resources. As a result, the government has to rely on the private sector to produce most of the goods society needs. To elaborate, the drastic reduction of the government's command over resources under NEP has seriously impaired its ability to invest in irrigation, flood control, agricultural R&D and so on to improve the performance of agriculture, which is directly and indirectly the source of livelihood for most of the poor people in India. It has significantly eroded the government's ability to also invest in education and health care and provide the common people these services at low costs. It has also substantially reduced the government's capacity to run a public distribution system to provide the poor masses with the basic necessities of life at affordable prices. Spending on old-age care or unemployment allowance is also a distant dream. The NEP is, therefore, to put it mildly, completely pro-rich and anti-poor. The NEP has hardly left any scope for the government to develop an indigenous technological or knowledge base. By reducing the government's command over resources to the minimum possible level, the NEP has deepened India's dependence on foreign technology and, therefore, on foreign intermediate and capital goods. This chapter focuses on one aspect of the fiscal deficit target that NEP has imposed on the government—an aspect that the existing literature on fiscal deficit target has largely overlooked. It seeks to show that fiscal deficit target magnifies manifold the adverse effects of inflation.

The kind of monetary policy being pursued these days all across the capitalist world, including India, is also a matter of grave concern for the poor, toiling masses, who are net lenders to the capitalists. This monetary policy consists in reducing interest rates drastically as soon as a recession strikes an economy and raising it in times of inflation to weaken inflationary forces. All the major capitalist countries have been in the grip of recession for a long period of time. Japan, US and most of the countries in Europe have been in recession since 1992, 2001 and 2008, respectively (see Table 6.1). Interest rates in all these countries were reduced to the minimum possible level immediately following the onset of recession, much to the detriment of the interest of the workers who are net lenders to the capitalists. However, this policy failed to make any impact on recession, which continued unabated (see Tables 6.2 and 6.3). It should be noted here that, even though risk-free interest rates dropped to the minimum possible levels in these countries, loans were available at these low interest rates only to the giant corporations or giant capitalists, whom Bernanke, Gertler and Gilchrist (1996) call 'quality borrowers'. In fact, with the onset of recession, interest rates rose steeply for the small and medium enterprises eroding substantially their competitive strength (see Mishkin [2011] in this context) vis-à-vis the giant corporations. We seek to show in this chapter that if interest rates are raised in times of inflation to tackle the same, it will significantly strengthen inflationary forces and amplify the adverse effects of inflation by many times, thereby causing grievous harm to the toiling masses.

Table 6.1: Annual percentage growth rate of GDP at market prices based on constant local currency

	1981	'82	'83	'84	'85	'86	'87	'88	'89	'90
China	5.2	9.0	10.8	15.2	13.6	8.9	11.7	11.3	4.2	3.9
France	1.1	2.5	1.3	1.5	1.6	2.4	2.6	4.7	4.4	2.9
Germany	0.5	−0.4	1.6	2.8	2.3	2.3	1.4	3.7	3.9	5.3
Greece	−1.6	−1.1	−1.1	2.0	2.5	0.5	−2.3	4.3	3.8	0.0
Ireland	3.3	2.3	−0.2	4.4	3.1	−0.4	4.7	5.2	5.8	8.5
Italy	0.8	0.4	1.2	3.2	2.8	2.9	3.2	4.2	3.4	2.0
Japan	4.2	3.4	3.1	4.5	6.3	2.8	4.1	7.1	5.4	5.6
Spain	−0.1	1.2	1.8	1.8	2.3	3.3	5.5	5.1	4.8	3.8
UK	−0.8	2.1	4.2	2.3	3.5	3.2	5.5	5.9	2.5	0.5
US	2.6	−1.9	4.6	7.3	4.2	3.5	3.5	4.2	3.7	1.9

	1991	'92	'93	'94	'95	'96	'97	'98	'99	2000
China	9.3	14.3	13.9	13.1	11.0	9.9	9.2	7.9	7.6	8.4
France	1.0	1.6	−0.6	2.3	2.1	1.4	2.3	3.6	3.4	3.9
Germany	5.1	1.9	−1.0	2.5	1.7	0.8	1.8	2.0	2.0	3.0
Greece	3.1	0.7	−1.6	2.0	2.1	2.9	4.5	3.2	3.1	4.2
Ireland	1.9	3.3	2.7	5.8	9.6	9.3	11.2	8.9	10.8	10.2
Italy	1.5	0.8	−0.9	2.2	2.0	1.3	1.8	1.6	3.7	1.8
Japan	3.3	0.8	0.2	0.9	1.9	2.6	1.6	−2.0	−0.2	2.3
Portugal	4.4	1.1	−2.0	1.0	4.3	3.5	4.4	4.8	3.9	3.8
Spain	2.5	0.9	−1.0	2.4	2.8	2.7	3.7	4.3	4.5	5.3
UK	−1.2	0.4	2.6	4.0	4.9	2.7	3.1	3.4	3.1	3.8
US	−0.1	3.6	2.7	4.0	2.7	3.58	4.5	4.4	4.7	4.1

	2001	'02	'03	'04	'05	'06	'07	'08	'09	'10
China	8.3	9.1	10.6	10.1	11.4	12.7	14.2	9.6	9.2	10.6
France	2.0	1.1	0.8	2.8	1.6	2.4	2.4	0.2	−2.9	2.0
Germany	1.7	0.0	−0.7	1.2	0.7	3.7	3.3	1.1	−5.6	4.1
Greece	3.8	3.9	5.8	5.9	3.8	3.9	5.8	5.1	0.6	5.7
Ireland	5.8	5.9	3.8	4.4	6.3	6.3	5.5	−2.2	−5.6	0.4
Italy	1.8	0.3	0.2	1.6	0.9	2.0	1.5	−1.0	−5.5	1.7
Japan	0.4	0.3	1.7	2.4	1.3	1.7	2.2	−1.0	−5.5	4.7
Portugal	1.9	0.8	−0.9	1.8	0.8	1.6	2.5	0.2	−3.0	1.9
Spain	4.0	2.9	3.2	3.2	3.7	4.2	3.8	1.1	−3.6	0.0
UK	2.8	2.5	3.3	2.5	3.0	2.7	2.6	−0.5	−4.2	1.5
US	1.0	1.8	2.8	3.8	3.3	2.7	1.8	−0.3	−2.8	2.5

(Contd)

Table 6.1 (Contd)

	2011	'12	'13	'14
China	9.5	7.8	7.7	7.3
France	2.1	0.2	0.7	0.2
Germany	3.7	0.4	0.3	1.6
Greece	−9.1	−7.3	−3.2	0.7
Ireland	2.6	0.2	1.4	5.2
Italy	0.6	−2.8	−1.7	−0.4
Japan	−0.5	1.8	1.6	−0.1
Korea Rep. (South)	3.7	2.3	2.9	3.3
Malaysia	5.3	5.5	4.7	6.0
Portugal	−1.8	−4.0	−1.1	0.9
Spain	−1.0	−2.6	−1.7	1.4
Thailand	0.8	7.3	2.8	0.9
UK	2.0	1.2	2.2	2.9
US	1.6	2.3	2.2	2.4

Note: Aggregates are based on constant 2005 US dollars.
Source: World Bank national accounts data, and OECD national accounts data files; see https://data.worldbank.org/indicator/NY.GDP.MKTP.KD?locations=AU (accessed March 2023)

Table 6.2: Interest rates and growth rates in the US

Year	R^1	Y^2
1994	7.15	4.0
1995	8.83	2.7
1996	8.27	3.8
1997	8.44	4.5
1998	8.35	4.5
1999	8.00	4.7
2000	9.23	4.1
2001	6.91	1.0
2002	4.67	1.8
2003	4.12	2.8
2004	4.34	3.8
2005	6.19	3.3
2006	7.96	2.7

(Contd)

Table 6.2 (Contd)

Year	R¹	Y²
2007	8.05	1.8
2008	5.09	−0.3
2009	3.25	−2.8
2010	3.25	2.5
2011	3.25	1.6
2012	3.25	2.2
2013	3.25	1.5

Note: ¹Average majority prime rate charged by banks on short-term loans to business
²Percentage increase in real GDP from the previous year
Source: Data on interest rates have been taken from the Board of Governors of the Federal Reserve System (2014)

Table 6.3: Average growth rate of real GDP and average interest rates in the US economy

Year	Average growth rate¹	Average prime lending rates of banks	Average interest rates on 30-year mortgage contracts
1994–2000	4.04	8.32	7.73
2001–07	2.5	6.03	6.25
2008–13	0.8	4.27	4.64

Note: ¹Simple arithmetic mean of the year-on-year growth rates of GDP
Source: Computed from the data given in Table 6.1

Inflation is a matter of grave concern to the people and the government. It inflicts enormous costs on society. The objective of this chapter is to develop a suitable macro model for India to study how inflation harms the economy. It does so to examine how the costs of inflation are affected in the presence of fiscal deficit target and inflation target. Even though Patnaik (2014) and Kaldor (1976) respectively warn of the costs of inflation getting aggravated by fiscal deficit target and inflation target, they have not used any model to rigorously establish their claims. We consider it worthwhile to analyse in greater detail and capture the destabilising effects of fiscal deficit target and inflation target rigorously within the framework of a macro-theoretic model suitable for India. We consider our endeavour necessary in view of the Government of India's (GoI) fiscal and monetary policy stance. In pursuance of the Fiscal Responsibility and Budget Management Act (FRBM) 2003, the GoI adheres to a strict fiscal deficit target. Following the recommendation of the Urjit Patel Committee Report (RBI 2014a), the GoI seeks to restrict fiscal deficit to around 3 per cent of GDP. The same committee recommended that inflation should be the nominal anchor for monetary policy framework. Following this recommendation, the RBI has set 4 per cent as the inflation rate target (RBI 2016). If inflation rate exceeds 4 per cent, the RBI raises its policy rates to bring down the inflation rate to its target level. If the inflation rate is less than 4 per cent, the RBI lowers its policy rates to give a boost to growth, if it is below the desired or potential level. It is important to know whether these policies, contrary to the policy makers' beliefs, act as automatic destabilisers and aggravate the costs of inflation as suggested by the authors cited above.

The chapter shows that the fiscal deficit target substantially reinforces adverse effects of inflation, if the government seeks to keep fiscal deficit under control by adjusting government consumption or administered prices of essential inputs such as services of railways, electricity, coal, etc., or by raising indirect tax rates. It also shows that inflation target also reinforces inflationary forces and magnifies manifold the costs that an exogenous increase in the inflation rate inflicts on a society.

The Model

In this section we formally build a model suitable for India that can capture the major costs of inflation and the effects of fiscal deficit target and inflation target on them. The model consists of a real sector and a financial sector. We consider the real sector first.

THE REAL SECTOR

Following the Keynesian tradition we assume that aggregate output is demand-determined. We shall now identify the major determinants of aggregate demand. Let us start with aggregate personal consumption demand. There are two classes of consumers: workers and capitalists. We shall first compute the incomes of these two classes of people. To produce 1 unit of Y, l amount of labour is required and W is the money wage rate. So, total wage income for producing Y units of output is WlY. The workers are net lenders. Their total outstanding loan at the beginning of the period is denoted by D. The average interest rate at which the loans were given is denoted by r_0. Total interest income of the workers in the given period is Dr_0. Total real income of the workers, denoted Y_w, is given by $Y_w = \dfrac{WlY}{P} + \dfrac{Dr_0}{P}$, where P denotes the domestic price level.

Total real income of the capitalists (Y_c) is, therefore, given by $Y_c = Y - \dfrac{WlY}{P} - \dfrac{Dr_0}{P}$. We assume that workers' and capitalists' incomes are taxed at the rates t_w and t_c, respectively. For simplicity, for the present we assume t_w and t_c to be equal and denote the common tax rate by t. Aggregate output is, accordingly, given by

$$Y = c_w \cdot \left(\dfrac{WlY}{P} + \dfrac{Dr_0}{P} \right)(1-t) +$$
$$c_c \cdot \left(Y - \dfrac{WlY}{P} - \dfrac{Dr_0}{P} \right)(1-t) + I(r, e) + G +$$
$$NX\left(p, c_c \cdot \left(Y - \dfrac{WlY}{P} - \dfrac{Dr_0}{P} \right), I(r, e), G \right) \qquad (1)$$

In equation (1), Y is NDP (Net Domestic Product), I is net investment, r is the interest rate, NX is net export and p is the real exchange rate given by (P^*e/P), where P^* denotes the price of foreign goods in foreign currency and e is the exchange rate. India being a small economy cannot influence the price of foreign goods prevailing in the world market and so P^* is assumed to be given. c_w and c_c are the fixed average and marginal consumption propensities of the workers and capitalists, respectively. It is standard to assume that $c_w > c_c$. Let us now explain the investment function. Investment in India depends not only on the interest rate but also on the nominal exchange rate, e, for the following reasons. Imported capital goods constitute an essential and important ingredient of investment in India. (To illustrate with an example, consider the import intensity of studying economics in India. Almost all the text books are imported, almost all the journals we refer to are foreign, all the computers and software we use are imported. Thus, to set up a college or a university or any other facility in India, almost all the knowledge inputs such as books, journals, etc., and high-tech products have to be imported.) Following an increase in exchange rate *ceteris paribus*, prices of foreign capital goods go up in domestic currency, cost of investment rises, which, given investors' expectations, lowers investment. Imported intermediate inputs constitute an essential and major ingredient of production in India. An increase in the exchange rate, therefore, generates a strong cost push. Large firms in India also have large stocks of external debt. An increase in exchange rate raises external debt service charges in domestic currency. All these adverse supply shocks dampen investor morale and lower investment. Data on exchange rates, growth rates and capital formation given in Tables 6.4 and 6.5 show that in all the years of recession (2011–12 to 2013–14), exchange rate increased substantially indicating a strong inverse relationship between the exchange rate, rate of capital formation and growth rate in India. For a more elaborate explanation of the reasons for the incorporation of e in the investment function and supportive empirical evidences, one may go through Ghosh and Ghosh (2016).

Table 6.4: Growth rate of GDP, net FDI, foreign portfolio investment, government consumption and gross fiscal deficit (GFD)

Year	Growth rate of GDP at factor cost (at constant prices; base 2004–05)	Net FDI (US$ million)	Net portfolio investment (US$ million)	Total (US$ million)	Government consumption (in Rs bn)	GFD[1] (% of GDP)	Rate of GDCF[2]	Rate of NDCF[3]
2000–01	5.3	3270	2590	5860	3247.27	5.65	24.6	16.7
2001–02	5.5	4734	1952	6686	3323.69	6.19	24.6	16.5
2002–03	5.0	3157	944	4101	3317.53	5.91	25.4	17.3
2003–04	8.1	2388	11377	13765	3409.62	5.48	27.3	19.5
2004–05	7.0	3712	9291	13003	3545.18	3.88	32.8	25.5
2005–06	9.5	3033	12492	15525	3860.07	3.96	34.9	27.8
2006–07	9.6	7693	6947	14640	4005.79	3.38	36.2	29.2
2007–08	9.6	15891	27434	43325	4389.19	2.54	39.0	32.2
2008–09	6.7	22343	−14032	8311	4845.59	5.99	35.6	27.9
2009–10	8.4	17965	32396	50361	5517.02	6.48	38.4	30.9
2010–11	8.4	11305	30292	41597	5843.52	5.87	39.8	32.5
2011–12	6.5	22006	17171	39177	6345.59	5.89	38.8	31.1
2012–13	4.5	19819	26891	46710	6620.33	5.06	38.9	30.9
2013–14	4.7	21564	4822	26386	6873.89	4.85		

Note: [1]Gross fiscal deficit, [2]Gross domestic capital formation, [3]Net domestic capital formation
Source: RBI 2014b

Let us now explain the net export function. C, I and G represent aggregate demand of domestic agents for both domestic and foreign goods. How these expenditures are allocated between domestic and foreign goods depends upon the real exchange rate. We assume here for simplicity that workers' consumption consists of domestic consumption goods only. Given this assumption, we make net export an increasing function of p, capitalists' consumption, G and I.

We assume, à la Kalecki (1954), that the domestic price level is set on the basis of cost and the most important determinant

Inflation and Stabilisation Policies in India 165

Table 6.5: Exchange rate of the Indian rupee vis-à-vis the US dollar (monthly average)

Year/Month	US$ average	Year/Month	US$ average	Year/Month	US$ average	Year/Month	US$ average
2008		Oct	46.7211	Jul	44.4174	Apr	54.4971
Jan	39.3737	Nov	46.5673	Aug	45.2788	May	55.1156
Feb	39.7326	Dec	46.6288	Sep	47.6320	Jun	58.5059
Mar	40.3561	2010		Oct	49.2579	Jul	60.0412
Apr	40.0224	Jan	45.9598	Nov	50.8564	Aug	64.5517
May	42.1250	Feb	46.3279	Dec	52.6769	Sep	64.3885
June	42.8202	Mar	45.4965	2012		Oct	61.7563
Jul	42.8380	Apr	44.4995	Jan	51.3992	Nov	62.7221
Aug	42.9374	May	45.8115	Feb	49.1671	Dec	61.7793
Sep	45.5635	June	46.5670	Mar	50.3213	2014	
Oct	48.6555	Jul	46.8373	Apr	51.8029	Jan	62.1708
Nov	48.9994	Aug	46.5679	May	54.4735	Feb	62.3136
Dec	48.6345	Sep	46.0616	June	56.0302	Mar	61.0021
2009		Oct	46.7211	Jul	55.4948	Apr	60.3813
Jan	48.8338	Nov	46.5673	Aug	48.3350	May	59.3255
Feb	49.2611	Dec	46.6288	Sep	54.3353	June	59.7143
Mar	51.2287	2011		Oct	52.8917	Jul	60.0263
Apr	50.0619	Jan	45.3934	Nov	54.6845	Aug	60.9923
May	48.5330	Feb	45.4358	Dec	54.6439		
June	47.7714	Mar	44.9914	2013			
Jul	48.4783	Apr	44.3700	Jan	54.3084		
Aug	48.3350	May	44.9045	Feb	53.7265		
Sep	48.4389	June	44.8536	Mar	54.5754		

Source: RBI 2014b

of cost in India, besides wage cost, is e. Let us now explain why the exchange rate is a major determinant of cost of production in India. Imported intermediate inputs such as petroleum and petroleum products, fertiliser, spares and components are essential ingredients of production in India (see Table 6.6). An increase in the exchange rate makes them costlier in domestic currency pushing up domestic cost of production substantially. Besides cost, price may also depend upon the degree of monopoly power enjoyed by the firms. If for some reason or the other, the degree of concentration increases in the domestic economy, domestic price level may go up, with the level of cost remaining unchanged. We denote the exogenous factors such as the degree of concentration in the domestic economy by ϕ. Thus, we make the domestic price level P an increasing function of e and ϕ. We do not consider the wage rate explicitly as a determinant of cost as we regard it as fixed in the short run. Thus,

$$P = P(\underset{+}{e}, \underset{+}{\phi}) \qquad (2)$$

Table 6.6: Commodity composition of India's imports percentage share

Commodity group	2000–01	2010–11	2011–12
Food and allied products	3.3	2.9	3.1
Fuel	33.5	30.9	37.4
POL[1] (a component of fuel)	31.3	28.7	31.7
Fertiliser	1.3	1.9	2.4
Capital goods	10.5	13.6	14.1
Others	52.5	49.6	49.0
Chemicals (a component of others)	5.9	5.2	5.1
Pearls, precious, semi-precious stones (a component of others)	9.7	9.3	6.1
Gold and silver (a component of others)	9.3	11.5	12.6
Electronic goods (a component of others)	7.0	7.1	7.1

Source: GoI 2013
Note: POL stands for petroleum, oil and lubricants

Our specification of the real sector is complete. We now turn to the financial sector.

THE FINANCIAL SECTOR

Interest rate is determined in the financial sector. In India, the RBI employs different means such as the liquidity adjustment facility, open market operations, etc., to keep the interest rate at a target level. We shall therefore regard r as a policy variable of the RBI and take it as given. Thus,

$$r = \bar{r} \qquad (3)$$

Incorporating (2) and (3) into (1), we rewrite it as

$$Y = c_w \cdot \left(\frac{WlY}{P(e, \phi)} + \frac{Dr_0}{P(e, \phi)} \right)(1 - t) +$$

$$c_c \cdot \left(Y - \frac{WlY}{P(e, \phi)} - \frac{Dr_0}{P(e, \phi)} \right)(1 - t) + I(\bar{r}, e) + G +$$

$$NX\left(p, c_c \cdot \left(Y - \frac{WlY}{P(e, \phi)} - \frac{Dr_0}{P(e, \phi)} \right), I(\bar{r}, e), G \right) \qquad (4)$$

We shall now explain how exchange rate is determined.

Table 6.7: Composition of India's external debt (as percentage of total external debt)

	Government (sovereign) external debt	Other external debt	Total external debt as percentage of gross national income
End September 2012	22.3	77.7	
2012			20.8

Source: GoI 2013

FOREIGN CURRENCY MARKET

In this section, we shall focus on the foreign currency market where e is determined. In India, the exchange rate is best regarded as flexible. There are wide variations in the exchange rate every year (see Table 6.5). Let us now turn to the determination of e. The BOP or balance of payments consists of trade surplus and net inflow of foreign capital, which we denote by K. We assume for simplicity and without any loss of generality that K

is exogenously given. We, therefore, write the BOP equilibrium condition, incorporating (2) and (3) into it and denoting the real exchange rate by p, as

$$NX\left(p, c_c \cdot \left(Y - \frac{WlY}{P(e, \phi)} - \frac{Dr_0}{P(e, \phi)}\right)(1-t), I(\bar{r}, e), G\right) +$$

$$\bar{K} = 0 \qquad (5)$$

From (5) we find that balance of payments denoted by B, given by the LHS of (5), is a function of Y, e and the exogenous variables such as ϕ, t, etc. We do not consider other exogenous variables explicitly, as they are not relevant for our purpose. We can, therefore, rewrite equation (5) as

$$B(e, Y; \phi) = 0 \qquad (6)$$

$$B_Y = NX_{cc} \frac{Wl}{P}(1-t) < 0 \qquad (6i)$$

In (6i), $NXcc$ denotes partial derivative of the net export function with respect to capitalists' consumption. Clearly, this is negative, as a unit increase in capitalists' consumption demand raises capitalists' consumption demand for imported consumption goods also. This lowers net export.

$$B_e = NX_p \left(\frac{P^*}{P} - \frac{P^*e}{P^2}\right) + NX_{cc} \frac{WlY + Dr_0}{P^2} + NX_I I_e \qquad (6ii)$$

Let us now explain (6ii). Following a unit increase in e, real exchange rate goes up, raising net export. However, the increase in the real exchange rate is likely to be insignificant as an increase in e raises P substantially. This is captured by the first term on the RHS of (6ii). An increase in e raises P and, thereby, redistributes income in favour of the capitalists at the expense

Inflation and Stabilisation Policies in India   169

of the workers. This raises capitalists' consumption demand for both domestic and foreign goods lowering net export. This is captured by the second term on the RHS. An increase in e also lowers investment demand raising net export. This is captured by the third term on the RHS of (6ii). We assume that this term dominates so that $B_e > 0$. This is necessary for stability of equilibrium. We have demonstrated this in A.1 in the appendix.

$$B_\phi = -NX_p \left(\frac{P^*e}{P^2} \right) + (NX_{cc}) \frac{WlY + Dr_0}{P^2} < 0 \qquad (6\text{iii})$$

Following an increase in the exogenous variable ϕ, P goes up for exogenous reasons. The increase in P makes domestic goods dearer relative to foreign goods. Since close substitutes of the goods India produces are available in plenty in the world market, the increase in P is likely to reduce export, raise import and, thereby, lower net export by substantial quantities. This is given by the first term on the RHS of (6iii). The increase in P also redistributes income in favour of the capitalists at the expense of the workers. This also reduces net export by raising import demand of the capitalists. This is captured by the second term on the RHS of (6iii). Thus, following an exogenous increase in P, NX is likely to fall by a large quantity.

The specification of our model is now complete. It consists of two key equations (4) and (5) or (6) in two endogenous variables e and Y. We solve them as follows:
We first solve (5) or (6) for e as a function of Y and the exogenous variables. Thus,

$$e = e(Y; \phi); \; e_1 > 0, \; e_2 > 0 \qquad (7)$$

(We assume that the adjustment in e is instantaneous but that in Y is sluggish. Given this assumption, we have shown in section A.1 in the appendix that the equilibrium value of e is stable, given Y and the exogenous variables, iff $B_e > 0$.)

Substituting (7) into (2), we get

$$P = P(e(Y; \phi); \phi) = \overline{P}(Y; \phi) \quad (8)$$
$$\phantom{P = P(e(Y; \phi); \phi) = \overline{P}(Y; \phi)} {\scriptstyle +\quad\quad +\quad\quad +\ +}$$

Signs of partial derivatives of (8) follow straightway from (2) and (7). Substituting (5), (7) and (8) into (1), we get

$$Y = c_w \cdot \left(\frac{WlY}{\overline{P}(Y; \phi)} + \frac{Dr_0}{\overline{P}(Y; \phi)} \right)(1 - t) +$$

$$c_c \cdot \left(Y - \frac{WlY}{\overline{P}(Y; \phi)} - \frac{Dr_0}{\overline{P}(Y; \phi)} \right)(1 - t) +$$

$$I(\overline{r}, e(Y; \phi)) + G - \overline{K} \equiv \overline{E}(Y; \phi) + G = 0 \quad (9)$$

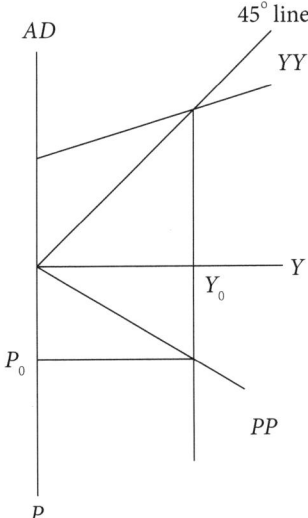

Fig. 6.1: Determination of Y and P

Source: Author

$$\overline{E}_Y = c_w \cdot \left(\frac{Wl}{P}\right)(1-t) + c_c \cdot \left(1 - \frac{Wl}{P}\right)(1-t) -$$

$$(c_w - c_c)\frac{1}{P^2}(WlY + Dr_0)P_Y - (-I_e)e_Y < 1 \qquad (9\text{i})$$

Note that $\overline{E}_Y$ may be negative also.

$$\overline{E}_\phi = -(c_w - c_c) + \frac{1}{P^2}(WlY + Dr_0)\overline{P}_\phi - (-I_e)e_\phi < 0 \qquad (9\text{ii})$$

We solve (9) for the equilibrium value of Y. Putting this equilibrium value of Y in (8) and (7), we get the equilibrium values of P and e, respectively. The solution of Y is shown in Figure 6.1, where YY schedule represents the RHS of (9), while the 45^0 line plots the value of the LHS against Y. The equilibrium value of Y corresponds to the point of intersection of the YY and the 45^0 line. The slope of YY is given by (9i), which may be negative also. However, for simplicity and without any loss of generality, we take it to be positive. The stability analysis carried out in section A.2 in the appendix shows that the equilibrium value of Y is stable iff $\overline{E}_Y < 1$. From (9i) we find that this condition is satisfied. In the lower panel, we measure positive values of P in the downward direction on the vertical axis. The PP line represents (8). The equilibrium P corresponds to the equilibrium Y on PP.

We are now in a position to use this simple model to identify the costs of inflation in India and how these costs are affected by the fiscal deficit target.

Inflation and its Costs in India

We shall examine here how inflation harms Indian economy. To identify the costs of inflation, we consider an exogenous increase in the rate of inflation, i.e., an exogenous increase in P, due to a rise, for example, in the degree of monopoly power of the firms in the Indian economy. The rise in the degree of concentration is indicated by an increase in ϕ. To derive the impact of an increase in ϕ on Y, we take total differential of (9) treating all exogenous variables other than ϕ as fixed and, then, solve for dY. This yields,

$$dY = \frac{\overline{E}_\phi}{1 - \overline{E}_Y} < 0 \tag{10}$$

The sign of (10) follows from the stability condition (see A.2 in the appendix) and (9ii). The result may be explained as follows. Following an increase in ϕ for exogenous reasons, P goes up redistributing income from the workers to the capitalists at the initial equilibrium (Y, e). It also reduces net export, which induces a rise in e that restores net export to its initial equilibrium value. However, the rise in e lowers investment demand and reinforces the redistribution effect by causing P to rise further. As a result, aggregate demand at the initial equilibrium Y falls engendering an excess supply of goods and services. Producers reduce Y to remove the excess supply. Per unit decline in Y, excess supply falls by $1 - \overline{E}_Y$. Hence, excess supply falls by $\overline{E}_\phi$, when Y goes down by the amount given by the expression on the RHS of (10).

To derive the impact on e and P, we take total differential of (7) and (8), treating all exogenous variables other than ϕ as fixed, substitute for dY its value as given by (10), and, then, solve for de and dP. This yields

$$de = -\frac{B_Y}{B_e}\left(\frac{\overline{E}_\phi\, d\phi}{1 - \overline{E}_Y}\right) + \frac{B_\phi}{B_e} d\phi \tag{11}$$

$$dP = \overline{P}_Y\left[\left(\frac{\overline{E}_\phi\, d\phi}{1 - \overline{E}_Y}\right)\right] + \overline{P}_\phi\, d\phi \tag{12}$$

Let us focus on the expression on the RHS of (11). It follows from (7) and (11) that the first term is negative, but the second term is positive. Hence, the direction of change in e is ambiguous. Let us now focus on the expression on the RHS of (12). It follows from (8) and (11) that the first term is negative, but the second term is positive. Hence, the direction of change in P is also ambiguous. However, we shall prove below that the new equilibrium P will be higher than its initial equilibrium value, though the new equilibrium e may be less.

Let us first explain the adjustment process. Following an increase in ϕ, P rises. The increase in P redistributes income from the workers to the capitalists and, thereby, lowers demand at the initial equilibrium (Y, e). It also reduces net export, which induces an increase in e that restores net export to its initial equilibrium value. The rise in e, however, lowers investment demand and reinforces the redistribution of income from the workers to the capitalists by causing P to rise further. Thus, there emerges a large excess supply at the initial equilibrium Y. Hence, Y begins to fall. However, the fall in Y raises net export bringing about a fall in e that keeps net export at its initial equilibrium level. The fall in e lowers P. The decline in e and P raises investment and consumption demand, respectively. Thus, through the fall in Y, e and P, the excess supply is removed. If the fall in Y is sufficiently large, e may fall below its initial equilibrium level. However, we shall now show that in the new equilibrium, P will remain above its initial equilibrium value. Let us prove. Note that the fall in Y does not directly lower P. It does so only by reducing e [see (8) and (2)]. Therefore, P can be less than its initial equilibrium value, only if e goes below its initial equilibrium value [see (8) and (2)]. From (9) it is clear that if e is below its initial equilibrium value and P is at or below its initial equilibrium value, the RHS will be greater than Y at every Y less than its initial equilibrium value. Therefore, even if e falls below its initial equilibrium value, P cannot be less than its initial equilibrium value in the new equilibrium. The results derived here may be summarised in the form of the following proposition:

Proposition 1: An exogenous increase in the inflation rate leads to a contraction in aggregate output and employment. It also makes the rate of inflation in the new equilibrium higher and, thereby, redistributes income from the workers to the capitalists. Inflation, thus, hurts the workers in two ways. Two, it redistributes income from the workers to the capitalists. One, it causes substantial recession and, therefore, unemployment. The recession thus hurts the capitalists as well.

Factors Worsening the Impact of Inflation

There are two important characteristics of fiscal and monetary policies being pursued by the GoI, namely, fiscal deficit target and inflation target. We examine below whether these targets act as automatic destabilisers and exacerbate the costs of inflation delineated in Proposition 1.

FISCAL DEFICIT TARGET: AN AUTOMATIC DESTABILISER

Fiscal deficit target is an integral part of the NEP. As mentioned earlier, the Urjit Patel Committee recommended a ceiling on the size of the fiscal deficit at 3 per cent of GDP (RBI 2014). GoI has several instruments for achieving its fiscal deficit target such as direct tax rates, indirect tax rates, amount of subsidy, government consumption, prices of essential inputs such as services of railways, power, coal, and so on. The GoI normally does not consider it politically prudent to raise direct tax rates to achieve its fiscal deficit target for reasons that we shall explain later. It uses the other instruments for the purpose. Since the effects of hikes in indirect tax rates, raising of the administered prices of essential inputs and lowering of subsidies are similar, and since the second measure implies the third one, we only explicitly consider here the first two of these three instruments.

Along with it, we also consider G as an instrument for achieving the fiscal deficit target.

G as the Instrument for Meeting the Government's Fiscal Deficit Target

We consider here the case where the government uses G as the instrument for meeting the fiscal deficit target. And it is often that GoI uses G for this purpose (see, for example, GoI 2014: 23). Fiscal deficit in our model is given by $G - tY$. Fiscal deficit target of the government is a given fraction a of Y. Therefore, government adjusts G in such a manner that the following equation is satisfied:

$$G - tY = aY \qquad (13)$$

Substituting (13) into (9), we rewrite it as

$$Y = \overline{E}(Y; \phi) + (t + a)Y \qquad (14)$$

To derive the impact of an increase in ϕ, we take total differential of (14) treating all exogenous variables other than ϕ as fixed and, then, solve for dY. This yields

$$dY = \frac{\overline{E}_\phi}{1 - \overline{E}_Y - (a + t)} < 0 \qquad (15)$$

Comparing (10) and (15), we find that the fall in Y is larger than that under no fiscal deficit target case. The reason may be explained as follows: Following an exogenous increase in ϕ, Y in the first round declines by $dY_1 = \frac{\overline{E}_\phi}{1 - \overline{E}_Y} < 0$. The contraction would have stopped here in the absence of any fiscal deficit target. However, under the fiscal deficit target, this lowers G by $(a + t)dY_1$, which will lower Y in the second round by $dY_2 = \dfrac{(a+t)dY_1}{1-\bar{E}_Y} < 0$. This will lead to further contraction in G and Y. In the third round, Y will go down by $dY_3 = \dfrac{(a+t)dY_2}{1-\bar{E}_Y} < 0$. This contraction in Y will continue until the contraction that takes place in each round eventually falls to zero. Thus, the total decrease in Y, using the value of dY_1, is given by

$$dY = dY_1 + \frac{(a+t)dY_1}{1-\bar{E}_Y} + \left[\frac{(a+t)}{1-\bar{E}_Y}\right]^2 dY_1 +$$

$$\left[\frac{(a+t)}{1-\bar{E}_Y}\right]^3 dY_1 + \ldots = \frac{\bar{E}_\phi}{1-\bar{E}_Y - (a+t)} < 0 \qquad (16)$$

From the above discussion it is clear that the contraction in Y that takes place following an exogenous increase in the inflation rate becomes substantially larger in the presence of the fiscal deficit target. This yields the following proposition.

Proposition 2: When the government adjusts its consumption expenditure to meet its fiscal deficit target, the recession caused by an exogenous increase in the inflation rate becomes more severe compared to the case where there is no fiscal deficit target. In the present case, therefore, fiscal deficit target acts as a strong automatic destabiliser.

When government expenditure is reduced in essential sectors to meet the fiscal deficit target, it goes against the poorer sections and inequality widens. This is what happens in India. In the budget of 2017–18, the government following its tradition of sound finance, fixed the target of fiscal deficit at 3.2 per cent of GDP. Budget estimates of government expenditure on defence stood at Rs 2,62,390 crore, while for essential sectors like education and health the budget estimates were Rs 79,686 crore and Rs 48,878 crore, respectively (GoI 2018: 4). Given such priorities of the GoI, if G has to be reduced to meet the fiscal deficit target in the face of inflation-induced recession, the part of G that is allocated to the poor will be cut first. This is an additional cost that inflation will inflict on the poor in India, when G is adjusted to meet the fiscal deficit target.

Administered Prices of Essential Inputs as the Instrument for Meeting the Fiscal Deficit Target

In India, government takes part in production. It produces essential intermediate inputs such as power, services of railways and other transport services, coal, oil, etc. Prices of these inputs, which we denote by P_0, are administered by the government. Profit from the production of these inputs is given by

$$\pi_g = P_0 Y \qquad (17)$$

where π_g denotes profit of the public sector. Let us explain (17). We assume that the fixed requirement of the output of the public sector as intermediate input per unit of Y is unity. We assume for simplicity that the public sector in India is vertically integrated. Even the wage cost is fixed in the public sector. Thus, there is no variable cost. We again assume for simplicity and without any loss of generality that the fixed cost is nil. Hence, (17) gives the profit of the public sector.

Since a part of the aggregate profit of the economy accrues to the government, total pre-tax real income of the capitalists (Y_c) is given by

$$Y_c = Y - \frac{WlY}{P} - \frac{Dr_0}{P} - \frac{P_0 Y}{P} \qquad (18)$$

GoI often uses administered prices of the essential inputs mentioned above as instruments for meeting fiscal deficit targets. To give a dramatic example, in September 2012, to reduce fiscal deficit, GoI hiked administered prices of diesel and cooking gas. To vindicate the act, which adversely affected the poor, the Prime Minister of India had to address the nation on 21 September 2012. We quote a few lines from the speech below,

> We are at a point where we can reverse the slowdown in our growth ... The decisions we have taken recently are necessary for this purpose. Let me begin with the rise in diesel prices and cap on LPG cylinders ... If we had not acted, it would have meant a higher fiscal deficit. If unchecked this would lead to a ... loss of confidence in our country ... and I would be failing in my duty as Prime Minister of this country if I did not take strong preventive action. (Singh 2012)

To examine how hikes in administered prices of essential inputs affect the economy, we assume t, D and a to be zero for simplicity and write the government's budget constraint as

$$PG = P_0 Y \qquad (19)$$

Using (19), we can write (18) as

$$Y_c = Y - \frac{WlY}{P} - G \qquad (20)$$

Again, from (19) we get

$$P_0 = \frac{PG}{Y} \qquad (21)$$

P_0 is an important determinant of cost of production and, therefore, that of price. Incorporating it in (2), we rewrite it as

$$P = P(e, P_0; \phi) \qquad (22)$$

However, to avoid unnecessary algebraic complications, we shall drop e from (22). This will not affect our results qualitatively in any way.

Substituting (21) into (22) and dropping e as a determinant of P, we rewrite it as

$$P = P\left(\frac{PG}{Y}; \phi\right); \quad P = P(0; \phi) > 0 \text{ and}$$

$$\frac{\partial P\left(\frac{PG}{Y}; \phi\right)}{\partial P} = P_{P_0}\frac{G}{Y} < 1 \text{ (by assumption)} \quad (23)$$

Given the assumptions stated above, we can solve (23) for P as a function of Y and ϕ, given G. Thus,

$$P = \tilde{P}(Y; \phi) \quad (24)$$
$$\quad\;\; - \;\; +$$

Note that, as follows from (23),

$$\tilde{P}_Y = \frac{-P_{P_0}\dfrac{P}{GY^2}}{1 - P_{P_0}\dfrac{G}{Y}} < 0, \; \tilde{P}_\phi = \frac{P_\phi}{1 - P_{P_0}\dfrac{G}{Y}} > 0 \quad (24\text{i})$$

To avoid unnecessary algebraic complications and put our result in the sharpest possible relief, we drop e from the investment function and assume D to be equal to zero. This will not affect our results qualitatively. Dropping e from the investment function, setting D and t equal to zero and substituting (24) and (20) in (9), we rewrite it as

$$Y = \left[c_w \cdot \left(\frac{Wl}{\tilde{P}(Y; \phi)}\right) + c_c \cdot \left(1 - \frac{Wl}{\tilde{P}(Y; \phi)}\right)\right]Y + I(\bar{r}) +$$

$$(1 - c_c)G - \bar{K} \equiv C(\tilde{P}(Y; \phi))Y + I(\bar{r}) +$$

$$(1 - c_c)G - \bar{K} = 0 \quad (25)$$

$$C = C(\tilde{P}(Y;\phi)) \equiv \left[c_w \cdot \left(\frac{Wl}{\tilde{P}(Y;\phi)} \right) + c_c \cdot \left(1 - \frac{Wl}{\tilde{P}(Y;\phi)} \right) \right] \quad (25i)$$

We are now in a position to examine the impact of an increase in ϕ on Y and P. Taking total differential of (25) treating all exogenous and policy variables other than ϕ as fixed and, then, solving for dY, we get

$$dY = \frac{C_P \tilde{P}_\phi Y d\phi}{1 - C - C_P \tilde{P}_Y} < 0 \quad (26)$$

Let us now explain (26). Note that in the absence of the fiscal deficit target, P_0 would have remained unchanged and P would have increased only on account of the increase in ϕ. Its increase would have been equal to only $P_\phi d\phi$ (see (2)) and $\tilde{P}_Y$ would have been zero. Hence, the value of dY, denoted by dY_0, as follows from (26), would have been given by the following:

$$dY_0 = \frac{C_P P_\phi Y d\phi}{1 - C} < 0 \quad (27)$$

Note that, as follows from (23),

$$\tilde{P}_\phi = \frac{P_\phi d\phi}{1 - P_{P_0} \dfrac{G}{Y}} > P_\phi d\phi \quad (28)$$

Let us explain (28). Following an increase in ϕ by $d\phi$, the desired value of P rises by $P_\phi d\phi$. However, as producers raise P from its initial value, per unit increase in P, fiscal deficit, as follows from (19), rises above the target by G and, hence to meet the fiscal deficit target, P_0 goes up by $\dfrac{G}{Y}$ raising the desired value

Inflation and Stabilisation Policies in India   181

of P by $P_{P_0} \dfrac{G}{Y}$. Thus, per unit increase in P, the gap between the desired and the initial value of P falls by $\left(1 - P_{P_0}\dfrac{G}{Y}\right)$. Hence, to remove the gap of $P_\phi d\phi$, P has to be raised by the amount given by the expression on the RHS of (28).

Clearly, the absolute value of (26) is much larger than that of (27). Let us now explain it in greater detail. Following an increase in ϕ by $d\phi$, P increases by $P_\phi d\phi$ in the absence of fiscal deficit target creating an excess supply of $-C_P P_\phi Y d\phi$ at the initial equilibrium Y reducing Y by dY_0. However, in the presence of fiscal deficit target, as we have already pointed out, P will increase by $\tilde{P}_\phi d\phi > P_\phi d\phi$ at the initial equilibrium Y creating a much larger excess supply of $-C_P \tilde{P}_\phi Y d\phi$ reducing Y by

$$dY_1 = \dfrac{C_P \tilde{P}_\phi Y d\phi}{1-C} = \dfrac{1}{1 - P_{P_0}\dfrac{G}{Y}} dY_0,$$ with P_0 remaining unchanged

at the level it was raised to at the initial equilibrium Y, following the increase in ϕ. Clearly, $-dY_1 > -dY_0$. However, with the decline in Y, fiscal deficit widens, inducing the government to raise P_0, which in turn will raise P further by $\tilde{P}_Y dY_1$ [see (24i)]. This will lower demand again by $C_P \tilde{P}_Y Y dY_1$. In the second round, Y will, therefore, fall by $dY_2 = \dfrac{C_P \tilde{P}_Y Y}{1-C} dY_1$. This will, again, lead to further increase in P_0 and P reducing Y in the third round by $dY_3 = \left(\dfrac{C_P \tilde{P}_Y Y}{1-C}\right)^2 dY_1$. Similarly, in the fourth round, Y will go down by $dY_4 = \left(\dfrac{C_P \tilde{P}_Y Y}{1-C}\right)^3 dY_1$. This process of contraction will continue until the excess supply created in each successive round eventually falls to zero. Thus, the total decline in Y is given by

$$dY = dY_1 + \frac{C_p \tilde{P}_Y Y}{1-C} dY_1 + \left(\frac{C_p \tilde{P}_Y Y}{1-C}\right)^2 dY_1 +$$

$$\ldots = \frac{C_p \tilde{P}_\phi d\phi}{1 - C - C_p \tilde{P}_Y Y} \tag{29}$$

Clearly, (29) tallies with (26).

The increase in ϕ and the cumulative contraction in Y that follows also bring about a cumulative increase in P or the rate of inflation. Taking total differential of (24) and substituting (28) into it we get

$$dP = \frac{1}{1 - P_{P_0} \dfrac{G}{Y}} P_\phi d\phi + \tilde{P}_Y \frac{C_p \tilde{P}_\phi d\phi}{1 - C - C_p \tilde{P}_Y Y} > P_\phi d\phi \tag{30}$$

The above discussion yields the following proposition.

Proposition 3: When the government adjusts administered prices of essential inputs to meet the fiscal deficit target, both the decline in Y and the increase in P that occur following an increase in P for exogenous reasons become much larger than what they would have been in the absence of the fiscal deficit target. Thus, the fiscal deficit target in the present case magnifies manifold the costs of an exogenous increase in the rate of inflation.

Indirect Taxes as the Instrument for
Meeting Fiscal Deficit Target

We shall now examine how costs of inflation are affected when indirect tax rates are used to meet the government's fiscal deficit target. Suppose an indirect tax is imposed at the rate τ on production or sales of goods and services. Following that, the market price of domestic goods and services denoted by P^m will be given by

$$P^m = P(1 + \tau) \tag{31}$$

where P denotes the producers' price. Assuming P to be an increasing function of ϕ alone, we rewrite (31) as

$$P^m = P(\underset{+}{\phi})(1 + \tau) \tag{32}$$

Total indirect tax collection in real terms denoted by T is given by

$$T = \frac{P\tau Y}{P(1+\tau)} = \frac{\tau}{(1+\tau)} Y \equiv (1-\gamma)Y \qquad \gamma \equiv \frac{1}{1+\tau} \tag{33}$$

Assuming t and a and government's profit to be equal to zero, fiscal deficit target implies

$$G = (1 - \gamma)Y \tag{34}$$

From (34) we get

$$\gamma = 1 - \frac{G}{Y} \equiv \gamma\left(\underset{+}{Y}\right) \tag{35}$$

Workers' and capitalists' real incomes in this case denoted by Y_W and Y_c respectively are given by (assuming D and t to be zero for simplicity)

$$Y_W = \frac{WlY}{P(1+\tau)} = \frac{Wl}{P}\gamma Y \quad \text{and}$$

$$Y_c = \frac{PY - WlY}{P(1+\tau)} = \left(1 - \frac{Wl}{P}\right)Y\gamma \tag{36}$$

Given the assumptions already specified, using (32), (35) and (36) and assuming investment to be a function of r alone, we write down the goods market equilibrium condition as follows:

$$Y = C(P(\phi))\gamma(Y)Y + I(\bar{r}) + G + NX\left(p, c_c\cdot\left(Y - \frac{WlY}{P(\phi)} - \frac{Dr_0}{P(\phi)}\right), I(\bar{r}), G\right) \quad (37)$$

where

$$\bar{C} \equiv C(P(\phi)) \equiv \left[c_w\cdot\left(\frac{Wl}{P(\phi)}\right) + c_c\cdot\left(1 - \frac{Wl}{P(\phi)}\right)\right] \quad (37i)$$

Substituting (5) into (37), we rewrite it as follows:

$$Y = C(P(\phi))\gamma(Y)Y + I(\bar{r}) + G - \bar{K} \quad (38)$$

To derive the impact of an autonomous increase in ϕ, we take total differential of (38) treating all exogenous variables other than ϕ as fixed and, then, solve for dY. This gives

$$dY = \frac{C'P'Y\gamma d\phi}{1 - \bar{C}\gamma - \bar{C}Y\gamma'} \quad (39)$$

In the absence of the fiscal deficit target, γ would have remained unchanged and the value of dY would have been

$$dY_1 = \frac{C'P'Y\gamma d\phi}{1 - \bar{C}\gamma} \quad (40)$$

Clearly, the fiscal deficit target magnifies manifold the recessionary impact of an autonomous increase in ϕ. Let us explain this point below.

Following an autonomous increase in ϕ by $d\phi$, with γ remaining unchanged, Y falls in the first round by $dY_1 = \dfrac{C'P'Y\gamma d\phi}{1-\bar{C}\gamma}$ raising fiscal deficit above the target level. This will induce a decline in γ by $\gamma' dY_1$, which will reduce consumption by $\bar{C}Y\gamma' dY_1$. This lowers Y in the second round by $dY_2 = \dfrac{\bar{C}Y\gamma'}{1-\bar{C}\gamma} dY_1$. This will again raise fiscal deficit above the target level inducing a decline in γ by $\gamma' dY_2$. This will lower consumption demand by $\bar{C}Y\gamma' dY_2$. In the third round, therefore, Y will fall by $dY_3 = \left(\dfrac{\bar{C}Y\gamma'}{1-\bar{C}\gamma}\right)^2 dY_1$. This process of contraction will continue until the fall in Y that takes place in each round eventually falls to zero. Thus, the total fall in Y is given by (putting the value of dY_1)

$$dY = dY_1 + \frac{\bar{C}Y\gamma'}{1-\bar{C}\gamma}dY_1 + \left(\frac{\bar{C}Y\gamma'}{1-\bar{C}\gamma}\right)^2 dY_1 + $$

$$\ldots = \frac{C'P'Y\gamma d\phi}{1-\bar{C}\gamma - \bar{C}Y\gamma'} \qquad (41)$$

(41) tallies with (39). It is clear from (41) that fiscal deficit target amplifies manifold the contraction in Y brought about by an exogenous increase in the rate of inflation, when indirect tax rate is adjusted to meet the fiscal deficit target.

Again, from (32), (33), (35) and (39) it follows that

$$dP^m = \left(P_\phi \frac{1}{\gamma} d\phi\right) + \left[-P(\phi)\frac{1}{\gamma^2}\frac{C'P'Y\gamma d\phi}{1-\bar{C}\gamma - \bar{C}Y\gamma'}\right] \qquad (42)$$

(42) gives the increase in the market price following the exogenous increase in ϕ. In the absence of the fiscal deficit target, the market price would have gone up by only the first term of the expression on the RHS of (42). However, the fiscal deficit target induces hikes in indirect tax rates in the face of inflation-induced contraction in Y. This engenders further increase in the market price. The increase in the market price that takes place on account of the fiscal deficit target is given by the second term of the expression on the RHS of (42). This substantially larger increase in P brings about a much larger redistribution of income from the workers to the capitalists. The above analysis yields the following proposition.

Proposition 4: When indirect tax rates are adjusted to meet fiscal deficit target, an exogenous increase in the rate of inflation brings about a substantially larger contraction in GDP and a significantly larger increase in the market price of goods and services making the redistribution of income from the workers to the capitalists much larger compared to the case where there is no fiscal deficit target.

INFLATION TARGET

As mentioned above, following the recommendation of the Urjit Patel Committee, which wanted to make inflation targeting the sole objective of monetary policy, the RBI has set 4 per cent as the inflation target. If inflation rate exceeds 4 per cent, the RBI raises rates to reduce the inflation rate. In what follows, we shall examine how this policy is likely to affect the costs of inflation. For this purpose, we shall consider only those situations where the inflation rate equals or exceeds the target rate of inflation. Suppose $\bar{p}$ is the price level that makes the rate of inflation in the given period equal to its target level, given the price level of the previous period. We make $\bar{r}$ an increasing function of $(P - \bar{P})$, when P exceeds or equals $\bar{p}$. Dropping $\bar{p}$ for simplicity and without any loss of generality, we write

Inflation and Stabilisation Policies in India 187

$$\bar{r} = r(P) \quad (43)$$
$$\phantom{\bar{r} = r(}_{+}$$

Note that producers take loans not only to finance investment but also to purchase intermediate inputs and to make factor payments. Interest charges on these loans constitute a component of the cost of production. An increase in $\bar{r}$, therefore, not only reduces demand but also generates a cost push. We shall, therefore, incorporate $\bar{r}$ into (22) (omitting e for simplicity, as it is no longer relevant for our purpose) and rewrite it as

$$P = P(\bar{r}, P_0; \phi) \quad (44)$$

Substituting (44) into (43), we rewrite it as

$$\bar{r} = r(P(\bar{r}, P_0; \phi)) \quad (45)$$

We assume that $r(P(0, P_0; \phi)) > 0$, and $r_p P_{\bar{r}} < 1$. Under these conditions, (45) will yield a unique solution for $\bar{r}$ and it will be stable. Thus, solving (45) for $\bar{r}$, we get

$$\bar{r} = \bar{r}(P_0; \phi) \quad (46)$$
$$\phantom{\bar{r} = \bar{r}(}_{++}$$

From (45) we find that

$$\bar{r}_\phi = \frac{r_p P_\phi d\phi}{1 - r_p P_{\bar{r}}} > 0, \qquad \bar{r}_{P_0} = \frac{r_p P_{P_0} dP_0}{1 - r_p P_{\bar{r}}} > 0 \quad (46i)$$

Substituting (46) and (44) into (38), we rewrite it as follows:

$$Y = [\tilde{C}(P(\bar{r}(\phi, P_0), P_0, \phi))] Y + I(\bar{r}(\phi, P_0)) +$$
$$G - \bar{K} = 0 \quad (47)$$

where

$$\tilde{C} = \tilde{C}(P(\bar{r}(\phi, P_0), P_0, \phi)) \equiv$$

$$\left[c_w \cdot \left(\frac{Wl}{P(\bar{r}(\phi, P_0), P_0, \phi)} \right) + c_c \cdot \left(1 - \frac{Wl}{P(\bar{r}(\phi, P_0), P_0, \phi)} \right) \right] \quad (47i)$$

Let us first focus on the case where the government adjusts G to meet its fiscal deficit target so that (13) is satisfied.

G as the Instrument for Meeting Fiscal Deficit Target in the Presence of Inflation Target

We shall examine here how in the presence of inflation target costs of inflation are affected, when government uses G to meet its fiscal deficit target. In this case, G is adjusted in such a way that (13) is satisfied. Substituting (13) into (47), we get

$$Y = [\tilde{C}(P(\bar{r}(\phi, P_0), P_0, \phi))]Y + I(\bar{r}(\phi, P_0)) +$$
$$(a + t)Y - \bar{K} = 0 \quad (48)$$

To derive the impact of an exogenous increase in ϕ, we take the total differential of (48), treating all exogenous variables other than ϕ as fixed and, then, solve for dY. This yields the following:

$$dY = \frac{[\tilde{C}'(P_r\bar{r}_\phi + P_\phi) + I_r\bar{r}_\phi]d\phi}{1 - \tilde{C} - (a + t)} \quad (49)$$

Let us now explain (49). Following an increase in ϕ, P rises only by P_ϕ in the absence of the inflation target, reducing aggregate demand by $\tilde{C}'P_\phi d\phi$ at the initial equilibrium Y. This lowers Y by $dY = \dfrac{\tilde{C}'(P_\phi)d\phi}{1 - \tilde{C} - (a + t)}$. This would have been the total contraction in Y in the absence of the inflation target [see (15)]. However, in the presence of the inflation target, following the increase in P by P_ϕ, the central bank will raise r by $\bar{r}_\phi = \dfrac{r_p P_\phi d\phi}{1 - r_p P_{\bar{r}}}$, which in turn will raise P by $P_{\bar{r}} \bar{r}_\phi d\phi$. At the given Y, this will lower demand by $(\tilde{C}' P_{\bar{r}} + I_{\bar{r}}) \bar{r}_\phi d\phi$ reducing Y further by $\dfrac{(\tilde{C}' P_{\bar{r}} + I_{\bar{r}} \bar{r}_\phi) d\phi}{1 - \tilde{C} - (a+t)}$. Thus, in the presence of the inflation target, the contraction in Y will be substantially larger. The increase in P will also be many times more. From (44) and (46), we find that

$$dP = (P_\phi + P_{\bar{r}} \bar{r}_\phi) d\phi \qquad (50)$$

In the absence of the inflation target, increase in the inflation rate is given by the first term of the expression on the RHS of (50). In the presence of inflation target, P increases by the sum of both the first term and the second term of the expression on the RHS of (50). We present our finding in the form of the following proposition.

Proposition 5: When government consumption expenditure is adjusted to meet fiscal deficit target, the contraction in GDP and the increase in the market price of goods and services that take place following an exogenous increase in the rate of inflation become substantially larger in the presence of inflation targeting, and bring about much greater suffering to the workers.

P_0 as the Instrument for Meeting Fiscal Deficit Target in the Presence of Inflation Target

We know that when P_0 is used as the instrument for meeting fiscal deficit target, equilibrium Y is given by (25) and the value of P, derived from (23), is given by (24). We also know that $\bar{r}$ is a determinant of P. Incorporating it in (23) and (24), we rewrite them respectively as (51) and (52):

$$P = \hat{P}\left(\bar{r}, \frac{PG}{Y}; \phi\right) \tag{51}$$

$$P = \overline{P}(\underset{+}{\bar{r}}, \underset{-}{Y}; \underset{+}{\phi}) \quad \overline{P}_{\bar{r}} = \frac{\hat{P}_{\bar{r}}}{1 - \hat{P}_{P_0}\dfrac{G}{Y}} > 0,$$

$$\overline{P}_Y = \frac{-\dfrac{P}{GY^2}}{1 - \hat{P}_{P_0}\dfrac{G}{Y}} < 0, \quad \overline{P}_\phi = \frac{\hat{P}_\phi}{1 - \hat{P}_{P_0}\dfrac{G}{Y}} > 0 \tag{52}$$

Substituting (52) into (25), we rewrite it as

$$Y = \left[c_w \cdot \left(\frac{Wl}{\overline{P}(Y, \bar{r}; \phi)}\right) + c_c \cdot \left(1 - \frac{Wl}{\overline{P}(Y, \bar{r}; \phi)}\right)\right]Y +$$
$$I(\bar{r}) + (1 - c_c)G - \overline{K} \equiv$$
$$\overline{C}(\overline{P}(Y, \bar{r}; \phi))Y + I(\bar{r}) + (1 - c_c)G - \overline{K} = 0 \tag{53}$$

$$\hat{C} = \overline{C}(\overline{P}(Y, \bar{r}; \phi)) \equiv$$
$$\left[c_w \cdot \left(\frac{Wl}{\overline{P}(Y, \bar{r}; \phi)}\right) + c_c \cdot \left(1 - \frac{Wl}{\overline{P}(Y, \bar{r}; \phi)}\right)\right] \tag{53i}$$

We also know that, under inflation targeting, $\bar{r}$ is given by (46). Incorporating (52) into it, we rewrite it as

$$\bar{r} = \bar{r}(\overline{P}(\underset{+}{\bar{r}}, \underset{-}{Y}; \underset{+}{\phi})) \tag{54}$$

To derive the impact of an exogenous increase in ϕ on Y, we take total differential of (53) treating all variables other than Y, ϕ and $\bar{r}$ as fixed and, then, solve for dY. This yields the following:

$$dY = \frac{\bar{C}'\bar{P}_\phi Y d\phi}{1 - \bar{C} - \bar{C}'\bar{P}_Y Y} + \frac{(\bar{C}'\bar{P}_{\bar{r}} Y + I')d\bar{r}}{1 - \bar{C} - \bar{C}'\bar{P}_Y Y} \tag{55}$$

It is clear that in the absence of inflation targeting, $\bar{r}$ would have remained unchanged and following an exogenous increase in the rate of inflation, Y would have contracted by only the first term of the expression on the RHS of (55). However, in the presence of inflation targeting, Y contracts further by the second term of the expression on the RHS of (55). We shall elaborate on this point below.

Under inflation targeting, $\bar{r}$ is given by (54). Taking total differential of (54) and solving for $d\bar{r}$, we get

$$d\bar{r} = \frac{\bar{r}_p(\bar{P}_\phi d\phi + \bar{P}_Y dY)}{1 - r_p \bar{P}_{\bar{r}}} \equiv R_\phi d\phi + R_Y dY$$

$$R_\phi \equiv \frac{\bar{r}_p(\bar{P}_\phi)}{1 - r_p \bar{P}_{\bar{r}}} > 0, \; R_Y \equiv \frac{\bar{r}_p(\bar{P}_Y)}{1 - r_p \bar{P}_{\bar{r}}} < 0 \tag{56}$$

Let us explain the expression on the RHS of (56). The numerator gives the excess of the desired value of $\bar{r}$ over the initial value of $\bar{r}$ following the increase in P due to the increase in ϕ and decline in Y by $d\phi$ and dY, respectively. The central bank will, therefore, raise $\bar{r}$ from its initial value to its desired value. However, per unit increase in $\bar{r}$, the desired value of P rises by $\bar{P}_{\bar{r}}$. Hence, per unit increase in $\bar{r}$, the excess of the desired value of P and the initial P falls by $(1 - \bar{r}_p \bar{P}_{\bar{r}})$, which we assume to be positive and less than unity. Therefore, to remove the excess of the desired P and the initial P, P has to be raised by the expression on the RHS of (56). Substituting (56) into (55) and solving for dY, we get

$$dY = \frac{[\overline{C}'\overline{P}_\phi + (\overline{C}'\overline{P}_{\bar{r}}Y + I')R_\phi]d\phi}{1 - \overline{C} - \overline{C}'\overline{P}_Y Y - (\overline{C}'\overline{P}_{\bar{r}}Y + I')R_Y} < 0 \qquad (57)$$

We shall now explain (57) and in the process show how the contraction in Y that occurs following an exogenous increase in ϕ gets magnified several times in the presence of an inflation target.

Let us delineate how the contraction of Y occurs following the exogenous increase in ϕ. At the initial equilibrium Y and $\bar{r}$, there takes place, vide (52), a cumulative increase in P and P_0 and, finally, P rises by $\overline{P}_\phi d\phi$ [see (24) and (24i)]. However, $\bar{r}$ does not remain unaffected. The increase in P by $\overline{P}_\phi$ induces an increase in $\bar{r}$, which engenders further increase in P and P_0. Thus, a cumulative increase in $\bar{r}$ takes place. Finally, $\bar{r}$ rises by $R_\phi d\phi$ at the initial equilibrium Y. This increase in $\bar{r}$ raises P by $\overline{P}_{\bar{r}} R_\phi d\phi$. Thus, the total increase in P that occurs at the initial equilibrium Y is $(\overline{P}_\phi + \overline{P}_{\bar{r}} R_\phi)d\phi$. This increase in $\bar{r}$ and P will reduce demand by $\overline{C}'(\overline{P}_\phi + \overline{P}_{\bar{r}} Y R_\phi)d\phi + I'R_\phi d\phi$ at the initial equilibrium Y. With $\bar{r}$ remaining fixed at its higher value, Y will fall by

$$dY_1 = \frac{\overline{C}'\overline{P}_\phi Y d\phi}{1 - \hat{C} - \overline{C}'\overline{P}_Y Y} + \frac{(\overline{C}'\overline{P}_{\bar{r}}Y + I')R_\phi d\phi}{1 - \hat{C} - \overline{C}'\overline{P}_Y Y} \qquad (58)$$

(58) gives the contraction in Y that takes place in the first round. In the absence of the inflation target, total decrease in Y would have been given by the first term of the expression on the RHS of (58) [see (26)]. We denote it by dY_{1F} and the second term by dY_{1R} and the increase in P in the absence of inflation targeting would have been only $\overline{P}_\phi d\phi + \overline{P}_Y dY_{1F}$.

Inflation and Stabilisation Policies in India 193

In the first round, $\bar{r}$ and P go up by (59) and (60), respectively:

$$d\bar{r}_1 = R_\phi d\phi \tag{59}$$

$$dP_1 = (\bar{P}_\phi + \bar{P}_{\bar{r}} R_\phi) d\phi + \bar{P}_Y dY_1 \text{ [see (52)]} \tag{60}$$

As Y contracts, fiscal deficit rises above its target and induces an increase in P_0 and, thereby, in P by $\bar{P}_Y dY$ [see (52)]. At the end of the first round, P increases by $\bar{P}_Y dY_1$. This will prompt the central bank to raise $\bar{r}$ by $R_Y dY_1$ (see [56]), which, in turn, raises P by $\bar{P}_{\bar{r}} R_Y dY_1$. The increase in P and r lowers aggregate demand by $[\bar{C}'(\bar{P}_{\bar{r}} Y R_Y) + I' R_Y] dY_1$. This leads to further contraction in Y in the second round by

$$dY_2 = \frac{[\bar{C}'(\bar{P}_{\bar{r}} Y R_Y) + I' R_Y] dY_1}{1 - \bar{C} - \bar{C}' \bar{P}_Y Y} \tag{61}$$

In the second round, the increases in r and P are given by

$$dr_2 = R_Y dY_1 \tag{62}$$

and

$$dP_2 = \bar{P}_{\bar{r}} R_Y dY_1 + \bar{P}_Y dY_2 \tag{63}$$

The increase in P in the second round will induce a further increase in $\bar{r}$ by

$$dr_3 = R_Y dY_2 \tag{64}$$

This increase in r, as in the second round, will lower Y in the third round by

$$dY_3 = \left(\frac{[\bar{C}'(\bar{P}_{\bar{r}} Y R_Y) + I' R_Y]}{1 - \bar{C} - \bar{C}' \bar{P}_Y Y} \right)^2 dY_1 \tag{65}$$

The increase in P at the end of the third round is given by

$$dP_3 = \bar{P}_{\bar{r}} R_Y dY_2 + \bar{P}_Y dY_3 \tag{66}$$

This process of contraction will continue until the fall in aggregate demand that takes place in each successive round eventually falls to zero. Thus, the total decline in Y is given by [upon substituting the value of dY_1 given by (56)],

$$dY = dY_1 + \frac{[\bar{C}'(\bar{P}_{\bar{r}} YR_Y) + I'R_Y]}{1 - \hat{C} - \bar{C}'\bar{P}_Y Y} dY_1 +$$

$$\left(\frac{[\bar{C}'(\bar{P}_{\bar{r}} YR_Y) + I'R_Y]}{1 - \hat{C} - \bar{C}'\bar{P}_Y Y}\right)^2 dY_1 + \ldots$$

$$= \frac{[\bar{C}'(\bar{P}_\phi + \bar{P}_{\bar{r}} R_\phi)Y + I'R_\phi] d\phi}{1 - \hat{C} - \bar{C}'\bar{P}_Y Y - [\bar{C}'(\bar{P}_{\bar{r}} YR_Y) + I'R_Y]} \tag{67}$$

The total increase in P is given by

$$dP = (P_\phi + P_{\bar{r}} R_\phi) d\phi + (\bar{P}_{\bar{r}} R_Y + \bar{P}_Y) dY_1 +$$

$$(\bar{P}_{\bar{r}} R_Y + \bar{P}_Y) dY_2 + (\bar{P}_{\bar{r}} R_Y + \bar{P}_Y) dY_2 + \ldots$$

$$= (P_\phi + P_{\bar{r}} R_\phi) d\phi + (\bar{P}_{\bar{r}} R_Y + \bar{P}_Y) dY \tag{68}$$

It is clear that (67) tallies with (57).

From the above it is evident that inflation target increases manifold both the contraction in Y and the rise in the price level following an exogenous increase in the inflation rate. The above discussion yields the following proposition.

Proposition 6: When administered prices of essential inputs are adjusted to meet the fiscal deficit target, inflation targeting increases manifold both the contraction in Y and the rise in the price level that take place following an exogenous increase in the inflation rate. It, therefore, substantially magnifies the deterioration in the economic conditions of the workers that an exogenous increase in the inflation rate brings about.

Following the line chalked out above, one can easily show that the result summarised in Proposition 6 will hold when indirect tax rates, instead of the administered prices of essential inputs, are adjusted to meet the fiscal deficit target.

Conclusion

The chapter develops a model suitable for India to identify the costs of inflation and to examine how these costs are affected in the presence of fiscal deficit target and inflation target. Normally, the Government of India uses its own consumption expenditure, administered prices of essential inputs and indirect tax rates to meet its fiscal deficit target. Under inflation targeting, when inflation rate rises above its target level, the central bank raises interest rates to bring inflation rate down. We show that when the government and the central bank behave in the ways mentioned above, both fiscal deficit target and inflation target magnify manifold the costs that an exogenous increase in the inflation rate inflicts on society. And these costs are principally borne by the workers.

REFERENCES

Bernanke, B., M. Gertler and S. Gilchrist. 1996. 'The Financial Accelerator and the Flight to Quality'. *The Review of Economics and Statistics* 78(1): 1–15.

Board of Governors of the Federal Reserve System. 2014. 'Average Majority Prime Rate Charged by Banks on Short-term Loans to Business', The Federal Reserve, United States.

Ghosh, C. and A. Ghosh. 2016. *Indian Economy: A Macro-Theoretic Analysis*. New Delhi: PHI Learning Private Limited.
GoI (Government of India). 2013. *Economic Survey 2012–13*. New Delhi: Ministry of Finance.
———. 2014. 'Public Finance'. In *Economic Survey 2014–15*, Volume 2, Chapter 2: 23. New Delhi: Ministry of Finance.
———. 2018. *Budget 2018–19*, Expenditure profile, Statement 2A: 4. New Delhi: Ministry of Finance.
Kaldor, N. 1976. 'Inflation and Recession in the World Economy'. *The Economic Journal* 86(344), December: 703–714.
Kalecki, M. 1954. *Theory of Economic Dynamics: An Essay on Cyclical and Long-Run Changes in Capitalist Economy*. London and New York: Routledge.
Mishkin, F. 2011. 'Over the Cliff: From the Subprime to the Global Financial Crisis'. *Journal of Economic Perspectives* 25(1), Winter: 49–70.
Oxfam India. 2018. *India Inequality Report 2018*. New Delhi.
Patnaik, P. 2014. 'On Controlling Inflation'. *Economic & Political Weekly* XLIX(45): 44–48.
RBI (Reserve Bank of India). 2014a. *Report of the Expert Committee to Raise and Strengthen the Monetary Policy Framework*, January.
———. 2014b. 'Handbook of Statistics on Indian Economy'. Available at https://www.rbi.org.in/Scripts/AnnualPublications.aspx?head=Handbook+of+Statistics+on+Indian+Economy (accessed March 2023).
———. 2016. *Monetary Policy Report*, October.
Singh, Manmohan. 2012. 'PM's Address to the Nation', Speech, 21 September, New Delhi. Available at https://archivepmo.nic.in/drmanmohansingh/content_print.php?nodeid=1226&nodetype=2 (accessed March 2023).

APPENDIX

A.1 Stability of the Equilibrium Value of e

The equilibrium value of e is given by (6) in the text. By assumption, adjustment in e is instantaneous, while that in Y is sluggish. The adjustment rule for e is given by

$$\frac{de}{dt} = -a.B(e, Y; \phi) \qquad a > 0 \qquad \text{(a.1)}$$

Linearising around the equilibrium value of e, which we denote by $\bar{e}$, treating Y and ϕ as fixed, we get

$$\frac{d\tilde{e}}{dt} = -a.B_e\tilde{e}_t \qquad \tilde{e}_t = e_t - \bar{e} \qquad \text{(a.2)}$$

From (a.2) it is clear that the equilibrium value of e is stable if $B_e > 0$.

A.2 Stability of the Equilibrium Value of Y

Equilibrium value of Y, which we denote by $\bar{Y}$, is given by (9) in the text. The adjustment rule for Y is given by

$$\frac{dY}{dt} = b.[\bar{E}(Y, \phi) - Y] \qquad \text{(a.3)}$$

Linearising (a.3) around the equilibrium value of Y treating ϕ as fixed, we get

$$\frac{d\tilde{Y}}{dt} = b.(\bar{E}_Y - 1)\tilde{Y}_t \qquad \text{(a.4)}$$

From (a.4) it is clear that the equilibrium value of Y is stable if $\bar{E}_Y < 1$.

7
INDIAN INFLATION
An Econometric Exploration with
Disaggregated Price Data

Dipankor Coondoo and *Paramita Mukherjee*

Introduction

The Reserve Bank of India has adopted inflation targeting as a goal of monetary policy since 2015 and with this, there has been a change in the way inflation is sought to be managed in India. The focus of policy has now shifted from tracking headline wholesale price (WP) inflation to tracking consumer price (CP) inflation and some new indicators of inflation (for example, inflation based on the new Consumer Price Index [CPI] for urban consumers, rural consumers, and rural and urban consumers combined) are also being examined. However, the design and mechanism of monetary policy depend on whether observed price movements are transitory or permanent in nature. Also the short- and long-run policy implications of observed price movements can be quite different. In this context, it is important for the RBI to ascertain which one of the two price indices, Wholesale Price Index (WPI) and CPI, is more appropriate as the indicator of price movements experienced by the economy, and hence shall be taken as target for monetary policy. For example, according to Cecchetti (1996), the commonly used CPI contains both transitory noise and bias—sources of noise are varying seasonal pattern, changing exchange rate, indirect taxes, etc., whereas a bias may arise due to the weighting diagram, the sampling scheme, and/or the method of quality adjustment implicit in the compilation of the CPI. While a noise causes a short-run change in measured inflation and that leads it to inaccurately reflect the true long-run trend of inflation, a bias leads to the average change in the CPI to be too high or too low. For example, when the structure of relative prices changes, expenditure on more expensive commodities is likely to fall. But the CPI, being based on a fixed set of weights, will show a rise in the aggregate/overall price level due to a change of relative prices, when no such rise in overall price level has actually taken place.

Rakshit (2011) notes that during 2006–11, the Indian economy experienced some curious and unusual features of inflation. For example, during this period the phasing of inflation and GDP are found not to match; even WPI and CPI inflation exhibit dissimilar patterns, varying from a cyclical movement to a steep trend rise, even when GDP falls. In some phases during this period, sometimes the gap between WP and CP inflation narrows and sometimes CP inflation stays systematically below WPI—phenomena that are not normally observed. Also, there is considerable mismatch between WP headline and CP headline inflation in terms of variation in prices of the component indices (Figures 7.1 and 7.2) and their weights. These imply that policy based on CPI and WPI as targets will have qualitatively different implications for the

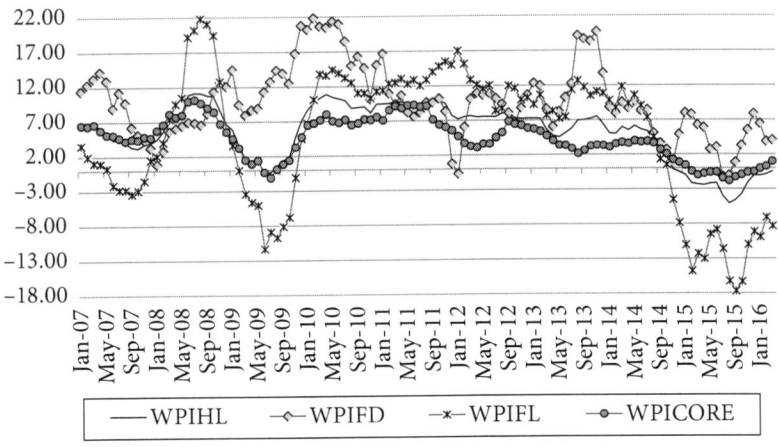

Fig. 7.1: Movement of WPI inflation components

Source: Authors' computation based on data from RBI (n.d.); Office of the Economic Adviser (n.d.) and National Informatics Centre (n.d.)

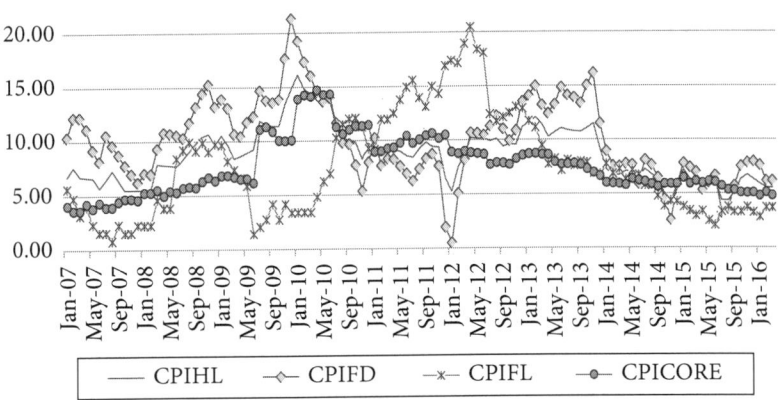

Fig. 7.2: Movement of CPI inflation components

Source: Authors' computation based on data from RBI (n.d.) and Labour Bureau (n.d.)

economy (see Table 7.1). Another important issue is that the relationship between different components of inflation points to the possibility of some adjustment in demand from one set of goods to another taking place, implying corresponding adjustments in terms of relative prices. Actually, inflation can result in absolute as well as relative price changes (relative price change for individual commodities being measured as the weight of a commodity in the price index times the corresponding commodity price change), and therefore, a careful investigation of an observed inflation should be done to examine this aspect of price change as well.

Table 7.1: Weights of components in inflation

WPI Headline	100	CPI-IW Headline	100
WPI Food	14.3	CPI Food	46.2
WPI Fuel and Power	14.9	CPI Fuel, Light, etc.	6.4
WPI Core	70.8	CPI Core	47.5
of which		of which	
WPI Manufacturing	65	Pan, Supari, Tobacco & Intoxicants	2.3
WPI Non-food & Minerals	5.8	Housing	15.3
		Clothing, Bedding & Footwear	6.6
		Miscellaneous Group	23.3

Source: Office of the Economic Adviser (n.d.) and MOSPI (n.d.)

Given the above, the present chapter examines the nature of recent inflation experienced by the Indian economy from two perspectives—(*i*) To understand the role of individual component indices in driving CPI- and WPI-based inflation through an empirical analysis of the interrelationship of these two price indices with their respective component indices (viz., food, fuel and core inflation); and (*ii*) examining (a) the temporal movement of relative prices at a disaggregated level for both WPI and CPI, and also (b) how overall inflation is related to such relative price changes. It may be noted that a comprehensive analysis of inflation based on a careful examination of relative price changes has not been done for India and it is hoped that this analysis will provide new insights about the nature of Indian inflation during the recent past.

The empirical analyses presented here are based on monthly inflation data (CPI for Industrial Workers[1] and WPI) for the January 2006–August 2018 period. For the study of movements of WPI and CPI, the components of WP and CP inflation are analysed based on the Vector Auto Regression (VAR) model framework.[2] The study of the movement of relative prices and its relationship with overall inflation is based on the methodology of Ball and Mankiw (1995) and examines how the asymmetry of the distribution of relative price changes may affect overall inflation.

In what follows, a brief review of the relevant literature is done. In the third section, the data and methodology of the present analysis are described. The results of the analysis are presented in the fourth section, which is followed by a concluding section.

Review of Relevant Literature

Choice of inflation as a target of monetary policy involves several considerations. First, whether core or headline inflation is to be chosen as target for policy can be a debatable issue. Mishkin (2007) suggests that a central bank may focus on headline inflation for medium term and on core inflation for longer term monetary policy. Since headline inflation reflects cost of living, a central bank generally uses this as target and uses core inflation as a supplementary indicator for internal use. However, Bank of Thailand targets core inflation and this seems to be an exception. Cecchetti (2010), contrary to Mishkin's view, suggests that if the target horizon is greater than a year or two, it should not matter whether the central bank targets headline or core inflation.

The next consideration is about whether WP or CP inflation shall be targeted by a central bank. To resolve this, one needs to ascertain which one of WPI and CPI more accurately tracks the observed price movements. While most central banks track

CPI-based inflation, it remains a question as to how accurately this index may reflect the actual inflation. In the Indian context, some experts recommend that the RBI should track CPI since it covers prices of services, has a large share of non-tradables over which monetary policy has significant influence, and reflects the food price movements correctly (Patnaik, Shah and Veronese [2011]). Raj and Misra (2011), in searching for an appropriate measure of inflation to be targeted by RBI, observe that non-food manufacturing price index that RBI uses as a measure of demand-side pressure is the only measure which satisfies all the properties of a core measure, and hence can be a short-term operational guide for monetary policy making. Mishra and Roy (2012), when analysing food price inflation based on a disaggregated high-frequency commodity-level price dataset, note that food price inflation is consistently higher than non-food price inflation, quite persistent, and has a significant pass-through to non-food inflation. Mukherjee and Coondoo (2019) observe that the determinants of CPI headline and core inflation are not the same and so, the central bank should track both of them.

A third and important strand of the inflation literature relates to the relationship between relative price change and inflation, which deals with price changes at the disaggregated level. There are alternative justifications for such relationship in terms of menu costs, asymmetric responses of prices to inflation, monetary search model, and so on. Menu cost models are based on the rationale that since a firm's decision to change price is not costless, it has a range of inaction in response to a shock. When the firm experiences a shock to its desired relative price, it will change price only if the desired adjustment is large enough to warrant paying the menu cost. So, firms respond only to large shocks (Ball and Mankiw [1995]). Thus, compared to a small shock, a large shock has a greater impact on the price level. Using annual data on US commodity prices, Ball and Mankiw (ibid.) show that years of substantial negative skewness in the distribution of relative price changes tend to be years of falling inflation and vice versa. However, a relationship between inflation and the standard deviation of price changes is found to be less obvious. In Ball and Mankiw (ibid.) too, it is shown that an increase in the variance of shocks raises aggregate inflation—even when the price change distribution is symmetric (like in the case of trend inflation), price adjustments become asymmetric. With such asymmetric adjustment, a greater dispersion in shocks raises prices on average because firms facing positive shocks adjust more quickly than those receiving negative shocks.

Another alternative explanation of the inflation-relative price variation relation is as follows: since prices are downwardly rigid and individual markets are affected by relative shocks, prices increase with increased demand, whereas prices do not fall with increased supply. Thus, with greater variability in shocks, inflation rises (Fischer 1981). Assarsson and Riksbank (2003) analyse the relationship between inflation and relative prices for the Swedish economy and observe a significant positive relationship between inflation and the second and third moments of the distribution of relative price changes. Among the few inflation studies involving relative price changes in the Indian context, Senapati and Trivedi (2017) explore the relationship between relative price variability (RPV) and aggregate inflation rate through parametric and semi-parametric methods and determine the optimal inflation rate that minimises RPV. Using monthly WPI data on 244 commodities for the February 1995–March 2014 period, they find a nonlinear relationship between inflation and RPV. An optimal value of inflation rate which minimises RPV is found to be 5.5 per cent. In a similar study, Rather et al. (2014) also find a similar nonlinear relationship for India with an optimal inflation rate of 4.5 per cent. Finally, there is hardly any study that looks into how CP or WP headline and core inflation are related to relative price changes in the Indian context. As a part of the present study, such an analysis is done and reported here, based on monthly data available at the disaggregated level for the new CPI and WPI, which examines if

Indian Inflation 205

for India also, skewness and standard deviation of relative price changes affect the overall inflation.

Data and Methodology

As already mentioned, the present study is divided in two parts. One part contains an examination of the relationship between CPI and WPI headline inflation and their components, and the other part examines the temporal pattern of relative price changes and how the overall inflation is affected by relative price changes. The data and methodology for these two parts are described below.

RELATIONSHIP BETWEEN INFLATION COMPONENTS

The first part of the study is based on monthly data for the January 2006–March 2016 period. The period is chosen keeping in mind that the results obtained will be compared with those of previous studies, in particular Rakshit (2011). A similar dataset is analysed by Mukherjee and Coondoo (2019), but the model specifications are not the same. The price indices considered are Headline CPI (CPIHL) and corresponding Core CPI (CPICORE), CPI Food (CPIFD), CPI Fuel (CPIFL), and Headline WPI (WPIHL) and corresponding Core WPI (WPICORE), WPI Food (WPIFD) and WPI Fuel & Power (WPIFL). CPI is for Industrial Workers is with base 2001 and WPI is with base 2004–05. Core WPI and Core CPI are calculated by stripping off the food and fuel components from the corresponding headline price index. Three macroeconomic variables, viz., agricultural GDP[3] (GDPAG), non-agricultural GDP (GDPNAG) and exchange rate (EXCHRT), are considered here as possible covariates of the price indices. GDPAG and GDPNAG are used as these may be closely related to food and non-food prices and hence may help understand the relationship among components of inflation.[4] Exchange rate is used because of its close link with the fuel price, a major volatile component of Indian inflation. Available data on these macroeconomic variables are converted into index form taking January 2006 as the base. For the purpose of analysis, logarithmic transformation is done of the data on price indices and macroeconomic variables. The basic data are sourced from Reserve Bank of India (RBI) *Handbook of Statistics on Indian Economy*, Office of the Economic Advisor, Government of India and National Informatics Centre (NIC) websites.

As a preliminary analysis, presence of unit root in the individual time series of the dataset is tested by Phillips–Perron (PP) test. Zivot–Andrews (ZA) test is also done for every time series of the dataset to detect presence of structural break in the data, if any. In case a deterministic time trend is found in the time series of a variable, the trend estimated by regression is removed and the residual series is obtained. These residual variables/series are denoted as rCPIHL, rCPIFD, etc. Next, stationarity of the residual series is checked. In case non-stationarity is detected, the first difference of the series concerned is tested further for unit root and its stationarity is confirmed. Note that these first-differenced series, denoted as drCPIHL, drCPIFD, etc., basically measure logarithmic price change, that is, inflation, for a price variable/EXCHRT and growth rate for GDPAG and GDPNAG. Briefly, except for CPIFD, for all the variables, the results of both stationarity tests agree (see Table 7.2).[5] For CPIFD, going by the result of PP unit root test, stationarity is confirmed after removing trend, that is, rCPIFD is stationary and this is used for further analysis. The ZA test results detect break for most variables at 2008–09 or between middle of 2011 to middle of 2013, which coincide with the time of worldwide financial crises.

For studying interrelationships, the variables in each of the following six groups are considered separately. Given the time series nature of the dataset used, for each group of variables a VAR model of appropriate order is estimated. The variable groups analysed are—(*i*) CPIHL components, viz., CPIFD, CPIFL, CPICORE; (*ii*) WPIHL components, viz., WPIFD, WPIFL,

Table 7.2: Summary of stationarity test results

Variable	ZA test statistic	ZA test critical value at 5% l.o.s.	Order of integration (ZA test)	Order of integration (PP test, 5% l.o.s.)	ZA test break points	Time-differenced variable	Presence of UR (PP test, 5% l.o.s.)	Differenced series	Order of integration
CPICORE	−4.51	−5.08	I(1)	I(1)	2009 M07	rCPICORE	I(1)	drCPICORE	I(0)
CPIFD	−5.08	−5.08	I(0)	I(1)	2009 M07	rCPIFD	I(0)		
CPIFL	−3.42	−5.08	I(1)	I(1)	2011 M05	rCPIFL	I(1)	drCPIFL	I(0)
CPIHL	−3.73	−5.08	I(1)	I(1)	2013 M06	rCPIHL	I(1)	drCPIHL	I(0)
EXCHRT	−3.36	−5.08	I(1)	I(1)	2012 M03	rEXCHRT	I(0)		
WPICORE	−4.00	−5.08	I(1)	I(1)	2013 M07	rWPICORE	I(1)	drWPICORE	I(0)
WPIFD	−4.49	−5.08	I(1)	I(1)	2013 M06	rWPIFD	I(0)		
WPIFL	−3.78	−5.08	I(1)	I(1)	2013 M06	rWPIFL	I(1)	drWPIFL	I(0)
WPIHL	−3.88	−5.08	I(1)	I(1)	2013 M06	rWPIHL	I(1)	drWPIHL	I(0)
GDPAG	−8.24	−5.08	I(0)	I(0)	2008 M04				
GDPNAG	−5.85	−5.08	I(0)	I(0)	2011 M10				

Source: RBI (n.d.), Office of the Economic Adviser (n.d.) and Labour Bureau (n.d.).

WPICORE; (*iii*) CPIFD, GDPAG, GDPNAG; (*iv*) CPICORE, GDPAG, GDPNAG; (*v*) WPIHL, WPIFL, EXCHRT; and (*vi*) WPICORE, WPIFL, EXCHRT. The rationale for this grouping of variable sets is as follows: Sets (*i*) and (*ii*) are explored to discover relationship, if any, among own components of CPI and WPI separately; sets (*iii*) and (*iv*) are analysed to examine sectoral linkages;[6] and sets (*v*) and (*vi*) focus on the role of fuel price and exchange rate[7] in temporal variation of inflation.[8]

INFLATION AND RELATIVE PRICE CHANGES

The analysis with disaggregated prices is done separately for WPI and new CPI. For both indices, monthly data (which are the highest frequency disaggregated level data available in public domain) are taken. For CPI headline and CPI core, data are taken for the new CPI, rural and urban combined,[9] for the January 2011–March 2018 period and the base year is 2012. Data on these price indices available for 23-item subgroups are sourced from Labour Bureau, Government of India. This new CPI (henceforth denoted as NCPI) is different from CPI for Industrial Workers taken for the first part of the analysis. For this disaggregated analysis, NCPI is chosen since RBI tracks this now.[10] For WPI headline and WPI core, the sample consists of monthly WPI data for 698 individual items for the April 2012–August 2018 period with 2011 as the base year. These data are sourced from the Office of the Economic Adviser and the National Informatics Centre websites. It is to be noted that the level of commodity disaggregation of the WPI data is much higher compared to that of the new CPI data. For the analysis, all price indices are taken with logarithmic transformation.

Following Ball and Mankiw (1995), we try to detect asymmetry in the distribution of relative prices by analysing separately annual and monthly data sets. For this purpose, commodity-specific relative prices are calculated as change in logarithm of the price index of a commodity times its weight in the new CPI or WPI, as the case may be. This is actually a cross-sectional analysis based on data for 7 (86) annual (monthly) time series of change in logarithm of new CPI and 6 (76) annual (monthly) time series of change in logarithm of WPI. The year-specific distributions of relative price changes are presented here in the form of a histogram for the new CPI and WPI (see Appendix for Figures A7.1 and A7.2, respectively). The extent of variation in relative prices underlying these two indices, measured as skewness (SK) and standard deviation (SD) of the respective distributions of relative price changes of all the commodities for each month, is calculated from the cross-section data of commodity relative price changes. Finally, the relationship between aggregate inflation (WPI and new CPI, headline and core, separately; Figure 7.3) and SD and SK of the relative price distributions are estimated by regression using monthly data set.

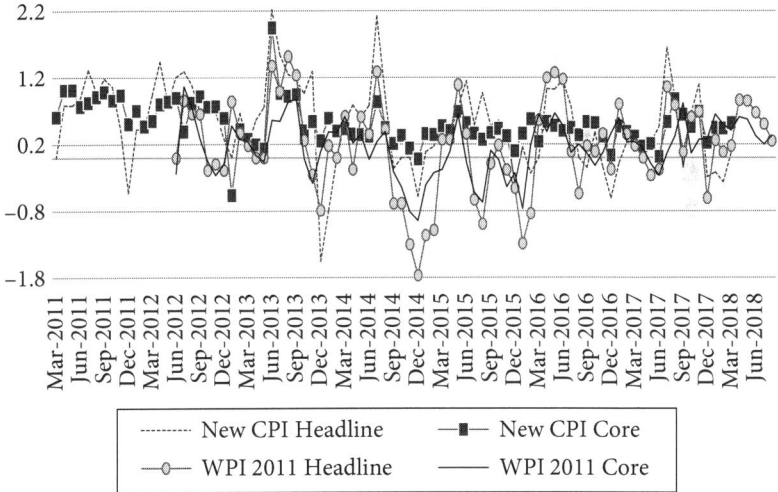

Fig. 7.3: Movement of new CPI and WPI 2011 inflation components (m-o-m)

Source: Authors' computation based on data from RBI (n.d.), Labour Bureau (n.d.), Office of the Economic Adviser (n.d.) and National Informatics Centre (n.d.)

Since a precondition for applying linear regression method to estimate a relationship involving monthly time series variables (like logarithm of WPI or new CPI in the present case) is that the variables have no seasonal unit root; HEGY test (Hylleberg et al. 1990) of seasonal unit root is done for logarithm of NCPIHL, NCPICORE, WPIHL and WPICORE.[11] The results reject the null hypothesis of seasonal unit root at non-zero frequencies. Also, they indicate acceptance of null hypothesis of non-seasonal unit root at zero frequency for most of the series suggesting presence of a stochastic trend in the specific cases. However, for WPIHL and CPIHL, seasonal unit roots at six and 12-month lags, and at 12-month lag, respectively, are detected (Table 7.3).[12]

As the seasonality test results detect non-seasonal unit roots in most cases, ADF (Augmented Dickey–Fuller) unit root test is done and all the series are found to be integrated of order 1. Hence in the subsequent regression analysis, these variables are taken in logarithmic difference form. However, in the text that follows, these variables are referred to as NCPIHL, NCPICORE, WPIHL and WPICORE inflation, respectively.[13] Finally, based on the ADF unit root test, the SK and SD series of both NCPI and WPI groups of commodity prices are found to be stationary. Such series are denoted as SK and SD in respective regressions.

Results

The results for the two sets of analysis described in the previous subsections are presented separately, in the following two subsections. Results in the first set of analysis corroborate some of the findings of Mukherjee and Coondoo (2019).

INFLATION AND ITS COMPONENTS

CPI and WPI Components

The estimated relationships among the CPI components are presented in Table 7.4. These show that CPICORE inflation, which depends on its own previous three-month levels, is not

Table 7.3: HEGY test results for WPIHL, WPICORE, NCPIHL and NCPICORE

Variable	log (NCPIHL)		log (NCPIHL, differenced by lag 12)		log (NCPICORE)		log (WPIHL)		log (WPIHL, differenced by lag 12)		log (WPICORE)	
Model	with intercept		with intercept		with trend and intercept		with trend and intercept		with trend and intercept		with intercept	
Null	Simulated P-value*	Statistical	Simulated P-value*	Statistical	Simulated P-value*	Statistical	Simulated P-value*	Statistical	Simulated P-value*	Statistical	Simulated P-value*	Statistical
Non-seasonal unit root (zero frequency)	0.004*	−3.741	0.424	−1.574	0.207	−2.626	0.825	−1.282	0.007*	−4.199	0.718	−1.019
Seasonal unit root (2 months per cycle)	0.007*	−2.827	0.008*	−2.797	0.021*	−2.285	0.136	−2.216	0.005*	−3.127	0.007*	−2.691
Seasonal unit root (4 months per cycle)	0.003*	4.557	0.009*	4.117	0.000*	7.215	0.001*	9.767	0.0001*	13.372	0.027**	3.329
Seasonal unit root (2.4 months per cycle)	0.001*	6.215	0.0001*	12.587	0.000*	7.660	0.02**	6.879	0.001*	7.495	0.0001*	7.293
Seasonal unit root (12 months per cycle)	0.228	1.337	0.0009*	8.621	0.046**	2.763	0.235	3.146	0.027*	3.312	0.029**	3.111
Seasonal unit root (3 months per cycle)	0.009*	4.333	0.001*	6.320	0.003**	4.681	0.08***	4.712	0.0002*	6.025	0.001*	6.788
Seasonal unit root (6 months per cycle)	0.00	12.998	0.00*	10.650	0.001*	5.565	0.231	3.013	0.006*	4.406	0.017**	3.473
*Monte Carlo Simulations	2000		2000		2000		2000		2000		2000	
Selected lag using AIC (Akaike Information Criteria)	0		5		0		4		3		0	

Note: *1% l.o.s., **5% l.o.s., ***10% l.o.s.

Source: Authors' computation based on data from Office of the Economic Adviser (n.d.) and Labour Bureau (n.d.)

affected by CPIFD or CPIFL inflation—two volatile components of CPI inflation. The CPIFD price is affected, in addition to its own previous two-month levels, by previous three months' CPICORE inflation. This dependence of CPIFD inflation on CPICORE inflation may be an indication of adjustment in demand taking place from one component to the other. There is an indication that it is also influenced positively by CPI fuel inflation. Finally, the only determining factor of the current CPIFL inflation turns out to be CPIFD inflation of three-month lag, apart from its own past lag. This reflects the autonomous

Table 7.4: VAR estimation on components of CPI inflation

	drCPICORE	drCPIFL	rCPIFD
drCPICORE(–1)	–0.206**	–0.056	–0.336**
Standard Error	0.100	0.119	0.145
drCPICORE(–2)	–0.203**	0.029	0.209*
Standard Error	0.101	0.120	0.147
drCPICORE(–3)	–0.152*	0.037	0.386***
Standard Error	0.103	0.122	0.148
drCPIFL(–1)	0.043	0.149*	0.17*
Standard Error	0.084	0.100	0.121
drCPIFL(–2)	0.065	0.095	0.075
Standard Error	0.085	0.100	0.122
drCPIFL(–3)	–0.079	0.004	–0.122
Standard Error	0.084	0.099	0.121
rCPIFD(–1)	0.039	0.039	1.409***
Standard Error	0.064	0.076	0.093
rCPIFD(–2)	0.067	0.101	–0.599***
Standard Error	0.105	0.124	0.151
rCPIFD(–3)	–0.013	–0.142**	0.064
Standard Error	0.067	0.197	0.252
C	–0.0001	0.0001	–0.0001
Standard Error	0.001	0.017	0.022
Adj. R-squared	0.068	0.023	0.870

Note: ***1% level of significance, **5% l.o.s., *10% l.o.s.
Source: Authors' computation based on data from Labour Bureau (n.d.)

nature of the CPIFL inflation. However, the estimated negative coefficient of the CPIFD inflation of three-month lag of the CPIFL inflation equation is not obvious as fuel price in India is mostly supply-driven.

Table 7.5 presents the estimated VAR equations for WPI components. Here, WPICORE inflation solely depends on its own level of one- and three-month lags. This is unlike Rakshit's (2011) observation that lagged fuel price has negative impact on core inflation. However, WPIFD prices, apart from being dependent on its own previous two months' level, turns out to be affected positively by lagged core and fuel inflation. This confirms the statement that in India, food inflation is well known to be not autonomous (ibid.). Interestingly, WPIFL inflation turns out to be dependent, in addition to its own previous-month level, on previous two months' WPICORE inflation. This is in contrast to the observation of Rakshit (ibid.) that fuel prices in India are autonomous as it is tagged to international prices and government policies.

CPI Food, CPI Core and GDP Components

Estimated results of VAR models linking CPI components to GDP components are given in Table 7.6. Panel 1 and Panel 2 of this table present the estimated VAR model comprising rCPIFD, GDPAG and GDPNAG; and drCPICORE, GDPAG and GDPNAG, respectively. Qualitatively the results of this table on the relationship of CPIFD and CPICORE inflation with GDPAG and GDPNAG are basically similar to those of Rakshit (2011) and Mukherjee and Coondoo (2019)—viz., there is evidence of CPIFD price being affected by lagged GDPAG as well as GDPNAG. The coefficient of GDPNAG is negative, like Rakshit (ibid.), though theoretically it should be positive. But interestingly, unlike Rakshit (ibid.), CPICORE inflation is positively affected by lagged GDPAG and it is also observed that it is influenced by lagged GDPNAG.[14] But, what is more interesting is that GDPAG influences CPICORE

Table 7.5: VAR estimation on components of WPI

	drWPICORE	drWPIFL	rWPIFD
drWPICORE(–1)	0.309***	0.747***	–0.163
Standard Error	0.091	0.316	0.344
drWPICORE(–2)	0.109	0.755**	0.200
Standard Error	0.096	0.331	0.360
drWPICORE(–3)	0.229***	0.383	0.519*
Standard Error	0.096	0.334	0.363
drWPIFL(–1)	0.023	0.135*	0.203**
Standard Error	0.030	0.102	0.111
drWPIFL(–2)	–0.033	0.048	–0.053
Standard Error	0.030	0.102	0.111
drWPIFL(–3)	–0.021	–0.119	0.053
Standard Error	0.029	0.100	0.109
rWPIFD(–1)	–0.023	–0.024	1.131***
Standard Error	0.026	0.088	0.096
rWPIFD(–2)	0.018	0.074	–0.280**
Standard Error	0.038	0.132	0.143
rWPIFD(–3)	0.008	–0.045	0.014
Standard Error	0.025	0.088	0.096
C	0.000	0.000	0.000
Standard Error	0.0005	0.002	0.002
Adj. R-squared	0.258	0.274	0.847

Note: ***1% level of significance, **5% l.o.s., *10% l.o.s.
Source: Authors' computation based on data from Office of the Economic Adviser (n.d.)

inflation positively, and CPIFD prices negatively. This suggests that income from agriculture (and also non-agriculture implied by negative coefficient on rCPIFD) is spent on non-agricultural goods by significant measure and is spent less on food. Also, there is a positive impact of GDPAG on GDPNAG, a result which is consistent with dual economy theories that suggest that a rise in agricultural output has a positive impact on the demand side of the non-agricultural sector, both directly and through a rise in the real income of workers.

Table 7.6: CPI inflation and components of GDP

	PANEL 1: CPI Food and GDP			PANEL 2: Core CPI and GDP			
	rCPIFD	GDPAG	GDPNAG		drCPICORE	GDPAG	GDPNAG
rCPIFD(−1)	1.259***	−3.151***	0.109	drCPICORE(−1)	−0.026	−1.835	0.164
Standard Error	0.092	1.167	0.153	Standard Error	0.105	1.829	0.251
rCPIFD(−2)	−0.548***	1.243	0.450**	drCPICORE(−2)	−0.011	−1.165	0.109
Standard Error	0.137	1.725	0.227	Standard Error	0.105	1.829	0.251
rCPIFD(−3)	0.206**	2.384**	−0.477***	drCPICORE(−3)	−0.070	6.417	−0.449**
Standard Error	0.092	1.156	0.152	Standard Error	0.094	1.629	0.224
GDPAG(−1)	−0.019***	0.722***	0.030**	GDPAG(−1)	−0.004	0.855***	0.019
Standard Error	0.008	0.100	0.013	Standard Error	0.005	0.095	0.013
GDPAG(−2)	−0.013	−0.007	−0.003	GDPAG(−2)	−0.002	−0.0003	0.0001
Standard Error	0.010	0.130	0.017	Standard Error	0.007	0.129	0.018
GDPAG(−3)	0.011	−0.773***	0.165***	GDPAG(−3)	0.021***	−0.685***	0.152***
Standard Error	0.009	0.120	0.016	Standard Error	0.007	0.118	0.016
GDPNAG(−1)	−0.094**	2.057***	0.459***	GDPNAG(−1)	−0.092**	2.708***	0.388***
Standard Error	0.050	0.630	0.083	Standard Error	0.038	0.668	0.092
GDPNAG(−2)	0.076	0.064	−0.013	GDPNAG(−2)	−0.013	−0.082	0.007
Standard Error	0.061	0.771	0.101	Standard Error	0.049	0.850	0.117
GDPNAG(−3)	0.021	−1.703***	0.466***	GDPNAG(−3)	0.099**	−2.277***	0.523***
Standard Error	0.048	0.606	0.080	Standard Error	0.037	0.649	0.089

(Contd)

Table 7.6 (Contd)

	PANEL 1: CPI Food and GDP				PANEL 2: Core CPI and GDP		
	rCPIFD	GDPAG	GDPNAG		drCPICORE	GDPAG	GDPNAG
C	0.084***	2.870***	−0.456***	C	−0.040	2.137***	−0.382***
Standard Error	0.032	0.401	0.053	Standard Error	0.021	0.373	0.051
Adj. R-squared	0.891	0.673	0.994	Adj. R-squared	0.066	0.646	0.993

Note: ***1% level of significance, **5% l.o.s., *10% l.o.s.
Source: Authors' computation based on data from RBI (n.d.) and Labour Bureau (n.d.)

WPI Headline, WPI Core and Exchange Rates

Table 7.7 presents the estimated VAR models involving WPIHL/WPICORE, WPIFL and EXCHRT in two panels. Panels 1 and 2 report the estimated models defined on WPIHL, WPIFL and EXCHRT; and WPICORE, WPIFL and EXCHRT, respectively. The following results are noteworthy: (*i*) EXCHRT is affected by WPIFL inflation in the model including WPICORE, but not in the model including WPIHL; (*ii*) WPIFL inflation is affected by EXCHRT and its lagged value—that is, exchange rate depreciation in previous one to three months has significant effect on WPIFL inflation;[15] and finally, EXCHRT shows no impact on WPICORE inflation, whereas its effect on WPIHL inflation is found to be negative (a result which is hard to justify). Results are similar to Mukherjee and Coondoo (2019).

INFLATION AND RELATIVE PRICES

The histograms of year-specific relative price change distributions estimated for NCPI and WPI are shown in Figures A7.1 and A7.2 (see Appendix). For NCPI (Figure A7.1) the relative price change distributions are (*i*) positively skewed for 2012 and 2013 that are years of rising inflation; (*ii*) almost symmetric (that is, SK is positive but close to zero) for the remaining years except 2017; and (*iii*) for 2017, which is a year of falling inflation, SK of the distribution is negative. This pattern of variation of SK of the relative price change distribution is more prominent for WPI (see Figure A7.2). Positive SK is observed for most of the sample years, except 2015 and 2016 for which high negative SK is observed. It may be noted that WPI inflation declined in 2015 and 2016. These observations are thus in line with the results of Ball and Mankiw (1995)—viz., the years of rising inflation have positive skewness of the relative price change distribution, whereas years of falling inflation have negative skewness (Figures 7.4a and 7.4b).

Table 7.7: WPI inflation and exchange rate

	PANEL 1: WPIHL and Exchange Rate				PANEL 2: WPICORE and Exchange Rate		
	drWPIHL	drWPIFL	rEXCHRT		drWPICORE	drWPIFL	rEXCHRT
drWPIHL(−1)	0.350**	0.653**	−0.023	drWPICORE(−1)	0.319***	0.869**	−0.379
Standard Error	0.120	0.306	0.365	Standard Error	0.091	0.301	0.368
drWPIHL(−2)	0.128	0.608	0.230	drWPICORE(−2)	0.103	0.725**	−0.323
Standard Error	0.124	0.317	0.378	Standard Error	0.0968	0.3191	0.3896
drWPIHL(−3)	0.218	0.345	−0.112	drWPICORE(−3)	0.216**	0.328	0.048
Standard Error	0.1236	0.3165	0.3773	Standard Error	0.0969	0.3194	0.3900
drWPIFL(−1)	0.035	0.073	−0.205	drWPIFL(−1)	0.017	0.127	−0.130
Standard Error	0.049	0.126	0.150	Standard Error	0.030	0.099	0.121
drWPIFL(−2)	−0.044	−0.031	0.230	drWPIFL(−2)	−0.038	0.0757	0.319**
Standard Error	0.0480	0.1229	0.1465	Standard Error	0.0290	0.0954	0.1165
drWPIFL(−3)	−0.098**	−0.244**	−0.109	drWPIFL(−3)	−0.029	−0.188	−0.129
Standard Error	0.048	0.123	0.146	Standard Error	0.0288	0.0949	0.1159
rEXCHRT(−1)	0.025	0.142	1.316***	rEXCHRT(−1)	0.020	0.226**	1.288***
Standard Error	0.031	0.080	0.096	Standard Error	0.024	0.079	0.097
rEXCHRT(−2)	−0.098**	−0.348***	−0.436***	rEXCHRT(−2)	−0.041	−0.393***	−0.427**
Standard Error	0.050	0.127	0.151	Standard Error	0.038	0.125	0.152
rEXCHRT(−3)	0.058	0.169**	0.050	rEXCHRT(−3)	0.013	0.140	0.066
Standard Error	0.031	0.079	0.094	Standard Error	0.024	0.078	0.096

(*Contd*)

Table 7.7 (Contd)

	PANEL 1: WPIHL and Exchange Rate				PANEL 2: WPICORE and Exchange Rate		
	drWPIHL	drWPIFL	rEXCHRT		drWPICORE	drWPIFL	rEXCHRT
C	−0.0002	−0.0002	−0.001	C	−0.0002	−0.00001	−0.001
Standard Error	0.001	0.002	0.002	Standard Error	0.000	0.001	0.002
Adj. R-squared	0.259	0.250	0.917	Adj. R-squared	0.206	0.297	0.919

Note: ***1% level of significance, **5% l.o.s., *10% l.o.s.
Source: Authors' computation based on data from RBI (n.d.) and Office of the Economic Adviser (n.d.)

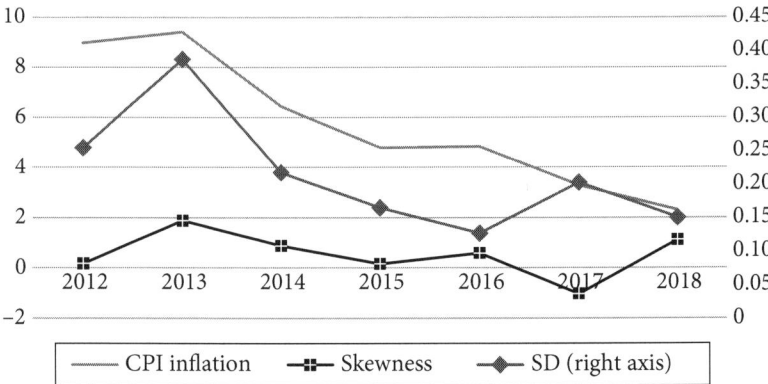

Fig. 7.4a: New CPI inflation and moments of relative price distribution
Source: Authors' computation based on data from Labour Bureau (n.d.)

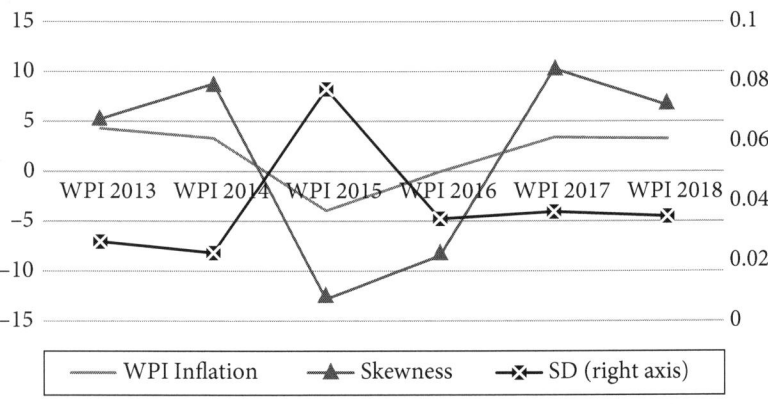

Fig. 7.4b: WPI inflation and moments of relative price distribution
Source: Authors' computation based on data from the Office of the Economic Adviser (n.d.) and National Informatics Centre (n.d.)

To examine if inflation gets significantly affected by SK and SD of relative price change distribution, a multiple linear regression exercise is done based on the available monthly data on inflation and corresponding monthly SK and SD measures of the relative price change distributions separately for NCPI and WPI (with base of 2011) components. The scatter plots for NCPIHL, NCPICORE, WPIHL and WPICORE inflation indicate a positive relationship with SK for all the indices considered except WPICORE. For NCPI, however, this relationship is less clear (Figures 7.5a and 7.5b).[16] The relationship between inflation and SD, however, is found to be much weaker for both the indices. The regression results for

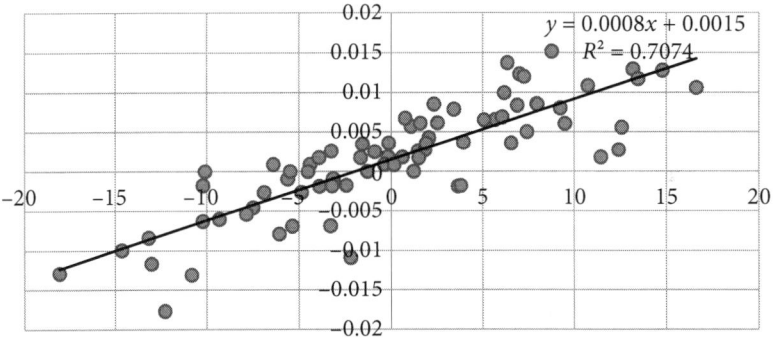

Fig. 7.5a: WPI headline inflation and skewness of relative price changes

Source: Authors' computation based on data from the Office of the Economic Adviser (n.d.) and National Informatics Centre (n.d.).

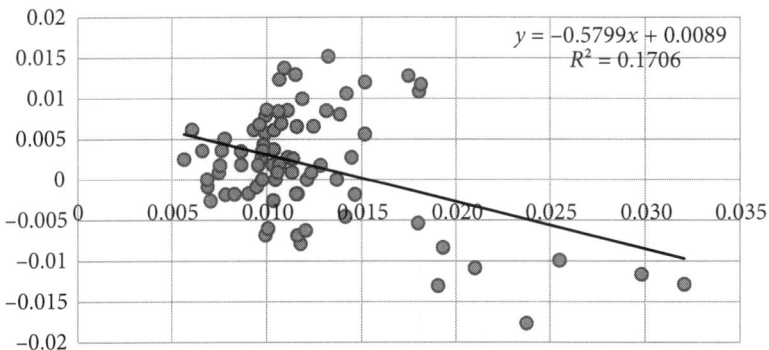

Fig. 7.5b: WPI headline inflation and SD of relative price changes

Source: Authors' computation based on data from the Office of the Economic Adviser (n.d.) and National Informatics Centre (n.d.).

WPIHL and WPICORE are presented in Table 7.8a and those for NCPIHL and NCPICORE are presented in Table 7.8b. In these regression equations, the dependent variable is taken as the first difference of logarithm of the price index concerned (hence the dependent variable measures inflation).[17]

Table 7.8a: Regression for WPI headline and core inflation

Dependent variable	(1) dlogWPIH	(2) dlogWPIH	(3) dlogWPIH	(4) dlog WPICORE	(5) dlog WPICORE
c	0.005	0.006	0.003	0.003	0.003
p-value	0.0002	0.0218	0.0079	0.0011	0.0147
SD	−0.251*	−0.583	−0.132	−0.163**	−0.114
p-value	0.006	0.090	0.118	0.035	0.174
SK	0.0007*	0.001*	0.0006*	0.0003*	0.0003*
p-value	0	0.008	0	0	0
SK*SD		0.008			
p-value		0.5612			
SD^2		16.929			
p-value		0.1475			
AR(1)				0.371*	
p-value				0.0038	
MA(1)		0.388*	0.229**		
p-value		0.0022	0.0404		
MA(2)		0.647*	0.422*		
p-value		0	0.0006		
MA(3)		0.263**			
p-value		0.036			
MA(8)			−0.283*		
p-value			0.009		
Adjusted R-squared	0.73	0.76	0.77	0.43	0.48
D-W Statistic	1.54	2.03	1.80	1.43	1.73

Note: ***1% level of significance, **5% l.o.s.
Source: Authors' computation based on data from Office of the Economic Adviser (n.d.)

Table 7.8b: Regression for NCPI headline and core inflation

Dependent variable	(1) dlogNCPIHL	(2) dlogNCPIHL	(3) dlog NCPICORE	(4) dlog NCPICORE
c	0.0043	0.0032	0.0043	0.0030
p-value	0	0.0006	0	0.0115
SD	0.0047	0.0365**	0.0098	−0.0022
p-value	0.5513	0.019	0.1529	0.9202
SK	0.0018*	0.0001	0.0003*	−0.0001
p-value	0.000	0.5587	0.0043	0.5492
SK*SD		0.0158*		0.004**
p-value		0		0.0474
SD^2		−0.0982		0.052
p-value		0.0935		0.537
AR(1)				0.371*
p-value				0.0005
MA(1)		0.382*		
p-value		0.0011		
MA(2)		0.260**		
p-value		0.0291		
MA(3)		0.297*		
p-value		0.0105		
Adjusted R-squared	0.70	0.88	0.08	0.21
D-W Statistic	1.75	1.96	1.37	2.11

Note: *1% level of significance, **5% l.o.s.
Source: Authors' computation based on data from Labour Bureau (n.d.)

From Table 7.8a, it is evident that marginal effect of skewness on inflation is positive—i.e., as skewness of the relative price change distribution increases, both WPIHL and WPICORE inflation rise. The standard deviation of the relative price change distribution also has a significant negative effect on these inflation measures.[18] However, this significant effect vanishes when seasonal AR/MA terms are introduced as additional regressors to take care of the autocorrelation of residuals.[19] However, the positive effect of skewness is always significant. The interaction term of skewness and standard deviation (introduced to detect nonlinearity of effect of these factors, if any) also fails to be significant. The corresponding results for NCPIHL and NCPICORE inflation are less interesting. As Table 7.8b shows, marginal effect of SK on both NCPIHL and NCPICORE inflation are quite weak. Although a significant positive marginal effect of SK is estimated, inclusion of seasonal MA/AR terms (for taking care of autocorrelation of residual) makes this marginal effect non-significant for both the CPI inflation measures. Interestingly, elimination of residual autocorrelation makes the effect of SD and that of interaction between SK and SD positive and significant for both new CPI inflation measures. However, compared to NCPIHL result, the adjusted R-square for the estimated NCPICORE equation is notably smaller.

Conclusion

This chapter empirically examines the recent Indian inflation from two different perspectives, that is, how the components of WPI and CPI inflation may be related among themselves, and whether the moments of the distribution of relative price changes of the respective constituent commodities of the price indices affect the inflation level. The first part of the analysis is done by estimating appropriately defined VAR models separately for WPI (with base 2004–05) and CPI for Industrial Workers (with base 2001), and the second part is done separately by examining relationship of WPI (with base 2011) and new CPI (with base 2012) with the skewness and standard deviation of the corresponding distribution of relative price changes by regression analysis. Needless to mention, results of both these studies are potentially important from the policy making point of view. An in-depth analysis of inflation and relative prices at the disaggregated level of this kind is new for India.

The findings from the two sets of analysis do indicate some interesting relationships. From the first part of analysis on aggregate inflation, it is observed that in an economy like India, where agriculture faces a lot of uncertainty, quite expectedly, CPI food inflation is explained by agricultural as well as non-agricultural output; but interestingly, it seems that increase in both agricultural and non-agricultural income leads to more spending on non-agricultural goods and less on food. Second, since India has moved to tracking CPI rather than WPI as a monetary policy target, the results of the present study perhaps suggest that the RBI needs to track CPI core inflation along with headline inflation, as the core inflation has influence on other components of headline inflation. For example, CPI food prices are influenced by lagged fuel and core inflation. Third, for WPI, both lagged core and fuel inflation explain food inflation and lagged core inflation influences fuel inflation as well. Unlike Rakshit (2011), neither lagged fuel inflation nor exchange rate has significant influence on WPI core inflation. Thus, WPI core inflation should also be tracked to assess its impact on other components. Fourth, it appears that the effect of exchange rate on overall (WPI) inflation is only through fuel inflation and not through other components like core inflation. But, perhaps the most interesting observation is that the relationships among different components of CPI and WPI inflation suggest the possibility of some adjustment in demand from one set of goods to another, leading to adjustments in terms of relative prices. This observation, in fact, justifies the analysis done in the second part.

The results of the second part also provide some curious insights. First, the distribution of relative price changes of new CPI and WPI exhibit significant positive skewness for most of the years during the sample period. As per Ball and Mankiw (1995) result, when menu costs lead to a range of inaction in response to shocks, overall price level is affected by the distribution of relative price changes. When the distribution is skewed to the right, the economy experiences an adverse shift in aggregate supply and the price level rises for given aggregate demand level. Interestingly, this holds for the Indian economy as observed during the sample period. Years of rising inflation are found to be years of positive skewness for both WPI and new CPI in India, although this positive impact of skewness of relative price change distribution on inflation is found more prominently in the case of WPI. Second, during the sample period of this study, the skewness of the relative price distribution has shown a significant positive correlation with the overall inflation level (particularly with WPI inflation). Third, significant amount of variation in both new CPI and WPI inflation is explained by skewness of relative price changes. Fourth, while WPI headline inflation is explained better by this skewness, WPI core inflation is not and this is not unexpected because the skewness and standard deviation are calculated by taking all commodities/subgroups for the respective indices, and core inflation consists of a subset of such commodities.

Thus, there exists significant asymmetry in the distribution of relative prices in India in the recent past and this skewness does have a significant influence on overall inflation. In the past few years, when the price changes were rising, it aggravated overall inflation and only in one or two years when price changes were falling, it reduced overall inflation. The policy implication of the results of the second part of our exercise may thus be that the headline inflation, which has a stronger relation with variation in relative price changes, needs to be given attention. However, the same analysis will be able to produce better insights for CPI if new CPI data are available at a more disaggregated level like the ones for WPI.

NOTES

[1] Consumer Price Index numbers for Industrial Workers is designed to measure cost of living for a defined population, that is, industrial workers. This index is compiled for industrial workers residing in 70 centres of industrial importance in the country. It

is based on retail prices and is used to determine the dearness allowance of employees in both the public and private sectors.

² In a similar analysis, Mukherjee and Coondoo (2019) considered the components of inflation and their interrelations among themselves and with macroeconomic variables, using VAR models.

³ The monthly time series data on the GDP variables have been constructed by repeating every quarterly value three times.

⁴ Dual economy theories suggest that a rise in agricultural output will have a favourable demand-side impact on the non-agricultural sector, both directly and through a rise in the real income of workers.

⁵ Similar findings on unit root test is observed in Mukherjee and Coondoo (2019), as they use a similar dataset.

⁶ The focus is on CPI food and CPI core inflation since compared to WPI inflation, food and core components have much higher weights in CPI.

⁷ The effect of exchange rate is examined for WPI as fuel price has much larger weight in WPI compared to CPI.

⁸ See also Mukherjee and Coondoo (2019) for some other such estimations of VAR models applied to the similar time period.

⁹ The new CPI has been adopted as the key measure of inflation in India in 2014. This is not computed for a specific group, but rather covers both urban and rural population; 310 towns and 1183 villages are included in the sample and the changing patterns of consumption are incorporated in the weighting scheme.

¹⁰ For the first part of analysis, we had to take CPI-IW for the sake of comparison with earlier studies.

¹¹ In each case, the HEGY test is simulated to examine robustness of the test result. The HEGY test stands for the Hylleberg-Engle-Granger-Yoo Test (Hylleberg et al. 1990).

¹² So, for both these series, 12-month seasonal differencing $(1 - B^{12}) X_t = X_t - X_{t-12}$ is taken and the test is redone. The differenced series are found free of seasonal unit roots.

¹³ In case of CPIHL and WPIHL inflation, the regression is estimated with the variables in seasonally differenced form as well.

However, that does not remove the autocorrelation of residual. Therefore, in these cases the equations are estimated in first differenced form, and seasonality is taken care of by incorporating AR (autoregressive) and MA (moving average) terms of appropriate order.

[14] The estimated coefficients of GDPNAG of lags 1 and 3 for CPI food and core inflation are negative and positive, respectively. In fact, barring the equation for GDPNAG, the sign of the coefficients of GDPAG and GDPNAG with lags 1 and 3 mostly have opposite signs and lag 2 is never significant. This may be due to the conversion of quarterly GDP into monthly GDP by repeating the same quarterly value for 3 months; and thus, the actual effect may not have been captured correctly. Theoretically, there should be a lagged positive impact on inflation.

[15] Again, it may be noted that while the positive sign of the coefficient of exchange rate at lag 3 or 1 on fuel price inflation makes economic sense, the negative sign at lag 2 does not.

[16] The scatters are given for WPIHL only. For CPI, data are available for a small number of commodity subgroups and therefore, the relative price change distributions cannot be obtained reliably. This seems to be the reason for not getting a clear relationship as obtained in the case of WPIHL.

[17] Despite evidences of the presence of seasonal unit roots in WPIHL and CPIHL inflation, these variables are not taken in seasonally differenced form for regression analysis because doing so will transform the equation disturbance term into one having a complex autocorrelation structure, thus complicating estimation of the regression equation. The regressions in first differenced form also suffer due to autocorrelation of residuals, which is taken care of by incorporating seasonal AR and/or MA terms.

[18] The adjusted R-square for these estimated equations are 73 per cent when WPIHL (or 43 per cent when WPICORE) is explained by SD and SK. This indicates a stronger observed relationship of inflation with SD and SK for WPIHL.

[19] The negative sign may be due to few outliers with high SD and negative WPIHL inflation (see Figure 7.5b).

REFERENCES

Assarsson, Bengt and Sveriges Riksbank. 2003. 'Inflation and higher moments of relative price changes in Sweden'. *BIS Papers* No. 19. Switzerland: Bank for International Settlements.
Ball, Laurence and N. Gregory Mankiw. 1994. 'Asymmetric Price Adjustment and Economic Fluctuations.' *The Economic Journal, The Journal of the Royal Economic Society* 104(423): 247–262.
_____. 1995. 'Relative-Price Changes as Aggregate Supply Shocks.' *The Quarterly Journal of Economics* 110(1), February: 161–192.
Cecchetti, Stephen G. 1996. 'Measuring Short-Run Inflation for Central Bankers'. *National Bureau of Economic Research*. Working Paper No. 5786, October.
_____. 2010. 'Monetary policy and the measurement of inflation: prices, wages and expectations'. *BIS Papers* No. 49: 111. Switzerland: Bank for International Settlements.
Fischer, Stanley. 1981. 'Relative Shocks, Relative Price Variability, and Inflation'. *Brookings Papers on Economic Activity* 2: 381–431.
Hylleberg, S., R. F. Engle, C. W. J. Granger and B. S. Yoo. 1990. 'Seasonal Integration and Cointegration'. *Journal of Econometrics* 44(1–2): 215–238.
Labour Bureau. n.d. Ministry of Labour and Employment, Government of India. Available at https://labourbureau.gov.in/ (accessed March 2023).
Ministry of Statistics and Programme Implementation (MOSPI). n.d. Government of India. Available at https://www.mospi.gov.in/ (accessed March 2023).
Mishkin, Frederic S. 2007. 'Headline versus core inflation in the conduct of monetary policy'. Speech at Business Cycles, International Transmission and Macroeconomic Policies Conference, HEC Montreal, Montreal, Canada.
Mishra, P. and D. Roy. 2012. 'Explaining Inflation in India: The Role of Food Prices'. *Indian Policy Forum* 8(1): 139–224.
Mukherjee, P., and D. Coondoo. 2019. 'The Indian Inflation 2006–2016: An Econometric Investigation'. *South Asia Economic Journal* 20(1): 46–69.

National Informatics Centre. n.d. Government of India. Available at https://www.nic.in/ (accessed March 2023).

Office of the Economic Adviser. n.d. Department for Promotion of Industry and Internal Trade, Government of India. Available at https://eaindustry.nic.in/ (accessed March 2023).

Patnaik, Ila, Ajay Shah, and Giovanni Veronese. 2011. 'How Should Inflation Be Measured in India?' *Economic and Political Weekly* 46(16): 55–64.

Raj, Janak and Sangita Misra. 2011. 'Measures of Core Inflation in India—An Empirical Evaluation'. *RBI Occasional Papers* 32(3).

Rakshit, Mihir. 2011. 'Inflation and Relative Prices in India 2006–10: Some Analytical and Policy Issues'. *Economic and Political Weekly* 46(16): 41–54.

Rather, S. R., S. Durai and M. Ramachandran. 2014. 'Inflation and relative price variability: Evidence for India'. *Journal of Asian Economics* 30: 32–41.

Reserve Bank of India (RBI). n.d. *Handbook of Statistics on Indian Economy*, various issues. Available at https://www.rbi.org.in/ (accessed March 2023).

Senapati, Manjusha and Pushpa Trivedi. 2017. 'Relationship between inflation and relative price variability in India'. *Macroeconomics and Finance in Emerging Market Economies* 11(4): 1–16.

APPENDIX

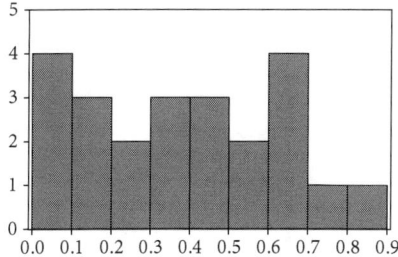

Series: WDLOG12
Sample 1 25
Observations 23

Mean	0.392264
Median	0.388957
Maximum	0.885440
Minimum	0.021748
Std. Dev.	0.254310
Skewness	0.176836
Kurtosis	1.941593
Jarque-Bera	1.193421
Probability	0.550620

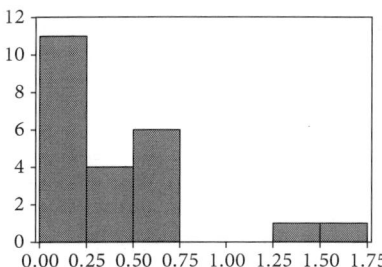

Series: WDLOG13
Sample 1 25
Observations 23

Mean	0.400926
Median	0.291186
Maximum	1.640175
Minimum	0.043984
Std. Dev.	0.386510
Skewness	1.880548
Kurtosis	6.382386
Jarque-Bera	24.52028
Probability	0.000005

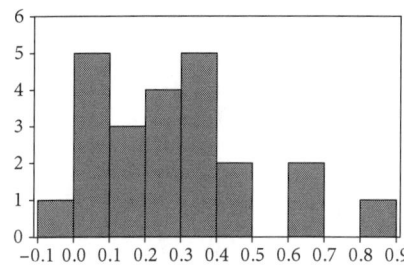

Series: WDLOG14
Sample 1 25
Observations 23

Mean	0.279991
Median	0.235889
Maximum	0.829413
Minimum	−0.018423
Std. Dev.	0.216783
Skewness	0.879359
Kurtosis	3.225774
Jarque-Bera	3.013063
Probability	0.221678

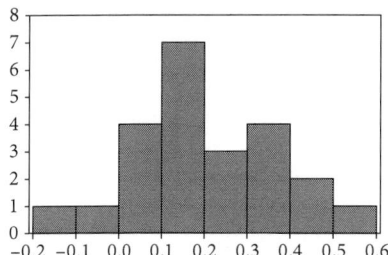

Series: WDLOG15
Sample 1 25
Observations 23

Mean	0.203497
Median	0.196687
Maximum	0.530135
Minimum	−0.107184
Std. Dev.	0.164383
Skewness	0.161719
Kurtosis	2.366088
Jarque-Bera	0.485354
Probability	0.784525

(Contd)

Fig. A7.1 (Contd)

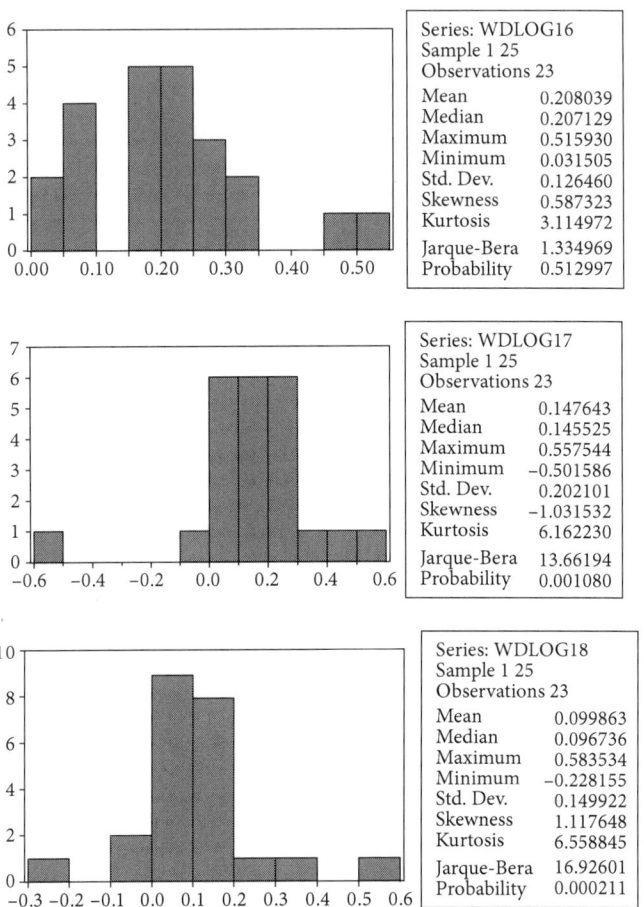

FIG. A7.1: Relative price distribution of new CPI commodities subgroups for 2012 to 2018

Source: Authors' computation based on data from Labour Bureau (n.d.)

Indian Inflation 233

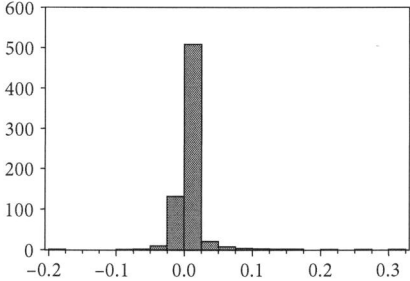

Series: WDLOG2013
Sample 1 700
Observations 698

Mean	0.005530
Median	0.000968
Maximum	0.323205
Minimum	-0.179583
Std. Dev.	0.026428
Skewness	5.226593
Kurtosis	57.25958
Jarque-Bera	88802.21
Probability	0.000000

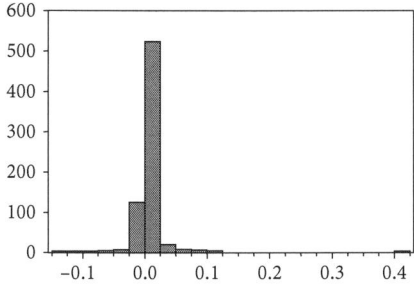

Series: WDLOG2014
Sample 1 700
Observations 698

Mean	0.004589
Median	0.001323
Maximum	0.417856
Minimum	-0.146028
Std. Dev.	0.022690
Skewness	8.778560
Kurtosis	165.8461
Jarque-Bera	780221.2
Probability	0.000000

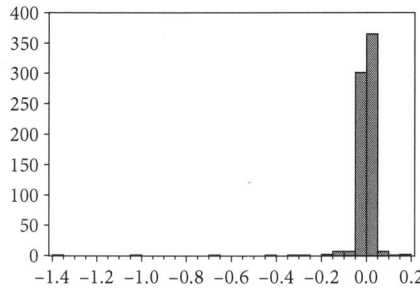

Series: WDLOG2015
Sample 1 700
Observations 698

Mean	-0.006920
Median	2.49e-05
Maximum	0.194054
Minimum	-1.384056
Std. Dev.	0.077388
Skewness	-12.81489
Kurtosis	198.8604
Jarque-Bera	1134778.
Probability	0.000000

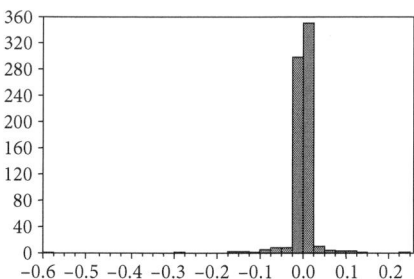

Series: WDLOG2016
Sample 1 700
Observations 698

Mean	-0.001397
Median	2.37e-05
Maximum	0.226669
Minimum	-0.597847
Std. Dev.	0.033988
Skewness	-8.484179
Kurtosis	150.1325
Jarque-Bera	637969.4
Probability	0.000000

(Contd)

Fig. A7.2 (Contd)

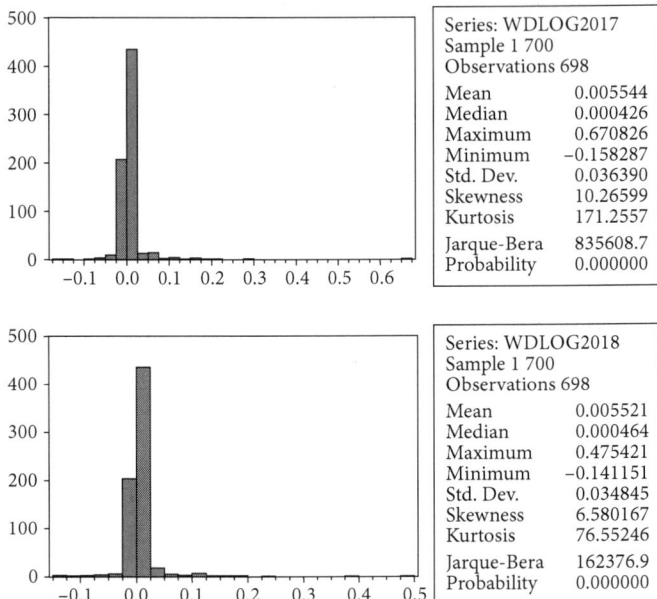

FIG. A7.2: Relative price distribution of WPI commodities for 2013 to 2018

Source: Authors' computation based on data from Office of the Economic Adviser (n.d.)

8
INDIA'S TRADE AND FOREIGN INVESTMENT POLICY
Evolution and Current Issues

Alok Ray

Introduction

India's trade and foreign investment policy has evolved over time. Like any other policy, this is in response to changes in the economic and political reality at home and abroad. This chapter focuses on the sharp break in India's trade and investment policy that took place as a part of the economic liberalisation experiment beginning in 1991. The other major focus of this chapter would be on the important debates in the sphere of trade and foreign investment policy of India at the current juncture when the benefits (and hence the sustainability) of globalisation and multilateralism are being increasingly questioned in many parts of the industrially developed world. Alongside, China is aggressively emerging to challenge the global leadership of the US, which has been the major architect of the post–World War II economic and political order. In this context, what should be the appropriate policy response of India? Among other things, should India switch to selective protectionism, greater exchange rate intervention and strategic regional groupings (instead of multilateralism as enshrined in WTO) in the pursuit of 'fair trade' instead of 'free trade'? As China is gradually vacating the space as a result of rising labour costs while the labour cost advantage of less developed countries in many sectors is being eroded by the emergence of new technologies, should India try to encourage the growth of exports of labour-intensive manufacturing (like textiles and consumer electronics)? If yes, then what kinds of policy reforms are needed in India? Given the rising attractiveness of Indian market, should India impose more conditions on allowing FDI (foreign direct investment) or go for further liberalisation of its foreign investment regime? This chapter will address these and other related questions.

In the following section, we trace the evolution of India's share in global trade and the changes in the commodity and market composition of India's foreign trade basket over time, especially since the economic liberalisation in 1991. We also discuss the process of India's emergence as a destination of FDI. In the third section, we focus on the reasons why Indian industry, despite the initial apprehensions, has been able to successfully cope with external economic liberalisation. The fourth section analyses the evolving global economic and political environment with its attendant challenges and opportunities for India. Next, in the fifth section, we take up the major current debates in the realm of India's trade policy. These are: (*i*) Should India join the proposed Asia-Pacific Regional Comprehensive Economic Partnership (RCEP)? (*ii*) Should India go for selective protectionism or rely exclusively on exchange rate protection? (*iii*) Is exchange rate the main culprit behind export stagnation or are there other factors? In the sixth section, we explore the policy initiatives needed for bringing about a quantum jump in Indian exports. The concluding remarks are presented in the last section.

Evolution of India's Share in World Trade and Composition of Trade and Markets

For more than three-and-a-half decades after Independence, Indian policy makers were believers in 'export pessimism', unlike the so-called East Asian Tigers who pursued a policy of export-led growth strategy. Consequently, India did not pay much attention to increasing exports. Imports were kept at the bare minimum through a stringent system of import control with high tariffs, quantitative restrictions (QRs) and foreign exchange licensing to allow only imports of bare necessities like food grains, oil, industrial raw materials (including gold and precious stones to be used for exports of gems and jewellery), and machinery which could not be produced in India even at high costs. As a result, India's share in world trade shrank from 2.4 per cent in 1951 to 0.5 per cent at the beginning of 1990s. In 1992, India's trade to GDP ratio stood at 17 per cent of GDP (imports at 9.3 per cent and exports at 7.7 per cent of GDP) (Heitzman and Worden 1995).

In the early 1990s, India's major export products were handicrafts, gems and jewellery, textiles and readymade garments, tea, cotton, iron ore along with some industrial machinery, leather products and chemicals. Major imports consisted of petroleum products, capital goods, chemicals, dyes, plastics, pharmaceuticals, uncut precious stones, iron and steel, coal, fertilisers, metals, pulp paper and paper products.

India's most important trading partners were the US, Japan, the European Union, and nations belonging to the Organization of the Petroleum Exporting Countries (OPEC). From the 1950s until 1991 when the USSR broke up, Soviet Union was also a major trading partner. In 1990, our top five export destinations were: Soviet Union (16.14 per cent of total exports), US (14.74 per cent), Japan (9.34 per cent), GDR (7.83 per cent), UK (6.54 per cent). Our topmost import partners consisted of US (10.68 per cent), GDR (8.01 per cent), Japan (7.5 per cent), UK (6.44 per cent).

In 1990, India's Maximum Tariff Rate was 520.93 per cent, Simple Average Tariff was 80.85 per cent while Trade-weighted Average Tariff stood at 56.36 per cent. The HH Market Concentration Index [1] was 0.13 and the Index of Export Market Penetration[2] was 6.22. Trade to GDP ratio stood at 15.67 (World Bank 2018a).

Now, fast forward to 2016 and compare the two snapshots of summary pictures taken in 1990 and 2016. Trade as per cent of GDP in 2016 is at a much higher level of 39.81 per cent compared to 15.67 per cent in 1990. Tariff rates have dramatically fallen with Maximum Tariff Rate coming down to 150 per cent, Simple Average Tariff to 6.91 per cent and Trade-weighted Average Tariff to 6.35 per cent. The value of HH Market Concentration Index has fallen from 0.13 in 1990 to 0.06 in 2016, indicating a fall in market concentration (or rise in diversification) of India's exports, which implies less vulnerability to trade shocks. Over the same period, the Index of Export Market Penetration has risen from 15.67 in 1990 to 39.81 in 2016, implying that India's ability to exploit potential export markets has significantly gone up over the years after economic liberalisation (World Bank 2018a).

The US still remains the top export destination (16.13 per cent) but the importance of other partners has changed drastically. The UAE now occupies the second position (11.54 per cent), next comes China (3.42 per cent), which, together with Hong Kong (5.07 per cent), accounts for 8.49 per cent of our exports and then UK (3.29 per cent). Japan, Soviet Union and Germany have all dropped from the list of top five—in fact Russia does not even figure in the list of top 15 of India's export partners. However, as for sources of imports into India, China occupies the top slot (16.96 per cent), way above the rest. Next in descending order, we have the US (5.72 per cent), the UAE (5.39 per cent), Saudi Arabia (5.18 per cent) and Switzerland (4.16 per cent). China has emerged as the country with which India now has a massive trade deficit (more than $60 Billion in 2017–18) causing trade friction between these two countries.

According to GoI (2018a, b), for 2016–17, manufactured goods account for 73.6 per cent, agriculture and allied products 12.3 per cent and petroleum, crude and coal 11.8 per cent of total merchandise exports of India. Contributions of some major sectors are as follows: gems and jewellery (15.7 per cent), textile, readymade garments and related products (9.4 per cent), transport equipments (7.7 per cent), machinery and instruments (6.9 per cent), metals (4.6 per cent). Textiles and readymade garments—a major creator of low-skill employment in the manufacturing sector in the early stage of economic development of the East Asian Tigers and China—have gone way down the list of India's exports while other countries like Bangladesh and Vietnam have emerged as the major exporters.

The major import products are POL (petroleum, oil, lubricants) accounting for 22.6 per cent of total merchandise imports, capital goods (13.6 per cent), electronic goods (11.2 per cent), gold and silver (7.6 per cent), chemicals (6.3 per cent), diamonds, pearls, semi-precious stones (6.2 per cent), food and allied products (5.6 per cent) and coal (4.1 per cent). The most significant recent addition to the import basket is electronic products (including mobile phones and many other types of consumer durables in finished form or components) and telecom instruments. On the export side, pharmaceutical products, automobiles and auto components have emerged as important export items for India. Balance of trade as a percentage of GDP was −1.46 per cent of GDP in 2016, pretty much the same as in 1990 (−1.42 per cent of GDP) (see Statistical Appendix, GoI 2018a, b).

Exports of services, particularly IT services, were negligible in the early 1990s but have assumed great significance after the year 2000 following the entry of Indian IT firms providing work related to transitioning to the new millennium (known as Y2K work). Once the reputation of low-cost Indian software professionals got established abroad, IT services have been an increasing source of export earnings.

In 2016–17, total service exports were US$ 163.1 billion out of which software services accounted for 45.2 per cent and business services 20.2 per cent of total. Service imports amounted to US$ 95.7 billion, leading to a *surplus* on service account of US$ 67.4 billion. Merchandise trade *deficit* in 2016–17, on the other hand, was US$ 108.5 billion. Thus, our service account surplus reduced the overall trade deficit in goods and services by some US$ 41 billion or 38 per cent of the merchandise trade deficit. However, one troublesome fact is that our service export surplus has been going down over the last few years. Also, India had the highest share of Information and Communications Technology (ICT) exports in total service exports in the world in 2006. Over the last decade of 2006–2016, India's share has marginally gone down from 68 per cent to 67 per cent while several other countries like Israel, China, Russia, Brazil, Philippines and Ukraine have significantly raised their shares. This implies that India is gradually losing its relative advantage over other countries in this area (see Figure 6, GoI 2018b: 160).

Trade (exports + imports) to GDP ratio for India remained virtually static for a long period before globalisation in 1991 but has got a significant boost after 1991. In fact, trade/GDP ratio (in per cent) for India was 15.1 in 1980, 15.2 in 1990, 26.4 in 2000, 41.4 in 2005, 48.3 in 2010 and 49.6 in 2014 (Table 8.1). It is interesting to compare the trade/GDP ratios of India and China over time since 1980.

Among large economies, India's trade ratio (49.6 per cent) in 2014 was higher than that of China (41.5 per cent), US (30 per cent), Japan (35.1 per cent) and Brazil (25.8 per cent) but less than that of Germany (84.8 per cent), UK (58.5 per cent), Russia (51.3 per cent), Italy (55.6 per cent), France (59.2 per cent) and South Africa (64.4 per cent). So, according to this metric of

Table 8.1: Trade/GDP ratio of India and China during 1980–2014

Year	India	China	Comment
1980	15.1	12.5	C < I, China starts to liberalise
1990	15.2	29.5	C becomes nearly double of I
2000	26.4	39.4	I picking up since 1990
2005	41.4	62.9	Peak for C and then falling
2010	48.3	49.3	C and I virtually equal
2014	49.6	41.5	I > C

Note: C stands for China's trade/GDP ratio; I stands for India's trade/GDP ratio.
Source: Different publications of World Bank

openness, India falls somewhere in the middle range of large open economies.[3] India's share in world trade of *merchandise* in 2014 was only 1.7 per cent, as against the other BRICS countries—China (12.1 per cent), Russia (2.9 per cent), Brazil (1.3 per cent) and South Africa (0.5 per cent). In exports of *manufactured goods*, India's share of world exports in 2013 was a meagre 0.7 per cent, compared to the corresponding shares of China (17.5 per cent), US (9.5 per cent), Japan (5.3 per cent), and South Korea (4.1 per cent). Clearly, even after more than two decades of economic globalisation, India is way behind in exports of manufactured goods, which is one of the main reasons for India's low per capita income and huge underemployment of workers in low productivity agriculture and related occupations. The picture changes dramatically if one looks at exports of computer and information services. Here, if we leave aside the 27-member EU (with share of 58.4 per cent in global exports), India ranks the highest in terms of per cent share in total world exports of these services. The shares of leading exporters are: India (19.7 per cent), US (7.3 per cent), China (6 per cent), Canada (3.3 per cent), Israel (1.8 per cent), Philippines (1.0 per cent), Russia (0.9 per cent), Malaysia (0.9 per cent), and Costa Rica (0.8 per cent).[4]

In addition to services, India is also emerging as an important exporter of agricultural products. The share of agricultural exports in total exports for India in 2014 was 15 per cent, as against the leading exporters: Uruguay (75 per cent), New Zealand (68 per cent), Kenya (54 per cent), Argentina (51 per cent), Brazil (37 per cent), Pakistan (22 per cent), Australia (15 per cent), Canada (14 per cent), US (11 per cent). China's share is only 3.2 per cent.

India's largest trading partners in terms of total trade (sum of imports and exports) for the financial year 2016–17 were as follows.

Table 8.2: India's top 7 major trading partners in 2016–17 (in US$ billion)

Rank	Country	Exports	Imports	Total trade	Trade balance
1.	China	16.34	68.06	84.4	−51.72
2.	US	48.6	25.7	74.3	22.9
3.	UAE*	30.29	19.45	49.74	10.84
4.	Hong Kong	13.7	20.34	34.04	−6.64
5.	Saudi Arabia	6.39	20.32	26.72	−13.93
6.	Switzerland	0.98	19.30	20.28	−18.32
7.	Germany	7.09	12.09	20.33	−5.25

Note: *UAE's large share in India's exports is partly because of trade conducted between India and Pakistan, through UAE.
Source: Wikipedia (n.d.); WITS (2016 and 2017)

In terms of India's trade deficit in 2016–17 (total exports = US$ 262.29 billion, total imports = US$ 381.01 billion, total trade balance = US$ −118.72 billion), the top trading partner countries were (in US$ billion): China (−51.72), Switzerland (−18.32), Saudi Arabia (−13.93), Qatar (−13.55), Iraq (−13.42), Kuwait (−12.8), Venezuela (−11.47), Nigeria (−11.0), Indonesia (−10.96), South Korea (−8.93), Australia (−7.47), Hong Kong (−6.64), Malaysia (−5.30), Belgium (−5.29), Germany (−5.25), Japan (−4.75), Iran (−4.78), South Africa (−3.40). By contrast, India had a trade surplus with US (US$ 22.9 billion), UAE (US$ 10.84 billion), UK (4.30) and Singapore (2.68).

So, except for China, Hong Kong (which can be considered an extension of China), South Korea, Japan and Germany (all are global powerhouses of manufacturing including sophisticated machinery, steel and chemicals), India's major trade deficit is with countries from which India imports crude oil, natural gas and other mineral resources like coal and agricultural products like edible oil. India's trade deficit vis-à-vis Switzerland and Belgium is largely due to imports of machinery, gold, diamonds and other precious metals, mostly used for jewellery. Though a lot of attention is given to the big and rising trade deficit with China, it should be clear from the figures above that our combined trade deficit against all the energy (oil, gas, coal, etc.,) exporting countries is much higher. With the help of foreign collaboration and development of indigenous engineering skills along with improved 'ease of doing business' and various 'Make in India' initiatives, India is making gradual progress in manufacturing sophisticated machinery, equipment and military hardware, which it has so far been importing from the developed counties of the West and the East. Imports of gold, diamonds and other precious stones and metals are mostly used for making jewellery which is exported.

Thus, the major problem area remains the high value of deficit in energy trade. Though India is a significant exporter of refined petro products, its oil import bill is much higher and is subject to wide variation due to fluctuations in global prices of petro products. For example, in (most of) 2014 when oil prices were particularly high, import of oil stood at US$ 177.5 billion (38.3 per cent of total commodity imports) while the export of refined oil was US$ 62.2 billion (19.2 per cent of total commodity exports), implying a net trade deficit in oil of US$ 116.3 billion. So, our topmost priority should be reducing this energy trade deficit by exploring new sources of fossil fuel like petroleum, natural gas, shale oil, coal along with the development of alternative energy sources like solar and wind power. National resources would be much better utilised if, instead of trying to send a human to space,[5] India uses these to develop alternative renewable energy sources like solar, wind and bio fuels. Unless the net energy import bill is contained, our overall trade deficit, exchange rate, inflation and fiscal deficit would remain subject to external forces beyond our control.

INDIA AS A DESTINATION OF FDI

The FDI data from different sources vary widely. Subject to this caveat, we can make some observations.

According to RBI data (from RBI Annual Reports of different years), India received US$ 9.3 billion of net FDI in 2006–07, US$ 22.6 billion in 2008–09, US$ 14.9 billion in 2010–11, US$ 23.4 billion in 2011–12, US$ 18.2 billion in 2012–13, US$ 16.1 billion in 2013–14, US$ 24.7 billion in 2014–15, US$ 36.1 billion in 2015–16, US$ 36.3 billion in 2016–17 and US$ 37.4 billion in 2017–18.

Clearly, FDI flows into India has fluctuated a lot over time—a big jump between 2006–07 and 2008–09 and then a fall in 2010–11, again a sharp rise in 2011–12, followed by a sharp fall and again a big boost between 2013–14 and 2015–16 and finally stabilising. That India has come a long way is evidenced by the fact that net FDI into India in 1990–91 was a negligible US$ 1.4 million. The ebbs and flows in FDI are linked to the overall global economic situation, changing attractiveness of different countries as investment destinations, lumpiness of some big investment projects, and India-specific factors like its future growth prospects, political stability and policy changes with respect to sectoral openings under FDI, domestic content requirements, export obligations, tax laws, tariff rates, simplification of procedures, and so on.

According to the *Financial Times*, in 2015 India overtook China and the US as the top destination for FDI (*The Times of India* 2015). But it is not clear how they came to this conclusion. According to UNCTAD (United Nations Conference on Trade and Development) data, in 2015 (see Annex Table 1 in UNCTAD 2017), FDI inflow, outflow, and hence net inflow for India were US$ 44.1 billion, US$ 7.6 billion and US$ 36.5 billion, respectively. The corresponding figures for the US were

US$ 348.4 billion, US$ 303.2 billion and US$ 45.2 billion while for China they were US$ 135.6 billion, US$ 127.6 billion and US$ 8.0 billion and for UK, US$ 33.0 billion, US$ 82.1 billion and US$ –49.1 billion. So, no matter whether we take the gross inflow or net inflow, India did not get the topmost slot as FDI destination in 2015, though in terms of net inflow it occupied the second position, just below the US.

If we take data on net FDI inflows for different countries in 2017 (latest available data) as compiled by World Bank from different sources (World Bank 2018b), India received US$ 33.9 billion as against US (US$ 354.8 billion), Netherlands (US$ 316.5 billion), China (US$ 168.2 billion), Hong Kong (US$ 122.4 billion), Germany (US$ 77.9 billion), Brazil (US$ 70.6 billion), UK (US$ 64.6 billion), Singapore (US$ 63.6 billion) and France (US$ 47.3 billion), thereby attaining tenth position among all countries.[6]

According to RBI (2018, see Table: Foreign Direct Investment flows to India), in 2017–18, India received FDI of US$ 37.4 billion out of which the major sources are: Mauritius (US$ 13.4 billion), Singapore (US$ 9.2 billion), Netherlands (US$ 2.6 billion), US (US$ 1.9 billion), Japan (US$ 1.3 billion), Cayman Islands (US$ 1.1 billion) and Germany (US$ 1.1 billion). That Mauritius (with virtually no manufacturing activity) and Singapore (primarily a trading and financial centre and now home to some service industries) together account for more than 60 per cent of FDI inflows into India gives rise to the suspicion that a large part of this money could be 'round tripping' of funds ('black' or 'white' in the first instance) by Indians who first send money to these countries (even ordinary Indians can remit up to $ 2,50,000 each year legally under the Liberalised Remittance Scheme) and bring back as 'foreign investment' (even without disclosing names by using P-Notes) to derive tax advantages.

It should also be mentioned that sometimes there is a wide discrepancy between the FDI data given by RBI and that announced by the Government of India. For example, in

2017–18, while RBI data mentions US$ 37.4 billion as FDI, Department of Industrial Policy and Promotion (DIPP), GoI, talks of US$ 61.96 billion (see *The Economic Times* 2018a).

Irrespective of the discrepancies in FDI figures from different sources, there is no doubt that India is gradually becoming a more attractive destination for FDI and foreign investors would bring in more funds if the sectoral caps on FDI are relaxed and more reforms are carried out in the areas of labour laws, land acquisition and administrative red tapes. In this context, despite the limitations of all such summary indices, the big improvement in India's ranking (by 65 positions from 142 in 2014 to 77 in 2018) in 'Ease of Doing Business' index of the World Bank, while China's ranking has gone down by 27 positions over the same period, is a big positive for India in attracting foreign investment (see Kant 2018, for more details). However, even here we should note that in some crucial areas like 'Enforcing contracts' and 'Starting business', India's rank in 2018 remains a lowly 163rd and 137th, respectively, leaving considerable scope for improvement.

How Indian Producers are Coping with Globalisation

A sharp break in India's trade and investment policy took place as a part of the economic liberalisation experiment beginning in 1991. Though there was a general consensus in favour of domestic liberalisation, external sector liberalisation was the most controversial component of the package at the time of its inception. The passage of more than a quarter century since then gives us the opportunity to look back and objectively evaluate the costs and the benefits of the experiment.

There were two major apprehensions. First, our meagre foreign exchange reserves would further dwindle and we would be at the mercy of the IMF and World Bank for our economic survival. Exactly the opposite has happened. Our foreign exchange reserves have gone up from $ 1.1 billion at the height of the 1991 economic crisis to more than $ 400 billion with India currently occupying the sixth position in terms of reserves after China, Japan, Switzerland, Taiwan and Hong Kong, and ahead of South Korea, Brazil, Russia and Singapore.

The second apprehension was that Indian producers (and exporters) would not be able to compete with established foreign producers and there would be deindustrialisation in India. But, again, Indian producers have proved the doubters wrong. No Indian industry has gone down, though some firms within an industry have gone bankrupt or have been taken over by more efficient Indian firms. That is part of the rules of the game in a competitive liberalised regime. Looking back, we can identify several factors that have helped Indian producers to cope with the process of globalisation.

Instead of following a 'big bang' approach, India has liberalised its economy in a gradual calibrated fashion, giving producers the time to adjust. To some extent, the pace of tariff reduction was also influenced by the resultant loss of tariff revenue that the government could withstand. Despite the huge reduction in peak (non-agricultural) customs duty, India's average tariff rates are still above the ASEAN (Association of Southeast Asian Nations) levels.

Indian government has maintained a high degree of agricultural protection (even as high as 50 per cent to 80 per cent tariff rates for some 'sensitive' products) to make globalisation politically acceptable in a country with about 60 per cent of the population (mostly small farmers and landless labourers) depending on agriculture with no alternative means of livelihood.

Along with the gradual import duty reduction, the exchange rate of the rupee has depreciated substantially since 1991. One dollar worth of imports which used to cost about Rs 15 in 1991 is worth Rs 80 now. So, an Indian producer of a similar product can now charge up to Rs 80 compared to Rs 15 in 1991. This implies 433 per cent [= {(80−15)/15} × 100%] uniform nominal protection (or 433 per cent uniform import duty plus export subsidy), relative to 1991. Basically, exchange rate protection has more than replaced the traditional tariff protection. Of course, the rate of real depreciation of the rupee has been less, to the extent the rate of inflation in India has exceeded that in the competing countries.

In the face of attempts to 'dump' goods by foreigners in Indian markets, temporary anti-dumping duties (ADDs) have been used liberally by the Indian government. As a matter of fact, at one time, India had the dubious distinction of imposing the highest number of ADDs imposed by any country.

Lower tariffs did not hurt all Indian producers. Any reduction in import duties on inputs (say, steel) benefits the user industry (say, the automobile industry) while the domestic producers of similar products (say, the domestic steel industry) face stiffer competition. Hence, some producers gained while others lost. For example, Tata Motors may gain while Tata Steel loses. Consequently, from the very beginning, Indian industrialists were divided on the issue of liberalising imports of goods, technology and FDI. In fact, with the passage of time, many of the initial opponents of globalisation (like Rahul Bajaj, the most prominent member of the so-called 'Bombay Club' opposing globalisation) turned into supporters as they learned (like Bajaj working out a joint venture to form Kawasaki-Bajaj to contain Hero-Honda) how to make use of the new opportunities thrown up by globalisation, often by forging strategic alliances with foreign partners.

The Indian market is not a homogeneous unified market. India is a vast country with people and regions with widely divergent income levels and 'tastes'. Entry of branded sophisticated products touches the huge mass market for indigenous products marginally. Here (for example) both Sony and Santosh (an Indian company manufacturing low-end audio systems), Frito Lays and traditional potato/ banana chips, Baskin Robbins and Kwality ice creams, Swiss chocolates and Amul chocolates can coexist, provided the price differential is right and the products are positioned correctly in the appropriate markets.

India is now the fastest growing big economy in the world. In a growing market it is not a zero-sum game. For instance, the markets for bicycles, two-wheelers and four-wheelers or flat-screen LED TVs and basic colour TVs are all expanding at the same time as, along with people graduating to higher income levels and buying higher-end products, more people are entering into the basic categories. Also, the scope for product differentiation is enormous in today's world. Hence, many competing firms are simultaneously prospering through product differentiation and catering to different market segments. Most of the major auto, consumer appliance and cell phone companies are setting up production facilities in India to exploit the huge potential market in India as well as using India as a cheap production location (specially after China is fast losing its low wage advantage) to sell in the neighbouring markets in South and Southeast Asia.

India has a long history of entrepreneurship. After liberalisation, energy and efforts have been released from lobbying/license hunting to improvement in productive efficiency. This has paid rich dividends. More competition has enforced greater efficiency on Indian producers. Competition has come from several sources—from other domestic players as industrial licensing (which used to limit competition by preventing expansion by the more efficient Indian firms) ended, from imports and from producing for the highly competitive export market. As a result, both the quality and the cost competitiveness of Indian products have improved a lot. After the substitution of product patent for process patents, several Indian pharmaceutical companies (like Ranbaxy, Lupin, Reddy's Lab) have changed their focus from reverse engineering ('copying') of technologies to development of new molecules, supplying bulk drugs to foreign companies, switching production to generic and off-patent drugs and doing contract research for big multinational pharmaceutical companies. Foreign sales of some of these firms exceed their domestic sales.

Indian companies have used FDI and strategic alliances (like joint ventures, licensing, franchising) to derive advantages of foreign brands, technologies and global marketing channels. For example, Indian car maker Maruti (a joint venture with Suzuki of Japan) was able to sell cars at home and abroad, on the initial strength of the Suzuki brand.

As the domestic market has become more competitive, Indian firms are being forced to go abroad in search of new markets, new sources of raw materials and cheaper production facilities with different technologies (in all five continents of the world), and to get rid of the 'Made in India' stigma. Also some Indian firms are locating production facilities near the foreign markets to modify products according to local tastes and to provide better servicing facilities.

As a result of more competition, we see both specialisation in a narrower range of products and diversification in new lines. Mergers and acquisitions (at home and abroad) are taking place to gain economies of scale, economies of scope (reduction in unit cost by producing a wider range of products) and access to ready markets, distribution channels, brands, raw materials (like captive iron-ore mines), complementary product-mix and already running production facilities with different technologies. For example, Tata Steel has acquired Corus, a giant Anglo-Dutch steel company, to consolidate its position in the global steel market (TATA Steel 2007). Tata Motors has purchased Jaguar and Land Rover brands. Tata Tea has acquired a stake in Energy Brands, a US company producing energy drinks (*The Economic Times* 2006a), and Tata Coffee has acquired some bestselling brands (like energy health drinks and Eight O' Clock Coffee) in the US (*The Economic Times* 2006b). There have been offshore acquisitions by Dr. Reddy's (*Equity Bulls* 2022), Ranbaxy, Godrej (*Business Standard* 2013), HCL Technologies, Escorts, Bharat Forge, AV Birla group, Apollo Tyres and a host of other Indian companies. Mahindra is selling SUVs in large numbers in US. Indian IT companies Infosys, Wipro and Tata Consulting Services (TCS) are now globally known. A part of the Tata group, India's largest multinational business group, TCS has over 556,000 of the world's best-trained consultants in 46 countries, representing a diverse workforce comprising 156 nationalities (TCS 2022). Foreign investment is no longer a one-way street.

As more and more countries are going for regional trading blocs, Indian companies are also undertaking tariff-jumping FDI. They are setting up factories within such blocs like NAFTA (North American Free Trade Agreement), the EU, ASEAN, in order to escape the discriminatory tariffs against non-member countries and to get unhindered access to big regional markets. In addition, India is in the process of signing FTAs (free trade agreements) and various other economic cooperation arrangements with its Asian neighbours (with appropriate safeguards for 'sensitive' agricultural and industrial products) which should facilitate more two-way trade and investment flows.

The process of outward FDI and foreign acquisitions has been helped by the relaxation of restrictions on foreign investment by Indian companies abroad (though there is not yet full capital account convertibility for Indian companies and residents), following the build-up of a comfortable foreign exchange buffer for the country. Moreover, reputed Indian companies are now able to borrow money abroad at cheaper rates to finance expansion plans in India and abroad.

Globalisation has also enabled a lot of learning through direct contacts. Indian companies and business people have been exposed to new products, different and in some cases better production, inventory, quality, personnel and marketing management techniques while visiting foreign companies and markets. Incorporation of new ideas has improved productivity and efficiency.

Availability of cheap engineering and other skilled (including R&D) workers is giving India an edge in services and high skill or brain-intensive manufacturing. Regarding the speed and cost of moving from a new concept to prototype to commercial production, India is more favourably placed than US and Europe in several areas. This has been proved by auto component manufacturers in India. This ability to constantly improve component design is one major reason why small car manufacturers like Suzuki and Hyundai have made India not only a hub for exports but for global R&D as well. In addition to simple call centre-type BPO (Business Process Outsourcing) activities, India's service industry is now moving up the value chain to higher value software development, design and re-engineering of products and processes and R&D services in various fields—collectively known as KPO or Knowledge Process Outsourcing. Many well-known foreign companies (like IBM, Microsoft, Google, Walmart, GM, Cisco Systems, Adobe and several pharma companies) have shifted or are in the process of shifting significant parts of their R&D centres to India which is providing thousands of high-value jobs to Indian professionals within India, more so after several US administrations are making the process of acquiring H-1B visas more difficult for Indian professionals.

Stiffer competition at home due to globalisation has forced foreign companies to search for cheaper production and service locations in countries like India and China. If today China is the world's factory, India is known as the global back office. In addition, the availability of natural resources like coal, iron ore, bauxite is attracting foreign steel and metal companies (like Korean steel giant POSCO, and Arcelor Mittal of Indian ex-patriate L. N. Mittal, and Vedanta Group of companies of ex-patriate Anil Agarwal) to set up factories in India.

It is no longer the case that all MNCs are thriving relative to Indian companies. For example, Bata, Glaxo, Daewoo, GM, IBM did not do so well compared to Indian (or Indian joint-venture) companies like Khadim, Ranbaxy, Reddy's Lab, Maruti-Suzuki and TCS. In a liberalised competitive market, the success of a company does not depend on whether it is primarily Indian- or foreign-owned. A lot hinges on the business strategies, areas of strength and alliances forged by the different companies.

The Global Economic Environment

The benefits (and hence the sustainability) of globalisation and multilateralism are being increasingly questioned, as reflected in the voting patterns as well as the rhetoric of politicians, in many parts of the industrially developed world. US President Donald Trump, in pursuing his 'America first' policy, undermined the multilateral foundations of global trade, as enshrined in WTO rules by taking unilateral actions in imposing tariffs and various other restrictions on trade against many countries of the world. It started with additional US tariffs on steel and aluminium imports from all countries of the world by invoking the seldom-used provision of 'national security' under WTO rules. But it did not stop there. The US is gradually escalating the trade war between US and China, by successively raising tariffs on additional imports, followed by retaliatory tariffs by China on US goods. Alongside, the US, in addition to coming out of the proposed Trans-Pacific Partnership (TPP), has forced Canada and Mexico to renegotiate the NAFTA and is in the process of renegotiating FTA with other countries like South Korea. US under Trump was in favour of bilateral negotiations with countries as it hoped to extract better deals favouring US interests than is possible under the multilateral non-discriminatory rules of WTO. The US is even threatening to disobey the rulings of WTO courts if the verdict goes against the US. The post–World War II goal of moving toward 'free trade' is being replaced by 'fair trade', variously interpreted by different countries. Though the Biden administration is apparently making efforts to reverse some of the steps taken under the Trump administration, it is not clear to what extent it would succeed, given the stronghold that hardline Republicans have in the US Congress (*Chatham House* 2021; *CNBC* 2020).

The Brexit decision by British voters is a major blow to economic unification of Europe and, more generally, to globalisation. Also, the idea of 'currency union' in the form of a single currency 'Euro' is increasingly coming under stress by economic crisis in several countries of the Eurozone like Greece, Italy, Spain, Ireland and Portugal. As a result, the prospect of Euro attaining the status of an international reserve currency at par with the US dollar has received a severe dent, which is giving further boost to the hegemony of US dollar. No doubt, with the rise of China as a super economic power with huge savings to lend abroad, the yuan is increasing in importance. But the chances of yuan challenging US dollar in a big way in international transactions and as a global reserve currency are not high in the near future.

The US economy has, at long last, recovered from the 'Great Recession' of 2007, clocking a respectable GDP growth rate while unemployment has reached the lowest level since 1969, putting upward pressure on inflation and wage rate. In response, the US Fed has started rewinding its soft money policy (known as *QE* or quantitative easing). This has important implications for capital flows to and from emerging economies like India, affecting their BOP and exchange rates.

China is aggressively emerging to challenge the global leadership of the US that has been the major architect of the post–World War II economic and political order. US, under Trump, was determined to thwart the rise of China, especially in high tech areas (like AI, robotics) where it wants to maintain its superiority. Consequently, the US apart from starting a trade war to reduce its massive trade deficit with China, is putting restrictions on transfer of technology by US firms to Chinese counterparts as well as Chinese investment in US, particularly in areas like telecom equipment where it fears security threat by China. The US administration is routinely accusing China of violating/stealing intellectual property rights (with some justification) (*Marketwatch* 2018) and undervaluing currency ('currency manipulator'; see US Dept. of the Treasury 2019) to derive an undue advantage (even when that is not true any more). The same policy is being pursued by the Biden administration, especially after China's increasingly aggressive attitude vis-à-vis Taiwan and the developing alliance between China and Russia in the wake of the Ukraine War of 2021.

Chinese economy has been slowing down for some time. No doubt, the recent trade war inflicted by the US on China has started to produce an additional adverse impact on Chinese economy. There are further problems for China in the form of rising debt burden of Chinese firms and local bodies financing huge infrastructure projects with debt in various ways like using shadow banking channels. In addition, China's massive infrastructure projects under Belt and Road Initiative (BRI) are facing increasing criticism in some of the host countries (like Malaysia, Sri Lanka, and now even China's 'all-weather friend' Pakistan [*The Diplomat* 2015]) over financing terms and non-transparent contract award process. China in the face of opposition from the US, India, Japan, South Korea and Australia (virtually emerging as a counterweight to China), is advancing an alternative infrastructure development initiative in the Asia-Pacific region and seems to be taking a more conciliatory stand vis-à-vis India. China is also changing its brand of globalisation. Faced with rising labour costs at home, greater competition in traditional manufactures from countries like Vietnam and Bangladesh and huge excess production capacity in steel, cement and glass, Chinese companies are trying to shift their production locations elsewhere (including India for consumer electronics like smartphones). Alongside, Chinese companies are using materials (along with Chinese labour where possible) in construction activities abroad supported by massive Chinese private and public investment (under the ambitious 'One Belt, One Road' initiative linking Asia to Europe and the transport corridor through Pakistan to the Iranian border) with funds infused through the China-led Asian Infrastructure Investment Bank (AIIB), an alternative to the US-led World Bank and the Japan-led Asian Development Bank.

China is also striving to become more like the Western powers by being a major producer and exporter of power plants, arms, missiles, nuclear submarines and aircraft carriers along with marshalling natural resources from Africa and Latin America. It is taking the lead to forge an alternative 16-nation mega trade agreement known as the Regional Comprehensive Economic Partnership (RCEP) in the Asia-Pacific region excluding US (but including ASEAN, Japan, South Korea, Australia and India). Basically, China is projecting itself as the champion of free trade, multilateralism and existing global institutions and the US as the disruptor.

The US–China trade war is opening a window of opportunity for India to export additional goods to US and Chinese markets to replace some of the Chinese and US goods subjected to higher tariffs. However, it is not an easy job as the quality and specifications of substitute Indian products may not exactly fit in the vacated space and working out new trading contracts is a time-consuming process. At the same time, China and several other countries (like Japan, Korea), faced with trade restrictions in US market (specially of steel and aluminium), are reportedly dumping some of their excess supply in Indian markets, raising clamour from Indian producers for additional ADD and safeguard duties. An additional negative development for Indian exports has been the recent US withdrawal of duty-free access to some of India's export products (like textiles, leather, dairy, chemicals) granted under Generalized System of Preferences (GSP) in the US market as India has graduated from the low-income status, along with some other countries like Thailand, Argentina, Pakistan, Turkey and Philippines, and does not qualify for the preferential treatment any longer.

The anti-globalisation forces in the West were kept in check by the powerful business lobbies arguing in favour of foreign investment, outsourcing, temporary immigration of high-skilled workers and integration into the more efficient global supply chain (which led to low inflation and consumer gains). This balancing of forces seems to be breaking down in recent years, beginning with the advent of the Great Recession in 2007 which exposed the risks of reckless financial globalisation, and the rising inequality of income and wealth in many parts of the world which is often blamed on globalisation, deregulation and the unchecked greed of business interests promoted by pliable government policies.

In times of economic distress, foreigners become the easy scapegoats. Along with blaming the immigrants for taking away jobs from the natives, the rise of religious fundamentalism, clash of cultures and terrorist activities have created additional resentment against immigration, especially of people with different cultural backgrounds. So, the traditional anti-trade sentiments of labour have now been combined with a strong anti-immigration sentiment among a rising section within political parties. As a result, apart from low-skilled workers, the movement of high-skilled Indian professionals (in areas like IT, academics, research labs) into the US and EU—a major source of income through remittances from abroad and for Indian IT companies—is being adversely affected by additional immigration restrictions (like granting of H-1B temporary work visas).

Several developed countries, led by the US, are now trying to 'reform' WTO by changing it from a multilateral to a plurilateral organisation and bringing some new issues for discussion like electronic commerce, investment facilitation, disciplines for micro, small and medium enterprises, trade's impact on gender issues, and domestic regulation in services, without resolving the old issues like agricultural subsidies and public stockholding of foodgrains. They are also planning to transition from the prevailing consensus mode of decision-making over all issues as a package deal ('Single Undertaking') towards majority voting among subgroups of countries over specific issues. In addition, the US is particularly keen to weaken the existing Dispute Settlement Body of WTO which has passed several rulings against the US in global trade disputes. Many developing countries including India are expressing strong reservations over the proposed changes in the WTO. These developments are further strengthening the case for countries like India to form/join trading blocs with like-minded countries, as the 'reformed WTO' (if it happens) would be less advantageous in the future.

Finally, sanctions on Iran and Russia (guided by geopolitical considerations) by the US and its allies are leading to problems as well as additional opportunities for India. Both Iran and Russia, being forced to lose some markets for its oil, gas and defence supplies due to Western sanctions, are turning towards the Indian market with more favourable terms. Since paying in US dollars is becoming difficult due to US sanctions, Iran and Russia are negotiating trade deals with India in local currencies (like rouble or rupee), which would basically be like barter deals in which Iranian and Russian goods will be exchanged against Indian goods and services. This may serve to increase India's exports to these countries, though the exact matching of exports and imports and fixing appropriate prices may well be a tricky job.

In this context of the prevailing global environment, let us now take up a few major current debates in the area of India's trade and foreign investment policy.

Current Debates in India's Trade Policy

SHOULD INDIA JOIN THE RCEP?

Though the current Indian government has decided to not join the Regional Comprehensive Economic Partnership for the time being unless India's concerns are properly addressed and adequate safeguards are provided by the other member nations, this may well be a bargaining strategy. In fact, the Indian government has not closed the door on further negotiations and has kept open the possibility that India may join at a later stage. Japan, in particular, is trying hard to include India as a counterweight to China's economic and political might. Hence, the debate on whether India should join and if so, under what conditions, continues to be a live policy issue. The pros and cons of India joining the RCEP are discussed below.

The RCEP is a proposed grouping of 16 countries consisting of 10 member states of ASEAN (Brunei, Cambodia, Indonesia, Laos, Malaysia, Myanmar, the Philippines, Singapore, Thailand, Vietnam) plus 6 other Asia-Pacific countries with which ASEAN already has free trade agreements (Australia, China, India, Japan, South Korea, New Zealand). The RCEP countries together have a population of 3.4 billion, with a combined GDP of nearly US$ 50 trillion or about 40 per cent of the world's GDP.

There are a number of thorny issues over tariff rates, market access, investments, regulations, rules of origin and lists of exemptions which are prolonging the process of negotiations which started back in 2012. As usual, opinions of analysts in India vary over the advantages and disadvantages of joining such a big preferential regional trading arrangement. Several arguments are offered in support of India joining the arrangement. First, the role of multilateral rules and the Dispute Settlement Body of WTO is fast eroding, especially after the unilateral actions taken by President Trump in the sphere of international trade and investment and countries are increasingly taking the route of bilateral or regional agreements. In the absence of the protection provided by the multilateral umbrella of WTO, RCEP offers India the opportunity to discipline the aggressive economic rise of China (a largely non-market economy with various types of non-tariff barriers) by using the rules of a regional grouping, instead of bilateral negotiations with China which is a much stronger economic power. Otherwise, India would be isolated and would be at a disadvantage. For example, currently China imposes 6 per cent MFN (Most-Favoured-Nation) tariff on Naphtha, 8 per cent duty on aluminium oxide, 5 per cent on cotton yarn exported by India whereas ASEAN countries (because they already have an FTA with China) pay zero duty (*The Economic Times* 2018b).

Second, India needs to be a member of some big regional free trade agreement in order to attract FDI which would use

India as a base for exports in sectors (like IT, pharmaceuticals, automobiles and components) where India may have competitive advantage in the region. Having many bilateral FTAs with disparate rules of origin and market access is not going to help here.

Third, a large part of the global supply chain of many dynamic products is located in the Asia-Pacific region. If India wants to get connected to this supply chain (which is needed for the success of the Make in India policy by providing easy access to cheaper and better quality intermediate inputs and increasing exports in today's world), it needs to be a member of this regional grouping.

Fourth, if India has to be a member of some big trading bloc, it is better to be a part of some bloc which excludes the US. America (specially under Trump) has become a much less reliable leader which is likely to insist on stricter labour and environmental standards as well more stringent restrictions on technology transfer, temporary migration of service professionals and independent dispute settlement mechanism. In fact, if the recent renegotiation of NAFTA and its conversion into USMCA (United States-Mexico-Canada Agreement) is any indication, the US may also change the terms of engagement at frequent intervals to suit its economic and geo-political interests. There is no clarity yet on whether the policy would change significantly under the Biden administration. However, given the emergence of QUAD (of which India is a member) as a counter to China's increasing economic power and military assertiveness, USA's stand with respect to these issues may somewhat soften vis-à-vis its alliance partners. All these considerations further strengthen the case for an Asia-Pacific trading bloc like RCEP.

On the other hand, the major counter arguments are the following. First, India already has FTA with several member countries (ASEAN, Japan and South Korea) of RCEP. The experience has been negative showing that India has lingering problems in competing with such countries. India's combined trade deficit with these three FTA partners has increased from $16 billion in 2009–10 (when these FTAs were concluded) to $ 31 billion in 2017–18. The situation is even more problematic with the other prospective members of the RCEP. In 2017–18, India's total trade deficit with all other members of RCEP stands at $104 Billion (up from $48 billion at the end of the last decade) which is 64 per cent of India's global trade deficit in 2017–19. These figures show that India has a big and rising deficit vis-à-vis the prospective partner countries of RCEP. There is no reason to believe that India would suddenly improve its performance just by becoming a member of the new RCEP (Dhar 2021).

Second, for both economic and political reasons, the Indian government cannot ignore the interests of millions of small farmers and SMEs. So, India has to provide protection to these vulnerable sections against import competition from lower cost producers of other RCEP members, even if gains of the gainers (of other producers and in other products) in some sense are more than the loss of the losers. That may not be an easy task.

Third, India needs special market access in services (in which India is believed to have competitive advantage) with free entry of more natural persons to render such services. Unless the gains there offset the losses in goods trade, India would be a net loser. Consequently, India needs to have special market access in services (like IT) with more free temporary immigration along with a longer breathing space vis-à-vis Chinese goods. Unless such concessions are forthcoming, India should abstain from joining.

One has to remember that a country with higher tariffs (like India) after the signing of FTA with lower tariffs countries (like the ASEAN) is likely to experience a bigger trade deficit with the member countries but lower deficit with the rest of the world as imports will be diverted towards the lower tariff member countries. What matters is the multilateral deficit. So, data in Dhar (2021) do not necessarily establish a case against RCEP. If anything, it underlines the urgency of having a low tariff regime so that India would have more balanced FTAs over time.[7]

Also, similar protectionist arguments were advanced against import liberalisation in pre-1991 India but subsequent events had proved the naysayers wrong. Indian producers have shown that they can compete with established foreign producers when they are forced to do so by improving their efficiency as well as working out strategic collaboration with foreign producers. Many of them have started exporting and setting up production facilities abroad in a big way (like Tata, other steel producers, auto, IT, pharmaceutical firms) only when forced by competition at home from both domestic and foreign players. The same may well happen after India becomes a member of RCEP, with some suitable safeguards (like income support, instead of price support) built in to protect the vulnerable small producers (particularly in agriculture) and if the exchange rate is allowed to provide protection in lieu of import duties. Given India's current status as the fastest growing big market in the world and the uncertainties of access for other countries in US markets, India is currently in a much stronger bargaining position to extract better terms from foreign producers and investors both before and after joining the RCEP.

Hence, waiting for an opportune time to join the RCEP by bargaining hard as long as possible is a good strategy. This is particularly so as the Indian economy has clearly slowed down, and growing unemployment and farm distresses have become major economic and political concerns. However, even though it is in India's longer term economic interest, opening domestic markets at this time (of inadequate aggregate demand and excess production capacity) to further import competition at a fast pace may well be politically suicidal for the current government.

DEBATE ON 'NEW PROTECTIONISM'

Indian government is increasingly taking resort to selective protection of industries by raising tariffs, partly to raise revenue to cover the fiscal gap but more importantly to stem the rising

CAD and sliding rupee. Exports have remained virtually stagnant in the 2015-19 period. The situation worsened in the Covid years starting with 2020 due to the onset of global recession and disruptions in supply chains. As a result, any adverse pressure on balance of payments—either due to a hardening of global oil price or rise in US interest rates and consequent capital flight, or fall in remittances from abroad—is being tackled mainly through a cut in 'non-essential' imports or imports of products (like consumer electronics and telecom equipments) which hinder the government's 'Make in India' initiative. These import duty hikes are in addition to the proliferation of temporary ADDs and safeguard duties being imposed by India on a variety of imported products.

Critics of this policy are apprehensive that this could be the beginning of a gradual reversal to the days of the pre-1991 protectionist era. They fear that some of the hard-fought gains of liberalisation for consumers (in the form of lower prices, better quality and wider choice) and producers (in terms of productivity and efficiency gains due to forced competition from imported goods and producing for the more competitive export market, access to a greater variety of inputs and technology, economies of scale, getting connected to global supply chains and strategic collaboration with foreign players) as well as overall growth rate of GDP in the post-liberalisation era would be lost if the current policy is continued.

Their objections to this 'new protectionism' rest on several planks. First, even if temporary protection to some industries can be theoretically justified on the so-called 'infant industry' considerations, protection—once granted—becomes very difficult to withdraw later.[8] Hence, the continuing loss to consumers through higher prices and to producers through excess cost of resources used up in protected production may very well offset any potential gain that may be accrued in the long run. Second, selective protection allowed to some industries (say, steel) would increase the cost of production of other goods (like automobiles and domestic appliances) if the imported products are used as inputs in other industries. In addition, selective protection would distort the structure of effective rates of protection or value added protection in an unpredictable and arbitrary manner, and the consequent resource reallocation in the economy would have no economic justification. The export industries would also suffer as a result of cost increases. The assurance of a domestic market sheltered from import competition would encourage both domestic and foreign firms to set up factories in India to cater to the more profitable domestic market rather than using India as a base for exports to other countries. 'Make in India' would be reduced to 'Make for India' with negative consequences for exports and balance of payments in the longer run. Third, selective protection to some industries is often used by lobbyists to argue for protection to other industries as well which leads to a snowballing effect.

So, these economists would argue for a market-determined exchange rate which would depreciate whenever the balance of payments deteriorates for whatever reason. A 10 per cent depreciation of the rupee is equivalent to a uniform 10 per cent import duty plus a uniform 10 per cent export subsidy. Hence, this would not distort the structure of effective protection but would provide uniform protection to all industries from foreign competition as well as an implicit export subsidy.[9]

According to most analysts, over time, the Indian rupee has become overvalued (mainly because of higher inflation rates in India as well as lingering disadvantages originating from less efficient infrastructure and land, labour and capital markets relative to some of its trade competitors); this needs to be offset by appropriate nominal depreciation. Export subsidies in whatever form, apart from being WTO-incompatible, are being increasingly challenged by the US under Trump. We are much too dependent on oil imports (around 80 per cent of domestic consumption). Hiking duty on gold imports encourages smuggling and diversion of imported gold meant for exports to a more lucrative domestic market through 'fake' exports of jewellery. Under such circumstances, depreciation of the rupee (which is WTO-compatible) can kill several birds with one stone.

Hence, the most sensible policy in the immediate run is to let the rupee fall as quickly as possible to find a new equilibrium level. If delayed (as RBI attempts to defend rupee by selling dollars), speculators would take advantage by buying dollars from the market now and later selling at higher rates at the expense of RBI. Countries like Thailand that tried to defend the local currency against speculative capital outflows during the Asian Crisis in the late 1990s learnt the bitter lesson. Free float of currency burns the finger of speculators as they have to buy dollars at an immediately higher price whenever they try to take out money in a big way. This serves as an automatic restraining influence on outflows, unlike a fixed exchange rate system where the speculators make assured gains. Even China, with more than $ 3 trillion reserves, allowed yuan to fall in the face of capital flight. Our war chest of more than $600 billion foreign exchange reserves should be scrupulously preserved, specially as a large part of our reserves are borrowed reserves rather than earned through current account surplus (as in China). At the same time, maintaining macro stability by sticking to fiscal deficit target is a must—otherwise, global portfolio managers (prompted by international credit rating agencies) would take more money out of India, worsening the BOP and exchange rate situation.

The recently announced measures to stem the fall in rupee like easing terms of short-term external borrowing and tax concessions on rupee-denominated bonds sold abroad may induce some short-term capital inflows but would increase external vulnerability in the longer term, creating bigger troubles in the not-too-distant future. Cutting 'non-essential imports', apart from running the risk of violating WTO rules and hence inviting retaliation by others, would take time to produce an impact. Reducing oil-import dependence by developing use of alternative energy sources and exploring new oil and gas discovery at home is always desirable but comes with its own set of challenges and is not an immediate solution. Thus, in the short run, we have no option but to let the rupee bear the brunt of adjustment to cope with the evolving realities at home and abroad.

Alongside, as citizens we need to accept that the exchange rate is like any other price determined by demand and supply which should not be linked to 'national honour'.

Even if one accepts that floating exchange rate is the best immediate option, does this mean that there is no case for selective tariffs? The supporters of selective protection may point to the empirical fact that the rise in basic customs duty on imported mobile phones and mobile parts in the Union budget has provided a boost to local production of mobile phones by both Indian and foreign (mainly Chinese and Korean) producers in India. According to industry watchers, this is forcing them to gradually reduce imports of components to cut costs and encourage component makers to set up production facilities in India. Samsung, for example, is setting up its biggest overseas manufacturing plant for mobile phones in India.[10]

Given that the demand for smartphones is going up by leaps and bounds in India, increasing localisation of manufacture of components and finished phones would go a long way to save foreign exchange and eventually induce the firms to go for exports to similar markets once they meet the domestic demand and bring down costs by reaping economies of scale and 'learning by doing'. Supporters of selective protection also point to the successful rise of the Indian pharma industry behind the protective wall of the pre-WTO 1970 Patents Act of India which allowed these firms to 'copy' patented formulations and develop indigenous ability. Now even after the Indian government has moved over to the post-WTO patents regime, Indian pharmaceutical companies are able to flourish by competing successfully with established global players. The same has happened in the auto components sector. Thus, there is empirical evidence of some successful growth stories of globally competitive industries in India (and elsewhere) behind the protective wall.

All these imply that along with a competitive exchange rate, selected tariffs in a few carefully identified growth industries of the future may be a sensible policy. This combines the 'infant industry' argument with the 'tariff factory' argument for protection. It basically says that temporary tariffs would induce foreign firms to set up production facilities ('factories') in the tariff-imposing country, which would be less costly than bringing in the finished product. However, extreme care should be taken against extending this argument to each and every industry asking for protection. This case for tariffs would be valid for only such industries where the producers producing behind the temporary protective wall would eventually be globally competitive and survive without tariff protection. Also, the policy makers must ensure that these initial tariffs are not set too high (like, say, not more than 20 per cent or so). Otherwise, there is the risk that grossly inefficient firms would set up factories and there would be big pressure in the future to maintain high tariffs indefinitely, leading to huge loss of consumers' surplus and production efficiency. There will also be the temptation to justify any additional tariff protection as reaction to increased protectionist tendencies in other parts of the world.

Is Exchange Rate the Main Culprit behind Export Stagnation?

Most analysts would agree that the long-term solution to our recurring BOP problem is increasing exports, rather than import compression. But, in reality, India's exports have been stagnant for the last several years. So, the important question is: What is causing this stagnation and what can be done about it?

Falling exports can be attributed to weak global demand and hence it is beyond the control of Indian policy makers. But, countries like Bangladesh and Vietnam have been able to increase their exports in dollar terms during the same period. So, we cannot put the blame entirely on deteriorating global demand or falling prices. There are basically two schools of thought here—one emphasises the structural/institutional features of the economy to be primarily responsible while the other holds the exchange rate to be the villain. The RBI, not surprisingly, subscribes to the former school (Khan 2016; Rajan 2016). The RBI view is that we should focus on improving our economic fundamentals and maintaining macroeconomic stability and the trend exchange rate should be left to market forces. For improving our international competitiveness, we need to remove infrastructural bottlenecks, enhance productivity and access to finance, increase domestic competition, keep inflation in check and improve the ease of doing business in India.

The Indian rupee has fallen relative to most other Asian currencies over 2015–19. Even the real exchange rate or the real effective exchange rate (REER) (both the six-currency and the 36-currency index variants)—which better captures the average price competitiveness of India's exports relative to its competitors—have remained flat over most of the period of falling exports. All these imply that the exchange rate was not the primary reason for stagnant Indian exports.

People who hold the exchange rate primarily responsible refer to cross-country empirical studies which show that relative exchange rates (with suitable lags) matter for export performance. Even if that is generally true, the fact that the real exchange rate has remained flat during the period of falling exports (January 2015 to March 2016) and, even more strikingly, had actually appreciated, in both nominal and real terms, during the earlier period of rising exports means that for at least the specific period and the Indian context under consideration, exchange rate was not the main factor.

In theory, other things remaining the same, currency depreciation should produce an effect on a country's exports. However, even here, one needs to make a distinction between demand- and supply-constrained situations. Depreciation helps exports particularly when the binding constraint is weak external demand and lower dollar prices sufficiently increase demand for exports (case of high price elasticity of demand). That may not be the case for all commodities. One can even postulate a Sweezy-type kinked demand curve for some export products. That means that when India reduces the prices by rupee depreciation, other countries also lower their prices by competitive depreciation, producing a situation of low price elasticity of demand. Depreciation would then fail to increase export earnings. However, appreciation of the rupee would not help either. Any rise in dollar price as a result of appreciation of the rupee would not be matched by other countries. As a result, Indian exports in dollars would fall again. Neither depreciation nor appreciation would be effective in such situations.

What if there is a supply constraint (like in most agricultural products)? In that case, when rupee falls but supply remains the same, Indian exports may rise temporarily as production is diverted from domestic market to export market (since exporting becomes more profitable relative to home sales). But more exports will push up domestic rupee prices of exports and the initial gain in international price competitiveness will be neutralised by higher inflation. Removing supply constraints calls for other kinds of reforms—not exchange rate adjustment.

A country's export performance also depends on the credit terms, brands, reputation about reliable product quality and maintenance of delivery schedules, quality of repair and servicing facilities (for consumer durables and machines), linkages with global supply chains, access to global marketing channels (often controlled by multinationals), trader networks (note the role of expatriate Chinese traders in expanding Chinese exports), membership of big preferential trading arrangements, labour market flexibility (in the face of sudden rise/fall in export demand), efficiency of storage and transportation facilities, trade facilitation at the customs, and so on.

Even if one accepts that the RBI should intervene to maintain a target (real exchange rate and hence an implied nominal exchange rate, given the inflation differential between domestic and foreign countries), the question is: how? Since we allow free movement of foreign capital into and out of India, there will be periods of sharp appreciation and depreciation. The best that the RBI can hope to do is to smoothen out excessive fluctuations around the trend, but it should not try to buck the trend. Further, there is an inherent conflict between exchange rate, inflation and fiscal deficit targets. For example, RBI currently has an inflation target. RBI monetary policy, especially interest rate policy, is primarily geared to a particular range of inflation rate. So long as the actual inflation is within that target zone, RBI is not going to raise interest rates to attract capital inflows and support the rupee. Similarly, a falling rupee (especially when the international oil price rises pushing up CAD) would raise the oil subsidy bill of the government to the extent it is not willing or able to pass on the higher rupee cost of oil to the consumers. In that case, the government, fixated on a fiscal deficit target, would not like to see the rupee fall.

The folly of trying to prevent a currency from falling in the face of big capital outflow, whatever the reason, has been amply demonstrated by the experience of countries such as Thailand during the East Asian financial crisis (see *Federal Reserve History* 2013; UNCTAD n.d.; IMF 1998).

Maintaining an undervalued exchange rate—as Japan, Korea and more recently China are alleged to have done (and some economists want India to do)—to artificially create a competitive cost advantage, run a big trade surplus and accumulate foreign exchange reserves, has its costs.[11]

Devaluation, by raising prices of imported final goods and intermediate inputs, pushes up domestic prices.[12] Thus, an undervalued exchange rate, in effect, taxes domestic consumers and subsidises domestic producers. Also, while it benefits the domestic producers of import-competing products, it penalises the firms that use the imported goods as inputs (for example, higher price of steel would benefit Tata Steel but would hurt Tata Motors). Accumulating foreign exchange reserves by running a big trade surplus deprives the current generation of a higher level of consumption while the savings held in the form of US government securities earn a meagre 0.5 to 1 per cent interest rate.

The upshot is that, in addition to global demand and exchange rate, falling exports could be the result of factors specific to individual products and markets. This may also explain why exports from Bangladesh and Vietnam, whose commodity compositions, markets and integration with global supply chains are different from India's, could be rising while Indian exports were falling.

India's service exports dipped at a much slower rate than goods exports during the period of falling exports. That again shows that product- and market-specific factors may be of more consequence than the exchange rate. Therefore, the causes of falling exports should be subjects for detailed product- and market-specific research. A general explanation such as global recession or overvalued currency is not enough.

How to Increase Exports?

It is widely recognised from the East Asian and Chinese experience of near double-digit growth sustained over decades that without a sufficiently high growth rate of exports, it is impossible to achieve the 8 per cent plus GDP growth rate target of India on a sustained basis. The question then is: How can India increase exports?

Our problems in the export sphere are typified by the experience in the textile and garments sector. This is a sector which is intensive in low-skilled labour and hence can be an antidote to jobless growth. In addition, India has a traditional advantage in textiles due to its low-cost labour, age-old expertise and the financial ability to invest in modern machines and factories. Yet, as China is vacating the space of labour-intensive manufacturing in simple consumer goods including textiles and garments, much smaller economies of Bangladesh and Vietnam have been able to surpass India in exports in this sector. Why is this so? Leaving aside the short-term disruptions caused by demonetisation and GST tax refunds, analysts point to several factors (Ranade 2018).

Both Bangladesh and Vietnam have greater labour market flexibility (in terms of ease of hiring and firing, use of contract labour, availability of cheap female labour willing to work in multiple shifts, labour discipline), which is important in an export product line where fashions and hence demand for specific products change rapidly. Bangladesh (but not Vietnam) has an additional advantage in terms of duty-free access to US and EU markets under GSP. India's higher per capita income does not entitle India to this benefit any longer.

The exchange rate is largely market-determined in India but that does not adequately explain why India lags behind in this sector, in particular. Hence, domestic factors would be primarily responsible for India's poor performance in a sector dominated by a large number of small and medium enterprises working as sub-contractors of bigger manufacturing and export firms, primarily to avoid the more stringent labour laws applicable to bigger firms. But these small firms suffer from huge infrastructural problems like unreliable power supply, inadequate quality control and standardisation, lack of information on changing tastes and designs, access to finance and marketing facilities. Some of these bottlenecks are sought to be tackled by providing common infrastructure in 'clusters' but their number and efficiency are quite limited in India. Smaller firms (compared to firms in China, Bangladesh or Vietnam) suffer from diseconomies of scale which raises the per unit cost and creates an international competitiveness problem. Bank credit is another major problem for small enterprises which have to depend on informal credit or remain captive to the traders for advance money. This deprives them the flexibility or the ability to innovate and venture into the more uncertain export markets on their own. Most of the smaller firms prefer to cater to the more reliable, safer and less-demanding domestic market. Not allowing multi-brand big global retailers like Walmart (that sources products from all over the world) also means absence of access to their global supply chains and marketing channels.

So, we suggest several steps to promote exports. First, we need to focus on labour-intensive exports like textiles and garments, agricultural products, footwear and leather goods, simple consumer goods like watches, toys and tourism (particularly medical tourism). But for that we have to improve the state of physical infrastructure (roads, ports, railways, air cargo, cold storage, power) and the working of labour, land, capital markets to bring down the cost of inputs and ensure safety of foreign tourists which are all in our domestic policy domain. For instance, a cut rose fetches double the price in the Amsterdam market if it can reach there within 24 hours. But to avail of that higher price, we need to have refrigerated vans transporting the cargo from the farm door to the airport terminal along speedy roads without time-taking interference by the customs officials at the airport and regular cargo flights to deliver these at the Amsterdam marketplace within the shortest possible time. This is true for many other perishable agricultural products (vegetables, fruits, flowers) where Indian prices are much below international prices but we lack the efficient physical infrastructure to make use of the opportunities. In fact, the poor state of physical infrastructure was one of the main reasons why India had to go for service-led exports (like IT and ITeS) where firms could use captive power generation facilities, state-of-the-art computers, abundant supply of non-unionised engineers and other white collar workers and fibre optics network to export the services over the wire. The IT firms could bypass the bad roads and ports, unreliable power supply and land acquisition issues as they can expand vertically, unlike manufactured exports which crucially depend on efficient physical infrastructure and flexible land and labour markets (as in China, especially in their SEZs in the coastal areas).

Second, we need to focus on industrial clusters (in textiles, readymade garments, leather goods, food processing, and so on) and provide aggressive government support to improve the working of common infrastructure, which would bring down the cost of production and delivery of these products by SMEs for the export market. This assumes particular urgency as the product- and market-specific export subsidies are being challenged as WTO-incompatible but cluster subsidies (which are provided to all producers in the cluster, irrespective of domestic sales and exports) are allowed.

Third, efforts must be made to link our firms to global supply chains. For this, India must have a seamless facility of imports, exports, re-imports and re-exports of components and goods at different stages of manufacture. High duties and subsequent time-consuming rebates of taxes cannot achieve this. Also, long-term stability of tariffs and other trade restrictions is an important consideration for setting up production facilities by global firms in a country. As the Chinese experience shows (like in Apple phones or Barbie dolls), it is not necessary to have a high degree of value addition per unit. More important is the total value creation (depends on scale of production and exports) and employment generation. For all these reasons, being a member of the Asia-Pacific RCEP (with appropriate safeguards), which would bring down tariffs and trade facilitation measures to the level of competing countries as well as guarantee some treaty-enforced stability to trade policy, could be an important step. There may well be production and employment loss in some products but it is a good long-term policy (with proper phasing over time and suitable compensation cum retraining mechanism in place for the losers) if this loss is more than offset by gains in other areas.

Fourth, we must give up looking towards tariffs as a revenue generating-measure. Customs officials have to change the mindset and transform themselves from being inspectors and revenue collectors to being facilitators of trade and exports. Stringent penalties should be meted out to guilty officers who hinder the flow of goods and services across international borders for enriching themselves.

Fifth, FDI can play an important positive effect on exports, not so much by providing additional investment funds, but by providing access to newer (proprietary) technologies and global marketing channels controlled by multinational companies. In this context, allowing global big retail chains to operate in India may provide a big boost to exports, even if it may also increase imports from other countries. Given the current status of the fastest growing economy in the world has made it easier for India (like China in the past) to impose more stringent domestic sourcing and export obligations on foreign firms than ever before. In addition, anti-dumping duties and safeguard duties can always be imposed in the face of any sudden surge in imports.

Finally, the Competition Commission of India and other regulators must maintain a highly competitive domestic market to force Indian and foreign firms setting up factories in India not just to exploit a sheltered high-margin market but also to export for survival and growth. Some technology experts, however, are skeptical about whether countries like India can replicate the labour-intensive manufacturing export-led growth strategy in the future. According to them, the labour cost advantage of low-wage countries is being eroded by technological developments which would 'reshore' some of the previously 'offshored' activities back to the developed countries. This may happen in both goods and services which means trouble not only for activities like garment manufacturing or shoe-making but also for reading x-ray images or legal drafting. But, then, the question is: Is it going to take place anytime soon? The probable answer is that this is more likely to happen first in higher value products (like assembly processes in consumer electronics where it has already started) than in the garment industry, particularly at the low end. But, then, even in the traditional labour-intensive manufacturing of shoes and sports gears, robots have already started making custom-made shoes and gears for athletes in the

Olympic Games and World Cups (in soccer). Basically, it is now more useful to think in terms of activities/tasks, rather than industries. Certain tasks within an industry are more routine than others and hence these are more likely to be taken over by robots. But there are other activities within the same industry that require more dexterity, spontaneous creativity or social interactions which will continue to be done by humans for a longer time. Hence, in our export policy, we should switch our focus from industries to activities to find out where our labour cost advantage (in both low-skill manufacturing and high-skill services) will last for a longer time.

India has already proved its prowess in several areas of exports like IT, ITeS, pharma (especially in generic and off-patent drugs) and auto component. Given that India is the largest importer of defence equipments in the world and has an abundant supply of relatively low-cost engineers, there exists considerable scope for manufacturing and eventually exporting components and arms (like missiles) and defence equipment (like fighter planes, helicopters, battleships), in collaboration with established global players. As a large buyer, India can use its leverage to force foreign suppliers to accept gradual localisation (or 'offset contracts' as in the Rafael fighter jet contract with the French supplier) over time. In the current geo-political environment, the Western powers would have less hesitation in transferring sophisticated defence technology to Indian collaborating firms in the interest of using India as a counterweight to contain the rise of China as a military superpower.

Medical tourism is another area of export with ample potential, given the relatively low cost and international quality medical services (specially surgeries) provided by a number of Indian hospital chains and the abundance of attractive tourist spots in India. Further boost to this avenue of forex earnings would require ensuring safety of foreign tourists in India which is lacking at present. Even a single instance of harassment, especially directed at women tourists/patients, which is given publicity on social media can dent a reputation built over years. In addition, there is need for standardisation and regulation of the quality of service, fees and billing. The foreign medical insurance providers need to be convinced that reliable international standard medical service can be provided in Indian hospitals at a fraction of the costs in the US and other developed countries, which would save a lot of money for the insurers.

Regarding potential exports, an IMF study on Indian exports (IMF 2015) provides some useful ideas. The basic approach of the paper is that exports are not an end in itself. It needs to contribute towards (present and future) growth of the economy and job creation. The growth effect of exports comes through several channels (on both demand and supply sides) like enabling imports of a greater variety of inputs and technology (made possible by foreign exchange earnings from exports); the forced efficiency effect of producing for the highly competitive global market (along with competition from imported products); the introduction of new products, quality improvements in existing products and creating new areas of comparative advantage through innovation and learning from trading partners (especially in richer and more technologically advanced countries) as well as learning by doing in export industries; and generating additional demand for domestically produced goods and services (and hence GDP) in a demand-constrained situation. All export products do not have the same dynamism. So, it is not the quantity of exports but the composition of the export basket which is crucial for the productivity/growth effect of exports.

After a careful and technically sophisticated analysis of the income-generating power of various goods and services in the export basket of India over the period 1991–2013 and comparing those with the export composition of other countries, the IMF study concludes that Indian service exports are already highly sophisticated and complex. However, even though the quality, sophistication and complexity of goods exports have increased, it remains below the level of peers or comparator emerging economies. Hence, improving the quality, sophistication and complexity of goods exports and further enhancing the complexity of service exports remain the key policy priorities. Regarding potential markets, the study finds that there is considerable scope for further expansion of trade with China, the ASEAN and South Asian countries. Further, India's exports with countries in East Europe, CIS (Commonwealth of Independent States), Latin America and Africa have remained largely unrealised.

The study recommends a number of policy initiatives which include fostering regional trade integration and connecting to global value chains, liberalising FDI regimes, improving export-related infrastructure, developing skills and liberalising labour markets, and improving the environment of innovation and entrepreneurship. Almost everyone would agree with these broad policy suggestions.

Concluding Remarks

India has come a long way in liberalising its economy and diversifying the commodity and market composition of its trade basket. It has also succeeded in becoming an attractive destination for FDI though there is considerable scope for improvement here. However, increasing exports is a prime requirement for sustaining an 8 per cent plus growth rate that is needed to provide its teeming millions a modicum of respectable living within the next couple of decades. In addition to analysing the current global scenario (with its challenges and opportunities) and the principal trade policy debates in India, this chapter has outlined the major steps required for a quantum jump in exports in the evolving global environment. One may say that these required policy initiatives are fairly well-known to knowledgeable observers. Even then it is useful to list out the required reforms in one place along with the logic behind the proposed steps clearly spelt out. Unfortunately, implementation remains the major hurdle which is largely beyond the scope of economists. In a chaotic and fragmented parliamentary democracy like ours, a political party, while supporting an initiative when in government, opposes the same when voted out of power.[13] The slow-moving bureaucracy and judiciary is a further hindrance to speedy implementation of ideas, unlike a single-party authoritarian regime like China. It seems that we, argumentative Indians, are never short of ideas but find it difficult to arrive at a consensus, or put our ideas into practice.

Postscript: To know more on some of the most recent developments and issues in the context of India's trade and investment policy, the interested reader may refer to: Aiyar (2023); Ahluwalia (2022); Ray (2022a, b, c).

NOTES

[1] Herfindahl–Hirschman (HH) Market Concentration Index is a measure of the dispersion of trade value across an exporter's partners. A country with trade (export or import) that is concentrated in a very few markets will have an index value close to 1. Similarly, a country with a perfectly diversified trade portfolio will have an index close to zero. Over time, a fall in the index indicates rising diversification of its exports and hence falling vulnerability to trade shocks.

[2] The Index of Export Market Penetration measures the extent to which a reporter's exports reach proven importers of those products worldwide. A higher index indicates that a country already exports to a greater percentage of existing markets for its products; a low value indicates potential for expansion. It is calculated as the number of countries to which the reporter exports a particular product divided by the number of countries that report importing the product that year.

[3] Not surprisingly, small trading nations like Hong Kong and Singapore are found to have trade to GDP ratio in the range of 300 per cent to 400 per cent. This is due to those countries having a large value of imports and re-exports (with small value added) which inflate the value of total trade but does not contribute much to GDP which consists of only value added.

[4] Source: WTO data. For India, for these calculations, data provided by RBI does not include ITeS (Information Technology Enabled Services) and BPO services in which India is a global leader. RBI includes these as 'software services' whereas WTO includes these under 'other business services'. If these were included in RBI data under 'computer and information services', India's share would have been a lot higher.

[5] This no longer holds any novelty since several countries have already done it. For India, the technological spin-offs of space exploration can be obtained at much lower costs by sending unmanned spacecrafts into outer space which involves much less risk, though it looks less spectacular.

[6] Some tax havens like British Virgin Islands (38.3 billion), Cayman Islands (37.4 billion) are big recipients of net FDI but with virtually no real production activities, which implies that their attractiveness as investment destination is entirely due to tax advantages.

[7] See Srivastava (2018) for a neat two-country example to illustrate this point.

[8] See Ray (1991) for a detailed discussion of the pros and cons of infant industry argument in the context of a country like India.

[9] See Ahluwalia (2018), Panagariya (2018), Maira (2021), Mehta (2018) for more detailed discussions in favour of or against selective protection in India.

[10] See *Mint* (2018) for more details on the emerging smartphone manufacturing scenario in India.

[11] Basu (2016) believes that China is realising the cost of maintaining an undervalued exchange rate indefinitely.

[12] Analytically, 10% devaluation = 10% import duty + 10% export subsidy. Also, 10% import duty = 10% consumption tax + 10% production subsidy. Combining, 10% devaluation = (10% consumption tax + 10% production subsidy) for importables + 10% export subsidy for exportables.

[13] A good example is FDI in retail which both the Congress and the BJP supported while in government but opposed when out of power. See Ray (2011) for more on the case for and against FDI in retail.

REFERENCES

Ahluwalia, Montek Singh. 2018. 'Hiking customs duty was the wrong move', *Mint*, 23 February. Available at https://www.livemint.com/Opinion/pktTlRtd6IrPPN6B1P0dHI/Hiking-customs-duties-was-the-wrong-move.html (accessed February 2023).

———. 2022. 'The trade policy India needs', *Mint*, 19 July. Available at https://www.livemint.com/opinion/online-views/redesigning-trade-policy-what-is-the-best-way-ahead-for-india-11658247066774.html (accessed July 2023).

Aiyar, Swaminathan S. A. 2023. 'Turn the White Collars Up', *The Economic Times*, 18 April. Available at https://economictimes.indiatimes.com/opinion/et-commentary/view-forget-production-linked-incentives-service-exports-represent-indias-future/articleshow/99593571.cms?from=mdr

Basu, Kaushik. 2016. *An Economist in the Real World: The Art of Policymaking in India*. New Delhi: Penguin/Viking.

Business Standard. 2013. 'Godrej buys US BPO company', 6 February. Available at https://www.business-standard.com/article/technology/godrej-buys-us-bpo-company-105040401064_1.html (accessed March 2023).

Chatham House. 2021. 'Lessons from Trump's assault on the World Trade Organization', 3 August. Available at https://www.chathamhouse.org/2021/08/lessons-trumps-assault-world-trade-organization (accessed March 2023).

CNBC. 2020. 'A return to multilateralism under Joe Biden is "extremely promising," OECD says', 14 December. Available at https://www.cnbc.com/2020/12/14/bidens-return-to-multilateralism-is-extremely-promising-oecd-says.html (accessed March 2023).

Dhar, Biswajit. 2021. 'RCEP deal can be disastrous for India', *Business Line*, 6 December. Available at https://www.thehindubusinessline.com/opinion/columns/rcep-deal-can-be-disastrous-for-india/article24936537.ece?homepage=true (accessed February 2023).

Equity Bulls. 2022. 'Dr. Reddy's Laboratories announces the acquisition of an injectable product portfolio from Eton Pharma'. Available at https://www.equitybulls.com/category.php?id=315840 (accessed March 2023).

Federal Reserve History. 2013. 'Asian Financial Crisis: July 1997–December 1998', 22 November. Available at https://www.federalreservehistory.org/essays/asian-financial-crisis (accessed March 2023).

GoI. 2018a. *Economic Survey 2017–18, Vol. I*. Ministry of Finance, Govt. of India. Available at https://www.im4change.org/docs/740economic%20survey%202017-18%20-%20vol.I.pdf (accessed March 2023).

———. 2018b. *Economic Survey 2017–18, Vol. II*. Ministry of Finance, Govt. of India. Available at https://www.im4change.org/docs/751economic%20survey%202017-18%20-%20vol.%20II.pdf (accessed March 2023).

Heitzman, James and Robert L. Worden. 1995. *India: A Country Study*. Washington D.C.: Federal Research Division, Library of Congress. Available at https://www.loc.gov/item/96019266/ (accessed March 2023).

IMF. 1998. 'The Asian Crisis: Causes and Cures', June. Available at https://www.imf.org/external/pubs/ft/fandd/1998/06/imfstaff.htm (accessed March 2023).

———. 2015. 'Make In India: Which Exports can Drive the Next Wave of Growth', Working Paper, May. Available at https://www.imf.org/external/pubs/ft/wp/2015/wp15119.pdf (accessed February 2023).

Kant, Amitabh. 2018. 'Ease of Business: What We Have Learned in Last Three Years', *The Economic Times*, 1 November. Available at https://economictimes.indiatimes.com/news/economy/indicators/ease-of-business-what-we-have-learned-in-last-three-years/articleshow/66456306.cms (accessed February 2023).

Khan, H. R. 2016. 'Global Economic Turmoil: Impact on Indian Economy and the Way Forward', Speech, *RBI Bulletin*, April.

Marketwatch. 2018. 'Why is the U.S. accusing China of stealing intellectual property?', 6 April. Available at https://www.marketwatch.com/story/why-is-the-us-accusing-china-of-stealing-intellectual-property-2018-04-05 (accessed March 2023).

Maira, Arun. 2021. 'Changing paradigm on economic policy', *Business Line*, 7 December. Available at https://www.thehindubusinessline.com/opinion/columns/changing-paradigm-on-economic-policy/article23474214.ece (accessed February 2023).

Mehta, Pradeep S. 2018. 'The role of competition policy for development', *Mint*, 8 April. Available at https://www.livemint.com/Opinion/hjwUWOw6j0UFH1lgopIPbI/The-role-of-competition-policy-for-development.html (accessed February 2023).

Mint. 2018. 'A bright spot for Modi's "Make in India": Smartphone manufacturing', 25 October. Available at https://www.livemint.com/Companies/UkSpqypNBO7Jb2LnZyCizL/A-bright-spot-for-Modis-Make-in-India-Smartphone-manufac.html (accessed February 2023).

Panagariya, Arvind. 2018. 'The Return of Protectionism: Panagariya sounds alarm over Modi's new trade template for India', *The Economic Times*, 12 February. Available at https://economictimes.indiatimes.com/news/economy/policy/budget-2018-has-ensured-the-return-of-protectionism/articleshow/62876012.cms?from=mdr (accessed February 2023).

Rajan, Raghuram. 2016. 'India in the Global Economy', Speech, *RBI Bulletin*, April. Available at https://www.rbi.org.in/Scripts/BS_ViewBulletin.aspx?Id=16164 (accessed March 2023).

Ranade, Ajit. 2018. 'India needs to fundamentally alter its export strategy', *Mint*, 18 April. Available at https://www.livemint.com/Opinion/rHODuZ18xX55H1tqPTBz2O/India-needs-to-fundamentally-alter-its-export-strategy.html (accessed February 2023).

Ray, Alok. 1991. 'The Infant Industry Argument for Protection: Theory, Policy Implications and Practice'. In Dipak Banerjee (ed.), *Essays in Economic Analysis and Policy*. India: Oxford University Press.

———. 2011. 'Gainers and Losers: FDI in Retail', *Deccan Herald*, 6 December. Available at https://www.deccanherald.com/content/209883/gainers-losers.html (accessed February 2023).

———. 2022a. 'Globalization: Slowing down or mutating?' *The Hindu Business Line*, 19 January . Available at: https://www.thehindubusinessline.com/opinion/globalisation-slowing-down-or-mutating/article64910221.ece (accessed July 2023).

———. 2022b. 'India needs to plug in to global value chains'. *Deccan Herald*, 21 September. Available at https://www.deccanherald.com/opinion/main-article/india-needs-to-plug-in-to-global-value-chains-1147135.html (accessed July 2023).

———. 2022c. 'A changed situtaion'. *Deccan Herald*, 16 November. Available at: https://www.deccanherald.com/opinion/comment/a-changed-situation-1163016.html (accessed July 2023).

RBI. 2018. *Annual Report for 2017–2018*, August.

Srivastava, Ajay. 2018. 'Reshaping India's trade policy', *Business Line*, 17 January. Available at https://www.thehindubusinessline.com/opinion/reshaping-indias-trade-policy/article8894080.ece (accessed February 2023).

TATA Steel. 2007. 'Tata Steel completes £6.2bn acquisition of Corus Group plc'. Available at https://www.tatasteel.com/media/newsroom/press-releases/india/2007/tata-steel-completes-62bn-acquisition-of-corus-group-plc/ (accessed March 2023).

TCS. 2022. 'TCS named a 2022 Global Top Employer'. Available at https://www.tcs.com/who-we-are/newsroom/press-release/tcs-named-2022-global-top-employer (accessed March 2023).

The Diplomat. 2015. 'China and Pakistan's All-Weather Friendship', 12 March. Available at https://thediplomat.com/2015/03/china-and-pakistans-all-weather-friendship/ (accessed March 2023).

The Economic Times. 2006a. 'Energy deal to give Tatas foothold in US water market', 24 August. Available at https://economictimes.indiatimes.com/brand-equity/brands-news/energy-deal-to-give-tatas-foothold-in-us-water-market/articleshow/1921292.cms?from=mdr (accessed March 2023).

———. 2006b. 'Tatas buy Eight O'Clock Coffee', 26 June. Available at https://economictimes.indiatimes.com/t-companies/tata-tea/tatas-buy-eight-oclock-coffee/articleshow/1679209.cms (accessed March 2023).

———. 2018a. 'FDI in India rises to $61.96 billion in 2017–18: Government', 08 June 08. Available at https://economictimes.indiatimes.com/markets/stocks/news/fdi-in-india-rises-to-61-96-billion-in-2017-18-government/articleshow/64506567.cms (accessed February 2023).

———. 2018b. 'India can seek duty cuts from China on 200 items', 30 October 30. Available at https://economictimes.indiatimes.com/news/economy/foreign-trade/india-can-seek-duty-cuts-from-china-on-200-items/articleshow/66424206.cms?from=mdr (accessed February 2023).

The Times of India. 2015. 'India pips US, China as No. 1 foreign direct investment destination', 30 September. Available at http://timesofindia.indiatimes.com/articleshow/49160838.cms?utm_source=contentofinterest&utm_medium=text&utm_campaign=cppst (accessed February 2023).

UNCTAD. n.d. 'The Financial Crisis In East Asia'. Available at https://unctad.org/press-material/financial-crisis-east-asia (accessed March 2023).

_____. 2017. *World Investment Report 2017: Investment and the Digital Economy*. Geneva: United Nations. Available at https://unctad.org/en/PublicationsLibrary/wir2017_en.pdf (accessed February 2023).

US Dept. of the Treasury. 2019. 'Treasury Designates China as a Currency Manipulator', 5 August. Available at https://home.treasury.gov/news/press-releases/sm751 (accessed March 2023).

Wikipedia. n.d. 'List of largest trading partners of India'. Available at https://en.wikipedia.org/wiki/List_of_the_largest_trading_partners_of_India (accessed March 2023)

WITS (World Integrated Trade Solution). 2016. 'India trade balance, exports and imports by country and region 2016'. Available at https://wits.worldbank.org/CountryProfile/en/Country/IND/Year/2016/TradeFlow/EXPIMP (accessed March 2023).

_____. 2017. 'India trade balance, exports and imports by country 2017'. Available at https://wits.worldbank.org/CountryProfile/en/Country/IND/Year/2017/TradeFlow/EXPIMP/Partner/by-country (accessed March 2023).

World Bank. 2018a. 'Trade Summary for India'. Available at https://wits.worldbank.org/CountryProfile/en/Country/IND/Year/LTST/Summary (accessed February 2023).

_____. 2018b. 'Foreign direct investment, net inflows'. Available at https://data.worldbank.org/indicator/bx.klt.dinv.cd.wd (accessed February 2023).

9
BALANCING THE PUSHES AND PULLS OF THE IMPOSSIBLE TRINITY
Capital Flows, RBI Intervention and Exchange Rate in India

Partha Ray and *Parthapratim Pal*

Introduction

As per the basic open-economy Mundell–Fleming model, no country can have three things simultaneously—(*i*) fixed exchange rate, (*ii*) independent monetary policy, and (*iii*) free capital flows. There are many instances in the real world where a country sacrifices one of the vertices of the impossible trinity of policy triangle at the altar of two others. However, in the real world, policy choices get extended beyond the three vertices. In fact, faced with the tensions of the impossible trinity, a country often picks up a combination of incomplete monetary policy independence with partial capital control. India is one such economy.

There have been two takes on the Indian stance of handling the tensions of the impossible trinity. There is an influential view that Indian efforts of capital control have deprived the Indian economy from reaping the benefits of financial globalisation and has led to substantial loss of monetary policy autonomy (Shah and Patnaik 2008). On the contrary, the view from the RBI has been that given the configuration of Indian fiscal and current account deficit, issues relating to quality of assets in the Indian banking sector, and the Indian inflation experience, the policy has served India well (Mohan and Kapur 2009).[1]

It is in this context that the present chapter chronicles the story of the Indian economy, which with a perennial current account deficit has experienced a two-way movement in its exchange (with some stability) in the presence of sporadic intervention by the RBI in the forex market. Faced with the fickleness of capital flows (in tune with global cycles), Indian authorities maintain a calibrated pace of capital account convertibility, making a distinction between short-term and long-term capital flows as well as between debt and equity. In particular, India has tried to avoid the 'original sin' of issuing foreign currency-denominated sovereign debt. It is important to acknowledge here that these policies adopted by India have significant implications on the real sector of the economy, especially on output, employment and inflation. Also, these policies through their impact on exchange rate movements, may have also influenced India's international trade. However, in this chapter we are not looking at real sectors of the economy and are focusing more on the policy measures adopted by the RBI to manage the complexities associated with the impossible trinity.

Rest of the chapter is organised as follows. While the following section discusses the various aspects of the tensions of the impossible trinity, the broad trends in Indian balance of payments (BOP) is taken up in the third section. The compromise between the three vertices of the impossible trinity is discussed in the fourth section as the fifth section concludes the paper.

Reconciling the Tensions of Impossible Trinity: A Digression

The impossible trinity or trilemma has entered the economic policy maker's toolbox in a significant way. It refers to the impossibility of attaining the following three things by any country simultaneously, viz., (*i*) fixed exchange rate; (*ii*) monetary independence; and (*iii*) free capital inflows (Figure 9.1). As mentioned above, the result is a direct derivative of the Mundell–Fleming model wherein under flexible exchange rate and perfect capital mobility, interest parity conditions will be valid and thus, no country can attain monetary independence unless it puts restrictions on its capital flows.[2] In an open economy, thus, exchange rate assumes the

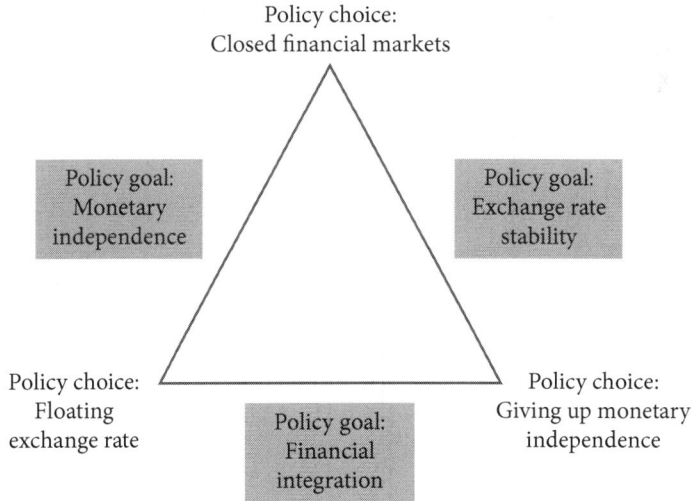

Fig. 9.1: The impossible trinity

Source: Aizenman (2013)

role of interest rate in a closed economy model, namely that of an equilibrator adjusting effective demand. Of course, the advantage of flexible exchange rates arises from the Marshall–Lerner condition, whereby depreciation improves trade balance of a country by making its exports more competitive. In other words, any country is confronted with 'three typically desirable, yet contradictory, objectives: (*i*) to stabilise the exchange rate; (*ii*) to enjoy free international capital mobility; (*iii*) to engage in a monetary policy oriented toward domestic goals' (Obstfeld et al. 2005).

In global economy, there are illustrations of each of the corners of the open economy policy triangle. For example, the US has perfect capital mobility with monetary policy, and hence it cannot have fixed exchange rate. On the contrary, many of the oil-exporting middle-east countries do have fixed exchange rate and capital mobility at the cost of monetary policy independence. Yet another example could be that of China which could maintain monetary policy independence and semi-fixed exchange rate through capital account restrictions.

These results are often seen as corner cases. But in reality, there could be intermediate cases whereby a country can sacrifice little of one objective and thereby gain some flexibility on account of another. Mundell (1963) himself was aware of this possibility and categorically stated:

> Of course the assumption of perfect capital mobility is not literally valid; my conclusions are black and white rather than dark and light grey. To the extent that Canada can maintain an interest rate equilibrium different from that of the United States, without strong capital inflows, fiscal expansion can be expected to play some role in employment policy under flexible exchange rates, and monetary policy can have some influence on employment and output under fixed exchange rates. But if this possibility exists for us today, we can conjecture that it will exist to a lesser extent in the future (p. 485).

Over the years, enough ink has flown to explain contours of the impossible trinity. Instead of attempting any detailed survey of the available literature, three comments are presented particularly, in the current context.[3]

First, in a detailed and careful analysis of cross-country policy experience, Obstfeld et al. (2005) came to a conclusion of a reasonable validation of the policy trilemma and observed,

> The overall lesson of our analysis is that the trilemma makes sense as a guiding policy framework. Exchange rate pegs do result in a substantially closer connection to the base country interest rate than do nonpegs. The interest rates of pegged economies react more to changes in the base rate; the base rate can explain more of the changes in the local rate for pegs; and, the pegs react more quickly and have a stronger long run relationship to the base than do nonpegs. Absent capital controls, countries choosing to peg lose considerable monetary independence. At the same time, nonpegs appear to have a reasonable amount of autonomy even when there are no capital controls. Pegs are rarely completely handcuffed (in any era) though, because of exchange rate bands and, possibly, arbitrage costs. Conversely, nonpegs are never purely free floats, as even countries that are not pegging their currencies do often choose to follow the base interest rate to some degree (p. 22).[4]

Second, more recently, Rey (2018[2015])studied the cyclical pattern of capital flows (both debt and equity) across the world and came to the conclusion, 'The global financial cycle transforms the trilemma into a "dilemma" or an "irreconcilable duo": independent monetary policies are possible if and only if the capital account is managed.' In fact, net capital flows in general and portfolio flows in particular, exhibited considerable volatility in the recent past and the latter has been on a downward trend since 2011 (Figure 9.2).

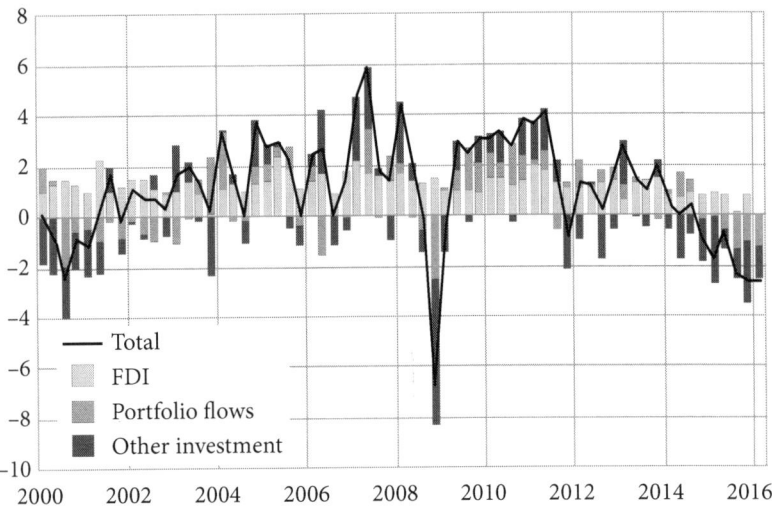

Fig. 9.2: Net capital inflows to EMEs (percentages of nominal GDP)
Source: ECB 2016

Third, more importantly, how does a country control capital flows? It is in this spirit that Aizenman (2013) tried to incorporate the importance of financial stability via 'reserves accumulation' in the context of the trilemma and noted,

> An unintended consequence of financial globalization is the growing exposure of developing countries to financial turbulences associated with sudden stops of inflows of capital, capital flights, and deleveraging crises. The significant output and social costs associated with financial crises, estimated on average about 10% of the GDP, added financial stability to the three policy goals framed by the original Trilemma, *changing thereby the policy Trilemma into the policy Quadrilemma* (emphasis added).

Thus, in view of the wide gyrations in capital inflows to emerging market economies (EME) and their adverse effects, some of the earlier orthodoxies are questioned. Even organisations like the IMF now recognise that in the policy tool box of an EME there is a legitimate place of 'macroprudential measures'.

What are macroprudential measures? While there is no universally accepted definition, macroprudential policy is interpreted as the use of 'prudential actions to contain risks that, if realised, could have widespread implications for the financial system as a whole as well as the real economy' (Orsmond and Price 2016). Generically, one can distinguish between the following four types of tools.

1. *Broad-based capital tools*, such as dynamic provisioning requirements, and time-varying leverage ratio caps;
2. *Sectoral capital and borrower-based tools* like restrictions on borrowers, such as caps on loans-to-value ratios (LVRs), debt-to-income ratios and debt-service-to-income ratios as well as restrictions on lenders such as risk-weight floors and sectoral capital requirements;
3. *Liquidity-related tools*, such as reserve requirements, the liquidity coverage ratio (LCR) requirement, the net stable funding ratio (NSFR) requirement and caps on loan-to-deposit ratios;
4. *Structural tools*, such as interbank exposure limits and additional loss-absorbing capacity for systemically important financial institutions.

It may be noted that the use of all four types of measures has increased across all types of economies over the past decade (Figure 9.3).

To sum up, notwithstanding the validity of the impossible trinity, there are ample policy tools available to manage the implicit tensions. It is against this backdrop that the rest of the chapter looks at how the Indian authorities negotiate the pushes and pulls of the impossible trinity.

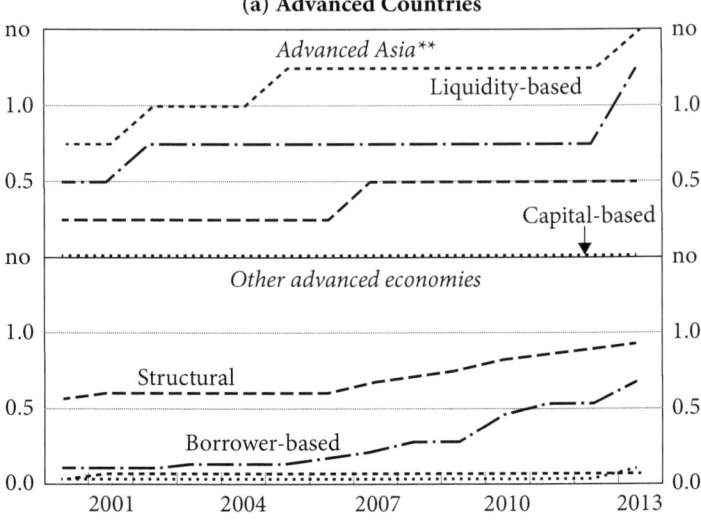
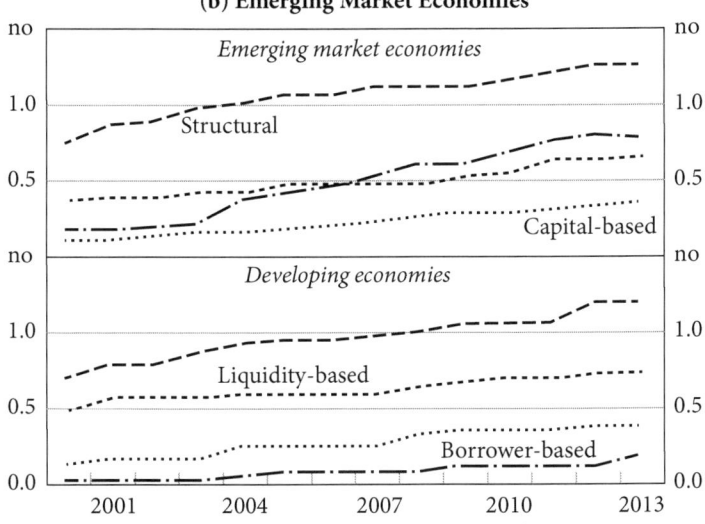

Fig. 9.3: Use of macroprudential tools

Note: Use is measured by the average number of tools used per economy type.
**Advanced Asia includes Hong Kong, Japan, Singapore and South Korea

Source: Orsmond and Price (2016)

Nature of India's BOP

In order to appreciate the extent of the tensions of the impossible trinity in India, we begin with a brief discussion on India's balance of payments. If one considers a long-run analysis, then the evolution of India's BOP reflected the changes in Indian economy and its policy contours and exogenous shocks. In the 60-year span, from 1951–52 till 2013, seven events had a lasting impact on our BOP: (*i*) the devaluation in 1966; (*ii*) first and second oil shocks of 1973 and 1980; (*iii*) external payments crisis of 1991; (*iv*) the East Asian crisis of 1997; (*v*) the Y2K event of 2000; (*vi*) the Global Financial Crisis of 2008; and (*vii*) the taper tantrum episode of 2013 (Mohanty 2012; Ray 2013). See Figure 9.4.

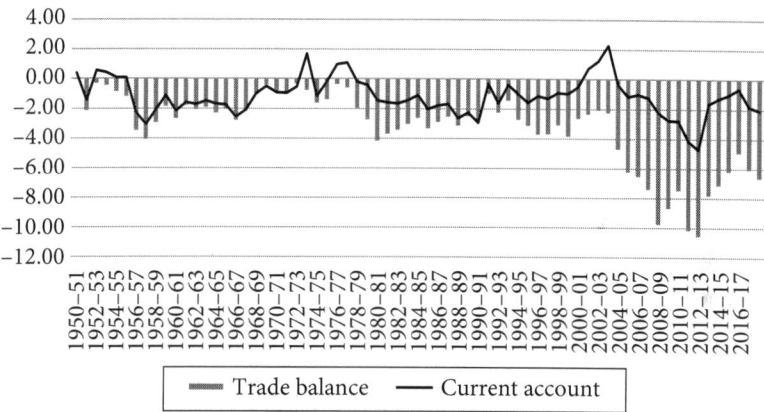

Fig. 9.4: Long-term trends in India's current account (% of GDP)
Source: RBI (n.d.)

However, in the present chapter we focus our attention to India's BOP since the beginning of the new millennium. It reveals a number of interesting stylised facts. First, unlike many of its East Asian neighbours, India has been experiencing a trade deficit consistently (Table 9.1). Various factors may be held responsible. Factors such as India's lacklustre industrialisation,

Table 9.1: India's balance of payments (US$ billion)

Year/Item	2000–01	2001–02	2002–03	2003–04	2004–05	2005–06	2006–07	2007–08	2008–09	2009–10	2010–11	2011–12	2012–13	2013–14	2014–15	2015–16	2016–17	2017–18	2018–19
A) Current Account	−2.7	3.4	6.3	14.1	−2.5	−9.9	−9.6	−15.7	−27.9	−38.2	−48.1	−78.2	−88.2	−32.3	−26.9	−22.2	−15.3	−48.7	−57.3
A.1) Merchandise	−12.5	−11.6	−10.7	−13.7	−33.7	−51.9	−61.8	−91.5	−119.5	−118.2	−127.3	−189.8	−195.7	−147.6	−144.9	−130.1	−112.4	−160	−180.3
A.2) Invisibles	9.8	15	17	27.8	31.2	42	52.2	75.7	91.6	80	79.3	111.6	107.5	115.3	118.1	107.9	97.1	111	123
o/w Software Services	5.8	6.9	8.9	12.3	16.9	22.3	29	36.9	43.7	48.2	50.9	61	63.5	67	70.4	71.5	70.1	72	77.7
o/w Private Transfers	12.9	15.4	16.4	21.6	20.5	24.5	29.8	41.7	44.6	51.8	53.1	63.5	64.3	65.5	66.3	63.1	56.6	63	70.6
B) Capital Account	8.8	8.6	10.8	16.7	28	25.5	45.2	106.6	7.4	51.6	63.7	67.8	89.3	48.8	89.3	41.1	36.5	91	−57.3
B.1) Foreign Investment	5.9	6.7	4.2	13.7	13	15.5	14.8	43.3	8.3	50.4	42.1	39.2	46.7	26.4	73.5	31.9	43.2	52	30.1
o/w Direct Investment	3.3	4.7	3.2	2.4	3.7	3	7.7	15.9	22.4	18	11.8	22.1	19.8	21.6	31.3	36	35.6	30	30.7
o/w Portfolio Investment	2.6	2	0.9	11.4	9.3	12.5	7.1	27.4	−14	32.4	30.3	17.2	26.9	4.8	42.2	−4.1	7.6	22	−0.6
B.2) Loans	5.3	−1.3	−3.9	−4.4	10.9	7.9	24.5	40.7	8.3	12.4	29.1	19.3	31.1	7.8	3.2	−4.6	2.4	17	15.9
B.3) Banking Capital	−2	2.9	10.4	6	3.9	1.4	1.9	11.8	−3.2	2.1	5	16.2	16.6	25.4	11.6	10.6	−16.6	16	7.4
B.4) Rupee Debt Service	−0.6	−0.5	−0.5	−0.4	−0.4	−0.6	−0.2	−0.1	−0.1	−0.1	−0.1	−0.1	−0.1	−0.1	−0.1	−0.1	−0.1	−0.1	0
B.5) Other Capital	0.3	0.8	0.6	1.7	0.7	1.2	4.2	11	−5.9	−13.2	−12.4	−6.9	−5	−10.8	1.1	3.3	7.6	6	1.1
C) Errors and Omissions	−0.3	−0.2	−0.2	0.6	0.6	−0.5	1	1.3	0.4	0	−2.6	−2.4	2.7	−1	−1	−1.1	0.4	0.9	−0.5
E) Forex Reserves (Increase −/ Decrease +)	−5.8	−11.8	−17	−31.4	−26.2	−15.1	−36.6	−92.2	20.1	−13.4	−13.1	12.8	−3.8	−15.5	−61.4	−17.9	−21.6	−43.6	3.3
Memo: Stock of Forex Reserves	42.3	54.1	76.1	113	141.5	151.6	199.2	309.7	252	279.1	304.8	294.4	292	304.2	341.6	360.2	370	424.4	412.8

Source: RBI (n.d.)

inability to develop a competitive export basket, a baggage of export pessimism and the strong focus on self-reliance in the first forty years of Indian planning, a huge dependence on the import of oil and gas, an insatiable demand for gold imports and adoption of a consumption-led growth model—all could have their share in this phenomenon of high and persistent trade deficit.

Second, notwithstanding the high trade deficit, India's current account deficit has been moderate. With the exception of 2012–13 it has never touched 5 per cent of GDP (Figure 9.5). This moderate current account deficit is an outcome of India's impressive performance in the invisibles front. Particularly, substantial inflows on account of software exports and private transfers (reflecting Indian remittances) led to sizeable surplus in the invisibles front.

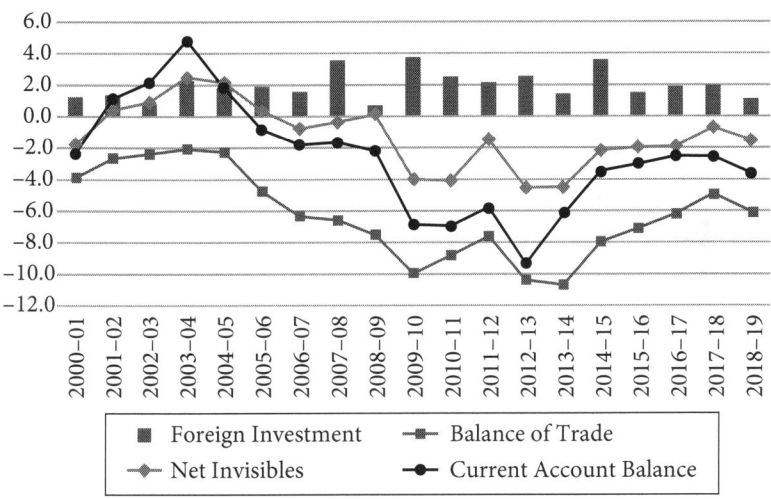

Fig. 9.5: India's BOP indicators (% of GDP)
Source: RBI (n.d.)

Third, such moderate current account deficits are turned into overall BOP surplus because of sizeable foreign investment inflows to India (Figure 9.5). There is, however, an interesting feature of the constituents of foreign investment, viz., foreign direct investment (FDI) and foreign portfolio investment (FPI). While FDI has been reasonably stable, FPI, in tune with the global cycles of capital flows to EMEs, has shown sharp gyrations (Figure 9.6). Illustratively, there were net outflows on account of FPI during March–September 2013 or September–December 2016. Such wide fluctuations happened both in debt and equity component of FPI (Figure 9.7). According to reports submitted to the Securities and Exchange Board of India (SEBI), from January 2018 to December 2019, India experienced net FII (foreign institutional investors) outflows in equities in 9 of the 24 months while net FII outflow in debt has also happened in most of the months of this period.[5]

Fourth, as a result of the moderate current account deficit and sizeable (but somewhat volatile) capital inflows, excepting 2008–09 and 2011–12, there were accretions in India's forex reserves (Table 9.1). However, largely due to the net outflow of foreign portfolio capital from the Indian market in the last few years, as of September 2022, the stock of India's forex reserves stood at little over US$ 532 billion with foreign currency assets at around US$ 473 billion.[6]

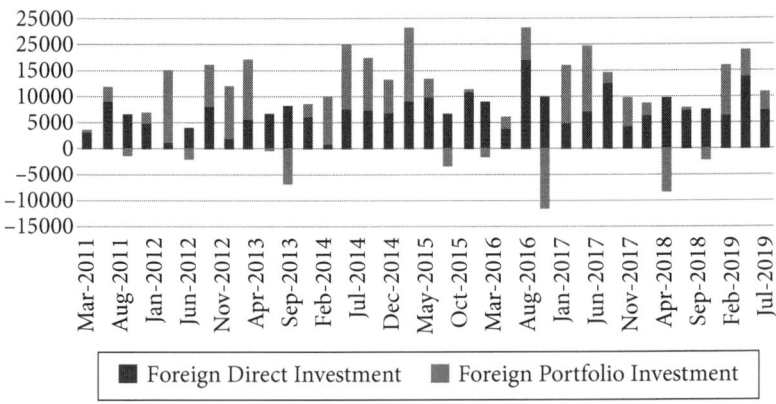

Fig. 9.6: FDI and FPI in India's capital account of BOP (US$ million)
Source: RBI (n.d.)

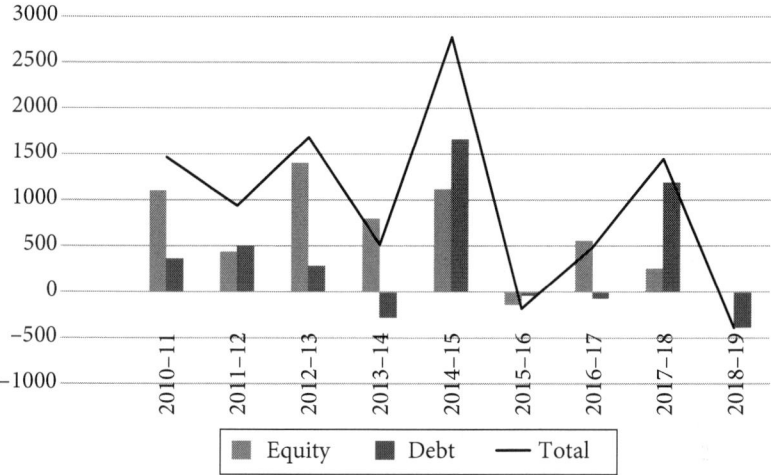

FIG. 9.7: Composition of FPI in India (INR billion)
Source: SEBI (n.d.)

Where does India stand in the triangle of the impossible trinity?

EXCHANGE RATES

What would be the implications of such BOP patterns on India's exchange rate? Admittedly, while the state of balance of payments is one of the key factors determining exchange, it is not the only one; factors such as inflation, interest rate, government debt and its composition, political stability, state of foreign capital inflows, terms of trade, speculation, and central bank intervention could all play a role. We have discussed some of these issues in Pal and Ray (2018). A survey of some recent empirical works on the same topic is covered in Sengupta (2015).

What has been the official stand of India on intervention in the forex market? RBI Governor Bimal Jalan in a speech in 2003 gave an authoritative description of the RBI's policy of intervention in the forex market.

In RBI's periodic credit policy statements, as well as other public statements, RBI has highlighted the main pillars of its strategy for the management of the exchange rate. These are: *RBI does not have a fixed 'target' for the exchange rate which it tries to defend or pursue over time*; RBI is prepared to intervene in the market to dampen excessive volatility as and when necessary; RBI's purchases or sales of foreign currency are undertaken through a number of banks and are generally discrete and smooth; and market operations and exchange rate movement should, in principle, be transaction-oriented rather than purely speculative in nature (Jalan 2003; emphasis added).

But what has been the pattern in India's exchange rate movement? Figure 9.8 depicts the exchange rate of INR with respect to four major currencies, viz., US dollar (USD), Euro (EUR), British Pound (GBP), and Japanese Yen (JPY). While it is not possible to explain the exchange rate of rupee with respect to each of these currencies, an interesting feature of these charts in Figure 9.8 is the presence of two-way movement in the exchange rate of the rupee, indicating significant play of market forces in the Indian forex market.

(Contd)

Fig. 9.8 (Contd)

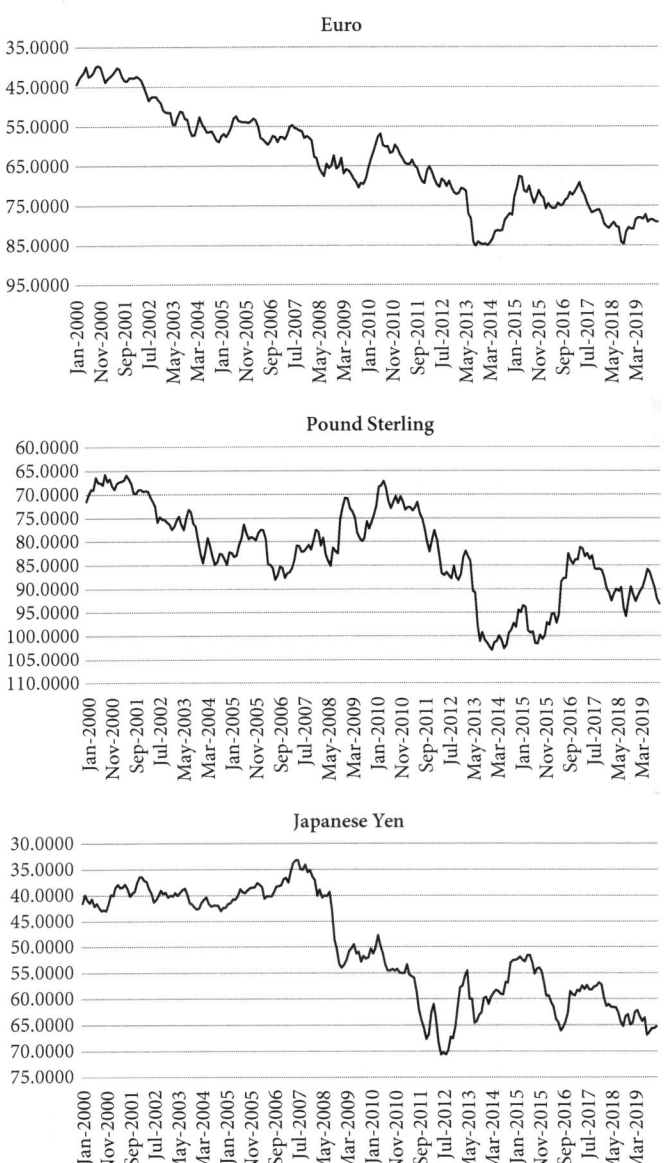

FIG. 9.8: Exchange rate of INR with respect to four major currencies (vertical axis values in reverse order)

Source: RBI (n.d.)

Strikingly the real effective exchange rate (REER) of India has been on an upward trajectory since September 2013. In fact, Joshi (2017) noted that while from 1993–94 to 2004–05, the real effective exchange rate moved within a fairly narrow band of +/– 5 per cent around a nearly flat trend, however, there has been a significant real appreciation from 2004–05 to 2017–18 (Figure 9.9). In fact, 'in the nine years after the 2008/09 global crisis, the REER has appreciated at a trend rate of about 2.5 per cent a year' (Joshi 2017). Indian economy with a low export growth, thus, posed a riddle as rarely there has been any high-growth economy without rapid growth in its net exports. India, so far, has been an exception to this general stylised fact (refer to the third section); after all, Indian growth has been driven primarily by domestic consumption followed by domestic investment. This could be reflective of the Indian pattern of industrialisation in the initial days of planning followed by service sector growth.

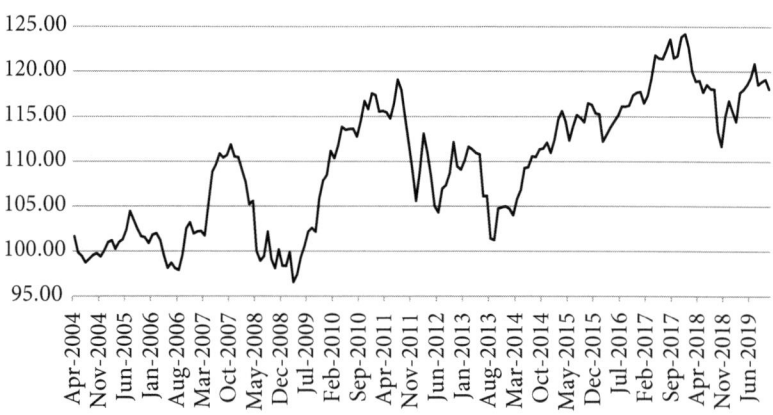

Fig. 9.9: Indices of real effective exchange rate (REER) of the Indian rupee (36-currency bilateral weights) (monthly average)

Source: RBI (n.d.)

Monetary Policy

As far as monetary policy is concerned, since 1998 and till recently India used to follow a multiple-indicators approach, whereby a number of quantity variables such as money, credit, output, trade, capital flows and fiscal position as well as rate variables such as rates of return in different markets, inflation rate and exchange rate are analysed for drawing monetary policy perspectives (RBI 2014). To the extent exchange rate and capital flows are taken into account for formulating monetary policy, some monetary independence could have been lost. In fact, there is an influential view that despite India's transition from relatively 'fixed exchange rate regime' to a 'managed float regime', India's exchange rate exhibited considerable stability and that such stability is due to large intervention by the central bank to manage exchange rate volatility (Mohanty and Bhanumurthy 2014).[7]

Subsequently, with the adoption of a flexible inflation-targeting regime, Indian monetary policy framework has undergone a major change since 2013—initially somewhat informally and later more formally when the inflation-targeting regime got statutory backing in 2016. Under the new regime, the Indian government set a target for the RBI: to bring down aggregate CPI inflation below 6 per cent by January 2016; the target for 2016–17 and all subsequent years was set at 4 per cent with a band of +/– 2 per cent (Mohan and Ray 2018).

While the broad philosophy of the exchange rate policy of the RBI remained more or less unchanged since the beginning of the new millennium, the extent of intervention in the currency market differed. For example, even if both the nominal and real exchange rates appreciated, accompanied by a widening trade and current account deficit until late 2011, the RBI hardly intervened in the foreign exchange market (Figure 9.10). However, it must be acknowledged here that the official intervention numbers by the RBI may not show the total government intervention in the market as the RBI also makes some public sector banks intervene in the foreign exchange market on its behalf. The RBI intervention data may be an underestimation of the actual intervention.

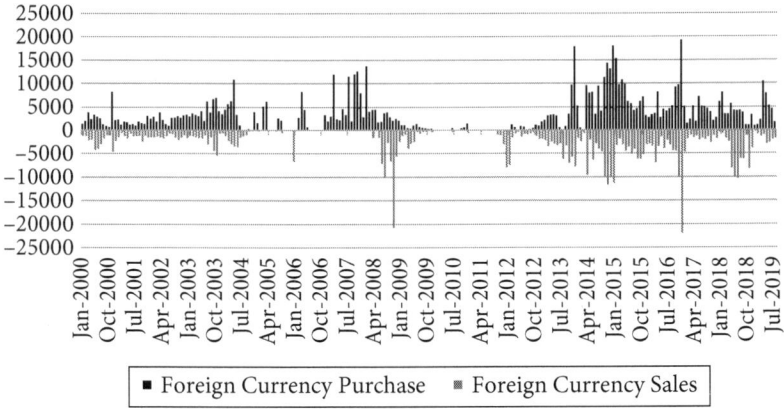

FIG. 9.10: RBI's sale and purchase of foreign exchange (US$ million): Outstanding net forward sales (–) / purchase (+) at end of month (US$ million)

Source: RBI (n.d.)

In spite of the caveat mentioned above, this hands-off approach to forex market intervention by the RBI during this period was also accompanied by loosening of restrictions on FPI in the domestic government securities and corporate debt markets: with falling global interest rates, debt portfolio inflows amounted to between 1.5 and 2 per cent of GDP in 2012 and 2013 until the taper tantrum. These flows added to the upward pressure on the exchange rate in the absence of intervention. Subsequently, the RBI changed its intervention strategy after being bitten by the taper tantrum as there were substantial capital outflows from India on account of both debt and equity.[8] This changed intervention strategy coincided with a change of guard in RBI with Raghuram Rajan taking over as RBI Governor on 5 September 2013 (Mohan and Ray 2018).

What is the qualitative judgment about the extent of the intervention of the RBI in the forex market? Was it excessive? Despite the official pronouncements, does RBI follow an interventionist strategy in its foreign exchange market? It is in this context that reference may be made to a recent report of the US Treasury titled *Macroeconomic and Foreign Exchange Policies of Major Trading Partners of the United States* (US Treasury 2018). Based on a few specific criteria, the US Treasury reviews exchange rate policies of its major trading partners—a euphemism for determining whether a country is a manipulator of its exchange rate. Three criteria were highlighted in particular, viz., (*i*) a significant bilateral trade surplus with the United States is one that is at least $ 20 billion; (*ii*) a material current account surplus is one that is at least 3 per cent of GDP; and (*iii*) persistent, one-sided intervention occurs when net purchases of foreign currency are conducted repeatedly and total at least 2 per cent of an economy's GDP over a 12-month period. Six countries were identified in the monitoring list, viz., China, Japan, Korea, Germany, Switzerland and India. The report discussed the case of India at length and made the following observation:

> India increased its purchases of foreign exchange over the first three quarters of 2017.... Notwithstanding the increase in intervention, the rupee appreciated by more than 6 per cent against the dollar and by more than 3 per cent on a real effective basis in 2017. India has a significant bilateral goods trade surplus with the United States, totalling $23 billion in 2017, but India's current account is in deficit at 1.5 per cent of GDP and the exchange rate is not deemed to be undervalued by the IMF. Given that Indian foreign exchange reserves are ample by common metrics, and that India maintains some controls on both inbound and outbound flows of private capital, *further reserve accumulation does not appear necessary* (US Treasury 2018: 4; emphasis added).

Admittedly, Indian forex reserves have increased nearly tenfold from about US$ 42 billion in March 2001 to about US$ 423 billion by March 2018 (Figure 9.11).[9] Does India have excess reserves? The US Treasury (2018) report thinks so—as it finds that as a percentage of short-term debt, India's forex reserves are more than 400 per cent of its short-term debt, just next to Brazil's whose forex reserves are more than 680 per cent of its short-term debt (Table 9.2). But as a percentage of GDP, India's forex reserves stood much lower (at around 15 per cent) than many of the emerging market economies.

FIG. 9.11: Foreign currency reserves (US$ billion)

Source: RBI (n.d.)

But India is a net commodity importing country with significant exposure to volatile foreign portfolio capital. The reserve adequacy numbers must consider these structural vulnerabilities of the economy. For example, some fraction of the stock of foreign portfolio investment (in mark to market pricing[10]) should be provisioned for when calculating adequacy of foreign exchange reserves. Similarly, some additional buffer should also be kept in the forex reserves as India is a big fuel importer. The IMF suggests that in countries with relatively open capital account, a fraction of the broad money (M2) may

Table 9.2: Some metrics of forex reserves of select countries, end of 2017

	FX reserves (% of GDP)	FX reserves (% of short-term debt)
Brazil	18	687
India	15	415
Mexico	14	321
Korea	25	319
China	26	307
Taiwan	80	278
Switzerland	112	72
Japan	25	45
Canada	5	13
Italy	2	4
UK	5	2
France	1	2
Germany	1	2

Source: US Treasury (2018)

also be included to estimate the potential of capital outflow threat from the country (see IMF 2016). As India has gradually opened up its capital account,[11] this also needs to be considered. It may also be noted that unlike most countries with high foreign exchange reserves, India is a country with significant current account deficit. Once these issues are factored in, it is doubtful whether India's foreign exchange reserves will still be considered as adequate. It is worth noting here that technically, the distinction between the current and capital accounts has to be drawn in terms of 'quid pro quo' obligations. While the current account transactions do not carry any repayment obligations, the capital transactions are distinguished precisely by such repayment obligations. The latter transactions transform themselves into some form of assets or liabilities whereas no such obligations arise in current transactions. Therefore, a foreign exchange reserve driven by current account surpluses is drastically different in nature than one primarily driven by capital account surpluses.

Moreover, in determining the objective of forex reserves, the professed policy of the RBI noted that the demands placed on the foreign exchange reserves might vary widely depending upon a variety of factors, such as the exchange rate regime adopted by the country, the extent of openness of the economy, the size of the external sector in a country's GDP and the nature of markets operating in the country (RBI 2017). Apart from safety and liquidity, optimising returns is also kept in view in focusing on the objectives of reserve management.

Also, admittedly, accumulation of forex reserves has a cost. But, it has been argued that as the result of the East Asian crisis and treatment that many of the East Asian nations got from the IMF and/or the conditionalities of the IMF loan, many of these countries realised the utility of self-insurance in the accumulation of forex reserves (Ray and Nag 2018). Countries like India or China who were not that affected by the East Asian crisis realised this. Mercantilist export promotion through currency management may be another positive fallout of building foreign exchange reserves but in the case of India it is likely that the insurance motive was the more dominant motive for building up the forex reserve.

Capital flows, of course, posed serious challenge to Indian monetary policy. A major challenge of increasing capital flows has been handled by the Indian authorities in an innovative way. The Market Stabilisation Scheme (MSS) was introduced in April 2004 for this purpose. The MSS is an innovative arrangement under which the Reserve Bank issues treasury bills/dated government securities by way of auctions and the cost of sterilisation is borne by the government. Visually a bond issued under MSS scheme is no different from any other bonds issued by the government but the proceeds from MSS are ring-fenced so that the government cannot use its proceeds. It is important to remind ourselves, the scheme works by impounding the proceeds of auctions of Treasury bill and Government securities in a separate identifiable MSS cash account maintained and operated by the RBI; the amounts credited into the MSS cash account are appropriated only for the purpose of redemption and/or buyback of the Treasury Bills and/or dated securities issued under the MSS (Mohan 2008).

Of course, the interest expenses on MSS bonds, being borne by the government, led to high cost of sterilisation.[12]

How independent is India's monetary policy? In terms of practice, monetary policy independence is often identified with the freedom to set monetary policy rates independently of those of other countries. Thus, a popular way to test monetary policy independence is via estimation of co-movement of short-term interest rates (Kharroubi and Zampolli 2016). In this spirit, Sen Gupta and Sengupta (2013) calculated a 'quarterly index of monetary independence' using weekly 3-month Treasury bill yields for India and the US. While the monetary independence index witnessed significant volatility, there is a perceptible upward trend since the early 2000s.

Another set of evidence on independence of India's monetary policy comes from the empirical literature on effectiveness of sterilisation operations by the RBI. Table 9.3 shows estimates of sterilisation coefficient as reported by different studies since 2004. A sterilisation coefficient measures the extent by which the net domestic assets (NDA) of a central bank change in response to a change in net foreign assets (NFA). The sterilisation coefficient can vary between 0 to −1, where −1 means that the impact of capital inflow on base money has been completely neutralised. On the other hand, a value of 0 implies that the intervention in the foreign exchange market has increased the reserve money by the same amount. Estimates of sterilisation coefficients in Table 9.3 show that the RBI has managed to calibrate the growth of reserve money to a large extent, in spite of the persistent capital inflows and regular intervention of the central bank in the foreign exchange market.

Table 9.3: Estimates of sterilisation coefficient

Author	Time Period	Estimates
Patnaik (2004)	Monthly data (April 1993–December 2003)	–0.82
RBI (2004)	Monthly data (April 1994–September 2003) (October 1995–September 2003)	–0.92 –0.65
Sen Gupta and Sengupta (2013)	Monthly data (January 1990–August 2010)	–0.21 to –0.61
Raj et al. (2018)	Monthly data for over a 20-year period (July 1997–October 2017)	–1.03
SBI (2018)	Monthly data (fiscal year 2013–2018)	–0.93

Source: Compiled by the authors

Restrictions on Capital Account

The third vertex of the impossible trinity triangle relates to capital mobility. India tended to have a number of draconian restrictions on capital account, which was codified by the Foreign Exchange Regulation Act (FERA), 1973. With the initiation of the economic reforms process, the foreign exchange market was also liberalised in a 'calibrated' (a RBI phrase) manner. First, the new Liberalised Exchange Rate Management System (LERMS) involving a dual exchange rate mechanism was instituted in March 1992; this dual exchange rate system was abolished later and a unified exchange rate system became effective from 1 March 1993 (RBI 2006). Subsequently, in 1994, a number of measures were announced for liberalising exchange control regulations; these were related to: (*i*) foreign currency accounts of exchange earners; (*ii*) basic travel quota; (*iii*) studies abroad; (*iv*) gift remittances; (*v*) donations, and (*vi*) payments due to certain services rendered by foreign parties. The current account was gradually liberalised in the 1990s with the elimination of quantitative trade restrictions and gradual reduction of tariffs and in 1994 current account convertibility obligations under Article VIII of the Articles of Agreement of the IMF were accepted (Mohan and Kapur 2009).

Capital account liberalisation was, however, much more gradual. In 1997, an RBI Committee with S. S. Tarapore as its

Chairman (the Tarapore Committee) constituted on capital account convertibility (CAC) and indicated the road map for CAC, pointing out that there needs to be three crucial preconditions for India: (a) fiscal consolidation; (b) low inflation; and (c) strong financial/banking system. Since it was followed by the East Asian crisis of the late 1990s, there was a lull in India's opening up of the capital account. Subsequently, in 2006, the Committee on Fuller Capital Account Convertibility (FCAC) (Chairman: S. S. Tarapore) went through the same issue and summarised the then existing status of capital account convertibility as follows:

> ... for foreign corporates, and foreign institutions, there is a reasonable amount of convertibility; for non-resident Indians (NRIs) there is approximately an equal amount of convertibility, but one accompanied by severe procedural and regulatory impediments. For non-resident individuals, other than NRIs, there is near-zero convertibility. Movement towards FCAC implies that all non-residents (corporates and individuals) should be treated equally. This would mean the removal of the tax benefits presently accorded to NRIs via special bank deposit schemes for NRIs (RBI 2006: 27).

Meanwhile the earlier draconian FERA 1973 was replaced by a more market-friendly Foreign Exchange Management Act (FEMA), 1999, which effectively discriminated between current and capital account transactions, the former unrestricted and the latter subject to regulations. Interestingly, 'While the overarching framework has not changed during the last 15 years, there have been significant changes in the operating procedure ... The process has been mostly in one direction; the capital account transactions have been progressively liberalised without any significant pause or regression' (Padmanabhan 2015).

What is the current status? The philosophy of capital controls had three distinctions: (*i*) non-residents and residents; under residents, households, corporates and FIIs; (*ii*) debt and equity;

and (*iii*) inflows and outflows (Gopinath 2005). At the current juncture the following broad specifics are worth mentioning:

- **Foreign direct investment (FDI)**: FDI is allowed through the automatic route into most sectors. FDI caps apply for certain sectors (see, https://dpiit.gov.in/foreign-direct-investment/foreign-direct-investment-policy).
- **Foreign portfolio investment (FPI) in equity**: Registered foreign institutional investors such as pension funds, mutual funds, investment trusts are allowed to invest in equity. The overall limit on residents' investments in companies listed abroad is $ 200,000 a year. Indian mutual funds are permitted to invest within an overall cap of $ 7 billion.
- **Foreign portfolio investment (FPI) in bond**: These are presently in the form of absolute size limits on (*i*) total FPI in domestic securities by asset class, with separate limits for Government of India securities, state development loans, and corporate bonds, amounting to around $ 39 billion, $ 6 billion and $ 36 billion, respectively, or a total of about $ 80 billion across the three asset categories; and on (*ii*) external commercial borrowings (ECBs) and rupee denominated bonds (RDB) (popularly called the *Masala* bonds) together, amounting to a total of about $ 130 billion (Acharya and Krishnamurthy 2018).
- **Derivatives**: These transactions are generally subject to limits and approval. Hedging of non-residents' investments in India is allowed. Commercial banks may purchase such instruments for their asset and liability management. Resident companies may use derivatives to hedge commodity price and foreign exchange debt exposures.
- **External commercial borrowing**: ECBs are allowed through automatic and approval route. ECBs through automatic route are subject to a cap of $ 20 million for a

minimum three-year average maturity and $ 750 million for a minimum five-year average maturity. External loans are subject to an all-in-cost ceiling and end-use restrictions. Lending abroad is generally subject to approval, except for certain trade credits and lending to foreign subsidiaries.

A key issue in Indian capital account convertibility has been the essential distinction between debt and equity. Indian authorities have been far more conservative in opening up the debt market.[13] Three principal kinds of external debt (excepting government debt from multilateral agencies and non-resident Indian deposits) can be distinguished: (*i*) FPI in domestic debt (in both Government of India securities at centre and state level, and corporate bonds); (*ii*) ECB; and, (*iii*) 'Masala bonds' (issued overseas by quasi-government entities or private firms, typically listed on the London Stock Exchange) (Acharya and Krishnamurthy 2018). These show remarkable volatility (see Figure 9.12).

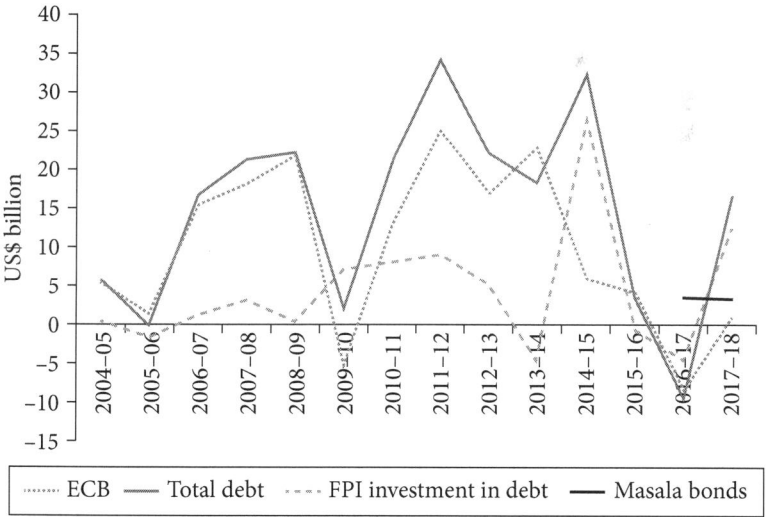

Fig. 9.12: Debt flows in various forms

Source: Acharya and Krishnamurthy (2018)

Concluding Observations

Policy choice in the real world is often messy and may not have the elegance of a theoretical construct. Taking the case of the impossible trinity or policy trilemma of exchange rate flexibility, monetary policy independence and capital controls, this chapter illustrates the case of the messy policy choice for India. It shows how in the presence of a peculiar configuration of significant and consistent current account deficit and substantial but volatile capital flows (often dominated by fickle portfolio flows), Indian monetary authorities have intervened in the forex market. Consequently, exchange rate of the rupee while experiencing episodes of volatility (such as the one associated with the taper tantrum) has shown some stability. The nature of intervention by the monetary authorities in India and the extent of capital controls have, however, been varied. Will it withstand the test of the times we live in? In the current scenario where the threat of a global slowdown and a trade war could be real (Lagarde 2019), will the Indian policy of selective intervention and making practicable compromises among the vertices of the triangle of impossible trinity be successful? It seems that these questions are going to be blowing in the wind in the days to come.

NOTES

Acknowledgements: The authors gratefully acknowledge the observations made by Ashima Goyal, Anindya Sen, Soumyen Sikdar and other participants of the conference on 'Perspectives on the Contemporary Indian Economy' held at IIM Calcutta (during 21–22 February 2019), in which this paper was presented. In particular, they are indebted to Rajat Acharyya for his insightful comments on an earlier draft of this paper. We are also grateful to S. L. Shetty for his insightful comments on an earlier draft. The views and opinions expressed in this chapter are personal views of the contributors and not of the organisations to which they belong.

[1] Interestingly, insofar as liberalising capital account is concerned, there was no monolithic view held by the Indian authorities; in fact, there was a difference in viewpoints between the RBI and the central government. It was most clearly seen in the 2005 report of the central government-constituted 'Expert Group on Encouraging FII Flows and Checking the Vulnerability of Capital Markets to Speculative Flows' (Ministry of Finance 2005) to which the RBI attached a dissent note. An instance of adding a dissent note from the RBI to a government-appointed committee was almost unheard of. The difference of opinion occurred along various issues, such as measures to contain large volatility in FII (foreign institutional investors) flows, threshold limits of different caps to be imposed on FDI and FII, treatment of Participatory Notes, or treatment of hedge funds. To the popular press, the debate was caricatured as a debate of pro-market and anti-market and was often interpreted as, 'RBI's yearning for more capital controls' (Shah 2006). See Ray (2013) for details.

[2] Under uncovered interest parity condition, $i = i^F + \frac{(\varepsilon - \varepsilon^e)}{\varepsilon^e}$; where ε is the exchange rate, expressed as domestic currency per unit of foreign currency, ε^e is the expected future exchange rate and i and i^F are the domestic and foreign interest rates, respectively. Under the basic Mundell–Fleming assumptions of perfect capital mobility and static exchange rate expectations, the above relationship gets reduced to $i = i^F$ and capital flows become absolutely sensitive to interest rate differentials.

[3] See Obstfeld et al. (2005) for a literature survey.

[4] Later Hosny, Kishor and Bahmoni-Oskooee (2015) reworked this with the dataset of Obstfeld et al. (2005) by using dynamic coefficients. Their regression results were in line with the conclusion of the latter.

[5] Data published by *Moneycontrol* based on data published by SEBI. This is available at https://www.moneycontrol.com/stocks/marketstats/fii_dii_activity/index.php (accessed February 2023).

[6] RBI Weekly Statistical Supplement dated 29 March 2019, which is available at https://rbidocs.rbi.org.in/rdocs/Wss/PDFs/2T_2903 20190B6E8691EE554EE19BADD23020B5DFC9.PDF (accessed February 2023).

[7] Investigating 'whether exchange rate stability in the so called managed float regime has led to lower inflation,' they found that

> it is not the exchange rate stability or volatility per se that has led to low inflation, but, rather, the sterilized intervention of RBI, which has kept a check on reserve money growth and its inflationary consequences resulting from its attempt to maintain a stable exchange rate (Mohanty and Bhanumurthy 2014: 21).

[8] On 22 May 2013, US Federal Reserve Chairman Ben Bernanke made the following statement in his testimony before the US Congress: 'Over the nearly four years since the recovery began, the economy has been held back by a number of headwinds. Some of these headwinds have begun to dissipate recently, in part because of the Federal Reserve's highly accommodative monetary policy' (Bernanke 2012). This statement was largely interpreted by the financial market players as a hint that the US Fed may soon start tapering off the size of the bond-buying programme. Subsequently, Chairman Bernanke indicated in as many words that the inevitable withdrawal of stimulus would happen sooner than expected and said in a press conference on 20 June 2013 (ibid.): 'If the incoming data support the view that the economy is able to sustain a reasonable cruising speed, we will ease the pressure on the accelerator by gradually reducing the pace of purchases.'

[9] Total foreign exchange reserves include foreign currency assets (FCA), gold reserves, Reserve Trench Positions (RTP) and Special Drawing Rights (SDRs).

[10] Mark to market (MTM) is a method of measuring the fair value of accounts that can fluctuate over time, such as assets and liabilities. Mark to market aims to provide a realistic appraisal of an institution's or company's current financial situation based on current market conditions.

[11] Under the Liberalised Remittance Scheme, all resident individuals, including minors, are allowed to freely remit up to US$ 2,50,000 per financial year (April–March) for any permissible current or capital account transaction or a combination of both. For more detail, see https://m.rbi.org.in/Scripts/FAQView.aspx?Id=115#Q1 (accessed February 2023).

[12] For example, Kohli (2011) estimated that the cost of sterilisation increased from Rs 7.6 billion per month in 2006 to over Rs 31 billion in 2007.

[13] This allows India to have some control on the sterilisation process. Without control on debt portfolio flows, sterilisation can become self-defeating.

REFERENCES

Acharya, Viral V. and Arvind Krishnamurthy. 2018. 'Capital Flow Management with Multiple Instruments', NBER Working Paper 24443.

Aizenman, Joshua. 2013. 'The Impossible Trinity—From the Policy Trilemma to the Policy Quadrilemma'. *Global Journal of Economics* 2(1).

Bernanke, Ben S. 2012. 'The Economic Recovery and Economic Policy', Speech at the Economic Club of New York, 20 November. Available at: https://www.federalreserve.gov/newsevents/speech/bernanke20121120a.htm (accessed March 2023).

ECB (European Central Bank). 2016. *Economic Bulletin* 5. Available at https://www.ecb.europa.eu/pub/pdf/other/eb201605_focus01.en.pdf (accessed March 2023).

Gopinath, Shyamala. 2005. 'Foreign Exchange Regulations—A Review', 26 November. Speech by Deputy Governor, RBI in FEDAI's Annual Conference. Available at https://www.rbi.org.in/Scripts/BS_SpeechesView.aspx?Id=220 (accessed February 2023).

Hosny, A. S., N. K. Kishor and M. Bahmani-Oskooee. 2015. 'Understanding the dynamics of the macroeconomic trilemma'. *International Review of Applied Economics* 29(1): 32–64.

IMF. 2016. 'Guidance Note on the Assessment of Reserve Adequacy and Related Considerations'. IMF Staff Report. Available at: https://www.imf.org/external/np/pp/eng/2016/060316.pdf (accessed February 2023).

Jalan, Bimal. 2003. 'Exchange rate management—an emerging consensus?', 14 August. Address by Governor of the Reserve Bank of India at the 14th National Assembly of the Forex Association of India, Mumbai. Available at https://www.bis.org/review/r030828c.pdf (accessed February 2023).

Joshi, Vijay. 2017. 'India's Economic Reforms: Reflections on the Unfinished Agenda', 11 December. Fifteenth L. K. Jha Memorial lecture delivered at the Reserve Bank of India, Mumbai. Available at https://rbidocs.rbi.org.in/rdocs/Speeches/PDFs/0 2SP10021840CF3ECE274447F1824D42D94C41A427C6775F9 F29584955961DB9121DD49F77.PDF (accessed March 2023).

Kharroubi, Enisse and Fabrizio Zampolli. 2016. 'Monetary independence in a financially integrated world: what do measures of interest rate co-movement tell us?' In BIS Papers No. 88, *Expanding the boundaries of monetary policy in Asia and the Pacific*, Basel, BIS.

Kohli, R. 2011. 'India's Experience in Navigating the Trilemma: Do Capital Controls Help?' ICRIER Working Paper 257, June.

Lagarde, Christine. 2019. 'A Delicate Moment for the Global Economy: Three Priority Areas for Action', 2 April. Speech by the IMF Managing Director, U.S. Chamber of Commerce, Washington, D.C. Available at https://www.imf.org/en/News/Articles/2019/03/29/sp040219-a-delicate-moment-for-the-global-economy (accessed February 2023).

Ministry of Finance. 2005. 'Report of the Expert Group on Encouraging FII Flows and Checking the Vulnerability of Capital Markets to Speculative Flows', Chaired by Ashok Lahiri, Government of India, New Delhi, November. Available at https://taxindiaonline.com/RC2/pdfdocs/Report%20EGFII.pdf (accessed March 2023).

Mohan, Rakesh. 2008. 'Capital Flows to India'. *RBI Bulletin* December: 2047–2079.

Mohan, Rakesh and Muneesh Kapur. 2009. 'Managing the Impossible Trinity: Volatile Capital Flows and Indian Monetary Policy'. SCID Working Paper No. 401, Stanford University.

Mohan, Rakesh and Partha Ray. 2018. 'Indian Monetary Policy in the Time of Inflation Targeting and Demonetisation'. Brookings India Working Paper 4.

Mohanty, Biswajit and N. R. Bhanumurthy. 2014. 'Exchange Rate Regimes and Inflation: Evidence from India'. NIPFP Working Paper No. 2014–130.

Mohanty, Deepak. 2012. 'Perspectives on India's balance of payments', 7 December. Speech by Executive Director of the Reserve Bank of India, at the School of Management, KIIT University, Bhubaneswar. Available at https://www.bis.org/review/r121210e.pdf (accessed February 2023).

Mundell, R. A. 1963. 'Capital Mobility and Stabilization Policy under Fixed and Flexible Exchange Rates'. *The Canadian Journal of Economics and Political Science* 29(4): 475–485.

Obstfeld, M., J. C. Shambaugh and A. Taylor. 2005. 'The Trilemma in History: Tradeoffs among Exchange Rates, Monetary Policies, and Capital Mobility'. National Bureau of Economic Research Working Paper No. 10396.

Orsmond, David and Fiona Price. 2016. 'Macroprudential Policy Frameworks and Tools'. *Reserve Bank of Australia Bulletin* December.

Padmanabhan, G. 2015. 'Is India ready for full capital account convertibility?', 16 May. Address by Executive Director of the Bank of India, at the MSNM Besant Institute of PG Management Studies, Mangalore. Available at https://www.bis.org/review/r150522e.htm (accessed February 2023).

Pal, Parthapratim and Partha Ray. 2018. 'Recent Downfall of the Indian Rupee'. *Economic and Political Weekly* 53(41).

Patnaik, Ila. 2004. 'India's Experience with a Pegged Exchange Rate'. *India Policy Forum* 1(1).

Raj, Janak, Sitikantha Pattanaik, Indranil Bhattacharyya and Abhilasha. 2018. 'Forex Market Operations and Liquidity Management'. *RBI Bulletin* August.

Ray, Partha. 2013. *Monetary Policy*, Oxford India Short Introductions. New Delhi: Oxford University Press.

———. 2016. 'The Relationship between the Reserve Bank and the Government of India: Political Economy of Central Banking in India'. In R. Nagaraj and Sripad Motiram (eds), *Political Economy of Contemporary India*. Delhi: Cambridge Press.

Ray, Partha and Biswajit Nag. 2021 'Two Crises Separated by a Decade: Political Economy of Trade Strategy and Reserves Accumulation in East Asia'. *Journal of Asian Economic Integration* 3(2): 169–189.

RBI. n.d. 'Online Handbook of Indian Economy'. Available at https://rbi.org.in/Scripts/AnnualPublications.aspx?head= Handbook%20of%20Statistics%20on%20Indian%20Economy (accessed March 2023).

———. 2004. *Report on Currency and Finance, 2002–03*. Mumbai: RBI.

———. 2006. *Report of the Committee on Fuller Capital Account Convertibility*. Mumbai: RBI.

———. 2014. *Report of the Expert Committee to Revise and Strengthen the Monetary Policy Framework*. Mumbai: RBI.

———. 2017. *Report on Foreign Exchange Reserves*, December. Available at https://rbi.org.in/Scripts/PublicationsView.aspx?id= 18084 (accessed February 2023).

Rey, Hélène. 2018[2015] 'Dilemma Not Trilemma: The Global Financial Cycle And Monetary Policy Independence', National Bureau of Economic Research Working Papers No. 21162.

SBI. 2018. *SBI Ecowrap*, 4 September. Available at https://www.sbi.co.in/documents/13958/14472/Ecowrap_20180904.pdf (accessed March 2023).

SEBI. n.d. 'FPI Investment Details (Calendar Year)'. Available at https://www.sebi.gov.in/statistics/fpi-investment/fpi-calendar-year/fpi-investment-details-calendar-year.html (accessed March 2023).

Sen Gupta, Abhijit and Rajeswari Sengupta. 2013. 'Management of Capital Flows in India', ADB South Asia Working Paper No. 17, March.

Sengupta, Rajeswari. 2015. 'The Impossible Trinity: Where does India stand?' Working Paper Number WP-2015-05. Mumbai: Indira Gandhi Institute of Development Research.

Shah, Ajay. 2006. 'RBI's yearning for more capital controls'. Available at https://blog.theleapjournal.org/2006/02/rbis-yearning-for-more-capital.html#gsc.tab=0 (accessed March 2023).

Shah, Ajay and Ila Patnaik. 2008. 'Managing Capital Flows: The Case of India'. NIPFP Working Paper No. 2008-52.

US Treasury. 2018. *Macroeconomic and Foreign Exchange Policies of Major Trading Partners of the United States*. Available at https://home.treasury.gov/system/files/206/2018-04-13-Spring-2018-FX-Report-FINAL.pdf (accessed March 2023).

10

CHANGING DYNAMICS OF INTERGOVERNMENTAL FISCAL RELATIONS IN INDIA
Emerging Issues and Challenges

Pinaki Chakraborty and *Shubham Gupta*

Introduction

India is a country of 28 states and eight centrally administered union territories. Though India is a Union of states and not strictly federal, it has a highly decentralised federal fiscal structure wherein state governments spend more than 56 per cent of total public spending when their share in combined revenue is only 38 per cent. Although, there are multiple channels of transfers, this gap in revenue and expenditure is met primarily through vertical transfers from the Union to the states through the statutory Finance Commission (FC) route. Federal fiscal relations in India have undergone significant changes in recent years. Three unprecedented changes in Centre-state financial relation since 2015–16 are: abolition of the Planning Commission in January 2015 and creation of the NITI Aayog; fundamental changes in the transfer system by providing higher tax devolution to the states based on the recommendations of the Fourteenth Finance Commission (FFC); and the constitutional amendment to introduce GST and the creation of GST Council. These changes have far-reaching implications on Union-state fiscal relations and provisioning of public services.

Since the announcement of the award of the FFC, there has been a considerable amount of debate over its impact on fiscal relations between the Union and the states. At the centre of this debate is the core recommendation of the FFC (see fincomindia.nic.in), which increased the states' share in the divisible pool (which comprises all the tax proceeds net of cess, surcharges, and cost of collection) of taxes from 32 per cent to 42 per cent, in the award period of 2015–20. Transfers from the divisible pool are unconditional transfers to the states as against most grants which are conditional. This increase in untied flow of resources is expected to provide greater fiscal autonomy to the states.

On the other hand, due to a substantial increase in the transfer from the divisible pool, the Union government had to roll back some of its spending commitments to the states, which were to be transferred in the form of grants. The net effect of this change has been asymmetric across states. The terminal year in the award period of the FFC was 2020. This chapter undertakes a detailed review of the changes in Union and state finance in recent years, with the objective of analysing the impact of the FFC's award on aggregate transfers to the states and associated changes on state-level fiscal space, and on Union-state fiscal relations.

Continuity and Change: Key Highlights

The FFC report has changed the nature and design of transfers fundamentally. Enhanced tax devolution has increased the flow of unconditional transfers to the states. This is expected to help in improving subnational fiscal autonomy. If we examine the composition of transfer post FFC award, more than 70 per cent of the total resources flowing to the states are in the form of untied transfers. Prior to FFC award, the share of untied transfer was less than 50 per cent of the total transfer. If we add the states' own revenues and the tax devolution, we get an estimate of the untied fiscal space of the states. This untied fiscal space is expected to help the states design their own programme for development. Own revenue of all states for the year 2014–15 (RE or revised estimate) was Rs 9,72,792 crore and tax devolution was Rs 3,37,808 crore. Together the untied fiscal resources for the same year was Rs 13,10,600 crore. As per 2015–16 (BE or budget estimate), the own revenue is Rs 11,18,834 crore and tax devolution is Rs 5,23,958 crore. The total untied fiscal space thus works out to be Rs 16,42,792 crore—an increase of Rs 3,32,192 crore. As a percentage of the previous year's (2014–15) untied fiscal space, the increase was to the tune of 25.35 per cent (from Union Budget: 2015-16 and authors' calculations; see indiabudget.gov.in). This was the base effect of the award of the FFC when compared with the year 2014–15, the terminal year of the Thirteenth FC award.

Second, the FFC has made two fundamental changes in the horizontal devolution formula. It has introduced 2011 population as an indicator of demographic change while retaining the 1971 population, as required under the terms of reference (TOR). Use of latest census data made assessment of expenditure needs more realistic. Also, FFC introduced forest cover with 7.5 per cent weight in the horizontal devolution formula. Forest cover reflects cost disability. Forest cover also provides ecological benefits beyond the state boundary and is a global public good. This is an innovative way to incentivise states to tackle climate change by preserving forests. This also shows how climate change issues can be accommodated in the distribution of federal resource to the subnational governments in a large federal country like India.

Third, the FFC did not recognise the distinction between Plan and non-Plan expenditure. It took an aggregate view of transfers and aggregate view of expenditure. This aggregate view should help in getting budgetary priorities right between development and maintenance expenditure. The incentive to have a large Plan size without appropriate concern for maintenance of existing assets had distorted budgetary priorities for long. Post FFC, transfer schemes introduced by the Union government should use this opportunity to have appropriate public expenditure management and budgetary practices.

Fourth, the FFC has provided flexibility to the states in borrowing without encouraging fiscal imprudence. Fiscal Responsibility Act (FRA) mandates that the subnational governments in India maintain a zero revenue deficit or revenue surplus and a fiscal deficit threshold of 3 per cent of GSDP (Gross State Domestic Product). The FFC envisaged that the quality of deficits is also equally significant as the levels. It, therefore, prescribed the following conditions for the enhanced borrowing limits of states:

(i) Fiscal deficit of all states will be anchored to an annual limit of 3 per cent of GSDP. States will be eligible for a flexibility of 0.25 per cent over and above this for any given year for which the borrowing limits are to be fixed, if their debt-GSDP ratio is less than or equal to 25 per cent in the preceding year.

(ii) States will be further eligible for an additional borrowing limit of 0.25 per cent of GSDP in a given year for which the borrowing limits are to be fixed if the interest payments (IP) are less than or equal to 10 per cent of the revenue receipts (RR) in the preceding year.

(*iii*) The two options listed above, under these flexibility provisions, can be availed of by a state either separately, if any of the above criteria is fulfilled, or simultaneously if both the above stated criteria are fulfilled. Thus, a state can have a maximum fiscal deficit-GSDP limit of 3.5 per cent in any given year.

(*iv*) The flexibility in availing of the additional limit under either of the two options or both will be available to a state only if there is no revenue deficit in the year in which borrowing limits are to be fixed and the immediately preceding year. This should help improve capital spending in states without violating fiscal sustainability. Flexibility in the FRBM framework is an issue which through appropriate designing of the rule of borrowing can go a long way to augment capital spending at the state level.

Fifth, it is the first time since the 73rd and 74th Constitutional Amendments, that around Rs 3,00,000 crores are being devolved to the local government largely as unconditional grants. If used effectively, this can strengthen the process of decentralisation further.

Finally, the FFC introduced a trust-based approach to devolution and public finance management in the Indian federal set up. The FFC refrained from giving policy advice to both the Union and states, reduced discretionary element in transfer and ensured provisioning fiscal space for each level of government to carry out constitutionally assigned functions. At the same time, the FFC fully acknowledged the role of Union government interventions on functions/programmes that have nationwide externalities within the framework of cooperative federalism. Cooperative federalism framework designed by the FFC is to ensure that central intervention does not result in the proliferation of one-size-fits-all centrally sponsored schemes (CSS) as was the practice in the past.

What are the Major Criticisms against the FFC Award?

The usual discontent is the relative decline in horizontal share of some of the states. These states have argued that the introduction of forest cover was not an appropriate indicator as it disproportionately benefitted a few states. It has also been argued that the large increase in vertical devolution has reduced the scope for financing nationally important CSS. Delinking of normal central assistance and backward region grant fund came under criticism though it was not an FFC recommendation. It is argued that not recognising special and non-special category states by the FFC may have adverse implications on the finances of special category states—an issue highlighted by many.

By taking aggregate expenditure for the purpose of assessment of need, the FFC has disregarded the process of planning and plan transfer. This has also been perceived as encroachment in policy space by the Finance Commission beyond its brief. The design of local body grants came under criticism for two reasons: (*i*) it was given only to the Gram Panchayats, not to Block and Zila Panchayats, and (*ii*) it was not given as a share of divisible pool of central taxes. It was also argued that the FFC did not give careful consideration to fiscal sustainability at the subnational level. Discontinuation of fiscal performance grant linked to fiscal prudence has come under criticism. It has also been argued that since aggregate expenditure was considered for the purpose of assessment, fiscally profligate states benefitted more than states which managed their finances prudently.

Before we discuss the fiscal impact of the FFC's recommendations, a brief history of recent trends in Union transfers to states would help understand the reason for the significant step-up in tax devolution. It has been articulated in the FFC report that the share of untied tax devolution in total transfer of resources declined over the years with a corresponding rise in conditional transfers. Conditional transfers through specific purpose grants emerged as a major driver of resource transfer to the states. Between 2011–12 and 2014–15, grants as a proportion of aggregate transfers to states varied between 53.39 per cent and 49.87 per cent of aggregate transfers. In other words, on an average, close to half of the resources transferred to states remained outside the Finance Commission's purview prior to the FFC award.

It has been mentioned in the FFC report that

> the aggregate transfers accounted for about 50 per cent of the gross revenue receipts of the Union. Keeping in view of the Union government's expenditure responsibilities, and the needs of fiscal adjustment at the Union level, we do not see the scope for increasing the transfers beyond the current level. However, we believe that there is a need to alter the existing composition of transfers by increasing the share of the untied transfers. This should provide enhanced fiscal flexibility to the states to meet their expenditure needs and make expenditure decisions in line with their own priorities. While doing so, we have ensured appropriate fiscal space to the Union to finance its own expenditure responsibilities and commitments, including continued transfers to States.

Thus, the FFC was of the view that there was an urgent need to restructure the mechanism of transfers in order to meet the following objectives without reducing the Union government's fiscal space: (*i*) providing higher state-level fiscal autonomy by reducing conditional transfers; (*ii*) aligning priorities according to the constitutional assignment of functions for Union and state governments; and (*iii*) moving towards Centre–state fiscal relations of greater fiscal cooperation through the institutional mechanism of 'cooperative federalism'.

Implications

Post the award of the FFC, transfers to the states from the Centre have undergone some structural changes. Distribution

Table 10.1: Devolution, grants and aggregate transfers to states

	2011–12	2012–13	2013–14	2014–15	2015–16	2016–17	2017–18 (RE)	2018–19 (BE)
Abs. no. (Figures in crores)								
Devolution of states' share in taxes	250522	291547	318230	337808	506193	608000	673005	788093
Grants	286994	285428	311612	336015	315792	359910	425372	461342
Aggregate transfers	537516	576975	629842	673823	821985	967910	1098377	1249435
Composition of transfers								
Devolution of states' share in taxes	46.61%	50.53%	50.53%	50.13%	61.58%	62.82%	61.27%	63.08%
Grants	53.39%	49.47%	49.47%	49.87%	38.42%	37.18%	38.73%	36.92%
Aggregate transfers	100.00%	100.00%	100.00%	100.00%	100.00%	100.00%	100.00%	100.00%
Growth								
Devolution of states' share in taxes	14.24%	16.38%	9.15%	6.15%	49.85%	20.11%	10.69%	17.10%
Grants	3.11%	−0.55%	9.17%	7.83%	−6.02%	13.97%	18.19%	8.46%
Aggregate transfers	8.02%	7.34%	9.16%	6.98%	21.99%	17.75%	13.48%	13.75%
% of GDP								
Devolution of states' share in taxes	2.87%	2.93%	2.83%	2.71%	3.68%	3.99%	4.01%	4.23%
Grants	3.29%	2.87%	2.77%	2.70%	2.29%	2.36%	2.54%	2.48%
Aggregate transfers	6.15%	5.80%	5.61%	5.40%	5.97%	6.35%	6.55%	6.71%
% of GTR								
GTR (in INR crores)	889177	1036235	1138733	1244886	1455648	1715822	1946119	2271242
Devolution of states' share in taxes	28.17%	28.14%	27.95%	27.14%	34.77%	35.43%	34.58%	34.70%
Grants	32.28%	27.54%	27.36%	26.99%	21.69%	20.98%	21.86%	20.31%
Total	60.45%	55.68%	55.31%	54.13%	56.47%	56.41%	56.44%	55.01%

Source: Union Budget Documents 2010–18, Ministry of Finance, Government of India

of central transfers to states has shifted significantly in favour of tax devolution (See Table 10.1, rows 6, 7 and 8). While in the years leading to and including 2014–15, close to 50 per cent of the transfers were effected through the devolution route, this increased to 61.58 per cent in the year 2015–16 (translating to an increase of Rs 1,68,385 crore in absolute terms) and have remained around the same level. On the other hand, the share of grants, which prior to 2015–16 made up close to half of the aggregate transfers, reduced to 38.42 per cent in the year 2015–16 (a decline of Rs 20, 223 crore in absolute terms over 2014–15 figures), and have reduced further to 36.92 per cent in 2018–19. Thus, untied funds constitute a relatively larger portion of the aggregate transfers than before.

As regards growth, tax devolutions grew to a sharp 49.85 per cent (row 10, Table 10.1) in 2015–16 compared to the average growth rate of about 11 per cent per annum during the previous four years. Thereafter, the growth rate in devolutions moderated, down to 20.11 per cent, 10.69 per cent (RE), and 17.10 per cent (BE) in the subsequent years. Table 10.1 also shows that aggregate transfers grew at a rate of 22 per cent in 2015–16 compared to 6.98 per cent in 2014–15. In the subsequent years as well, aggregate transfers exhibited a robust growth of 17.75 per cent, 13.48 per cent, and 13.75 per cent. As a proportion of GDP as well, tax devolution increased considerably from 2.71 per cent of the GDP in 2014–15 (the terminal year of the Thirteenth Finance Commission (TFC) award period) to 4.23 per cent (BE) for the year 2018–19, thus, exhibiting a 150 per cent rise in the four-year period. However, it should be noted that a large part of this increment is derived from a reduction in grants, which have shown a steady decline, falling from 2.70 per cent of the GDP in 2014–15 to 2.48 per cent (BE) in 2018–19.

From the preceding discussion, it appears that more resources are being transferred to states through the tax devolution route while reducing the share of grants. But this does not automatically imply that on an aggregate level, the quantum of resources available to states from the Centre has increased. Before the FFC award, aggregate transfers as a proportion of GTR (gross tax revenues) of the Union declined gradually—from 60.94 per cent in 2011–12, they decreased to 54.55 per cent in 2014–15. However, the trend reversed in 2015–16, when aggregate transfers increased to 56.88 per cent of GTR, and they have remained at around 57 per cent in the subsequent years. Aggregate transfers as percentage of GDP increased to 5.97 per cent in 2015–16 after declining from 6.15 per cent to 5.40 per cent of the GDP between 2011–12 and 2014–15. It improved further to 6.55 per cent in 2017–18 (RE) and to 6.71 per cent for the year 2018–19 (BE). However, aggregate transfers as a proportion of GTR are budgeted at 55.01 per cent in 2018–19, a decline of 1.43 per cent from the previous year.

Implications of Cess and Surcharge

Cess and surcharges are part of the non-divisible pool of resources. According to the FFC, the share of cess and surcharges in gross tax revenue of the Union has increased from 7.53 per cent in 2000–01 to 13.14 per cent in 2013–14. The states have argued that this denies them their rightful share in the devolution. However, constitutionally, cess and surcharges cannot be included in the divisible pool, 'as under Article 270, taxes referred to in Article 268 and 269—surcharges on taxes and duties and cesses levied for specific purposes—should not form part of the divisible pool'. The report notes how earlier Finance Commissions had recommended the Union government to review the current position with respect to the non-divisible pool arising out of cess and surcharges and take measures to reduce their share in the gross tax revenue. However, this has not happened till date. It further articulates, 'There are two ways of addressing this legitimate concern of the States—by amending the Constitution to include these items in the divisible pool, or increasing the share of the divisible pool to compensate States on this account. We ruled out the first option given the record of experience so far'.

Revenue from the various cess and surcharges is presented in Table 10.2, based on the methodology given in Chakraborty and Gupta (2016). Two rows are important in the table, one for the ratio between net cess and surcharge (NCS) and GTR (see the row on NCS as a % of GTR), and the other on the year-on-year growth rate of NCS. NCS is calculated by deducting the amount of the GST compensation cess from the total collections under cess and surcharges for the years 2017–18 and 2018–19. This is due to the fact that the proceeds from this cess are meant to be distributed to the states and will not stay with the Union. First we look at the ratio of NCS to GTR. In the year 2011–12, NCS formed 11.15 per cent of GTR. This increased to 14.43 per cent by 2014–15. When the FFC recommendations took effect, the Union government seems to have used cess and surcharges significantly to make up for the extra money going to the states. The increase in NCS in 2015–16 was 2.04 per cent over the previous year to 16.47 per cent. In absolute terms, this represents an increase in earnings of Rs 60,135 crore. Such an increased dependence is also reflected in the y-o-y growth figures of NCS. In the year 2012–13, their growth was 18.40 per cent, which increased to 32.28 per cent in 2014–15. In the year 2015–16, NCS grew to 33.48 per cent. However, this trend has been on the retreat in the last few years. While in 2016–17 and 2017–18, NCS as a percentage of GTR declined to 14.87 per cent and 13.69 per cent (RE), its growth fell drastically to 6.43 per cent and 4.40 per cent (RE), respectively. While the NCS to GTR ratio reduced further to 12.70 per cent, growth is budgeted to increase to 8.29 per cent. The growth in NCS has reduced to 6.37 per cent on average in the years after 2015–16. Similarly, NCS as percentage of GTR has averaged 13.76 per cent in the same period. A similar trend is visible in NCS as a percentage of GDP as well. While this ratio increased till 2014–15 and reached its peak in 2015–16, at 1.74 per cent, it remained around 1.55 per cent of GDP in 2018–19.

Table 10.2: Cess and surcharge

	2011–12	2012–13	2013–14	2014–15	2015–16	2016–17	2017–18 (RE)	2018–19 (BE)
Gross Tax Revenue	889177	1036235	1138733	1244886	1455648	1715822	1946119	2271242
States' Share in Divisible Pool	250522	291547	318230	337808	506193	608000	673005	788093
Divisible Pool	782881.3	911084.4	994468.8	1055650	1205221.42	1447619	1602392.85	1876411.90
Cost of Collection	7138.92	7751.84	8464	9593.38	10648.57	13000.46	15965.7	16315.02
Cess and Surcharge	99156.83	117398.80	135800.3	179642.6	239778	255202.5	327760.44	378515.07
GST Compensation Cess	–	–	–	–	–	–	61331	90000
Net Cess and Surcharge (NCS)	99156.83	117398.8	135800.3	179642.6	239778	255202.5	266429.44	288515.07
NCS Growth Rate	–	18.40%	15.67%	32.28%	33.48%	6.43%	4.40%	8.29%
NCS as a % of GDP	1.13%	1.18%	1.21%	1.44%	1.74%	1.67%	1.59%	1.55%
NCS as a % of GTR	11.15%	11.33%	11.93%	14.43%	16.47%	14.87%	13.69%	12.70%

Source: Union Budget Documents 2010–18; Author's own calculations
Notes: 1. Figures in crores.
2. Decimals in INR figures can be rounded off.

Emerging Issues

Although no Finance Commission award can satisfy all the states, the structural shift in the framework of award has the potential to fundamentally change the future of Centre-state relations in India. Also it needs to be recognised that a few states have received less in terms of horizontal share due to the inclusion of forest cover. Ex post one needs to analyse whether this resulted in decline in aggregate resource flows to states. In most cases, the decline in horizontal share has been offset by large increase in vertical devolution. Of course, the counterfactual would be that if the horizontal share was maintained, a particular state would have received more funds.

On the Plan and non-Plan distinction, it needs to be emphasised that this distinction is not mentioned in the Constitution. On the issue of Plan expenditure, state governments were unanimous in their view that proliferation of CSS under various Plans had reduced fiscal autonomy of states and distorted state budgets. It was argued by all states that CSS be rationalised and the share of conditional grants be reduced in total transfers. Even within plan transfers, the share of normal central assistance under the Gadgil formula reduced to less than 10 per cent in recent years. In other words, not only CSS, but all plan transfers in aggregate became conditional. In the past, it had been the Finance Commissions' job to ensure that tax devolution and grants-in-aid covered non-Plan expenditure in revenue account. The distinction between Plan and non-Plan expenditure resulted in significant distortion in expenditure allocation, wherein the focus continued to be on the new Plan schemes accompanied by a complete neglect of non-Plan operation and maintenance expenditure.

Criteria of transfer from Plan to non-Plan also changed and became arbitrary and at times confusing. Finance Commission award periods and Five Year Plan periods continued to be different. For example, the Twelfth Plan's terminal year is 2016–17, but the FFC award will continue up to 2019–20.

Finance Commissions in the past tried eliminating non-Plan revenue deficits of states through tax devolution and non-Plan revenue deficit grants. Proliferation of CSS and new Plan schemes continued to increase the Plan expenditure in a particular Plan period, which eventually increased non-Plan revenue expenditure of states.

In a significant departure from the past, terms of reference of the FFC did not make specific mention of gross budgetary support to Plan as a committed expenditure of the Union government. The TOR also did not bind the FFC to only look at non-Plan revenue expenditure. The increase in vertical devolution to 42 per cent of the divisible pool needs to be viewed from the perspective of total revenue expenditure, not the non-Plan revenue expenditure.

On the matter of population data, FFC's TOR required that,

> in making its recommendations on various matters, the Commission shall generally take the base of population figures as of 1971 in all cases where population is a factor for determination of devolution of taxes and duties and grants-in-aid; however, the Commission may also take into account the demographic changes that have taken place subsequent to 1971.

Views of the states on the use of 1971 population were deeply divided. It is important to note that changing demographic realities are an issue and need to be factored in while deciding allocation across states. For the first time, this was recognised by the TOR.

Commission took the view that weight assigned to the population should be decided first and an indicator of demographic change be introduced separately. The FFC has used 1971 population in horizontal devolution formula and given it a weightage of 17.5 per cent. It has also given 10 per cent weightage to demographic change, using 2011 population as the indicator reflecting demographic change. This in a way captured both age structure as well as migration, which has taken place in the country since 1971.

On the local government transfer, it needs to be mentioned that Panchayats and municipalities are in the Directive Principles of State Policy and are under states' jurisdiction. The 73rd and 74th Constitutional Amendments do not supersede that position. Since centrality of state governments in deciding the process of decentralisation continues even after the 73rd and 74th Constitutional Amendment, the FFC approach remained sensitive to this aspect. The FFC did not recommend one-size-fits-all policies for the local governments.

The FFC's fundamental approach was to recognise the asymmetric assignment of function and finance across levels of government. The FFC report also emphasised the unique role the Union government has to perform for macroeconomic stability and countercyclical fiscal policies. Symmetry, as understood by the FFC, was to provide each level of government with adequate fiscal space to carry out its constitutionally assigned functions with a degree of fiscal autonomy, as mentioned earlier. This was to correct imbalances observed in the analysis of expenditure functions across Union List, State List and Concurrent List subjects. To quote the FFC report,

> Our examination of the past data shows that between 2002–05 and 2005–11, revenue expenditure by the Union Government on State List subjects increased from an average of 14 per cent to 20 per cent and on Concurrent List subjects from an average of 13 per cent to 17 per cent. This implies a reduction in expenditure in percentage terms on Union List subjects. Expenditure functions under the Union List fall predominantly under General and Economic Services. The share of expenditure on these has progressively declined from 66.3 per cent in 2001–02 to 53.2 percent in 2014–14 (BE). Our assessment of Union finances has taken note of this and provided appropriate fiscal space to the Union to carry out its constitutionally assigned expenditure responsibilities.

Impact of Goods and Services Tax

Introduction of Goods and Services Tax also has fundamentally changed the Union-state fiscal relation. Prior to the introduction of the GST, our Constitution allowed the Union to collect taxes on production and states were allowed to tax consumption. The Union government was also taxing services; the states did not have the power to tax services at all. Post the introduction of GST on 1 July 2017, separate tax powers of the Union and the states have been merged and both the levels of government are now allowed to tax from the common tax base. The original plan was to introduce GST from 1 April 2010, but the process got delayed by more than seven years. This delay is a reflection of the fact that political economy of tax reform is not an easy job in a complex federal country like India with multiple stakeholders.

GST and the Constitution of India

The GST also required a constitutional amendment (122nd Constitutional Amendment) to enable the Union government to tax consumption of goods and allow states to tax consumption of services. Post the constitutional amendments, both the central and the state tax bases have been merged and from this common base, both the levels of government collect taxes. The constitutional amendment also enabled the creation of the GST council. The Council's chairperson is the Union Finance Minister and states have their ministerial nominees as members of the council. Since creation of the Council in November 2016, the Council has met 32 times. This shows that the Indian federal system has transformed itself as a matured federation where both Centre and states have learnt to trust each other and give up their exclusive taxation rights with respect to a particular tax base for a better tax system. This common tax base creation has resulted in the abolition of a fragmented tax regime, and in the development of a common market, elimination of cascading of taxes, and it should help increase the growth of GDP by promoting trade, business and investment.

Taxes Subsumed Under GST

The central taxes subsumed under GST include: central excise duties; additional duties of excise; additional duties of customs; special additional duties of customs; service tax and central cess; and surcharges so far as they relate to the supply of goods and services. Similarly, the various state taxes to be subsumed under GST are: state VAT; central sales tax; luxury tax; entry tax; entertainment tax; taxes on advertisement; purchase tax; taxes on lotteries, betting and gambling; and state surcharges and cesses so far as they relate to the supply of goods and services.

This list shows that petroleum products, alcohol for human consumption, real estate sector and electricity duty are kept out of the purview of GST. In other words, though most indirect taxes have come under GST, a large part of it also remained outside the purview of GST. Incomplete coverage of goods and services indeed is an issue that the country needs to resolve as we move further on the path of reform of indirect taxes to get the full benefit of GST with a comprehensive coverage. However, the GST structure when it was first introduced was a vast improvement on the design prevalent previously.

Destination Principle

The GST gets rid of the age-old regressive central sales tax (CST). The CST was a regressive levy at the point of production. This practice resulted in significant tax exportation from richer producing states to poorer consuming states, thus contributing to fiscal inequality in the country. This precisely is the reason why some of the richer producing states are not happy with the abolition of CST and were initially opposed to the idea of GST, and some continue to be unhappy with GST. It is expected that the revenue gain due to the expansion of base due to the destination principle of taxation at the point of consumption and additional taxation of services should result in significant revenue gain to consuming states, after the input tax credit adjustment and loss of CST revenue.

Has GST Compromised Federalism?

It is certainly true that the right to taxation is intimately linked with the right to decide on the rate of taxation. Post GST, individual state governments would not be able to decide on the rate structure of GST in a particular state. That way for the sake of tax harmony, fiscal autonomy is compromised. This is true for the central government as well. The Centre also cannot change anything without the approval of the majority of the states in the GST Council. But if we examine the big picture in a globalising world, fiscal policy, especially tax policy has become in a way ineffective long ago. To consider an example, to attract global investment, India really cannot have a corporate income tax rate which is way above the rates in other emerging market economies trying to attract the same investment. The same thing is being reflected here, that is, a process of harmonisation of tax rates across the country through a process of negotiation in the GST Council. In the former case, it is the market that forces a country to align rates to a particular reference, and in the latter case, it is happening through a process of negotiations. Even with floor rates, states would have ultimately converged to a particular rate. The larger question is whether rate harmonisation alone is sufficient to attract trade and investment? Probably not. We need to have harmonisation of processes. If business and trade have to face different kinds of complexities in complying with the tax laws in different states, rate harmonisation would become ineffective.

Finally, post-GST fiscal architecture is an outcome of the 101st Constitutional Amendment. Autonomy of all levels of governments including that of Union government has been tied to the GST Council on matters of indirect taxation. It is the responsibility of the Council to work in a manner that preserves and strengthens fiscal autonomy of all the levels of governments. The Union government would have to take the lead in this regard.

Conclusion

In the context of fiscal relation between the Union and the states, the larger question is not of arithmetic but rather of a shift in policy towards a greater fiscal autonomy for the states by ensuring that a greater proportion of funds flow through the Finance Commission. Simultaneously, it is also important that the fiscal space of the Union is preserved so that it can perform its functions. The increase in the award from the divisible pool to 42 per cent gives the states the much needed fiscal autonomy. It ensures that the states have a greater say in determining their priorities.

Finally, the Finance Commission's fundamental task is fiscal equalisation. Fiscal equalisation principle, in a way, tries to provide certain levels of resources for equal provision of public services across states. Hopefully, post FFC changes, the Centre-state financial relations would evolve to a stronger framework of non-Finance Commission grants. This is critically important. In the absence of the Planning Commission and discontinuation of Plan and non-Plan distinction from 2017–18 (announced in the Union Budget 2016–17), clarity is required on the treatment of non-Finance Commission grants post 2016–17. Discussion on a new framework of grants outside Finance Commission transfer should start among the stakeholders at the earliest. The new framework of grants should ensure stability in resource flows to the states, determined outside the Finance Commission award.

REFERENCES

Chakraborty, P. 2015. 'Finance Commission's Recommendations and Restructured Fiscal Space'. *Economic and Political Weekly* 50(12).

Chakraborty, P. and M. Gupta. 2016. 'Evolving Centre–State Financial Relations: Role of the New Framework for Grants'. *Economic and Political Weekly* 51(16).

11
THE NATURAL ENVIRONMENT IN INDIA
Good Laws, Bad Practices

Anup Sinha

Introduction

The importance of preserving the natural environment cannot be over-emphasised. The problem is how to ensure the required degree of protection in a manner that is acceptable to all and does not come at the cost of employment and livelihoods of people. There are two distinct aspects of this problem. Economists have long believed that Nature is a bottomless gift hamper from which we can draw resources. Yes, a resource can become scarce. In that event the price of the resource will go up and a signal will be sent out to look for a substitute of that resource. Nature is also looked upon by economists as a free garbage bin, where wastes emanating from production and consumption of goods and services can be dumped—in the air, in the oceans, beneath the soil. Economists are so used to analysing problems through marginal (incremental) changes that global issues are quite often overlooked. In the context of the discussion here, economists seldom factor in the fact that the planet is a closed energy system and matter cannot be created or destroyed. Hence there are limits to the extent of resources we can use as well as the amount of pollutants we can dump. If the limits are crossed, tipping points are likely to be reached and the chances of catastrophic changes would become very high leading to large costs—both for those who are living, as well as for those who are yet to be born.

The natural environment is a global public good. It does not belong to any nation nor is it limited by political boundaries. Hence solutions, for most of the larger problems of pollution and resource depletion, have to be global and acceptable to all. In some of these instances, even if the global solution is elusive, each nation (or even each individual) may choose to behave responsibly. Take climate change for example. An accepted solution to the problem is to reduce carbon emissions. If only a few countries do it then the solution would be ineffective because emissions may rise in other countries and the problem may actually magnify. Even then, taking a strong Kantian ethical position, a nation may reduce its carbon footprint knowing it to be the correct thing to do, even if other nations do not follow its example. There are other kinds of environmental problems that are local and can be handled by local solutions. Take for instance toxic effluents being discharged by a factory into a river, thereby polluting the water and causing harm to downstream users. This problem can be tackled by imposing a cost on the company by means of a tax. Alternatively, the company could be given a monetary incentive to reduce pollution. As a consequence of these issues, and greater awareness of the need to protect the natural environment, all nations have laws and regulations for these purposes. India is no exception. We have a large number of laws and regulations since the 1970s. Laws have been added; laws have been amended. Penalties for non-compliance have been revised. Indeed the written laws regarding these issues often look impressive and comprehensive. Yet, like in many cases in India, actual practice and the law diverge significantly. This applies to the natural environment as well.

In this chapter we will first attempt a brief review of the regulations in a chronological manner in the following section. Next, in the third section, we will comment on the fairly frequent instances of judicial activism, where courts and judges have passed comments and orders to ensure protection of the natural environment. This will be followed in the fourth section by a discussion on the changing public opinion and various people's movements that have taken place in India. The fifth section has a brief discussion of the state of implementation of these laws, both at the national as well as the state level. The sixth section will take a quick look into the future and provide a reality check of matters on the ground before the final section concludes the paper.

Review of Regulations

Since ancient times, human beings have had a tradition of looking at Nature as something beyond everyday materialism, almost akin to God. The common belief was that humans were part of Nature. Not only that, communities, when they used natural resources like water and forests, often ensured proper management and preservation. Decisions pertaining to these were taken by the community of users. The management was in terms of voluntary work undertaken for communal benefit. It was only after the industrial revolution and the Enlightenment that Nature became a thing: 'it', to be used by humanity for its own benefit. Modernity, as defined by an industrial society's lifestyle and consumption patterns, created an almost insatiable demand for resources from the natural environment, and waste began to increase at the same rate. The natural environment came under the threat of irreversible damage (Jodha 2012). In India specifically, the colonial experience enhanced the threat further (Rangarajan 2012). The imposition of the western way of life stifled the body of local knowledge of how to manage the environment. The commercial interests of the colonial regime needed protection from the local users of natural resources. Laws were enacted that protected forests for exclusive commercial use. The government claimed all unoccupied waste land. Bureaucracy became the chief decision-maker regarding the use of natural resources—the claims and the rights. Much later, it was only in the second half of the twentieth century that awareness about the need to preserve the environment began to grow.

In India the first ever mention of the need for environmental protection in policy documents appeared in the Fourth Five Year Plan (1969–74). The need for assessing the environmental impact of projects was articulated. Internationally, the platform where global leaders met and discussed the environment as a major issue for the first time, was at the United Nations Conference on the Human Environment at Stockholm in June 1972. It was from this conference the United Nations Environmental Programme (UNEP) was started. India's Prime Minister at the time, Indira Gandhi, announced that poverty was the greatest polluter (*The Wire* 2018), thus explicitly tying up the natural environment and its degradation with the persistence of human poverty. Actually, extreme inequality contributes to environmental degradation in an acute way. The very poor have little access to resources. Therefore, they over-intensively use natural resources like land, water and forests, often inspite of knowing that their actions could jeopardise the long-term availability of the resources since their present need is much more urgent than their concern for the future. On the other hand, the very rich have access to a lot of resources and they know full well that even if they over-consume and waste resources, there will still be enough for their children and grandchildren to thrive on. Hence on both counts, responsible use becomes a problem and the natural environment gets degraded, often beyond repair.

India, in the 1970s, became one of the first developing nations to enact serious legislation (Dwivedi 1997). All the major legislations were about the control of pollution rather than the depletion of resources. The first three laws were the Water (Prevention and Control of Pollution) Act (1974), the Air (Prevention and Control of Pollution) Act (1981) and the Environment (Protection) Act (1986). The laws were framed with the help of experts and bureaucrats. Implementation was entirely in the hands of administrators. Essentially, the approach was top-down and piecemeal in the sense that the interactions between the different aspects of ecosystems and the entire natural environment were left unaddressed.

WATER ACT 1974

In the Water Act, the definition of pollution was anything that altered the properties of water in a way that was injurious to the health of all living beings, as well as unsuitable for agriculture and industrial use. During the enactment of the legislation, the Central and State Pollution Control Boards were set up. The framework of the law was borrowed from the rubric provided by the United Nations framework. There were certain features of the approach that warrant comments. For example, in the process of putting the piece of legislation together, no public debate or community feedback was entertained nor was there any political debate. Hence, in the absence of such citizens' involvement, the definition of the problem of water pollution and its solution were both entirely set by the government.

Indira Gandhi had a personal interest in and a commitment to environmental improvement and she contributed significantly to the formation of these laws. The implementation was left entirely in the hands of civil servants. This background of the law-making process and its inception implied that there was little involvement of the public as stakeholders. The law, fearing possible political repercussions, kept penalties for violation very low, which could be easily ignored. In many instances it was cheaper to pay the penalty and pollute rather than spend on equipment to treat water before discharging as effluent. In amendments made in 1988 the penalties were made a little more stringent whereby industries required a clearance for their water usage and effluence. The budgetary support that the Pollution Control Boards (PCBs) received was meagre and inadequate which limited their monitoring capabilities. Hence, as happens so frequently in India, opportunistic behaviour of PCB officials was quite common. It may be noted here there was no Right to Information (RTI) Act in the 1970s or 1980s.

Air Act 1981

Following the lessons of the Water Act, the Air Act was passed in 1981. There was a pressure on the Union government to make laws that were in alignment with international treaties. Pollution was defined as concentrations of substances in the air that was injurious to the health of all living beings and property. The standards of emission and ambient air quality were set up by the PCBs who were now given the additional charge of managing air pollution. Industries required licences from PCBs to ensure that there were no violations of standards. Many of the problems that made the Water Act ineffective continued in the case of the Air Act too. It was again a top-down approach in inception as well as implementation. It required a lot of resources to monitor and in the absence of monitoring, it was easy to trigger opportunistic behaviour such as bribery and favours exchanged. Penalties were low hence they were conducive to non-compliance.

Environment Act 1986

The Environment Act of 1986 was a reaction to the tragic disaster at the Union Carbide Factory in Bhopal in 1984. The

Union Carbide disaster was a typical example of how large multinationals looked at safety and security of potentially dangerous parts of their operations (Ravi Rajan 2012). If the large companies were negligent, what could be expected from the smaller companies operating within national boundaries? This Act introduced several fundamental changes. The environment was defined more comprehensively as comprising of air, water and land, *and* their interrelationships with humans, all living beings and property. Pollutants were defined as anything that could be injurious to health. In widening the scope of the environment and admitting the importance of the interactions between different components, it tightened the Air and the Water Act. Penalties were reviewed, and increased upto Rs 2,00,000 monetary fine and even up to five years in prison depending on the nature of the environmental crime. While the implementation of the law continued to be in the command and control mode, the citizens were given the right to ask for information regarding the environment and were allowed to sue firms or even industries in a court of law.

A very wide definition of the environment is a double-edged sword. In one sense, it allows many harmful effects to be brought under the purview of legal action. It also allows new pollutants that may emerge through the use of new technologies to be included without having to amend the law books. However, on the other hand, too wide an ambit might stifle many technologies where there might be a new pollutant but its effects cannot be ascertained positively. A precautionary approach to the possible risk might prevent the new technology or the new good from being used at all. Pollutants have different characteristics. A pollutant may be injurious with a certain probability. How does one view the probability? Is a 1 per cent chance of injury unacceptable, but a 0.01 per cent chance acceptable? Some pollutants like allergens may not affect every living being in the same way. Some may be allergic to pollen while others are not. Should pollen be taken as a pollutant? Similarly, some pollutants may be created in the air or water when two or more non-polluting substances are mixed. Finally, if a pollutant is non-injurious to human beings but injurious to some small living being, say some species of birds, what do we do about the pollutant? Do we prioritise from an anthropocentric point of view?

OTHER LAWS AND REGULATIONS

There have been a number of other laws passed over time which has addressed more specific aspects of the natural environment. The laws are the Wildlife (Protection) Act 1972, Forest (Conservation) Act 1980, Public Liability Insurance Act 1991, Biological Diversity Act 2002, Forest Rights Act 2006, National Green Tribunal Act 2010 and the Coastal Regulation Zone Notification 2011. As the economy has progressed, toxic wastes that were non-existent two or three decades ago had to be regulated. Some of these regulations are: Bio-medical Waste (Management and Handling) Rules 1998, Municipal Solid Wastes (Management and Handling) Rules 2000, Batteries (Management and Handling) Rules 2001, Hazardous Wastes (Management, Handling and Transboundary Movement) Rules 2008 and E-Waste (Management and Handling) Rules 2011.

THE SPECIAL IMPORTANCE OF BIODIVERSITY
AND FOREST RIGHTS

The preservation of biodiversity and forests are important considerations in sustainable development, where human and non-human interactions are considered important in ensuring that the natural environment remains a resource for future generations too.

The importance of biodiversity has been stressed by biologists and ecologists for the simple reason that we are still not fully aware of the role of different species in the web of life. Ecosystems have a keystone species around which many processes of the ecosystem revolve. Similarly the extinction of any species can have unforeseen consequences on other species and ecosystem services. It may be noted that species extinction is a part of natural change. However, if the species extinction is due to anthropogenic interventions and actions then the consequences can be adverse for life in general. Hence biologists and ecologists would strongly suggest that biodiversity be preserved. In this context, it may be pointed out that economists treat biodiversity as one form of natural capital. There are many different kinds of productive capital like human-made capital, human capital, social capital and knowledge as well as natural capital. Sustainable development is defined by economists (Dasgupta 2001) as the bequest of a non-diminishing stock of productive capital to the future generations. Therefore, the total was important, not the components. This implied that capitals were substitutable. Biologists have refuted this claim due to the reasons given above as far as living beings are concerned. Hence, there is a special need to preserve biodiversity (Sarkar and Sinha 2017).

FORESTS AND LAWS

During the colonial period the British government had made all forests the exclusive property of the state and protected them for commercial use. Commercial use was mainly of two kinds—for use in the railways for manufacturing sleepers, and for teak wood which was sold as timber for profit. In 1927 the British enacted the Indian Forest Act which classified forests in to three distinct categories. The first was part of National Parks looked after by the Union government. The second comprised Reserve Forests notified under the Indian Forest Act, where all activities were prohibited unless permitted by the state. State governments had the authority to notify a bounded area as Reserve Forest and a Forest Settlement Officer was appointed. The Forest Settlement Officer would have three months to hear and settle all claims people might have over the Reserve territory, people such as indigenous tribes living there for a very long period of time. Some rights were usually granted such as right of way, right of pasture, right to non-timber forest produce and right to water contained in water bodies. Any other claim could be overridden by the Settlement Officer and the claimants' land could be acquired as forests. The third category of forests was under the administrative control of a village—usually adjacent to a relatively densely populated area. There were forest panchayats (*van panchayat*) that looked after it and managed the communal benefits that accrued to the local residents.

What the 1927 Act virtually did was to make the forest dwellers, most of them belonging to tribes, trespassers in their own homesteads. The officers of the Forest Service would strongly discourage them from staying in Reserve Forests. Until 2006, there were generations of tribes who lost claims on their ancestral land. In 2006, after decades of people's movements and social activism, the new Forest Rights Act called the Scheduled Tribes and Other Traditional Forest Dwellers (Recognition of Forest Rights) Act 2006, was enacted as a landmark legislation for forest-dwelling communities of India. The Act recognised the land rights of the communities living in forests, legally ending the control of the government's forest department. The total area estimated where such land rights might have to be recognised, and claims sorted out legally, was of the order of 34.6 million hectares.

Judicial Activism

The 42nd Amendment to the Indian Constitution in 1976 introduced into the Directive Principles the words that '... it is the duty of every citizen to protect and improve the environment and to safeguard the forests and wildlife of the country.' Despite this hugely forward-looking stance of the government, it is amazing to see the despoiling of India's natural environment even after more than 40 years since the constitutional amendment took place (Shrivastava and Kothari 2014). The Environment Act of

1986 allowed citizens to take the government to court through Public Interest Litigation and later by using the Right to Information Act (2005). A number of cases, big and small, have been fought in courts of law with different results. Sometimes the judgement has gone in favour of those seeking protection while in other cases the courts have ruled in favour of activities that appeared to have adverse impact on the natural environment. The guiding objectives of the courts have been: ensuring a wholesome environment, using the precautionary principle of risk management, invoking the 'polluter pays' principle, and laying the burden of proof on developers to demonstrate that their actions are environmentally benign.

There have been a number of key cases where the courts have enabled environmental preservation. A few important ones are the stopping of illegal mechanised mining of riverbeds in Dehradun (*Hindustan Times* 2022), the Shriram Food and Fertilizers gas leak case where the Supreme Court, in a pioneering move, applied the 'principle of absolute liability' of the company, but allowed the factory to reopen under 11 conditions so that employees' livelihoods were not dealt an abrupt blow (*Law Times Journal* 2021), and the Ganga Pollution case where tanning factories (primarily) discharging effluents without treatment could be closed or monetarily penalised to help restore environmental damage (Kumari n.d.). The case involving ambient air pollution around the Taj Mahal helped provide better pollution control in and around Agra (*Indian Kanoon* n.d.). In the Sardar Sarovar Dam on the Narmada case, the importance of rehabilitating the displaced people arising from a public project was affirmed (*The Indian Express* 2017). Finally the control of diesel pollution in New Delhi emitted by auto-rickshaws was curbed by the courts forcing them to switch to gas (CNG) (Tiwari n.d.). There have been a number of legal instances where the court's ruling has revealed that the judges believed in development first, environmental concerns later. For example, the Narmada Dam was actually allowed to be built. However, the trend of court verdicts has been in favour of preserving the natural environment.

People's Movements and Environmental Activism

Apart from judicial activism there have been a number of movements which have received a lot of public support and media attention. The players in these movements are usually non-governmental organisations (NGOs), political parties, the media or just citizens' groups. In recent times the Chipko movement, which started in 1973 in the hills of Uttar Pradesh, captured the imagination of public and policy makers alike. It was led by Sunderlal Bahuguna and was aimed at forest preservation through prevention of tree-felling for timber. Similarly, the Narmada Bachao Andolan led by Medha Patkar along with adivasis, environmental activists, NGOs and human rights activists protesting against the construction of large dams across the river Narmada, flowing through the states of Maharashtra and Gujarat, led to a lot of media attention, and public support in India and abroad. The dam was built but the decades-long people's struggle led to the establishment of the importance of rehabilitation of displaced people and the ecological damage done by large dams in the development discourse in India. There are lots of other smaller groups working at local levels on issues like better water conservation, improved urban waste management, the importance of hygiene and cleanliness, and preserving water bodies and open spaces. There has also been growing research on environmental issues, both the scientific aspects as well as the social and cultural aspects of environmental problems. At the policy-making level there has been much more advocacy and lobbying along with media involvement. Large specialised institutions have come up too, such as The Energy and Resources Institute (TERI), the Centre for Science and Environment (CSE), Green Peace and think tanks like Development Alternatives. Compared to even two decades ago, the general level of awareness among people with different social and educational backgrounds has increased substantially. Climate change, the need to plant and preserve trees, the disutility of air and water pollution, are things almost every citizen has heard of and generally believes to be important issues.

If the nation's laws are comprehensive, courts sympathetic, and citizens aware, we would expect that over the last four decades India's natural environment would have improved if not significantly, then at least discernibly from the past. Has it been so? To seek an answer to this question, let us take a look at the institutional apparatus that is available to implement the laws, and also to see whether the laws thread together into an all-inclusive thinking about the natural environment and sustainable development.

State of Implementation

Implementation of laws and regulations depend on many factors. A main aspect of this is the quality of governance, which includes the accuracy of monitoring and the speed and decisiveness of action along with a continuous updating of scientific standards and limits, as new research output becomes available. The second factor of importance is the clarity in the written laws so that ambiguous interpretations are minimal. The laws should also not overlap with each other. Also, there should not be any possibility of contradictory provisions regarding what is permissible and what is not. Finally, the institutional set-up for executing the laws should not be too complex regarding overlapping jurisdictions, and weak monitoring of the possibility of opportunistic behaviour, in the form of bribes and other leniencies shown by the administrators (Shrivastava and Kothari 2014).

The institutional set-up is unduly complex in the federal polity of India. There is at the head of the pyramid of authority the Union Ministry of Environment, Forest and Climate Change, the NITI Aayog, Ministry of Science and Technology, the Central Pollution Control Board, and State Pollution Control Boards in each state. The Ministry of Environment, Forest and Climate Change has four major departments with overlapping commands: National River Conservation Directorate, National Afforestation and Eco-Development Board, the Environmental Wing, and the Forests and Wildlife Wing. For instance, the country's afforestation plans, which have often led to the planting of only one species of trees, have conflicted directly with the provisions in the Forest Rights Act of 2006 (Kukreti 2018). So much so that millions of forest dweller livelihoods are affected and they are suffering malnutrition from lack of food. The Forest Department is supposed to look after both the rehabilitation of traditional forest dwellers as well as removing them for the plantation targets to be fulfilled. Little wonder that since 2006 only 3 per cent of the claims made by forest dwellers have been settled so far.

In 1994 the Environmental Impact Assessment Notification required all projects to submit an Environmental Impact Assessment (EIA) for approval. This assessment includes public hearing to ensure that people's participation is guaranteed in the final drawing up of environmental management plans. The EIA is now accepted as a farce with extremely poor execution. The process is influenced by large industries with strong vested interests, inadequate data, ambiguous definitions and no meaningful participation of the community of people who would be affected by the project. Hence it is not difficult to get a clearance at all and very often poor people hardly get to know about the project or comprehend its impact at all.

RESULTING STATE OF THE NATURAL ENVIRONMENT IN INDIA

Despite the long list of India's environmental laws and legislations, India's track record of environmental performance has been quite dismal. In the latest report on Environmental

Performance Index (Wolf et al. 2022), India ranked last out of 180 nations. There seems to have been a systematic decline in its performance over the years. According to the report, India has deteriorated in biodiversity conservation, ecosystem services, fisheries, acidification, and climate change parameters over a period of 10 years. More detailed analysis and data can be found in *Down To Earth Annual* reports (2021 and 2022). According to the article titled 'State of The States' (*Down to Earth* 2022: 23), India's rank as per the Sustainable Development Report 2021 had slipped 3 places down to 120 out of 192 nations. We were below all South Asian countries barring Pakistan.

In terms of air pollution, India has an alarming situation. In 2021, according to IQ*Air* (n.d.), India had 35 of the most polluted cities and out of the top 15, 10 were in India. All the polluted Indian cities in the top 10 have particulate matter which are far above the accepted international standard of 10 micrograms per cubic metre. In India, the average is 40 micrograms, and the worst cities have levels around 110 micrograms. In many parts of North India, the level of air pollution is alarmingly high. All of these problems exist and deteriorate despite having a National Clean Air Programme. In terms of carbon emissions and greenhouse gases, the nation is now the third worst polluter after China and the US.

The Ministry of Drinking Water and Sanitation launched a *Har Ghar Jal Yojana* to provide piped water to every Indian household by 2030. By December 2021 (see *Down To Earth* 2022: 47), the achievement was only 45 per cent. There is also a shortage of groundwater resources emerging in many parts of India. Even in 2018, 88.9 per cent of rural households did not have piped water supply (see Sengupta and Verma 2020).

Renewable Energy in India had a strong support from governments, especially in the promotion of investments in solar power, wind energy and hydro-electric projects. The initial target was to install 175 GW of renewable energy by 2002, which it did achieve. India has an ambitious target of reaching 450 GW by 2030. In many of these projects there are serious challenges regarding land identification and allotment (Jhawar 2021: 214-218).

Forests play an important role in preserving biodiversity, providing ecosystem services and controlling local climate. In India, forests have been traditionally the home of indigenous people. In the twenty-first century, there has been a constant tension between the territorial rights of the indigenous people, conserving Nature and using forests as a commercial resource for development. The Forest Rights Act of 2006 had tried to give rights to communities but the NDA government had proposed an amendment to the Indian Forest Act that gave the usufructuary rights of forests to the bureaucracy. In November 2019, the proposed amendment was withdrawn after it generated much controversy (see Kukreti 2020a). Forests are viewed by the government, like the colonial rulers of the past, as revenue sources and not as an ecological foundation for lives and livelihoods. Hence, the judiciary and the executive continue to view forest dwellers' rights from the perspective of encroachment and eviction (see Kukreti 2020b). The FRA was supposed to create a narrative that undid the story of colonial times where the indigenous people were looked upon as encroachers. Ironically, the same act, through recent amendments might be used to legitimise the old narrative. In a Consultation Paper released on 2 October 2021, the Union Ministry of Environment, Forests and Climate Change proposed amendments to the Forest Conservation Act of 1980. Amongst many points proposed, one was to provide full relaxation to entities such as safaris, zoos, resorts, and mines undertaking non-forest activities on forest land, while restricting access and traditional ownership of the local communities that have resided there for centuries.

A Regressive Metamorphosis

By the turn of the century the Forest Rights Act, Right to Food and the Mahatma Gandhi National Rural Employment

Guarantee Act (MGNREGA), 2005, promising right to 100 days of paid work along with the Right to Information had raised expectations about improvements in the natural environment along with the rise in economic wellbeing of the poor. This has been belied. The current National Democratic Alliance (NDA) government has dragged its feet over managing the environment. Some observers claim that even the lip service paid by the government regarding solving environmental problems is on the wane.

There are a number of instances that indicate this lack of interest. The government has been much more concerned about economic development and growth as well as the ease of doing business. Many industrialists considered the EIA a waste of time and money to get the clearance. The government has considered amendments in many vital laws so that the perceived constraints on doing business get eased, and investments are promoted. As early as September 2014, a high-powered committee was formed under the Cabinet Secretary to consider changes in the Indian Forest Act 1927, The Forest Conservation Act 1980, the Wildlife Protection Act 1972, Water Act 1974, the Air Act 1981 and the Environmental Protection Act 1986.

Recently, the Union government has proposed the revamping of the Indian Forest Act 1927, which was known for its notorious clauses which curtailed the rights of millions of forest dwellers. This was partially rectified after decades in the Forest Rights Act (FRA) of 2006. The draft legislation of the Indian Forest Act 2019 is much more draconian than the colonial version of the 1927 Act (*Down to Earth* 2019). The draft proposes veto powers of the forest bureaucracy over the Forest Rights Act 2006, which would enable the bureaucracy to extinguish rights over forest land already granted under the Forest Rights Act of 2006. It would also allow the officers to reduce or restrict the use of non-timber forest produce (which indigenous people own according to the FRA), and restrict the role of *gram sabhas* over village forests. There would be a parallel system where the forest officers would have the last say.

As far as federal powers are concerned, the draft proposes that the Centre can intervene in any matter of the management of forest lands that it deems fit.

The law proposes that the Centre can open up any patch of forest for commercial plantations, either through public investments or through private agencies. In order to augment its supervisory policing powers, the law proposes that state governments should create adequate infrastructure in the form of lock-up rooms, articles for restraining the accused, transportation of the accused, armouries and safe custody of arms, ammunitions, helmets, and modern wireless equipment. Certain previously bailable offences under the FRA have been made non-bailable. Finally, in perhaps the most draconian measure, the onus of proving innocence has been left to the accused. The accused are going to be presumed guilty until proven otherwise. On the other side of this provision, the forest officers cannot be arrested for any crime alleged to have been committed in the discharge of his official duties. A case once registered cannot be withdrawn. The law re-introduces a relic from the colonial past, whereby if any offence is seemingly perpetrated by a member of a village, the entire village can be collectively punished and all rights of the village dwellers to the forest will be suspended. In a way it makes the 1927 colonial act look very lenient and overturns the entire spirit of the FRA. The 2019 Act will prepare the way for massive commercial use of forests through plantations. Plantations are a collection of trees, and a plantation is not considered a forest by ecologists since its properties and biodiversity is completely different. It will also jeopardise the livelihoods of millions of adivasis, disposing them of the little resources and rights they possess. Forests have already been de-notified as being part of the protected area.

The current government has been arguably the most hostile to protecting the natural environment in independent India. It has strictly sought development-as-usual at the expense of the environment. There have been amendments to the EIA in 2014 and again in 2016 whereby state governments have now powers over bigger projects, of sizes varying from 5000–50000 hectares, compared to 2000–10000 hectares, previously. This amendment pertains to mining and river valley projects. States have typically their own political interest groups. As a result of this amendment, regional outcomes could be very different from state to state. Similarly in a notification of 2016, the Ministry of Environment, Forests and Climate Change had moved the Supreme Court of India against the National Green Tribunal to exempt the real estate sector from environmental laws (*Business Standard* 2017). The sector produces a little less than a quarter of all carbon emissions in the country.

The stance of the government is clear even in the interim budget of the Union government presented in February 2019. The minister in presenting the budget had claimed three environmental objectives as part of its Vision 2030, namely the ease of living, pollution-free India and clean rivers. Yet there were no measures stated in the budget and since 2014, with the advent of the NDA government, there has been a 25 per cent reduction in the environment ministry's budget allocation.

Some Points to Ponder on for the Future

The NDA government has revealed without reasonable doubt that it prefers to put economic development above environmental concerns. This is often claimed to be justified because of the urgency of reducing widespread acute poverty. However, developing now and cleaning up later has many problems. In societies where economic inequalities are acute like in India, environmental degradation hurts the poor the most because they are directly dependent on ecosystem services and natural capital like forests for survival. It is also true that their vulnerabilities are more and the ability to defend themselves from disasters very limited. Hence cleaning up later will have created a large human social cost by then. Postponing the cleaning up of the environment until we are rich is risky too. China is a much polluted country too, but has a per capita income that is about three times India's. If we catch up with China in terms of income, we will be far more polluted than China is now. We will become a global problem, and the environmental damages done will be irreversible.

The approach of accepting the western model of industrial development as the only one available reflects a laziness to think about available alternatives that can marry the wellbeing of citizens to improvements of the natural environment (Gerber and Raina 2018). We all talk about sustainable development but policy makers often show a lack of understanding of the fact that the economy is only embedded in the environment and not the other way around. Even the business-as-usual model of development has not been that spectacular because of our exclusive concern with GDP growth rather than employment and livelihoods. Hence we have a myopic vision about our national future. We refuse to accept no-build decisions in project appraisals and we refuse to impose stricter standards and penalties.

Concluding Remarks

India started well in the 1970s with *Garibi Hatao* and an attention to preserving the natural environment in all its dimensions. Somewhere we lost the way with exclusive focus on material growth where Nature was a free gift hamper-cum-garbage bin. The environment was considered a constraint on growth, and such constraints would have to be overcome through public debate and consensus-building. Investment projects got delayed. Policy makers got restless as quick returns were missing. Now, the environment is considered as something that is best ignored in the discourse of development. It may at best be kept on show for the optics. We seem to refuse to realise that environmental safeguards are not a drag on development. It can prevent irreversible damage to ecosystem resilience and ecosystem services like the bio-geo-chemical cycles, local climate control, waste management and maintaining the fertility of the top soil, apart from recharging fresh water and cleaning up the air. Without essential life support systems, neither can the economy be sustained nor human welfare improved.

REFERENCES

Business Standard. 2017. 'NGT challenged for objecting to EIA exemption to real estate', 23 January. Available at https://www.business-standard.com/article/news-ians/ngt-challenged-for-objecting-to-eia-exemption-to-real-estate-117012301213_1.html (accessed March 2023).

Dasgupta, P. 2001. *Human Well-Being and the Natural Environment.* New Delhi: OUP.

Down to Earth. 2019. 'Unsettled: Despite a historic settlement legislation, India's forest dwellers face eviction, again' 27(21), March 16–31 print issue. New Delhi: Centre for Science and Environment.

———. 2021. *State of India's Environment Report 2021.* New Delhi: Centre for Science and Environment.

———. 2022. *State of India's Environment Report 2022.* New Delhi: Centre for Science and Environment.

Dwivedi, O. P. 1997. *India's Environmental Policies, Programmes and Stewardship.* London: Macmillan Press Limited.

Gerber, J. and R. Raina. 2018. *Post-Growth Thinking in India: Towards Sustainable Egalitarian Alternatives.* Hyderabad: Orient BlackSwan.

Hindustan Times. 2022. 'Uttarakhand HC prohibits mechanised mining in riverbeds across state', 19 December. Available at https://www.hindustantimes.com/cities/dehradun-news/uttarakhand-hc-prohibits-mechanised-mining-in-riverbeds-across-state-101671451623224.html (accessed March 2023).

Indian Kanoon. n.d. 'M.C. Mehta vs Union Of India & Ors on 30 December, 1996'. Available at https://indiankanoon.org/doc/1964392/ (accessed March 2023).

IQAir. n.d. 'World's Most Polluted Cities (Historical Data 2017–2022)'. Available at iqair.com/in-en/world-most-polluted-cities (accessed March 2023).

Jhawar, P. 2021. 'Let's Renew Our Energy Pledge'. *Down to Earth Annual: State of India's Environment Report 2021*: 214–218. New Delhi: CSE.

Jodha, N. 2012. 'Common Property Resources and the Environmental Context: Role of Biophysical Versus Social Stress'. In M. Rangarajan and K. Sivaramakrishnan (eds), *India's Environmental History: Colonialism, Modernity, and the Nation*, Volume 2. Ranikhet: Permanent Black.

Kukreti, Ishan. 2018. 'Policy V. Policy Government's afforestation schemes are undermining the Forest Rights Act'. *Down to Earth Annual: State of India's Environment Report 2018*: 181–184. New Delhi: CSE.

———. 2020a. 'FRA is for People not for Government'. *Down to Earth Annual: State of India's Environment Report 2020*: 316–318. New Delhi: CSE.

———. 2020b. 'Colonial Hangover'. *Down To Earth Annual: State of India's Environment Report 2020*: 312–315. New Delhi: CSE.

———. n.d. 'Pollution of River Ganga, Case Study'. *Legal Service India e-Journal*. Available at https://www.legalserviceindia.com/legal/article-1177-pollution-of-river-ganga-case-study.html (accessed March 2023).

Kumari, Navnit. n. d. 'Pollution of River Ganga, Case Study', *Legal Service India e-Journal*. Available at https://www.legalserviceindia.com/legal/article-1177-pollution-of-river-ganga-case-study.html (accessed March 2023).

Law Times Journal. 2021. 'Shriram Food and Fertilisers Gas Leak Case', 1 April. Available at https://lawtimesjournal.in/shriram-food-and-fertilisers-gas-leak-case/ (accessed March 2023).

Rangarajan, M. 2012. 'The Raj and the Natural World: The Campaign against "Dangerous Beasts" in Colonial India 1875–1925'. In M. Rangarajan and K. Sivaramakrishnan (eds), *India's Environmental History: Colonialism, Modernity, and the Nation*, Vol. 2. Ranikhet: Permanent Black.

Ravi Rajan, S. 2012. 'Disaster, Development, and Governance: Reflections on the "Lessons" of Bhopal'. In M. Rangarajan and K. Sivaramakrishnan (eds), *India's Environmental History: Colonialism, Modernity, and the Nation*, Vol. 2. Ranikhet: Permanent Black.

Sarkar, R. and A. Sinha. 2017. *The Economics of Sustainable Development*. New York: Business Expert Press.

Sengupta, S. and R. Verma. 2020. 'India's Piped Dream'. In *Down to Earth Annual State of India's Environment Report 2020*: 292–295. New Delhi: Centre for Science and Environment.

Shrivastava, A. and A. Kothari. 2014. *Churning the Earth: The Making of Global India*. New Delhi: Penguin Books.

The Indian Express. 2017. 'A short history of the Sardar Sarovar Dam on river Narmada', 17 September. Available at https://indianexpress.com/article/research/a-short-history-of-the-sardar-sarovar-dam-on-river-narmada-4847807/ (accessed March 2023).

The Wire. 2018. 'Poverty Is the Greatest Polluter: Remembering Indira Gandhi's Stirring Speech in Stockholm', 19 November. Available at https://thewire.in/books/indira-gandhi-nature-pollution (accessed March 2023).

———. n.d. 'MC Mehta v Union of India, AIR 2002 SC 1696 (CNG Vehicles Case), Case Note'. *Legal Service India e-Journal*. Available at https://www.legalserviceindia.com/legal/article-4863-mc-mehta-v-union-of-india-air-2002-sc-1696-cng-vehicles-case-case-note.html (accessed March 2023).

Tiwari, Anamika. n. d. 'MC Mehta v Union of India, AIR 2002 SC 1696 (CNG Vehicles Case), Case Note', *Legal Service India e-Journal*. Available at https://www.legalserviceindia.com/legal/article-4863-mc-mehta-v-union-of-india-air-2002-sc-1696-cng-vehicles-case-case-note.html (accessed March 2023).

Wolf, M. J., J. W. Emerson, D. C. Esty, A. de Sherbinin, Z. A. Wendling, et al. 2022. *2022 Environmental Performance Index*. New Haven, CT: Yale Center for Environmental Law & Policy.

Notes on the Contributors

ASIS KUMAR BANERJEE is former Vice-Chancellor and former professor of economics, University of Calcutta. At various stages of his career, he has also been associated with Presidency College (now Presidency University), Kolkata; Indian Statistical Institute, New Delhi; and the University of California, Riverside, California. He works in the fields of development economics, welfare economics, choice theory, measurement of poverty and inequality.

DEBASHREE CHAKRABORTY has recently completed her PhD from the Department of Economics, Jadavpur University, Kolkata. She specialises in open economy macroeconomics and macroeconomic problems of the Indian economy.

PINAKI CHAKRABORTY is currently working for the Asian Development Bank on post-Covid fiscal recovery in South Asia, and on public financial management and governance reforms. He was Director, National Institute of Public Finance and Policy, New Delhi and Economic Advisor to the Fourteenth Finance Commission.

DIPANKOR COONDOO is retired professor of economics, Indian Statistical Institute, Kolkata. He served as the President of Indian Econometric Society, and was a member of several committees of the World Bank, UNDP, National Sample Survey and Government of West Bengal.

AMBAR GHOSH is professor of economics, Jadavpur University, Kolkata.

ASHIMA GOYAL is professor emeritus at IGIDR, Mumbai. She is widely published and is currently a member of Reserve Bank of India's Monetary Policy Committee. *Business Today* selected her as one of the most powerful women in Indian business in 2021 and 2022.

SHUBHAM GUPTA has worked as a consultant at the National Institute of Public Finance and Policy, and Deloitte. He has a bachelor's in commerce from the University of Delhi and a master's in economics from Gokhale Institute of Politics and Economics, Pune.

PARAMITA MUKHERJEE is professor of economics, Narsee Monjee Institute of Management Studies, Hyderabad. She was visiting faculty at Indian Institute of Management Ranchi and Presidency College, Kolkata. Her research interest lies in financial economics and applied econometrics.

ABHISHEK NARESH is currently working as assistant professor of economics in Goa Institute of Management. Previously, he was associated with Birla Institute of Technology, Mesra. His research interests include monetary policy in emerging nations and international macroeconomics.

PARTHAPRATIM PAL is professor in the Economics Group at the Indian Institute of Management (IIM) Calcutta. He has a Master's, MPhil and PhD in Economics from the Jawaharlal Nehru University, New Delhi. He has also received education from Cambridge University and Harvard Business School. With more than 25 years of research and teaching experience, his areas of interest include international economics, macroeconomics, and development economics.

MIHIR RAKSHIT retired as professor of economics from Indian Statistical Institute, Kolkata. He has taught at Burdwan University and Presidency College, Calcutta and held visiting faculty positions at Jawaharlal Nehru University, Delhi School of Economics and Erasmus University Rotterdam. He served as a member of the Monetary Policy Advisory Board of Reserve Bank of India. A globally acknowledged expert on the Indian economy, both pre and post economic reforms, he has published widely in the areas of macroeconomics and finance.

ALOK RAY is former professor of economics, Indian Institute of Management Calcutta. He obtained his PhD from University of Rochester, US. Prof. Ray has also taught in the University of Calcutta, Delhi School of Economics, Cornell University (US),

University of Rochester (US), University of Pittsburgh (US), Portland State University (US), Queen's University (Canada), and Monash University (Melbourne, Australia). He writes columns regularly on current economic issues in several English dailies. He has served as a consultant to United Nations, World Bank, Government of India, and a number of private sector companies.

PARTHA RAY is Director, National Institute of Bank Management, Pune. He was a professor of economics at the Indian Institute of Management Calcutta from December 2011–April 2021. Between 2007–2011, he was Adviser to the Executive Director (India) at the International Monetary Fund, Washington D.C. Earlier (1989–2006), he had worked in the specialist cadre of Economists at the Reserve Bank of India (RBI); his last position was Director, Department of Economic and Policy Research, RBI. Educated in Kolkata, Mumbai and Oxford, he has written extensively on issues relating to various global economic issues.

ABHIRUP SARKAR is retired professor of economics, Indian Statistical Institute, Kolkata. He has also taught at the University of Florida, Concordia University, Brigham Young University, and the Indian Institute of Management Calcutta.

AGNIRUP SARKAR is assistant professor of economics at the Indian Institute of Technology, Guwahati and a former Research Officer at the Central Bank of Slovenia.

JONG KOOK SHIN is associate professor of economics at Korea University, Sejong Campus. His research and publications are in the domain of financial economics, macroeconomics and human capital.

ANUP SINHA retired as professor of economics from the Indian Institute of Management Calcutta. He is Chief Mentor, Heritage Business School, Kolkata, and also the Chairman of the Board of Directors, Bandhan Bank Limited. He did his PhD from the University of Southern California, USA.

CHETAN SUBRAMANIAN is professor of economics at the Indian Institute of Management Bangalore, with decades of experience in teaching and publishing in top-tier journals of macroeconomics and international macroeconomics.

SOUMYEN SIKDAR is retired professor of economics, Indian Institute of Management Calcutta. He is visiting faculty at Presidency University, Kolkata; Indira Gandhi Institute of Development Research (IGIDR), Mumbai; Osaka University, Japan; and Aarhus University, Denmark. Educated at Presidency College(now Presidency University), University of Calcutta, Kolkata and the University of Minnesota, US, his teaching career spanned almost four decades. His areas of research interest and publication include globalisation, international trade and macroeconomic issues.

Index

1991 economic crisis 246

adjustments
  price 10, 204
  process 10, 173
  structural 41, 43
aggregate investment 8, 23, 25
aggregate output 7, 162, 174
agricultural
  bottlenecks 38
  goods 10, 23, 214, 225
  labourers 91–92
  protection 247
  R&D 155–56
  surpluses 53
agriculture xxviii, 4, 7, 9–10, 19–20, 23, 29, 31, 49–50, 52–55, 69, 155–56, 214, 225, 239, 241, 247, 262, 346
  performance of 23, 156
Air (Prevention and Control of Pollution) Act, 1981 346–58
anti-dumping duties (ADDs) 248, 256, 263, 275
appreciation 9–10, 25, 31, 41, 43, 47, 50–51, 61, 65, 69, 269–70, 302
  real 43, 47, 50–51, 65, 69, 302
approximation 13–14, 79, 84, 86–87, 98
Asian Development Bank 256
Asian Infrastructure Investment Bank (AIIB) 255–56
Asia-Pacific region 255–56, 260

Asia-Pacific Regional Comprehensive Economic Partnership 236
asset-liability mismatch 40, 48
asset pricing model xxxiii, 109, 119
  consumption-based 109, 119
assets xxxiii, xxxv, 26, 28, 38, 40, 48, 50, 52, 56, 60, 68, 108–09, 119, 140, 156, 288, 299, 307, 312, 325
  financial 50, 68
  stressed 26, 28
Association of Southeast Asian Nations (ASEAN) 247, 251, 256, 259, 261, 278
automatic destabiliser 161, 174, 176
Ayushman Bharat 64

balance of payments (BOP) 23, 36, 49, 167–68, 254, 263–65, 267, 289, 295–99
  problem 267
balance of trade 239, 297
Ball and Mankiw methodology 202
Bangladesh 57, 239, 255, 268, 271–72
bank/banking xxvii, 11, 27–28, 40, 47–48, 58, 107, 155, 189, 191, 193, 195, 202, 255, 288, 299, 303, 309, 311
  advances 28

central 130, 203
public sector 26, 41, 48, 60, 304
bankruptcy 28, 48
bargaining 45, 258, 262
Belt and Road Initiative (BRI) 255
biodiversity 349–50, 356–57, 359
Biological Diversity Act 2002 349
Bio-medical Wastes (Management and Handling) Rules 1998 349
Bombay Club 248
bond 24, 26, 143, 265, 308–09, 312–13
   acquisition of 26
   corporate 312–13
   rupee-denominated 265
bond yield 131, 135, 136
   government 131, 135–36
Bretton Woods institutions 40
BRICS xxiii, 241
BSE Sensex 66
'business as usual' model xxxv
business cycle xxxii, 130, 132–35, 147, 151
business lobbies 256

capacity utilisation 22–23, 26, 28
capital xxvi–xxvii, xxxiv, 4, 8–9, 13, 21–27, 29–30, 36, 39–40, 44, 45, 47, 52, 54, 63, 65–66, 68, 107, 154–55, 157, 163–64, 167, 237, 239, 251, 254, 263–65, 270, 273, 287–93, 298–99, 303–11, 313–14, 326, 350, 360
   fixed 8, 13

   flows 49, 308
   foreign 39, 68, 163, 167, 270, 299
   natural 350, 360
   private 29, 305
capital account 307
   controls 47
   restrictions on xxxvi, 290, 310
Capital Account Convertibility (CAC) 39, 44–45, 47, 65, 251, 288, 311, 313
   Indian 47
capital adequacy ratio 26
capital control xxxvi, 40, 288, 291, 311, 314
capital flows xxvi, 65–66, 68, 154–55, 254, 287–89, 291–92, 298, 303, 308, 314
   cross-border 154–55
   management 65–66, 68
capital formation 13, 21–22, 24–25, 107, 163–64
capital markets 24, 47, 264, 273
capital outflow 270, 307
capital-output ratio 36, 52
capital stocks 24–25, 27, 30
   composition of 25, 27, 30
   infrastructural 24–25
catch-up growth 36, 38, 45, 69
   Indian 69
centrally sponsored schemes (CSS) 326–27, 334–35
Central Pollution Control Board 355
Central sales tax (CST) 338–39
Central Statistics Office (CSO) xxix, 7

Centre for Development and
 Environment Policy xxv
Centre for Science and
 Environment (CSE) 353
Centre-state and private
 partnership 64
Centre-state relations xxvi,
 xxviii–xxix, xxxvii, 323, 328, 340
 financial xxvi, 323, 340
 fiscal xxiv, xxvii, xxxv, 328
certification 52, 62
cess and surcharges 331–33
 implications of 331
China xxv–vi, xxviii–ix, xxxi,
 35–36, 43–51, 53, 57–58, 67,
 158–59, 236, 238–46, 249,
 252–56, 259–60, 265, 270, 272,
 274–76, 278–79, 290, 305,
 307–08, 356, 361
 economic might 259
 economic rise of 259
 political might 259
 reforms process 46
 rise as a formidable economic
  force xxiii
 rise as an economic
  superpower xxvi
 trade ratio 240
China and India xxix, xxxiv,
 43–44, 49, 58, 239–41, 252
 comparison 49
 growth strategies 44
 trade deficit 239, 243
 trade/GDP Ratios 240–41
China and Russia 255
China and US 253, 256
 trade deficit 254
 trade war 253–56

Chinese
 depreciated real exchange
  rate 69
 economy(ies) 255
 goods 261
 investment 254
 labour 255
 markets 256
climate change 53, 324–25, 343,
 354–57, 360
Coastal Regulation Zone
 Notification 2011 349
Committee on Fuller Capital
 Account Convertibility
 (FCAC) 311
commodity(ies) xxxv, 46, 49,
 55, 154, 166, 199, 201, 203–04,
 208–10, 224, 226, 232, 234,
 236, 243, 269, 271, 278, 306,
 312
Commonwealth of Independent
 States (CIS) 278
comparative advantage 47, 277
competition xxvii, 40, 45–51,
 63–64, 70, 248–50, 252, 255,
 261–64, 268, 277
 domestic 51, 268
competitive advantage 260–61
competitiveness 41, 249, 268–69,
 272
Constitution of India 331, 334,
 337, 351
 42nd Constitutional
  Amendment 351
 73rd and 74th Constitutional
  Amendments 326, 336
 101st Constitutional
  Amendment 339

122nd Constitutional
Amendment 337
Concurrent List 336
Directive principles 351
Directive Principles of State
Policy 336
State List 336
Union List 336
constraints 5, 10, 14, 22–23, 38,
40–41, 46, 48, 52, 60, 269, 358,
361
budgetary 48
political 41, 60
structural 22, 40
supply 5, 10, 269
construction sector 30, 58, 63,
255, 353
Consumer Price Index (CPI)
xxxiv-xxxv, 11, 19–21, 31,
91–92, 142–43, 146, 198–203,
205, 208–10, 212–13, 215–16,
220, 224–26, 232, 303
inflation xxxiii, 11, 20, 31, 143,
199, 212, 215, 220, 224, 303
Consumer Price Index for
Agricultural Labourers (CPI-
AL) 91–92
Consumer Price Index for
Industrial Workers (CPI-IW)
91–92, 201
consumers xxxii, 11, 53, 61, 79,
88–89, 91–92, 111, 115, 119–20,
127, 162, 198, 236, 239, 249,
255, 257, 263, 267, 269–73, 276
consumption xxx, 5, 8, 11, 13–19,
29, 41–43, 45, 46, 48–51, 67, 70,
88, 90, 109–11, 115–16, 119–20,
142–43, 145, 154–55, 161–64,
168, 173–74, 176, 185, 189,
195, 265, 271, 297, 302, 337–38,
343–44
domestic 46, 51, 143, 164, 265,
302
government 16, 18, 29, 161,
174, 189
household 8, 11, 14–16, 17
contract award process 255
corporate debt markets 304
corporate social responsibility
60
corruption 48, 57, 59
costs
advantage 58, 236, 270,
275–76
labour 58, 236, 255, 275–76
push 163, 187
Covid-19 pandemic xxvi–xxviii,
37, 66–67, 263
creativity 51, 62, 276
credit 22, 27–28, 40–41, 47–49,
56, 107, 155, 265, 269, 273, 300,
303, 339
bank 27–28, 40, 48, 107
growth 40, 48–49
credit markets 56
credit ratings 22
crisp theory 79, 85
crude oil 11, 20, 23, 46, 67, 243
currency(ies) 23, 27, 30, 42–43,
46, 51, 142–43, 158, 163, 165,
167, 254–55, 258, 265, 268–71,
288, 291, 299–301, 303,
305–06, 308, 310
appreciation of 51
cheap 46
depreciation of 42

domestic 142–43, 163, 165
Euro 254, 300–301
foreign 23, 27, 163, 167, 288, 299–300, 305, 310
GBP 300
INR 298, 300–301, 329
Japanese Yen 300–301
local 258
overvalued 271
reserve 254
rouble 258
undervaluation of 43, 255
union 254
USD 19–20, 254, 300
yuan 254, 265
current account 36, 41, 46, 51, 265, 288, 297, 299, 303, 305, 307, 310, 314
Current Account Balance 297
Current account deficit (CAD) 36, 41–43, 46–47, 49–50, 65, 67–69, 263, 270, 288, 297, 299, 303, 307, 314
Current account surplus (CAS) 46, 49, 51, 265, 305, 307

data and methodology xxviii, 133–34, 136, 202, 205, 332
annual 208
comparability of 88
computed 134
detrended 133
faulty xxviii
historical 134
HP-filtered 146
Indian 132, 140, 145
monthly xxxv, 204–05, 208–09, 220

debt xxxvii, 23, 26–28, 30, 39–40, 44–45, 47, 65–66, 163, 167, 255, 288, 291, 293, 296, 298–99, 304, 306–07, 311–13, 325
external 163, 167, 313
financing 26–27
financing of investment 26
flows 47, 65
government 299, 313
inflows 65–66
private 26, 39
short-term 39, 306
debt-equity ratio 26
debt/GDP ratio 45
debt-service-to-income ratios 293
debt-to-income ratios 293
decoupling hypothesis 132
deficiency 3, 8, 24
demand
  aggregate 3–4, 7–9, 11, 13–18, 22, 28, 69, 140, 162, 164, 172, 188, 193–94, 225, 262, 376
  components of 12, 14
  effects on 10
  excess 39, 41–44, 69
  export 52, 67, 270
  price elasticity of 11, 269
demand and supply 4–5, 9–10, 12–13, 140, 266, 277
demand and supply constraints 5
democracy xxxii, 44, 51, 58, 60, 70, 279
demographic dividend xxxi, 37
demonetisation xxvi, xxix, 2, 37, 57, 272
dependency ratio 37

374 Index

development xxv, xxix, xxxiii,
    xxxvi–vii, 28, 47, 55, 59, 61,
    106–09, 154–55, 239, 243, 249,
    252, 255–56, 312, 324–25, 337,
    349–50, 352–54, 357–62, 378
  economic 106, 154, 239, 358,
    360
  financial 106–07, 108
  sustainable 349, 354, 361
devolution xxxvii, 60–61, 323–24,
    326–28, 330–31, 334–35, 378
  horizontal formula 324, 335
digital land-title records 60
disturbances 132, 143–44
diversity 38, 51, 52, 66–69
dollar debt 65
domestic
  demand 15, 43, 50, 52, 68–69,
    266
  income 8, 11
  investment 15, 302
  market 25, 27, 39, 107, 250,
    262, 264–65, 269, 273, 275
  monetary policy 130, 151
  monetary shock 144
  retail debt markets 66
  sales 27, 249, 274
  savings 44, 47, 50, 67–68
  securities 66, 312
drugs, generic and off-patent
    249, 276
duty free access/entry 57, 256,
    272

'Ease of Doing Business' index/
    ranking 59, 70, 246
East Asian crisis 36, 295, 308,
    311

East Asian Tigers 237, 239
economic
  activities xxv, xxxvii, 11, 130,
    132, 135, 140, 146, 149, 151,
    154–55, 369
  inclusion xxxii, 44, 58–59
  interests 262
  performance xxviii, 2, 7, 108
  well-being xxviii, xxxii–iii,
    76, 88, 91, 93, 98–99, 369
economy(ies) xxv–xxxvi, 2–7,
    9–12, 15–18, 20, 22–23, 25, 28,
    30–31, 37–39, 41, 43–45, 50–52,
    55–56, 58–59, 61, 63–67, 70,
    76–78, 80–81, 96, 106, 108–11,
    114, 116–17, 119–20, 124,
    129–33, 140–49, 151, 157, 160,
    163, 166, 171–72, 177–78,
    199–201, 204, 206–07, 209,
    214, 216, 219, 225–26, 240–41,
    247–48, 250, 254–55, 259,
    262–64, 266, 268, 272, 275,
    277–78, 287–95, 302, 305–06,
    308, 337, 339, 349, 361–62
  behaviour of xxviii, 3, 5, 12,
    28, 30
  developing xxx, xxxiii
  domestic 16, 25, 30, 67, 166
  emerging xxiv, 129, 254, 278
  foreign 140, 141
  global xxxiii, 41, 290
  high cost 59, 70
  labour intensive 43
  large 140, 146–47, 149
  macro xxv, 2–3, 10–11, 17, 31
  open 45, 131–32, 140–42,
    144, 146, 151, 241, 289–90
  performance of 22, 108, 124

real xxiv, 108–09, 124, 130, 293
  small 148–49, 163
economies of scale 58, 250, 263, 266
education 38, 44–45, 62–64, 69, 90, 101, 155–56, 177
  quality of 62, 64, 69
efficiency 39, 56, 77–78, 96, 249, 251, 262–63, 267, 270, 272, 277
electricity 24, 54, 60–61, 161, 338
  generation 25, 273
electronic commerce 257
electronics 63, 236, 255, 263, 276
e-markets 55
Emerging Market Economies (EMEs) xxv, xxxiii, 23–24, 292–93, 298, 306, 339
Emerging markets (EMs) xxv, xxxiii, xxxvi, 39, 44, 65, 67, 133, 292, 294, 306, 339
empirical analysis 28, 109, 119, 201
empirical model 132–33, 138
employment xxix, 23, 37, 42, 46, 53–54, 61–64, 174, 239, 274, 288, 290, 342, 361
  rural 53, 61
energy 46, 67, 69, 243, 249–50, 266, 343, 353, 356–57
  alternative 243, 266
  renewable 243, 357
  solar power 356
  sources 243, 266
  wind 356
environment xxvii, xxxii, xxxvii, 4, 14–15, 18, 24, 52, 236, 253, 258, 276, 278–79, 342–46, 348–49, 351–55, 357–61
  economic 4, 14–15, 18
  global 258, 279
  natural 342–46, 349, 351–54, 358–59, 361
environmental
  concerns 352, 360
  degradation 345, 360
Environmental Act of 1986 347
Environmental Impact Assessment (EIA) 355, 358, 360
Environmental Performance Index 355–56
Environment (Protection) Act 346
equity 26–27, 45, 47, 66, 77–78, 96, 107, 250, 288, 291, 298–99, 304, 311–13
equity to debt ratios 27
Essential Commodity Act 55
estimated model 145, 147, 151
Euler equation 112, 142
European Union (EU) 57, 237, 241, 251, 257, 272
'Everything But Arms' (EBA) scheme 57
E-Waste (Management and Handling) Rules 2011 349
exchange rate xxvii, xxxvi, 19–20, 40, 49, 65, 69, 143, 163–65, 167–68, 199, 205, 208, 217–19, 225, 236, 244, 247, 254, 262, 264–72, 287–91, 299–305, 308, 310, 314
  fixed 265, 287, 289–90, 303
  flexible 65, 289–90
  floating 65, 266
  nominal 143, 163, 270
  protection 236, 247

real 69, 143, 163–64, 168, 268, 270
Re/US$ 20
undervalued 69, 270–71
expectations hypothesis 130, 141–42, 144
expenditure xxx, xxxiii, 3–5, 8–9, 13–14, 16, 21, 29, 65, 76–82, 84, 86, 88–89, 96, 101, 164, 176, 189, 195, 199, 322, 324–25, 327–28, 334–36
  autonomous 3, 5, 13–14
  components of 5, 8
  consumer 79, 88
  consumption 16, 88
  distribution of 77, 88
  government 14, 65, 176
  non-plan 325, 334
  per capita 80, 82, 88
  plan 325, 334–35
export-intensive sectors 51
export market 238, 249, 263, 269, 273–74
  competitive 249, 263
exports 8, 11, 13–16, 18–19, 23, 29, 40–41, 43–46, 49–52, 55, 57–58, 63, 65, 67, 69, 154–55, 162, 164, 168–69, 172–73, 236–44, 247, 249, 252, 256, 258, 260, 263–79, 290, 295, 297, 302, 308
  expansion 51, 67
  growth 16, 65, 302
  net 162, 164, 168–69, 172–73
  obligations 244, 275
  pessimism 237, 295
external commercial borrowing (ECB) 27, 292, 312–13

external payments crisis of 1991 295

factors
  costs 3, 7–8, 12–13, 20
  demand side 13
  domestic 16, 65, 272
  external 15, 18
  structural 23
  supply-side 4, 9–11, 376
farmers 4, 10, 53–55, 247, 261
farm sector 20, 23
Fast-moving Consumer Goods (FMCG) 53
Finance Commissions xxxv, 323, 326–28, 330–31, 334, 340, 367
  award 324, 334, 340
financial development 106–08
financial intermediation 50, 106–07
financial sector xxix, xxxi, 3, 22, 27, 30, 68, 155, 161, 166, 372
firms 26–28, 36, 41, 51–52, 56, 60, 140, 163, 166, 172, 203–04, 240, 247, 249–50, 254–55, 262, 264, 266–67, 271–76, 313, 348
  foreign 264, 267, 275
  Indian 41, 51, 247, 249–50, 275
  infrastructural 27
  large 56, 163
  small 56, 272
fiscal
  autonomy 323–24, 328, 334, 336, 339–40
  consolidation 40, 45, 61, 311
  deficit xxxiv, 14, 21, 39, 156–57, 160–61, 164, 171,

174–78, 180–86, 188–89,
193–95, 244, 265, 270,
325–26
  target 157, 160–61, 171,
  174–77, 180–86, 188–89,
  194–95, 265, 270
  -deficit-GDP ratio xxxii
  deficit ratio 14
  prudence xxxii, xxxiv, 327
  stimulus 27, 48, 65
Fiscal Responsibility Act (FRA)
  325, 357–59
Fiscal Responsibility and Budget
  Management Act (FRBM) 2003
  161, 326
Five Year Plan 334–45
flood control 155–56
fluctuations 4–6, 16, 18, 22, 65,
  124, 146, 243, 270, 298
  cyclical 4–5, 16
food 4, 10, 19–20, 23, 29, 31, 36,
  43, 45–46, 53, 55, 63, 89–90,
  155, 201, 203, 205, 213–14, 225,
  237, 239, 274, 355, 370, 374
  inflation 19, 29, 53, 203, 213,
  225
food grains 10, 23, 237
food prices 4, 20, 36, 45–46, 53,
  55, 203, 205, 225, 370
  inflation 20, 203
food processing 63, 274
foreign commerce and
  investment xxiv
foreign companies 249, 251–52
foreign currency reserves 306
foreign debt 66
Foreign Direct Investment (FDI)
  46, 49, 67, 164, 236, 244–46,
  248–49, 251, 260, 275, 278,
  292, 297–98, 312
  inflows 244–45
  net 164, 244–45
  outflow 244
  tariff-jumping 251
foreign exchange buffer 251
Foreign Exchange Management
  Act (FEMA) 311
foreign exchange market 303–05,
  309–10
Foreign Exchange Regulation
  Act (FERA) 310–11
Foreign Institutional Investors
  (FII) 299, 311–12
foreign portfolio capital 299, 306
Foreign portfolio inflows (FPI)
  47
Foreign Portfolio Investment
  (FPI) 49, 65, 164, 297–98, 306,
  312
Forest (Conservation) Act 1980
  349, 357–58
forest rights 349
Forest Rights Act of 2006 349,
  351, 355, 357–58
forests 324, 327, 334, 344–45,
  349–51, 353, 355, 357–60
Forests Act 1927 350, 357–58
forex market 288, 299–300,
  304–05, 314
forex reserves 296, 299, 306–08,
  369
formal sector 52
Fourteenth Finance Commission
  (FFC) xxxv, 323–28, 330–32,
  334–36, 340
  award 324, 326, 328, 330, 334

recommendations of xxxv,
   323, 332
report 324, 327–28, 336
Terms of Reference of 335
franchising 249
Free Trade Agreements (FTAs)
   57, 251, 253, 259–62
   bilateral 260
   regional 260
Fuller Capital Account
   Convertibility (FCAC) 311
fuzzy dominance 86–87, 97
fuzzy Lorenz-dominance xxxi,
   79, 84–87, 98, 100

Garibi Hatao 361
Generalized System of
   Preferences (GSP) 256, 272
Gini coefficient 77, 96
Gini inequality index 87
Global Financial Crisis, 2008-09
   xxiii, xxvii, 2, 17, 36, 40, 47–48,
   50–51, 61, 65, 67–68, 295
globalisation xxxiii–iv, 235,
   240–41, 246–48, 251–57, 288
   financial 257, 288
global monetary policy 129
global recession xxx, 263, 271
goods
   consumer 61, 272–73
   domestic 142, 164, 169, 182
   domestically produced 277
   foreign 142, 157, 163–64, 169
   imported 168, 263, 271
   intermediate 46, 51, 69, 157
   manufactured 239, 241
   non-traded 41–43, 53, 68
   public 44, 58, 60

tradable 41–42, 56, 68
traded 41–43, 53, 68
goods and services xxxiii, 4,
   9–10, 14–15, 17–18, 22, 29,
   172, 182, 186, 189, 240, 258,
   275, 277, 338, 343
   exports of 15, 18
   industrial 4, 10, 29
Goods and Services Tax (GST)
   xxvi, xxviii, xxxvii, 2, 56–57,
   60–61, 272, 323, 332–33, 337–39
   impact of 337
governance 44, 48, 57, 59–60, 354
government
   bond 131, 135–36
   deficits 44, 65
   intervention 22, 303
   securities 66, 271, 304, 308
government final consumption
   expenditure (GFCE) 8, 13–14,
   16–18
Government of India (GoI) 66,
   161, 166–67, 174–75, 177–78,
   195, 206, 208, 239–40, 245,
   247–48, 258, 261, 263, 303,
   312–13, 329
   fiscal and monetary policy
      161
Gram Panchayats 327
grants 24, 323, 326–27, 329–30,
   334–35, 340
Great Recession 2007 254, 257
Greece 158–59, 254
Green Peace 353
Gross Domestic Product (GDP)
   xxiv, xxvii–ix, xxxii, 1–10,
   12–21, 23, 28–30, 35–37, 40,
   45, 50, 52, 56, 68, 107, 121–22,

Index 379

133, 146, 150, 156, 158–61,
164, 174, 176, 186, 189, 199,
205, 213, 215–16, 237–41, 254,
259, 263, 271, 277, 292, 295,
297, 304–08, 329–33, 338, 361
  at market prices 7, 12, 19, 158
  changes in 3, 6, 8–9, 14
  components of 7–8, 17–18,
    29, 215
  fall in 20–21, 29
  growth xxvii–viii, 1–4, 6–9,
    12, 15–21, 23, 28–29, 107,
    150, 158, 164, 254, 263, 271,
    338, 361
  growth rate of xxvii, 2, 158,
    164, 263
  per capita 37, 107
  quarterly xxix, 3–4, 7, 12–13,
    29–30, 133
  variations in 2–3, 5, 9, 12, 28
Gross Fiscal deficit (GFD) 164
gross fixed capital formation
  (GFCF) 13–16, 19, 21–23
Gross Tax Revenue (GTR)
  329–33
Gross Value Added (GVA) 7,
  9–10
growth
  cycles xxix, 2, 5–6
  drivers 52, 55
  long-run 106–08, 124
  medium-term 17, 21
  per capita 108, 122–23
  q-o-q 6, 12–13, 15
  rate xxvii, 2, 13, 17, 21, 35–39,
    41, 54, 119, 122, 133, 150,
    158, 160, 163, 206, 254, 263,
    271, 278, 330, 332

  recovery 56
  short term 3, 13–14, 21
  slowdown in 2, 57
  sustained (real) xxix
  volatility of xxvi
growth cycle 4, 12–13, 17–18, 20,
  25, 29, 133
  phases of 17, 20, 25, 29
growth cycle approach 133
growth-oriented approach 44
GSDP 325–26
GST Council 60, 323, 337, 339

H-1B temporary work visas 252,
  257
Har Ghar Jal Yojana 356
Hazardous Wastes
  (Management, Handling and
  Transboundary Movement)
  Rules 2008 349
HH Market Concentration
  Index 238
household 5, 8, 10–11, 14–17,
  29, 50, 53, 66–68, 80, 88–90,
  94, 140, 311, 356
  consumption 8, 11, 14–17
  expenditure on 16, 88
  Indian 10, 66
  investment 11, 15
housing 25, 29–30, 56, 63, 201,
  373
  low-income 56, 63
human capital xxvii, 4, 350

imbalances xxvii, xxix, 3, 12,
  21–28, 30–31, 336
  real and financial sector xxix,
    3, 26–27, 30

structural 21–23, 25, 30
immigration 256–57, 261
  temporary 256, 261
import duty 247, 263–64
imports 8, 11, 14, 18–19, 23,
  44–47, 49–52, 67–70, 154–55,
  163, 166, 169, 237–40, 242–43,
  247–49, 253, 258, 261–67, 271,
  274–75, 277, 297
  commodity 46, 243
  control 237
  dependence 51, 266
  duties 248, 262
  merchandise 47, 239
  substitution 44, 52
impossible trinity xxvi, xxxiv,
  287–89, 291, 293, 295, 299,
  310, 314
incentives 25, 39–40, 41, 55–56,
  61, 63, 107, 325, 343
inclusion xxx, xxxvi, 44, 58–59,
  61, 224, 334
  political xxx, 44, 58
income 1, 10, 25, 36, 44, 49, 53,
  57, 116, 121, 162, 167, 183
  distribution of xxx, 38, 76, 156
  effect 5, 109, 115–16, 120
  fall in 109, 116
  per capita xxxi, 44, 57,
    109–10, 112, 114, 116–19,
    121–22, 241, 272, 361
  real 108–09, 162, 177, 183,
    214
  redistribution of 173, 186
  source of 110, 257
  trap 49, 62
Index of Export Market
  Penetration 238

India
  economic activities in 130,
    132, 140, 146, 149, 151
  economic well-being in xxvi,
    xxxi, 88, 91, 98–99
  exchange rate 299–300, 303
  exports 15, 57, 237–39, 242,
    256, 258, 267–69, 271,
    277–78
  external debt 167
  FDI flows into 244
  forex reserves 299, 306
  GDP 1, 7, 28
  growth xxvii, 3, 9, 13, 15, 18,
    37, 56, 58
  growth path 56
  imports 11, 166, 238
  inflation in 171, 248
  labour participation rate 37
  Maximum Tariff Rate 238
  National Democratic Alliance
    (NDA) government 357–58,
    360
  post-reform period in 132–33
  recession 132, 134–39
  trade deficit 242–43, 261
India and US 131–32, 134–35,
  140, 151
  bond yield 131
  yield curves 134–35
  yield spreads 151
Indian
  business cycles xxxii, 132, 135,
    151
  companies 248–52
  democracy xxx, 58
  economy xxiii, xxv–vii, xxx,
    2, 4, 10–11, 18, 20, 23, 38,

56, 76–77, 129, 146, 151, 171–72, 199–201, 206–07, 209, 216, 219, 262, 288, 295, 302
  contemporary xxiii, xxvii macro xxv, 2, 10–11
  exports 237, 256, 268–69, 271
  goods 69, 258
  growth xxiv, xxviii, 44, 69, 302
  inflation xxxii, 201, 206, 224, 288
  markets 236, 248, 256, 258, 299
  professionals 252, 257
Indian Forest Act 350, 357–58
Indian Medical Council 63
Indian recession 135–36, 138–39
  forecast of 139
  periods of 137–38
  predictive power for 138–39
  probabilities of 138
Indian rupee xxiv, xxxiv, 20, 28, 47, 65, 165, 247, 263–66, 268–70, 296, 300, 302, 305, 312, 314
  depreciation of 28, 247, 265
  exchange rate 165
  volatility 65
Indian yield spread xxxii, 134–35, 137–38, 146, 149, 151
indicators 19, 26, 30, 54, 121, 130, 136, 159, 198–99, 202, 297, 303, 324, 327, 335, 373, 380
indifference curve 41
industrialisation 295, 302
industry(ies) 7, 9, 23, 41, 46, 48, 55–58, 62–63, 70, 155, 236, 245, 247–48, 252, 263–64, 266–67, 276–77, 347–48, 355

  domestic 46, 70, 248
  growth 23, 37
  infant 263, 267
inequality xxiv–vii, xxx–xi, xxxv, 23, 76–77, 80–83, 85, 87, 94, 96, 127, 156, 176, 257, 338, 345
  index 81, 87
  indices 81, 87
  problem of 76–77
inflation xxiv–xiii, 11, 19–20, 29, 31, 37, 43–46, 50–51, 53, 67–69, 91, 131, 141, 143–47, 157, 160–61, 171, 174, 176–77, 182, 185–86, 188–92, 194–95, 198–206, 208–10, 212–13, 215, 217–18, 220–26, 244, 248, 254, 257, 264, 268–70, 288, 299, 303, 311
  aggregate 204, 209, 225
  analysis of 201, 224
  components of 200–202, 205, 209–10
  core xxxiii, 201–02, 204, 213, 222–23, 225–26
  costs of xxxii, 160–61, 171, 174, 182, 186, 188, 195
  CPI xxxiii, 11, 19–20, 31, 143, 146, 199–201, 212, 215, 220, 224, 303
  CPICORE 210, 212–13
  CPIFD 212–13
  CPIFL 212–13
  effects of 43, 91, 157, 161, 174
  flexible 68, 303
  food price 20, 203
  fuel 19–20, 212–13, 225
  headline xxxv, 199, 202, 205, 225–26

382 Index

measures xxv, 199, 203, 223–24
overall xxxiii, 201–02, 205, 226
price 20, 143, 203
target 160–61, 174, 186, 188–89, 192, 194–95, 270
targeting xxiv–xv, xxxii, 51, 68, 131, 145, 186, 189–92, 194–95, 198, 303
WPI 200–201, 220
WPI-based 201
WPICORE 210, 213, 217, 221, 223
WPIFL 213, 217
WPIHL 210, 217, 221, 223
inflationary pressure 11, 20
inflation rate 37, 141, 161, 174, 176, 186, 189, 194–95, 204, 264, 270, 303
inflation target/targeting xxiv–xv, xxxii, 51, 68, 160–61, 174, 186, 188–92, 194–95, 198, 270
informal sector 52–53, 62
Information and Communications Technology (ICT) 61, 240
infrastructure xxvii, 15, 24–25, 27–28, 30, 40, 44–49, 54, 56, 58, 64, 255, 264, 272–74, 278, 359
  fetishism 24
  investments in 15, 24–25, 27–28, 40, 45
  physical 273–74
infrastructural facilities 23–25, 27

innovations xxxi, 51, 58, 61–62, 277–78
inputs
  essential 161, 174, 177–78, 182, 194–95
  intermediate 163, 165, 177, 187, 260, 270
Insolvency and Bankruptcy Code (IBC) 56
institutions
  democratic xxiv
  domestic 24
  financial 24, 48, 155, 293
  inclusive 58
insurance 55, 64, 155, 277, 308
intellectual property rights (IPR) 254
interaction xxv, xxviii, xxxi, 10, 31, 224
interest cover ratios (ICR) 28
interest rates xxxi–xii, 26, 40, 47, 50–51, 57, 65, 130–33, 140–42, 144–47, 149, 151–52, 157, 159–60, 162–63, 167, 195, 263, 270–71, 290–91, 299, 304, 309
  average 162
  correlations 132, 140, 149, 151
  domestic 132, 145
  foreign 145
  Indian xxxii, 65, 130, 151
  long-term xxxi, 130–33, 142, 144–45, 147, 149, 151
  low 47, 65, 157
  near zero 65
  nominal 130, 141–42, 146–47
  real 50, 57, 130, 142
  risk-free 157

short-term 130–33, 144–45, 309
US xxxii, 129, 263
International credit rating agencies 265
International Monetary Fund (IMF) xxviii, 26, 40, 65, 155, 246, 270, 277–78, 292, 305–08, 310
   Articles of Agreement of 310
Internet 51–52, 62, 64, 379
Inter-State GST Council 60
investments xxiv–vi, xxxiii–iv, 4, 8, 11, 13–16, 18–19, 21–30, 36, 40, 45–46, 48–50, 52, 55–57, 59, 65–68, 70, 107, 124, 154–55, 162–64, 169, 172–73, 179, 183, 187, 235–36, 244–46, 251, 254–59, 275, 292, 296–98, 302, 306, 312–13, 338–39, 356, 358–59, 361
   fixed 8, 16
   foreign xxv–vi, xxxiv, 235–36, 245–46, 251, 256, 258, 296–97
   government 45, 59
   infrastructural 15, 24–25, 27, 30, 56
   private 8, 15, 19, 21, 25, 27–30, 48
   private corporate 21, 29
   public 8, 15, 19, 21, 29, 40, 45, 255
investors 22, 24–25, 51, 66, 107, 163, 246, 262
   expectations 22, 163
   foreign 51, 66, 246
irrigation 15, 54, 155–56

IT 239–40, 250, 257, 260–62, 273, 276

jobs 36–38, 52, 63–64, 146, 151–52, 252, 256–58, 277, 334, 337
   creation 63, 277
joint ventures 248–50, 252

Kerala floods relief effort 60
Keynesian
   analytical framework xxvi
   framework xxxii, 5
   model 13
   remedies 23
   theory 3
Knowledge Process Outsourcing (KPO) 252

labour/labourer xxvii, 4, 9, 36–38, 41, 43–44, 46, 52–54, 56–60, 62–63, 69–70, 140–41, 162, 236, 246–47, 255, 257, 260, 264, 270–76, 278
   allocation of 52
   anti-trade sentiments of 257
   educated 4, 52
   growth of 4
   hired 54
   inputs 36
   intensive sector 57
   landless 247
   low-skilled 271
   market 40–41, 70
   reform 70
   surplus 44
   underemployed 69
labour participation rate 37, 369

land
    market xxvii, 41, 59–60, 70, 274
    records 55, 70
    reform 70
    rights 351
laws and regulations xxxv, 45–46, 55, 60, 63, 70, 142, 244, 246, 259, 272, 310–11, 339, 343–44, 346–50, 352, 354–55, 358–60
    domestic 257
    farm 70
    financial sector 68
    implementation of 354
    labour 63, 70, 246, 272
    land 70
least developed countries 57
liberalisation xxvi, xxxiii–iv, 35, 39, 44, 47, 59, 65–66, 70, 235–36, 238, 246, 249, 262–63, 310
    capital account 66, 310
    economic 235–36, 238, 246
    external 47, 246
Liberalised Exchange Rate Management System (LERMS) 310
licensing 237, 249
life
    necessities of 155–56
    quality of 70
liquidity 26, 48, 52, 166, 293–94, 308
liquidity coverage ratio (LCR) 293
livelihood 10, 156, 247, 342, 352, 355, 357, 359, 361

loans 24, 26–28, 30, 40, 56, 157, 160, 162, 187, 293, 312–13
    bank 27
    external 313
    housing 56
    infrastructure 40
    restructured 26
    stressed 28
    term 26, 160
loans-to-value ratios (LVRs) 293
lobbies 55, 256
lobbying/licence hunting 249, 353
localisation 266, 276
London Stock Exchange 313
Lorenz Consistency (LC) 81–82, 85, 96, 100
Lorenz curve xxx–xi, 78–80, 82–84, 86–88, 91, 94–99
    generalised 82, 94–96
Lorenz diagram 82, 87
Lorenz dominance 78–82, 84–87, 98, 100
    crisp 84, 85
    fuzzy 79, 84–87, 98, 100
    generalised 78, 82, 85
    notion of 80–82, 84

macroeconomic
    management xxxvi
    stability 40, 268, 336
    tightening 38, 48, 50
macroeconometric models 5
macroprudential measures 293, 374
Mahatma Gandhi National Rural Employment Guarantee Act (MGNREGA) 54

Make for India 264
Make in India 243, 260, 263–64
manufacturing xxviii, 23, 46,
  50–52, 62–63, 203, 236, 239,
  243, 245, 248, 251, 266, 272,
  275–76, 350
  labour-intensive 62–63, 236,
    272, 275–76
market capitalisation xxxi,
  107–22, 124
market capitalisation ratio
  108–10, 112, 114, 117–18, 122
Market Stabilisation Scheme
  (MSS) 308–09
markets
  access 259–61
  clearing 10, 142
  debt 26, 66, 304, 313
  domestic 25, 27, 39, 107, 250,
    262, 264–65, 269, 273, 275
  economy xxiii, xxxi, xxxiv,
    259, 292, 294, 306, 339
  financial 41, 70, 129
  foreign currency 167
  global 129, 277
  goods 142, 184
  integration, failures of 70
  international 11, 23
Markov chain 112
Marshall-Lerner condition 290
Masala bonds 312–13
Maximum Tariff Rate 238, 369
mergers and acquisitions 250
Micro Small and Medium
  Enterprises (MSME) 63
migration 55, 61, 260, 336
minimum support prices (MSPs)
  53, 55

mixed recall period (MRP)
  89–90
Modified Mixed Reference
  Period (MMRP) 90
monetary-fiscal coordination 51
monetary policy 141, 303
  autonomy 288
  domestic 130, 151
  independent 68, 287
  indicator of 130
  tightening 130
Monetary Policy Committee
  (MPC) 51
monetary search model 203
monetary tightening 17, 28–29,
  130, 376
Monthly per capita expenditure
  (MPCE) 88, 91–95, 97–99
  average 88, 91–93, 95, 97–99
  distribution of 88, 93–95,
    97–98
Most-Favoured-Nation (MFN)
  259
multilateralism xxv, xxviii, xxxvi,
  236, 253, 256
municipalities 60, 336
Municipal Solid Wastes
  (Management and Handling)
  Rules 2000 349
mutual fund 66

NABARD 53
Narmada Bachao Andolan
  353
National Afforestation and
  Eco-Development Board 355
National Bureau of Economic
  Research (NBER) 133, 136

National Clean Air Programme 356
National Company Law Tribunal (NCLT) 56
National Green Tribunal Act 2010 349
National Informatics Centre (NIC) 200, 206, 208–09, 220–21
National Sample Survey (NSS) xxviii, 53
National Sample Survey Office (NSSO) 77, 79, 88–89, 91–92, 97
   surveys 53, 88–89, 91, 97
natural resources xxvii, xxxv, 252, 256, 344–45
Negotiations 253, 258–59, 339
Net cess and surcharge (NCS) 332–33
Net Domestic Assets (NDA) 309, 357, 360, 369
Net Domestic Product (NDP) 162
Net exports (NE) 8, 302
Net Stable Funding Ratio (NSFR) 293
New CPI (NCPI) 208–10, 217, 220–21, 223
New Economic Policy (NEP) xxxii, 155–57, 174
NITI Aayog xxxiv, 323
non-agricultural sector 20–21, 24, 214
non-bank financial institution (NBFCs) 48, 61
non-governmental organisations (NGOs) 60, 353
non-infrastructural productive capacity 25
non-infrastructural sector 25
Non-performing Assets (NPAs) 22, 26, 48, 56
non-tariff barriers 259
North American Free Trade Agreement (NAFTA) 251, 253, 260
North-Atlantic financial crisis 36
nutrition 58, 69

octroi 61
oil price/pricing 11, 19–20, 23, 28–29, 36, 38, 46, 50, 57, 65, 67, 243, 263, 270
   domestic 67
   global 67
   international 11, 29
oil shocks of 1973 295
'One Belt, One Road' initiative 255
open economy 45, 132, 140–42, 144, 146, 151, 289–90
   large 141, 146
   small 132, 140, 142, 144, 146, 151
Organisation for Economic Cooperation and Development (OECD) 7, 12, 159
organised sector 61, 68
Organization of the Petroleum Exporting Countries (OPEC) 67, 237
output
   aggregate 7, 162, 174
   agricultural 10, 20, 214, 225
   demand-determined 4, 6, 162

growth 7, 29–30, 48
quarterly 5, 7, 15
outsourcing 51–52, 58, 252, 256
Oxfam India 156

Panchayats 60, 327, 336, 351
Patents Act of India 266
Petroleum, Oil, Lubricant (POL) 166, 239
Phillips equation 141
planning xxxiv, 52, 59, 257, 297, 302, 323, 327, 340
Planning Commission xxxiv, 323, 340
  abolition of xxxiv, 323
policy changes of 1991 xxiii
policy(ies)
  assessment of efficacy xxvi
  changes xxiii, 3, 58, 244
  choices 287, 289, 314
  exchange rate xxv, 305
  export 55, 276
  failures xxix
  fiscal and monetary xxix, 17, 22, 36, 161, 174, 339
  formulation xxix
  goal 289
  governments' 14
  implications 31, 199
  independence 288, 290, 309, 314
  initiatives xxvii, 8, 14, 237, 278–79
  macroeconomic 36–37, 39, 49, 51, 67–69
  macroprudential 293
  makers xxiv, xxvi, 30–31, 161, 237, 267–68, 353, 361

  measures xxix, 2, 288
  money 11, 254
  pragmatic 44
  tightening 50, 130
  trilemma 291, 314
political
  concerns 262
  constraints 41, 60
  economy 67, 337
  environment 236, 276
pollution 69, 343, 346–47, 352, 354, 356, 360
Pollution Control Boards (PCBs) 346–47, 355
Population Replication Invariance (PRI) 81–82, 85–86, 96, 100
portfolio flows 65, 291–92, 314
poverty xxvii, 38, 59, 77, 345, 360
power
  economic 254, 259–60
  monopoly 166, 171
  Western 256, 276
preferential trading arrangements 270
Prevention of Corruption Act 60
price/pricing xxvi, xxxiii, 67, 109, 119
  administered 161, 174, 177–78, 182, 194, 195
  affordable 10, 155–56
  agricultural 10–11
  changes xxxiii, 199, 201–05, 208–09, 217, 220, 223–26
  current 91–92
  deflator 91–92

domestic 142, 162, 164, 166, 270
food 4, 20, 45–46, 53, 55, 205, 225
index xxiv–xv, 11, 201, 203, 205, 208, 222
indices 199, 201, 205–06, 208, 224
international 20, 55, 67, 213, 269, 273
market 3, 7–8, 10, 12, 19, 158, 182, 186, 189, 306
movements xxxiii, 23, 199, 203
relative xxxiii, 4, 9, 23, 199, 201–05, 208–09, 217, 220, 223–26
stickiness 141–42
variation in xxxiii, 199
volatility 55, 66
price change distribution 204, 217, 220, 223, 226
primary health centres 64
private participation 48–49
privatisation 44, 59, 70
production 9, 43, 49
   capacity 255, 262
   cost of 165, 178, 187, 264, 274
   demand-determined 4–5
   domestic 42, 46, 69
   facilities 249–50, 262, 266–67, 274
   possibility 41, 43, 50–51
   supply-constrained 9–10
productivity 36–37, 39, 43, 46, 52–54, 56, 61, 107, 144–45, 241, 251, 263, 268, 277

products
   agricultural 29, 241, 243, 251, 269, 273
   differentiation 249
   high-tech 163
   imported 263–64, 277
   indigenous 248
   industrial 10, 31, 251
   non-agricultural 4, 29
   non-farm 11
profits 22, 24, 26, 28, 140, 177, 183, 350
protectionism xxxvi, 236, 263
   selective xxxvi, 236
public distribution system 155–56
Public Interest Litigation 352
Public Liability Insurance Act 1991 349
public-private partnership (PPP) 15, 24, 36, 49
public sector 26, 41, 44, 48, 60, 177, 304
public sector banks (PSBs) 26, 41, 48, 60, 304
public services xxxv, 45, 58, 60–61, 69–70, 323, 340
   delivery 59
   poor 69
   provision and quality of 58, 61, 58, 340
purchasing power parity (PPP) 35, 38

QUAD 260
Quantitative Easing (QE) 65, 137, 254

Ratio of gross savings to GDP
  68
RBI Committee 310
RBI Handbook of Statistics on
  Indian Economy 200, 206–07,
  209, 216, 219
R&D 155–56, 251–52
readymade garments 237, 239,
  274
Real Effective Exchange Rate
  (REER) 268, 302
real estate 65, 68, 338, 360
real sector 30, 161, 166, 288
recapitalisation 40, 48
recessions xxx, 22, 25, 129–30,
  132–39, 157, 163, 174, 176–77,
  263, 271
  periods of 134–39
reforms xxiii, xxvii, xxix–x,
  xxxii, 35–41, 43–49, 52–53,
  56–57, 59–61, 63, 68, 70,
  132–33, 236, 246, 257, 269,
  279, 310, 337–38
  domestic 44, 47
  feasible 37, 59, 68
  labour market xxvii, 40
  land 37, 41, 70
  opportunistic 59–60
  structural xxx, 37, 56, 59, 70
regional
  agreements 259
  markets 251
  trading blocs 251
Regional Comprehensive
  Economic Partnership (RCEP)
  236, 256, 258–62, 274
regional groupings xxxiv, 236,
  259–60

regression 122, 137–38, 206,
  209–10, 220, 222, 224, 311
relative prices xxxiii, 4, 9, 23,
  199, 201–05, 208–09, 217, 220,
  223–26
  changes xxxiii, 201–05,
  208–09, 221, 224–26
  commodity-specific 208
  distribution of xxxv,
  208–09, 220, 226, 232,
  234
relative price variability 204
remittances 11, 15, 67, 257, 263,
  297, 310
  non-resident 11, 15, 67
repayment obligations 307
repo rates 57
reserve accumulation 40, 47,
  305
Reserve Bank of India (RBI)
  xxvi–iv, 2, 7–9, 28, 56, 66, 131,
  135–39, 148, 161, 164–67, 174,
  186, 198–200, 203, 206–09,
  216, 219, 225, 244–45, 265,
  268, 270, 287–88, 295–306,
  308–11
  analysis of aggregate demand
  8
  analysis of supply-side factors
  9
  exchange rate policy of
  303
  guidelines 56
  interventions xxxiv
  Monetary Policy Reports 7
  monetary tightening 17
  performance xxxiv
reserve forests 350–51

resources xxvii, xxix xxxv, 39–40,
    42–44, 51, 70, 110, 154–57, 243,
    252, 256, 264, 323–25, 327–28,
    330–31, 334, 340, 342–47, 349,
    356–57, 359
  access to 345
  allocation of 39–40, 154, 155
  commercial 357
  demand for 344
  depletion of 346
  domestic 43, 51
  federal 325
  fiscal 324
  government command over
    156–57
  mobility 40
  productive 155
  reallocation 264
  scarce 155
  underutilised 43
  utilisation of 51, 70
  waste 345
restrictions xxxiv, 154–56, 237,
    251, 253–54, 256–57, 260, 274,
    289–90, 293, 304, 310, 313
  relaxation of 251
  stringent 154, 156, 260
  trade 256, 274, 310
revenue 27, 36, 45, 247, 263, 275,
    322, 324–26, 328, 331, 334–36,
    338–39, 357
  deficit 325–26, 335
revenue receipts 325, 328
Right to Education (RTE) Act 64
Right to Information (RTI) Act
    347, 352, 358
risk xxxi, 38, 47, 49–50, 53,
    64–67, 109, 111, 114–16,
    119–20, 122, 127, 143, 157,
    257, 266–67, 293, 348, 352
  aversion xxxi, 109, 111,
    114–16, 120, 122
  external 38, 65–66
  financial 38
  global 50, 65
  sharing 143
Rupee Denominated Bonds
    (RDB) 312
rural sector 88, 91–92

safeguard duties 256, 263
salaries 52–53, 64
Sardar Sarovar Dam 352
savings 36, 40, 44–45, 47, 49–50,
    52, 67–68, 109, 116, 119, 124,
    155, 254, 271
  current 109
  domestic 44, 47, 50, 67–68
  financial 50, 67–68
  foreign 68
  household 50, 67–68
Say's Law 4
Scale Monotonocity (SMON)
    81–83, 85–86, 96
Scheduled Tribes and Other
    Traditional Forest Dwellers
    (Recognition of Forest Rights)
    Act 2006 351
seasonality test 210
sectoral bottlenecks 50, 69
Securities and Exchange Board
    of India (SEBI) 298–99
self-reliance 155, 295
services sector 58
shadow banking 47, 255
share prices 22, 26

shocks xxix, 4–5, 10–11, 28–9,
    36, 38, 40–41, 45, 47–48, 65,
    67, 69, 140, 144–46, 148–49,
    151, 163, 203–04, 225, 238, 295
  demand 141, 144, 149
  domestic 28, 144–46, 148, 151
  external 28–29, 38, 40–41, 48,
    65, 69
  foreign 144–46, 148, 151
  monetary 141, 144
  oil 11, 20, 45, 67, 69, 295
  price 11, 36, 38, 67, 69
  supply xxix, 10, 36, 140, 163
  technology 141, 149
skewness xxxiii, 203, 205, 209,
    217, 220–21, 223–26, 231–34
  negative xxxiii, 203, 217
  positive xxxiii, 217, 225–26
skill/skilling 46, 52, 54, 58,
    62–64, 239, 243, 251, 276, 278
small and medium enterprises
    (SMEs) xxvii, 61, 157, 257, 261,
    272, 274
smart cities 60
soft money 254
Solovian growth models 4
South Asian countries 278, 356
Soviet Union 237–38
special purpose vehicles (SPVs)
    27
spending 3, 39, 47, 53, 56, 225,
    322–23, 326
  commitments 323
  government 53, 56
  induced 3
  public 322
stabilisation xxvi, 38, 41, 50,
    69–70

stabilise, liberalise, privatise
    40
stagnation xxxi, 2–3, 237, 268
standard generalised system of
  preferences 57
standard monetary business
  cycle models 130
State Pollution Control Boards
    346, 355
Statutory Liquidity Ratio (SLR)
    26
sterilisation xxxiv, 308–09
stock(s) 8, 24–25, 27, 107–11,
    115–16, 119, 163
  exchanges 107
  price 66, 108, 116, 124
  market xxiv, xxvi, xxxi, 66,
    106–10, 123–24
  development 106–09
strategic alliances 248–49
strategic regional groupings
    xxxiv, 236
subsidy(ies) xxiv, 9, 20–21, 53,
    55, 57, 174, 247, 257, 264, 270,
    274
  agricultural 55, 257
  export 247, 264
  growth 44, 237, 275
  industry-specific, WTO ban
    on 57
  Nehru-Mahalanobis 154–55
  petroleum 21
  reform 43
supply chain 257, 260, 263, 269,
    271, 273–74
  disruptions in 263
  global 260, 263, 269, 271,
    273–74

Supreme Court of India 352, 360
sustainability xxxiv–v, 235, 253, 326–27
  debt xxxv

Tarapore Committee 311
tariffs 57, 237, 244, 247–48, 251, 253, 256, 259, 261–63, 266–67, 274–75, 310
  discriminatory 251
  high 237, 267
  protection 247, 267
  rates 244, 247, 259
  reductions 57
  retaliatory 253
  revenue 247
  selective 266
  US 253
tax/taxation xxiv, xxxv, 8–9, 17, 24, 29, 36, 56, 61, 63, 65, 90, 155–56, 161–62, 174, 177, 182–83, 185–86, 195, 199, 244–45, 265, 271–72, 274, 311, 323–24, 327–31, 333–35, 337–39, 343
  base 63, 337
  central 327–38
  concessions 17, 265
  devolution xxxv, 323–24, 327–28, 330, 334–35
  direct 155–56, 174
  indirect 9, 17, 29, 156, 161, 174, 182–83, 185–86, 195, 199, 338–39
  input 56, 339
  rates 17, 155–56, 161, 174, 182, 186, 195, 339
Taylor rule 141

technology(ies) 51–52, 58, 60–62, 64, 70, 141, 144, 149, 157, 236, 240, 248–50, 254, 260, 263, 275–77, 348, 355
  defence 276
  foreign 157
  internet and communication 51
  new 64, 236, 275, 348
  telecom 58, 239, 254, 263
term spread 136–38, 150–51
  Indian 137, 150
  US 138, 150–51
terrorist activities 257
The Energy and Resources Institute (TERI) 353
Thirteenth Finance Commission (TFC) 324, 330
time series 3, 6–7, 12–13, 121, 206, 209–10
tourism 273, 276
trade xxiii, xxv–vi, xxxiii–iv, 5–6, 11, 45–46, 51, 56–57, 65, 111, 142–43, 146, 156, 167, 235–43, 246, 251, 253–61, 264, 270–71, 274–75, 278, 288, 290, 295, 297, 299, 303, 305, 310, 313–14, 338–39
  agreement 256, 260
  balance 146, 156, 242, 290
  cycle 5–6
  fair 236, 253
  foreign xxvi, xxxiii, 11, 236
  free 57, 236, 253, 256, 259–60
  global 236, 253, 258, 261
  international 259, 288
  world 56, 65, 237, 241

trade deficit 51, 239–40, 242–43, 254, 261, 295, 297, 369
trade to GDP ratio 237–38
trade war 253–56, 314
trading blocs 251, 258, 260, 376
training 52, 62–64
transactions xxxiii, 52, 107, 254, 300, 307, 311–12
transfers 8, 55, 296–97, 322–25, 327–31, 334
  aggregate 323, 327–31
  conditional 327–28
  system xxxiv, 323
  unconditional 323–24
transition matrix 112
transitivity 85
Trans-Pacific Partnership (TPP) 253
Treasury rate 134, 379
Treasury securities 134–35

Ukraine War 255, 379
unemployment 43, 156, 174, 254, 262
Uniform recall period (URP) 89, 90
Union Carbide disaster 347–48
Union government 323, 325–26, 328, 331–32, 335–37, 339–40, 347, 350, 358, 360
Union–state relations xxv, 323, 337
United Nations Conference on the Human Environment 345
United Nations Conference on Trade and Development (UNCTAD) 244, 270

United Nations Environmental Programme (UNEP) 345
United States (US) xxxi–ii, 15, 25, 30, 35, 45, 57, 61, 65, 67, 121, 123, 129–40, 145–47, 149–51, 157–60, 165, 203, 236–42, 244–45, 250–58, 260, 262–63, 265, 271–72, 277, 290, 300, 305–07, 309, 356
  Biden administration 253, 255, 260
  Chinese investment in 254
  expansionary policy 15
  financial tightening 65
  goods 253, 256
  growth rates in 159
  interest rates in 159
  markets 262
  monetary policy 67
  per capita GDP 146
  political actions 65
  sanctions on Iran and Russia 258
  Treasury rates 134
  Trump administration 252–54, 259–60, 265
United States-Mexico-Canada Agreement (USMCA) 260
unorganised sector 23, 61, 68
urbanisation 40, 61
urban sector 88, 91–92
Urjit Patel Committee 161, 174, 186
US Treasury 134–35, 305–07
  Macroeconomic and Foreign Exchange Policies of Major Trading Partners of the United States 305

value chains 55, 252, 278
Vector Auto Regression (VAR) 202, 206, 212–14, 217, 224
variables
 dependent 122–23, 222–23
 exogenous 168–69, 172, 175, 180, 184, 188
 independent 110, 122, 137
 macroeconomic 202, 205–06

wages 9, 53, 162, 165–66, 177, 249, 254, 275
 low 249, 275
Washington consensus 39
waste 43, 343–45, 349, 353, 358, 362, 377
Water (Prevention and Control of Pollution) Act, 1974 346–48, 358
welfare xxvii, xxx–xxxi, xxxv, 362
 concept of xxvii
 social xxx, xxxv
well-being xxv–xxvii, xxx–xxxi, 76–83, 86, 88, 91, 93–94–101
 aspects of 77, 96
 comparisons 79–80, 83, 86
 economic xxvi, xxx, xxxi, 76, 88, 91, 93, 98–99
 level of 78–79, 81, 83, 95–96, 98–100
 measurement of 76–78, 80, 94, 96
 trend of 76–77, 79
Wholesale Price Index (WPI) xxxiv–xxxv, 19, 198–202, 204–05, 208–10, 213–14, 217–22, 224–26, 231, 234

inflation xxxiii, 19, 217–18, 225–26
Wholesale price (WP) xxxiii, 198–99, 202, 204, 211
Wildlife (Protection) Act 1972 349
workers 23, 62, 64, 91–92, 157, 162–64, 168–69, 172–74, 183, 186, 189, 195, 205, 208, 214, 224, 241, 251, 256–57, 273
 industrial 91–92, 205, 208, 224
workforce 53, 62–63, 251
World Bank xxviii–xxx, 38–40, 47, 59, 121, 123, 159, 238, 241, 245–46, 256
 World Development Indicators 121
world trade xxiii, 56, 65, 237, 241, 380
World Trade Organization (WTO) xxiii, xxvi, 55, 57, 236, 253, 257–59, 264–67, 274
 Dispute Settlement Body 257, 259
 rules 253, 266
World War II 22, 131, 236, 253–54

Y2K 61, 240, 295
yield curve xxxi, 130, 132, 134–37, 140, 149–51
yield spread(s) xxxii, 130–40, 146, 149, 151, 369

zero revenue deficit 325
zero sum game 248
Zila Panchayats 327
zone of ignorance 100